THE
OXFORD BOOK
OF
AUSTRALIAN
SCHOOLDAYS

Edited by

BRENDA NIALL AND IAN BRITAIN

with

PAMELA WILLIAMS

D0912718

Melbourne

OXFORD UNIVERSITY PRESS

Oxford Auckland New York

OXFORD UNIVERSITY PRESS AUSTRALIA
Oxford New York
Athens Auckland Bangkok Bogota Buenos Aires
Calcutta Cape Town Chennai Dar es Salaam
Delhi Florence Hong Kong Istanbul
Karachi Kuala Lumpur Madrid Melbourne
Mexico City Mumbai Nairobi Paris Port Moresby
Singapore Taipei Tokyo Toronto Warsaw
and associated companies in
Berlin Ibadan

OXFORD is a trade mark of Oxford University Press

National Library of Australia
Cataloguing-in-publication data:

The Oxford book of Australian schooldays
ISBN 0 19 550805 X
1. Education—Australia—literary anecdotes. 2. Students—Australian—literary collections. I.
Niall, Brenda, 1930– . II. Britain, Ian, 1948– .
A820.80355

Edited by Cathryn Game
Text and cover designed by Steve Randles
Cover photograph: Austral International/FPG International
Typeset by Steve Randles
Printed by Kyodo, Singapore
Published by Oxford University Press
253 Normanby Road, South Melbourne, Australia

Contents

Preface

Ellipses in square brackets ([...]) indicate a cut that has been made by the editors. Minor typographical errors have been corrected, but the original spelling and punctuation have been retained in the extracts.

For help and advice on this project the editors thank: Marie-Louise Ayres, Elaine Barry, Ann Brothers, Verona Burgess, the *Canberra Times*, Michael Collins-Persse, Richard Cook, Kate Cregan, Denise Cuthbert, Robin Gerster, Gordonstoun School, Sarina Greco, Geoffrey Hiller, Nicholas Jose, Francis King, Sarah King, Maureen Kohlman, Margaret Le Mire, Aliki Mahon, Douglas Muecke, Hugh Niall, Frances O'Neill, Terry O'Neill, Barbara Perry, Peter Rose, Philippa Ryan, Heather Scutter, Jennifer Strauss, John Thompson, Liz Yandell.

We acknowledge with gratitude the support of the English Department, Monash University, the History Department, University of Melbourne, and the Australian Research Council. To Pamela Williams, research assistant throughout this project, we give special thanks: the project has gained immeasurably from her skill and discernment.

Brenda Niall and Ian Britain

Introduction

In Virginia Woolf's novel, *The Waves* (1931), the upper-class English artist, Bernard, declares to a stranger sitting opposite him at a restaurant table:

> in order to make you understand, to give you my life, I must tell you a story — and there are so many, and so many — stories of childhood, stories of school, love, marriage, death and so on; and none of them are true. Yet like children we tell each other stories, and to decorate them we make up these ridiculous, flamboyant, beautiful phrases.

Putting schooldays on a par with love and death constitutes a powerful tribute to their significance in the human lifecycle. Bernard's declaration here also suggests the irresistible attraction of schooldays as a source or focus of myths about the self; and he is not just talking about his own compulsions in this respect, or those of his particular nationality, class, and sex. The 'I' in one sentence turns to 'we' by the next. Moreover, his own creator is female, and the whole of her novel bears out his claims, is in itself a dramatisation of his thesis. It consists of the reflections of six characters, all of them at school when the book begins and for much of the rest of the book as well. Three are female. One of the male characters, Louis, is an Australian, who has been dispatched from his home in Brisbane to receive some English schooling before going out into the business world. And he turns out to be even more obsessed with school than the rest.

The subject of this anthology is Australian schooldays, as connoted in every sense of that term, and as represented in a wide variety of literature. The selected extracts mainly reflect the experiences of native-born Australians educated at institutions in their own homeland. But they don't exclude the stories of Australians (like the fictional Louis) who had at least a part of their schooling overseas. And they include multifarious accounts of the experiences of Australian schooling by those who were not native-born — who came to Australia as young immigrants or (in one exalted instance represented here) as visitors.

The word 'schooldays', as applied in these pages, is limited to the years of infant, primary and secondary education (unlike Americans, Australians don't use the word 'school' in everyday speech to refer to their time at universities or other places of higher learning); but the range of schools and schooling so defined embraces as many varieties as could be found in literary accounts: institutional and non-institutional, private and public, denominational and secular, orthodox and progressive, and all shades in between. We hope we have given as much considera-tion as the available sources allow to the different periods, social classes, sexes, races, and regions involved in the subject, but we have not sacrificed idiosyncrasy of perspective or expression to some ideal of representativeness. That is probably an unattain-able ideal anyway, and not an appropriate one for what is pre-eminently a literary anthology rather than a systematic chronicle.

The choice of material is based on the editors' judgment of what may be of interest in the literature of Australian schooldays as distinct from what could be considered important to an understanding of Australian educational history. But we don't wish to press this distinction too far. We have interpreted the term 'literature' as broadly as we have the terms 'Australian' and 'schooldays', so that it includes — and freely jumbles up — nov-els and poems, biography and autobiography, letters and diaries, newspaper reporting and official reports of governmental or other institutional authorities. (Plays, screenplays and television scripts relating to schooldays, though richly abundant, have been excluded here because they depend for their full flavour on so much more than reproduction on the printed page.) All the chosen extracts are as much historical as they are literary documents: records of impressions, of emotions, of memories, where not 'true' renderings of lived experience in the manner that Bernard, in *The Waves,* seems to hanker after. They suggest something about people's consciousness of the past — how this has been regulated, manipulated, shaped by them — if not something about the past itself.

Schooling figures prominently in most Australian autobiographies, and in accounts of childhood it is often the most vividly rendered phase. This may be because it is at school that the child first becomes conscious of the self as social being. Perhaps, too, it is easier to express the strong emotions roused by neglect, injustice or exclusion when these are experienced outside the family. And when memory marks out the first day at school as the first experience of separation from home, it is confirmed by some precise historic moments or motifs. The date, place, buildings, and uniforms are matters of verifiable record that the autobiographical self can retrieve and muse upon.

We have chosen a broadly chronological framework, the most conventional mode of historical representation. We might have opted for a more 'thematic' framework, as favoured by some anthologies on other subjects. The themes or areas of interest most commonly explored in the writings represented here include: travelling to school; landscapes and buildings; rules and rituals; misdemeanours and discipline; uniforms; food; the curriculum; friendships and sex; sports and recreations; conformists, eccentrics and rebels, among both teachers and students; and questions of personal, social and cultural identity faced by individuals at school. But in practice it proved very difficult to categorise our materials thus without breaking them up into unsatisfyingly small titbits, arbitrary-seeming fragments that distorted their shape, interrupted their flow, altered or obscured their original context. So we abandoned the thematic structure, trusting that the recurrent themes would emerge, and all the more tellingly, in cumulative form.

Our chosen extracts provide too small a sample to be more than suggestive about historical trends and patterns in Australia's schooling, but the suggestions are not without interest, and have implications for other, broader processes in the nation's development. These things, too, emerge most clearly perhaps within a chronological framework.

One obvious development is the general movement away from the British base or orientation of Australian society in the years since World War II as a consequence of large-scale migration from continental Europe and (in more recent decades) from Asia. 'As well as being Australians we were also British,' recalls one of our authors, Donald Horne, in evoking the milling throngs in his primary school playground of the late 1920s. 'By British, of course, was meant English and certain kinds of Scots,' explains the poet and academic Vincent Buckley when talking of the reading material to which he was exposed while at primary school in the 1930s. (Buckley's is one of hundreds of memoirs that, for reasons of space and balance, we unfortunately could not reproduce here.) This blanket label 'British' could hardly be applied to any facet of Australian playgrounds or Australian classrooms today, and especially not to their denizens. Most of the instruction, most of the casual chatter, might still be conducted in English; but just a look down the list of authors' names in our table of contents gives some idea of the general shifts, complications, and enrichments that have taken place in the ethnic composition of those attending Australian schools in the past four or five decades.

On the other hand, a close reading of our extracts suggests that there have always been some such 'complications' or sources of enrichment: the Aboriginal presence, for all the attempts to marginalise or suppress it from the earliest days of British settlement; the presence of the Chinese following the gold rushes of the 1850s; and the admixture of Irish and French influences in the various Catholic schools founded in the nineteenth century. A spokesman for Australia's indigenous peoples whom we invoke towards the end of this volume draws our attention to various kinds of schooling that have their origins long before any Britishers ever arrived on Australian shores; although it is not clear how far he would endorse the application of what he terms 'white people's categories' to those experiences, whether in their ancient or modern incarnations. He mentions instruction in ceremonial life, the teaching of hunting and fishing techniques, and the telling of 'stories that had a strong lesson for us kids'.

Other extracts towards the end of this volume serve to remind us that while multicultural influences have been much more pervasive in Australian schooling, and Australian society generally, over the last half century, they have not eroded the values, prejudices and rituals that characterised the Anglo-Australian 'mono-culture' of previous times. Helen O'Shea observes preparations for a school Christmas concert in a small country town at the beginning of the 1990s, but most of the detail she provides would not seem out of place in vignettes of a bush Christmas from much earlier in the century. The festive cornucopia she describes — consisting of 'fizzy drinks and fairy bread', 'cups of tea and cream puffs', 'plates of sandwiches, party pies, scones, slices, a couple of sponges' — is uncannily redolent of the fare served up at Donald Horne's Empire Day school picnic in the 1930s ('sandwiches, jellies and lemonade'). There's not a samosa in sight, no whiff of a pizza or souvlaki, no sign of a crumb from a panettone or panforte.

Is this just a case of vestigial rural innocence or provincial backwardness or country conservatism? Before accepting any such interpretation, it might be worth listening to some of the stories we have reproduced of migrant childhoods in Australia's major cities. According to Sonia Mycak's account of her brother's first day at a Sydney primary school, he was surrounded at lunchtime by a crowd of other children chorusing their repugnance at his 'dirty sandwich'. The teacher could only agree with them that 'a nice vegemite sandwich' would be infinitely preferable to the black bread and salami his mother had provided. Sonia was to have similar experiences that taught her of the existence of 'a definable quintessential Australian culture', which would go on eluding her as long as she retained any attachments to her family. For young 'Lucia', dispatched to a school in Melbourne following the arrival of her family from Italy, food became the 'biggest problem'. Plied with mortadella and frittata by her mother, she soon learned she would have to graduate to a ham and tomato roll to make herself 'more acceptable' to her schoolmates.

Exactly when such episodes are supposed to have taken place is not always clear. It might be assumed that they happened in the dreaded 1950s before we all learned there could be no worse thing than sliced bread. But complacency on this score should be a little troubled by the last of our pieces, from 21-year-old Aimée Tse, who tells a remarkably similar lunchtime story set at a Melbourne school in the 1980s.

Lunch looms large in our pieces. As it is the major break from classroom routine — particularly for day-school pupils who have their other meals at home — this is not surprising. But as well as being light relief, it has been something of an ordeal in the experience of many Australian schoolchildren. Where the contents of the lunchbox have not been a test of true Australianness, they have been a sign of status and social class. Sally Morgan tells us how as a seven- or eight-year-old at her primary school in Perth during the 1950s she had developed her 'infallible Look at the Lunch method for telling which part of Manning [her home suburb] my class-mates came from'. This was at a state school that serviced a largely working-class-cum-lower-middle-class area; but the nuances in social rank among its clientele seem to have been as clearly observable, and as keenly observed, as in the somewhat more privileged milieu of another of our authors, John Funder, who was educated in private Catholic schools on the other side of the continent. 'Melbourne's millefeuille society in the fifties' is his marvellous phrase for this milieu (although it's no reflection on the contents of his own school lunchbox, which were rather more bland, as he records them). His stress is not so much on the social distinctions within schools as on those between them.

The multilayering of Australian society, and its reflection in a hierarchy of schools, provides a theme that can be traced back to some of the earliest extracts in this volume. In spite of her initial unhappiness there, and the rough conditions compared to those of her early upbringing in Melbourne's highest social echelons, Eliza Chomley recalls of the Sydney boarding school to which she was dispatched in the 1850s that it was 'the best and most select'. A parliamentary School Commissioner in New South Wales in the same decade finds a disturbing congruity in the conditions of lower-class homes in country areas and the schoolhouses to which the children of these homes are being sent: 'framed of the rudest material and without the slightest regard for decency, comfort, or convenience', such establishments are 'evidence of what their superiors consider good enough for them'. When the novelist Martin Boyd remarks on his parents' insouciance in sending him, half a century later, to an establishment that was 'less "public school" than ... Geelong, now the Australian Eton', it is fairly clear that he himself has not been so insouciant. Moreover, the Boyds never dreamed of sending their son to one of the state schools, which had been in existence for more than thirty years.

Louis' self-consciousness in *The Waves* regarding his school and his class, as well as his nationality, is all the more comprehensible in this context. The extracts in our anthology also help us to understand — or they prompt us to consider further — his friend Bernard's sense of school as a distillation of life and the stuff of life's necessary myths and self-constructions. Look at Barry Oakley's memoir of his experience at a Christian Brothers' college in Melbourne in the 1940s. He seems to be speaking in as general terms as Bernard, if not in quite the same terms, when he pauses to reflect on school that 'like the stage, it's an image of life: life accelerated, life concentrated, life more formidable'.

A little earlier Oakley observes: 'School to us had nothing to do with education'. That is not meant to be the message of this anthology; there is a great deal here about teaching and learning and 'the getting of wisdom', if this process — in the narrowest or widest senses — can be equated with education. But we have certainly hoped to remind readers that schooldays are about a lot more than this.

The seat of happiness

ELIZABETH MACARTHUR (1766–1850), PASTORALIST, WIFE OF JOHN MACARTHUR, WRITES OF THE NECESSITY OF SENDING THE MACARTHUR CHILDREN 'HOME' TO SCHOOL IN ENGLAND.

This Country possesses numerous advantages to persons holding appointments under Government; it seems the only part of the Globe where quiet is to be expected. We enjoy here one of the finest Climates in the world. The necessaries of life are abundant, & a fruitful soil affords us many luxuries. Nothing induces me to wish for a change but the difficulty of educating our children, & were it otherwise it would be unjust towards them to confine them to so narrow a society. My desire is that they may see a little more of the world, & better learn to appreciate this retirement. Such as it is the little creatures all speak of going home to England with rapture — My dear Edward almost quitted me without a tear. They have early imbibed an idea that England is the seat of happiness & delight, that it contains all that can be gratifying to their senses, & that of course they are there to possess all they desire. It would be difficult to undeceive young people bred up in so secluded a situation, if they had not an opportunity given them of convincing themselves. But hereafter I shall much wonder if some of them make not this place the object of their choice.

ELIZABETH MACARTHUR TO BETSY KINGDOM, 1 SEPTEMBER 1795

Buttered toast under the pillow

SIR JAMES HASSALL (1823–1904), CHURCH OF ENGLAND CLERGYMAN, WAS ONE OF THE FIRST PUPILS AT THE KING'S SCHOOL, PARRAMATTA, NEW SOUTH WALES.

As only the Established Church was recognised at the time [the King's School] was made a Church of England school, as it has remained ever since, although boys of all classes and denominations were to be admitted. It was said that Governor Bourke, a few years later, refused to lay the foundation stone of the present school buildings, as he was endeavouring at the time to introduce a national system of education. Captain Westmacott, consequently, performed the ceremony.

The school began in a brick house in Lower George-street, Parramatta. I entered in April, 1832, three months later [...]

I wish I could present my readers with some portraits of the boys who came to the school. Knickerbockers were unknown. Short jackets were worn and often the little fellows had the jacket buttoned up and the trousers, or 'pantaloons,' as Mrs. Forrest called them, buttoned over it; the suit generally made of blue cloth. One boy had jacket and trousers all in one, made of brown holland, with buttons only at the back of the neck and waist. This suit gave him a cool appearance on a hot summer's day, and Parramatta was as hot a place as I was ever in.

Some of the boys wore large pinafores. At nine years old, I used to wear, over my long-trousered cloth suit, a brown holland pinafore, down to my ankles nearly. All we pinafore-wearing boys had girls' names given us, by way of nickname.

The caps worn were of a peculiar style, having small leather peaks and large crowns with a cane round them, the pleats drawn into the centre to a button. After a time, these canes would be taken out, and then the caps used to hang loose at the side of the head. One boy, John Antill, who at once received the nickname of 'Magpie,' came with a home-made cap, the upright made of square pieces of cloth — black, white, and red, with an immense cane top, no peak, and a ribbon at one side. Older lads wore what were called 'black billies' — the usual beaver or silk hats.

We walked to church two-and-two, in great order, while the soldiers marched there with a band playing and a crowd following, listening to the music. What I would not give to hear the old bugle-call again that used to summon us at nine o'clock at night to leave our lessons and go to bed.

School opened at seven a.m. and closed at nine p.m., but, morning, noon, and night, we had to learn the everlasting Eton Latin Grammar — parrot-like, as we learnt the Church Catechism. Of course there were some boys that read the Greek and Latin classics, but as I had not advanced so far I must confine my reminiscences to outside events.

We paid only £28 per annum, so we could not be expected to fare as well as schoolboys of the present day. For breakfast and tea we had merely dry bread, with tea in large basins containing about a quart apiece. Green tea alone was used then in the colony. The quantity allotted for our tea was very scant, but a liberal supply of brown sugar, about the colour of coffee, and a dash of milk, made it into a kind of syrup. Two or three basinfuls were considered necessary to wash down the dry bread, and the consequence was that the small boys became like podgy calves. For dinner we had roast beef one day and boiled the next, the boiled beef quite fresh, never corned or salted, sometimes mutton, and 'duff,' that is, suet puddings — with lumps of suet an inch in diameter, and not very nice either. I have never liked duff since. We never tasted butter, unless by means of a shilling tip to the housekeeper, when one might find some buttered toast under his pillow at night.

In Old Australia: Records and Reminiscences from 1794 (1902)

Orphan boys

IN HIS EVIDENCE TO THE BIGGE COMMISSION OF ENQUIRY INTO THE STATE OF THE COLONY ON 22 JANUARY 1821 THOMAS BOWDEN (1778–1834) REPORTED ON THE SCHOOLING OF MALE ORPHANS IN SYDNEY.

How long have you been Master of the Male Orphan School?
    Two years on 1st Jany last.

What school did you manage previous to that time?

 The first Public School to which I was appointed in England on the recommendation of the Revd. Mr. Marsden, & took upon me the superintendance of it on the 28 Jany 1812, when I arrived.

How have the schools been supplied with books?

 As the Public school was taught on the Lancastrian plan, only Bibles & Testaments were used; and on my removal to the orphan School, the Papers & cards that were used in the Public School I removed with me.

Did you find that the attendance of the boys was regular?

 Not quite so much as in England, owing to inattention on the part of the parents.

Were the children taught Gratuitously?

 I was allowed a Prisoner as Assistant & was allowed to receive 2d. per week from each child as a remuneration for his services. This sum was very ill paid.

What was the average number of scholars that you had in the school?

 About 110, & this average was greater, before the regimental school was established.

Who were the members of the Committee who superintended the schools & visited them at the period of which you speak?

 The Revd. Mr. Cowper.

How often in a week did he attend?

 Generally once a week; sometimes he was not so often.

Did the Rev. Mr. Marsden ever attend?

 I never recollect seeing him but once, & that was when he Introduced me to the school.

Were the accounts of the school settled & inspected by a Committee?

 They were quarterly.

Whom did you see in attendance in the Committee, when you presented your accounts?

My accounts were not presented personally, so I do not know who the Committee were.

Did Govr. or Mrs. Macquarie ever visit your School?

Not to visit the Children or inspect their progress, but to see soon after my arrival whether it was fit to be repaired.

Did they ever enquire after its Progress?

Occasionally.

Was the school ever repaired during your time?

It was & a kitchen built for my accommodation...

What is the nature of the subsistence & Diet of the Male Orphan School boys, & how is the Diet provided?

Their cloathing is given them when wanted. They are allowed for breakfast four days a week half a lb of bread, a pint of tea with sugar & milk, the other three mornings they have plain boiled rice with sugar and some milk, for dinner they have half a lb of fresh meat & 1 lb of potatoes but no bread each for four days in the week two days in the week plain suet puddings allowing ¾ lb of flour to each boy, the other day they have fish Ox head soup with pease in it. They have for supper every evening ½ lb of bread and a pint of tea with sugar & milk. Bread, meat & flour are provided by open contract — potatoes we buy in the market.

What are the hours of School & exercise?

They work in the Garden from rising till 8. They go into school from 9 till 12. Till 2 they dine & play — from 2 till 5 they work at their trades of Taylor and shoemaker & some in the garden.

Are they healthy in general?

Yes they are.

What Medical attendance have they?

> The Governor I believe recommends a Surgeon to the Comm^ee & he has £30 Pr. ann.

Who performs this duty?

> Mr. Redfern did till he left Sydney on resigning his appointment of Asst. Colonial Surgeon; on this occasion for some weeks we had no regular attendant until Mr. Stephenson Surgeon of the 48 Regt. was appointed.

During that interval did you ever apply to Mr. Bowman Principal Colonial Surgeon for Medical aid and was it granted?

> I frequently did & he invariably attended to my applications...

JOHN RITCHIE (ED.), The evidence to the Bigge Reports (1971)

Learning before landing

JOHN MACKRELL, A 25-YEAR-OLD EMIGRANT FROM BERKSHIRE, WAS PAID £10 FOR ACTING AS SCHOOLMASTER ON THE SHIP *PESTONJEE BOMANJEE*, WHICH SAILED FROM SOUTHAMPTON ON 18 JUNE 1854.

We had bad weather for the first few days, and most of the people were sea sick. As soon as possible which was on the 23rd I got the children together for school which was held on the main deck, a very bad place, as we were continually interrupted by people going into the hospital, and cabin, and by the sailors working the ship. The Poop would have been a far better place, but as there were 52 young women on board it was set apart from them. Our School hours were from 9 till 12 when the children went down to write and from 2 till 4. According to my instructions as soon as possible I began to form Classes for instruction of the Adults. But as the majority of the men on board were Mechanics, men who would sit for hours reading a book (being more or less educated) but who felt indisposed to attend school. To such men the Library

was of the greatest service. I however got some of the more ignorant of the Emigrants to attend my classes. At first they were
pleased with the idea of being instructed but after the novelty of
the thing had worn off, some from a feeling of false shame, others from finding the road to knowledge not so easily climbed as
they imagined, began one by one to fall off, and I am sorry to have
to report that here my efforts ended in a failure, with the exception of a few who got on well with their writing. They would sit
for half an hour writing a copy, but would get tired at a little mental exertion; particularly if they found any difficul[t]ies in the way.
But if the Emigrants were ever so disposed to receive instruction,
unless more books are sent out, it must prove a failure, as the
Schoolmaster is placed in the position of a workman without his
tools. And for this reason. There were 52 young women to be
instructed by my sister, and nothing provided for their use. As
soon as the Childrens school was over the books and slates were
required for them from 12 till 1 and from 4 till 5 which was tea
time, and as soon as tea was over, in the latitudes of fine weather
it was dark when nothing could be done. My Books were 18 First
Books very slightly put together, which from the wear of small
children, and exposure to the wind soon got out of order, 12
Second Books, 3 sequel to Ditto. 4 Third, 3 Fourth, 3
Supplement to Ditto and 3 Reading Books. These two last are
almost useless, as they are too hard, and at least 6 books of each
sort should be sent as less will not serve to form a Class. There
were some English Grammars & Geographys sent, these are useless as there is neither time nor place to get up the Exercises.
Instruction in these subjects should be given orally. Of Ink &
Copy Books I had plenty, but only one box of very bad Steel Pens;
there should be one box of each hand of Gillott's School Pens. The
Ceder Pencils were the worst that I ever saw, only 2 Inches of
some black substance in each, the rest was wood. The books sent
out should be 1st 2nd and 3rd Irish Books with some arithmetics,
and cards for the small children, the rest are useless except for the

Library where 2 of each sort would be very useful. As the books with care are not worn out, a good supply should be sent, and they might when the Vessel arrives in port be given with great advantage to the National Schools on shore. I consider the Library to be the great means of Adult education on board ship. The books most read are History, Biography, Travels, Tales and above all books treating of the Colonies. The exclusively religious books the people will not read; they are therefore useless for the purpose intended. I have experienced the same thing in Lending Libraries at home. The number of days it was possible to hold school was 50. One of my Sisters assisted me with the Girls and an intelligent young man with the Boys. The attendance was good and regular, and the Parents anxious that their children should learn. And I am happy to report that the Children generally made marked progress. On Sunday I held Divine Service, with a Sermon in the morning at 11 and Prayers in the afternoon at ½ Past 3. In fine weather from the Capstan head, in bad between decks. I also read the Burial Service over the dead of which there were [blank]. I have drawn up my report at some length, believing that from my experience at home and on board ship I am competent to give an opinion. My object being to serve the cause of Education, I trust that the freedom with which I have expressed my opinions will not give offence.

I am, Sir
your Obed.ᵗ Serv.ᵗ
John Mackrell

ANDREW HASSAM (ED.), *No Privacy for Writing: Shipboard Diaries 1852–1879* (1995)

Governesses, guitars and grammar

ANNABELLA BOSWELL (1826–1916), NÉE INNES, DESCRIBES HER SCHOOLING IN NEW SOUTH WALES, AND REPRODUCES A LETTER SHE WROTE AT THE AGE OF TEN UNDER THE GOVERNESS'S SUPERVISION.

But to return to Saltram. We stayed there till October 1835, and soon after our return home we were happy in being put under the care of an excellent governess. Her name was Miss Willis, and I am sure no children ever had a kinder or more painstaking teacher. My mother, too, found her helpful in many ways, and an acquisition in our isolated home. We children threw ourselves with zeal into our work. I panted for information, and read greedily every book I was allowed to have. We read many times the histories of England, Scotland, Greece, and Rome. The story of *Elizabeth, or the Exiles of Siberia* was an especial favourite, and we had many other nice books, considering the time and the place.

Miss Willis had a guitar; she was not very proficient, but she taught us to play nicely and to sing some simple songs. For grammar she had a mania. I think I learned every word of a large Murray by heart; her zeal never flagged. We played at spelling lessons; the spelling Bees of recent years would, I am sure, have been a joy to her. One of our amusements was that we each wrote a letter every week. I have a few of these compositions beside me now; many were to imaginary people. Those we really wrote and sent had also to be copied into the letter-book. In those days of exorbitant postage very few went beyond it. I have seen a letter for which seven and eightpence postage was paid. I shall give an example of one of the letters that was sent. It is number fourteen, dated 16th April 1836, and was addressed to my uncle, Major Innes, Lake Innes, Port Macquarie:

It gives me very great pleasure to write to you, my dear uncle, and papa tells me I must send you the little drawing I have just finished this afternoon. Had I known it was to be sent to you I would have taken more pains with it.

We have got a governess now. I like it much better than being at school, because I do not require to leave dear papa and mamma. I am learning to play the guitar; I found it very difficult at first. I made my fingers so sore and my arms ache, but now my fingers have got quite hard at the points, and I am getting on very well with it. I can play the accompaniment to 'Ye Banks and Braes' and to 'Ah Vousdirais', 'Rondo', and a few other little airs. I am reading the history of England, and have got the length of James the First, who began the reign of the family of the Stuarts in England. I like my studies very much indeed; they are a pleasure to me. Miss Willis explains them as I go on, which makes them easy to be understood. I think I like geography better than any of my other lessons. I have gone through the four quarters of the globe with Miss Willis, and I begin again on Monday at the map of Europe and through each country, beginning at England. My sister gets on very well with her lessons. She writes very well indeed, and seems to have a great taste for drawing. She is also learning to play the guitar. I wrote to Grandmamma in December, and since then I have written to Aunt Jane. They cannot have got my letters yet, and very much pleased I shall be if my aunt writes to me. I intend to write to one of my aunts soon. I hope my dear little cousins are well. I suppose Gordina begins to run about now. Papa, Mamma, and Margaret join me in sending their love to you and my aunt, and kisses to my dear cousins. Goodbye, my dear uncle. — Believe me, etc.

A.A.C. Innes

MORTON HERMAN (ED.), *Annabella Boswell's Journal* (1965)

Port Phillip pastoral

FROM THE DIARY OF **GEORGE GORDON MCCRAE** (1833–1927), SON OF PORT PHILLIP SETTLERS GEORGIANA AND ANDREW MCCRAE. WITH HIS THREE YOUNGER BROTHERS GEORGE HAD LESSONS FROM TUTOR JOHN MCLURE, MA (GLASGOW). THE BOYS AND THEIR TUTOR BUILT THEIR OWN SCHOOL HUT AND SHARED OUTDOOR WORK ON THE MCCRAE CATTLE RUN AT ARTHUR'S SEAT, VICTORIA, WHILE LEARNING LATIN, GREEK, MATHEMATICS AND HISTORY, ACCORDING TO THE PATTERN OF BRITISH PUBLIC SCHOOL EDUCATION.

Friday December 11th, 1846

We rose early went to the sea-side and bathed. After breakfast we went to lessons and finished Goldsmith's Roman History, read a part of Cornelius Nepos's life of Hannibal, began a list of the plants in the garden and then went out. Mr McLure was cutting the grass from before the house and I wheeled some away. After a short time we went to school again, studied the map of the world, learned some of the Latin Syntax, and heard Mr McLure read a part of the Botany book to us. It then began to rain heavily accompanied by thunder. The dinner-bell rang and we ran down to dinner. After dinner we went back to school and worked a few sums in the square root and then went out for the remainder of the day. I brought down my list of plants to make some addition to it and also the *Saturday Magazine* to read. About this time the rain ceased and the sky cleared up and everything promises a fair tomorrow.

Thursday December 17th, 1846

We rose early and awakened the servants. Tom went to the yard to milk and we took the dogs and drove away the black bull. Wind blew from south-west. Mr McLure and I went to the field and planted two furrows of potatoes. We observed a ship going out today. After breakfast we went to lessons. We learned a part of the French history. I learned a part of the third book of the

Æneid. Willie and Sandy learned a part of Caesar. And Perry read a part of the English history. After these we wrote some more in our lists of plants. We then went out and began to plant potatoes which we continued until 12 o'clock. We then went to school and wrote a part of our *Latin Delectus* etc. until dinner-time. After dinner, Tom went for the cows so that we could not immediately begin ploughing. Accordingly we went to lessons again and worked until Tom came home. Mr McLure sent Perry down to the house to see whether Tom was ready and upon Perry's assurance that he was; we went down but found that no potatoes had been cut so we had to go up to school again. We worked some more sums in the square root. Mr McLure proved the use of the square root to us by making us find the height of his hut in this manner. Willie went up on the roof and held a line there while I measured a certain distance on the ground. Mr McLure stretched the line as far as I had measured so making a perfect triangle, the ground being the base, Willie being the top, the line being the long side and the wall of the hut being the short side. We then went down to the field to plant potatoes. Mr McLure allowed Tom and me and Willie to try to plough but none of us could manage it. We soon finished planting and went out with Tom and brought in a cart load of wood. Mr McLure had gone along Mr Smith's road to dig up orchids, a large kangaroo jumped so close to him that he struck him with the spade. Mr McLure informed us that there are plenty of cherries along the road so the boys start early tomorrow morning in quest of them.

Saturday December 19th, 1846

This morning was rather rainy; Mr Barker called on his way to town. He told us that there were some blacks at the foot of the fence. We accordingly went down and recognized several of our old friends and amongst them Ben-Benjie who readily agreed to shoot ducks for us. We gave the gun to him after he had breakfasted and he set out. After breakfast we went to school and went over all the French history and we came out. Mr McLure went to dig potatoes for dinner with Willie. After dinner Ben-Benjie returned without the ducks and gave me the charge, and three bommerings as he was to go away tomorrow.

Monday December 21st, 1846

Sandy and I arose early. We walked up along the beach and gathered some currants for a tart. After we returned we bathed and walked up to breakfast. Having breakfasted we went to school. We learned part of our French history, read a chapter in the Bible. I learned a part of the *Æneid,* while Sandy began a new book in *Caesar's Commentaries* and Perry learned a part of the English history. We all wrote part of our lists of plants and went out. Sandy went to the lower garden to cut some lettuces for dinner while I ran up and called Ellen from the wash-house. We soon went to school. Mr McLure asked us a few questions on the map of Scotland, but the bell soon rang and we ran to dinner. Lucy brought into the house a salmon-coloured Mantis having a claret tinge and striped with white. Tom turned out 'Duncan' this day. The school bell soon rang and we went to lessons. We read a part of Cornelius Nepos's life of Hannibal, a part of our *Latin Delectus.* We worked a few sums together tonight. Mr McLure and I went to Ellen's well and thinned the lettuces. Mamma gave me a book to sketch in but I have not as yet used it. Tom and the boys went to the beach and caught four small fishes resembling sprats and two or three flounders.

Hugh McCrae (ed.), *Georgiana's Journal: Melbourne 1841–1865* (1992; first published 1934)

A select academy

Eliza Chomley née à Beckett (1842–1932), niece of Sir William à Beckett, first Chief Justice of Victoria, was sent from home in Melbourne to a boarding school in Sydney.

So to Sydney we went, and after a very happy week or two at my Uncle Arthur's, I was left at Miss Moore's boarding school in Lyons Terrace — the best and most select in Sydney. For the first week or two I was very homesick, lonely and miserable. I managed to keep my composure through lesson time, but when it was over I would have many a 'weep' in my ugly bare little room, so unlike home. Though, as time went, I got accustomed to my new surroundings, I was never happy at school, I only made one real friend — my room mate — though I got on well enough with all the girls.

There were about 40 boarders, most of them squatters' daughters, some very handsome girls, all of them coming, like myself, from well appointed homes. Our way of living was very rough. We had our meals down in the basement, a cobblestone floor, two long narrow tables with a coarse cloth, and the commonest crockery and table appointments. We had forms instead of chairs — for breakfast and tea, roughly cut bread and butter — dinner equally plain. At breakfast there was a dish of some kind of meat or fish, sufficient for the teachers and about six of the girls, and in rotation we had this addition to our meal — about once in every week. There were no baths, no hot water for washing — in the coldest weather we would put our heads under the pump in the yard.

There were no sports of any kind, sometimes on Saturday evening we danced for about an hour — every day we went for a walk in a long procession, three abreast. If we met any acquaintance on these walks we were not to overtly recognise them, but eyes often were more expressive than a bow could be, and were not under control.

To my great surprise I was asked, as a new girl, on my first Sunday, to petition Miss Moore that we should attend church three times that day — not at all my ideal Sabbath. I found later, that church going was our only possible opportunity of seeing our fellow creatures — a little excitement and change — but twice a day was always enough for me personally.

In warm weather we went to the baths every day. All the Sydney girls could swim, and I was eager to learn, but there was too much ducking and splashing for my efforts to be successful. We had one outing while I was at school, all driving out in cabs to Coogee early on a lovely summer morning to see an eclipse of the sun over the sea. As it gradually became darker, the governess in charge, fearing a storm, hurried us all into a house near, where we remained till the sun shone again — to find that the threatened storm had been the eclipse! However, we enjoyed the drive through Sydney, going and coming [...]

[E]xcept for one teacher, I was not 'educated' at all, I had merely dry lessons set me which I learnt, and repeated in a perfunctory way, with neither comment or explanation given. I think my very early teaching must have been good, for I remember nothing of learning to read, and I must too have acquired more historical knowledge than is usual at eight years old, for I remember well, at our visit to Madam Tussaud's before we left England, the rapture with which I recognised not only various Kings and Queens of England, but notably Marie Antoinette with the Dauphin, whose tragic history had recently thrilled me — even the blood-stained shirt of Henry of Navarre, in its glass case, with the rent of the assassin's dagger in it, and all the Napoleonic trophies had a definite meaning for me, as well as plaster casts of the victims of the guillotine, with realistic blood stained necks ranged in the Chamber of horrors — an unsuitable place for an impressionable child.

Our first school in Melbourne, was with a Mrs Casperson, a tall, dark woman, with long elf locks hanging to her waist. Then we had a series of governesses who live chiefly in my memory by copious records they gave us of their own personal history, and the untoward events which necessitated their teaching. But the 'lessons' were always the same, writing — in a copy book — one or more pages a day, with moral or didactic copy steps, reading Little Arthur's History of England — later on, Mrs Larkham's English History, with conversations at the end of each chapter between her and her ineffably priggish children, who we always despised. I think those two historians must have had a very strong bias, social and sectarian. For a long time 'Bloody Mary', Cromwell, and every struggle of the 'common' people stood for all that was evil with me, while Elizabeth was perfect, and the Stuarts, root and branch, especially Charles I 'Saint and Martyr', were invested with a halo of romance.

In my later schooldays we read Pinnock's Goldsmith's English, Greek and Roman Histories. No questions — no remarks — no explanations — were given.

Arithmetic was just 'sums' up to the Rule of Three. Fractions were unknown to me till I taught my own children, though later, at school, I tackled successfully various arithmetical puzzles near the end of the book. French I think we were well taught, of course rule of thumb teaching, mostly from Ollendouk. The rest of our 'education' in Art, Science, Literature — in short every branch of learning, was comprised in 'Mangall's Questions' a fattish book, a series of short catechisms, or merely catalogues, with the briefest explanations or barest facts. It did contain a great deal of valuable information which I suppose made it the classic it undoubtedly was in all schools.

Once a week we had to write a 'theme' or letter. I always chose the latter as requiring nothing but the baldest commonplaces — just a page of 'exercise book'. Of course we had music lessons, but that was a labour of love, quite outside other work — then, too, beyond the value of notes, there was no study of 'theory' (which I confess is still a mystery to me).

When I was about 12 we went to 'Miss Polystack's day school' — held in high repute. She was a fat, middle-aged German — really Madam Damm. Her husband was rather fat and elderly, but he was the only teacher with whom I ever felt in sympathy. He did try to instil some love for literature and poetry into us. Chambers English Literature was added to 'Mangall's', and we had really interesting lessons on it. He was an enthusiastic lover of poetry, and I can see him now declaiming patriotic verses 'The Mariners of England', 'Battle of the Baltic', 'The Isles of Greece', et cet, to at least one hearer thrilled by them — he would always look my way for a response he knew he would find.

We learnt German then, and he was equally impressive in some of Schiller's or Goethe's poems. Our English readings were better selected, and gave us something to think about — if we wanted to.

A more practical but useful lesson was to teach us to read aloud coherently, and without stammering. Everything was taught in classes by him. The head of the class began with the first sentence, whether short or long. At the least mistake or hesitation, she was promptly stopped and it passed onto the next in class — if successful she went 'up', if not, the same rule was observed, a long or difficult sentence sometimes going almost the length of the class. This sounds a very elementary process, but I venture to say, many young and even adult persons, now would not stand the test brilliantly.

Mental Arithmetic we also took in class, in the same way, and indeed almost every subject, and the prizes were awarded by the places in class recorded in the 'Location Book' at the close of each lesson — the 'Absents' given on the average of class positions. Of course Latin and Mathematics then were unheard of subjects for girls, or any branch of physiology, botany, et cet, but we did have a little 'History of Europe' generally, linking England up more or less with the rest of the

world, and our readings, poetry or prose, enlarged our range
of vision [...]

I think school girls now could scarcely imagine so utterly
empty a life apart from our lessons, which could be in a large
measure avoided. During my year's stay, there was not any kind
of concerted movement in sport or work, or amusement, on the
part of the girls or the teachers. Even at the baths, our one recreation, the idea of competitions or swimming matches was never
dreamed of. We had no working club for ourselves or others, no
school library, knew nothing of other schools. Lessons over, we
had only our daily walk and idle gossip to fill the time till the
evening's 'silence hour', from seven to eight, to prepare the next
day's work — then prayers — then bed.

We had a few books among us openly, and a good many more
smuggled in, for even unexceptionable fiction was not allowed.
Very rarely, by good luck, a governess would take one or two of
us into Sydney for some shopping, or we would give the house-
maid a commission to buy us cakes or sweets — she did very well
out of it. Sometimes on Saturday evening we danced for an hour
or two — no visitors ever came to the school.

Lessons began from seven to eight in the morning, then
prayers, and breakfast. I forget the actual hours for morning and
afternoon, but with some skill one could evade many of them.
There were five pianos in the house and we had to practice an
hour daily. There were also two school rooms, and extra classes
in another room. By a judicious use of the practice hour, it
could stretch into two, and absence from one school or class
room might mean work in another.

During my first half year I was a successful absentee nearly
half my time. The course of study was on the same lines as in
Melbourne. I had Italian lessons and 'Use of the Globes' as
extras. Our French teaching was good — we had a lively, pleasant, Parisian lady as mistress, who encouraged us to French
conversation by various pieces of news or gossip, which we had

to persuade her to detail and to reply to; we liked those lessons.

Dancing and drilling too, we learnt — our only exercise as we had quite a small paved yard as recreation ground.

Prizes were given very sparingly, only one in each class for what was termed 'General Proficiency'. I think the only extra prizes were for French, Music and Dancing. The system of awarding them was very bad. We all had 'ticket books'. Pages headed with all our different subjects 'Conduct' included. Marks by the teachers of each subject varied from none to 10 or 20 after each lesson — there could be the grossest favouritism in awarding marks. I determined to gain this Proficiency prize, but had to work very hard for it, for my conduct marks were often nil, and if in any way I annoyed a teacher, my work marks for the day would be confiscated. I used to write page after page of translating — a little French History — for extra marks, every day, often in the dinner hour. The crowded slates were nearly always taken on trust, not a word read by the teacher. I was honest over them, and my 'French Translation' page mounted up big figures. But I really did work hard and went well all round, and felt I had honestly earned the prize I gained — a small copy of Coleridge's poems, which looked most inadequate as a First and only prize in the First class.

We were all very fond of the Headmistress, Miss M[oore], a kind gentlewoman who was uniformly just and considerate with us. Of the other teachers, the only one I cared for was a very crabbed old maid, severe in school, but a kindred spirit in loving poetry. I had bought Tennyson's poems — then little known — with me, and we enthused together over Locksley Hall and the Lotus Eaters, or wept over the May Queen.

'MY MEMOIRS' (1920)

Elbows and attitude

SIR JOSEPH VERCO (1851–1933), MEDICAL PRACTITIONER, CLINICAL TEACHER AND CONCHOLOGIST, BEGAN HIS EDUCATION IN A SMALL PRIVATE SCHOOL IN ADELAIDE. THIS EXTRACT COMES FROM HIS AUTOBIOGRAPHY IN WHICH 'FOR SOME MODEST REASON' HE REFERRED TO HIMSELF IN THE THIRD PERSON.

In the school-room — there was only one — with an outlook on the street over a little garden there were two Misses Tilney who were teachers, and their somewhat aged mother. She sat close by the window in her black suit and employed herself in doing netting with a shuttle and a mesh. The starting point of this work was fixed by a loop of cotton which went over the front of one foot. One of the rewards of good behaviour was to be allowed to stand before her and hold her skein of cotton on out-stretched hands while she wound this into a ball.

One of the three sisters Anna Maria looked after the domestic arrangements of the house, two others conducted the education department. One of the latter was somewhat delicate and had a taste for entomology, and the collection of all sorts of curios, and encouraged the scholars to bring anything of interest to her, to be placed in her 'Cabinet of Curiosities'. In Franklin St, was a very large open space opposite Mellor's Implement Works, and along its southern boundary was a long 'paling fence' somewhat bleached by the sun, and on this could occasionally be found a very large locust longer than a man's finger, of almost the same greyish tint as the bleached 'paling fence' but with great hoppers of a deep purple tint along their inner surface. This would be taken and given to Miss Charlotte for her 'Museum' and be pinned inside her glass fronted box of insects, and would be rewarded by a smile and cordial thanks. So also with any curiously shaped pebble, or strangely marked piece of stone from the hills' quarries, showing what were regarded (of course erroneously) as the markings of fossil ferns, but were really stains from the trickling in between the slatey layers of water holding some mineral in solution.

The boys and girls would sit on forms on each side of a long wooden table, and go through their various exercises and perform their several tasks with one of the teachers at the head, and the other to walk from one of the boys and girls to another and direct them and help them as might be required. They received marks according to merit and these were entered to their credit or otherwise. [Verco] used to relate how one afternoon the Principal asked him towards the close of the afternoon — 'Have I had to ask you to-day to take your elbows off the table?' and he meekly and happily was able to answer 'No! Ma'am' and was gratified to hear her reply 'Then I will give you five marks for 'Attitude'.' Is it any wonder that he received at the end of the year a prize for good conduct.

A Colonial Boy-Hood: Some Recollections of Sir Joseph Verco, 1858–1867 (1930)

Marking time

THE ORDER OF OCCUPATION FOR THE CHILDREN IN **MRS DARLING'S FEMALE SCHOOL OF INDUSTRY** IN THE LATE 1820S.

6 o'Clock	The children to rise, dress, and wash themselves.
20 min. past 6	Prayers, and the Psalms for the day read.
7	Breakfast.
30 min. past 7	Play.
55 min. past 7	The Monitors see that the children's hands are clean, form the classes for work, give out the work, needles, thimbles, etc.
8	All at work excepting the Monitors of each Class.

30 min. past 10	The children fold up their work, the Monitors collect needles etc.
33 min. past 10	The Monitors form writing classes, give out slates and pencils.
36 min. past 10	Writing or summing.
6 min. past 11	Monitors collect slates and pencils, and form reading classes, give out lesson books and cards.
10 min. past 11	Reading and spelling.
10 min. past 12	Play.
1	Dinner.
30 min. past 1	Play.
50 min. past 1	The children wash their hands, and return to School.
55 min. past 1	The Monitors give out lesson books, and form classes.
2	Reading.
30 min. past 2	The Monitors question the children on what they have been reading.
45 min. past 2	The books to be collected and the classes formed for needlework.
5	Play.
6	Supper.
7	The children to work or prepare work for the next day, during which time one of the monitors of the 4th reading class is to read some instructive tale.
8	The Matron to read prayers.
30 min. past 8	The children go to bed.

Rules of the Aboriginal Institution at Black Town
1. The Children to be up and dressed by 6 and set to work.
2. To wash themselves at ½ past 7, go to prayers and breakfast at 8.

3. To work until 10 o'Clock.
4. To wash and go to school from 10 till 12. Write one Copy, read ½ an hour, cypher 1 Hour.
5. To dine at ¼ after 12 and play till 1.
6. To School at 1 read and cypher till 2.
7. To work from 2 till 6, the boys at carpentering, the girls sewing and knitting.
8. To play and wash and ready for supper at 7.
9. To Prayers at ½ past and to be in bed at 8.
10. On Saturday morning to be devoted to instruction of Sunday Service.
11. The following rewards to be given tickets for
    1. Good Behaviour
    2. Good Work
    3. Religious Knowledge in which they are to be examined every Sunday of one Ticket at each time at the discretion of the master and mistress and for every 10 Tickets an account shall be kept in a book entitling the children to sixpence to be laid out for their benefit at the discretion of the Visitor.

GRAEME DAVISON, *The Unforgiving Minute* (1993)

A desire for neatness

THIS EXTRACT FROM A REPORT FROM THE **SCHOOL COMMISSIONERS** TO THE **NSW LEGISLATIVE COUNCIL** (1856–57), ASSESSES THE PHYSICAL CONDITIONS OF SCHOOL BUILDINGS AND THE LIKELY MORAL CONSEQUENCES OF UNKEMPT SURROUNDINGS.

Many [school-houses] are built of slabs, floored with mud, and roofed with bark. In addition to the dirt and discomfort of such structures they are objectionable for other reasons. The wretched hovels in which the humbler classes are content to live in the country districts, are of a nature to prevent their attaining common decency, much less comfort or neatness in their dwellings. Their habits and their education, in the widest sense of the term, would doubtless be greatly improved, if they could be induced to build neater and more commodious residences. But when the school-houses present them with examples of everything to be avoided rather than imitated; when they are framed of the rudest material, and without the slightest regard for decency, comfort, or convenience; when, in short, they resemble the miserable homes of the lower classes, it cannot be expected that the children will become more refined in their domestic arrangements when they grow up. The school is an evidence of what their superiors consider good enough for them; there is consequently no inducement to improve. There is nothing to remind them that better residences are attainable, or to excite a desire for neatness in and about their dwellings. And there can be no reasonable ground for hoping that they will be imbued with that respect and regard which it is of the utmost importance they should feel towards their Teacher. In a new country it is absolutely necessary, in order to prevent the people from retrograding in civilization, that these matters should be constantly borne in mind [...]

The condition of the Schools as regards instruction is deplorable in the extreme. Prepared as we were to find serious defects in the mode of instruction, and of course unsatisfactory results in the progress of the children, the actual state of things surprised and grieved us, and we are reluctantly compelled to report that few schools are worthy of the name. Whether viewed in relation to the extent of the instruction imparted, or the advancement of the children in each subject, the result is equally disappointing. The obstructions presented by the want of proper school buildings, furniture, apparatus, and books, have undoubtedly been the means of preventing many subjects from being taught, and of hindering the progress of the scholars; still, after making every allowance for deficiencies of this kind, the conviction remains that more ought to be done for the education of the Colony, and that it could be done better. The Colonial youth are by no means dull or incapable of cultivation; on the contrary, we have found them acute, apt to learn, and when properly managed, not deficient in industry and application. The Teachers also seem to be industrious, and in many cases zealous. The inference, therefore, is, that the methods of teaching employed are unsuitable and ineffective; and it will be perceived from other portions of this Report that the want of training on the part of the Teachers countenances this conclusion. 'As is the Master so is the School,' is a maxim now fully proved to be correct, […]

Intimately connected with the foregoing subject is the *government* of a school. We shall here limit the meaning of that word to the means of maintaining order and ensuring obedience. There are two modes of securing that object; first, by the infliction of corporal punishment, and, secondly, by moral influence […] In the country the children are almost invariably diffident and shy, and therefore require to be encouraged, which can be accomplished only by patient and gentle treatment — personal chastisement having the very opposite effect. On the other hand, the children in large towns — and we should here be understood to refer principally to Sydney — present a distinct phase of character. Keen, bold, and self-confident, corporal punishment indiscreetly administered, aggravates the offence it is intended to subdue; but from their impressibility, an appeal to their *understandings* or *right feelings* is seldom unsuccessful. We are persuaded, therefore, that government by the rod may in the majority of cases, be dispensed with, and the use of moral influence greatly extended […]

A gentleman of wealth and position, distinguished by the liberality of his views, and the favorableness of his sentiments in regard to education, established a school on his estate for the benefit of his tenantry. On visiting the school, situated almost within sight of his residence — we found the building to be a miserable slab hut, in such bad repair as to be unfit even for a stable. The Master's apartment contained fewer of the conveniences of civilized life, than the hut of the rudest shepherd. The only school furniture consisted of three forms, made by placing rough slabs upon blocks of wood. There was no apparatus whatever, and but one book, if a few spelling books, tattered and soiled, be excepted. No register had ever been kept or provided, and the usual Return must have been fabricated. The Teacher assured us he had been trained in the mother country, but his unkempt locks, and rude attire, left the impression upon our minds that he was wholly unfit for his office. The five children present were listless, dirty, and ignorant. Doubtless this is an extreme case, but the spirit which leads to such a state of things is universal.

A.G. AUSTIN (ED.), *Select Documents in Australian Education 1788–1900* (1972; FIRST PUBLISHED 1963)

It's never too hot to dance

CATHERINE HELEN SPENCE (1825–1910), BORN IN SCOTLAND, MIGRATED TO SOUTH AUSTRALIA IN 1839. HER NOVEL OF SOUTH AUSTRALIAN LIFE IN THE GOLD-RUSH YEARS OF THE 1850S, *Clara Morison*, IS BASED PARTLY ON HER OWN EXPERIENCES AS A GOVERNESS.

Clara had by this time reached the door, at which she knocked. Louisa Jane whispered to the children that most likely this was the new governess coming, at which news they hurried in at the back door, to get into the parlour as soon as she did, and have a good look at her before their mamma made her appearance. So by the time Clara was ushered into the sitting-room the whole of the juvenile Denfields were there ready to inspect her. There was the eldest, Caroline, who seemed to be about fifteen; then James; then the three whom Clara had seen in the garden, and

Robert and Emily, first merely looking at her, and then asking her questions.

'What a pretty frock you have on,' said Caroline, 'though you have got it rather dusty with the walk; and your bonnet is very nicely trimmed. Have you been long in the colony, or have you just come out?'

'I only landed last week,' said Clara.

'Then why do you wear your hair in ringlets? they are quite out of fashion. All new comers wear their hair crimped and stuck out in wavy bands, and it looks so stylish. If you stay here you must wear your hair like that, for ma does not like curls at all. What is your name?'

'Clara Morison,' was the reply.

'It is a nice name, I like it. Our last governess was called Bridget Dobson; wasn't it a horrid ugly vulgar name? but she was a vulgar creature altogether.'

'I do not think it such a vulgar name,' said Clara. 'There was a Mrs Dobson who translated Petrarch beautifully.'

Miss Denfield stared, and continued, 'If you are to be our governess you must give us nice short lessons, and let us play a great deal. I am not too old for play yet, though I am so tall, and I don't mean to give it up till I come out, and I hope that will not be long. There is Miss Robertson came out at fifteen, and I wish you would help me to persuade ma to let me accept the next invitation I get. It would be delightful to dance till daylight. It is never too hot to dance you know, and I would never miss a dancing lesson for the world, but I do hate learning spelling and grammar, and doing horrid sums when it is as hot as this. Ma says she is fit for nothing to-day, and what can you expect of me? Master James, don't break the chairs, swinging upon them like that; and do, Miss Eliza, keep Emily from ma's work-box. She has got everything out of it; and there now, if she has not run the scissors into her hand. Oh Emily, don't cry, it is not very bad. What will ma say?'

But Emily was of opinion that it was very bad indeed, and screamed so that Caroline was forced to take her out of the room to her mamma. Clara saw the other children do a good deal of mischief, and when she mildly hinted that they had better not, they merely stared at her, and went on. Three quarters of an hour elapsed before Mrs Denfield entered, and with considerable dignity requested Clara to resume her seat when she rose to accost her. Mrs Denfield prided herself on two things in particular; first, that she was lady-like, and secondly that she was decided. Her manner was cold, her eye critical, her mouth hard in its expression, and her gait stiff; but still she was, in the opinion of those twenty people who formed her world, such a lady-like superior woman. She was anxious that her children should be as lady-like and firm as she was, but neither precept nor example had hitherto succeeded in producing that result. She had at last adopted the opinion that mothers were not the best instructors of their darlings, but that they needed a subordinate educating machine, such as a governess, to act under their orders, and to cram the minds of children with useful knowledge, without either inspiring any of the respect, or winning any of the affection which was due to the mother, and the mother alone.

Her cold grey eyes looked Clara over; the result was not satisfactory. As Clara's colour rose at the inspection, she supposed that she had not been accustomed to good society; and as her flexible mouth did not close like a vice, she was of opinion that she wanted firmness. Besides, she was too young, and what some people would think too pretty for a governess, though there was no mind whatever to be found in her face.

'You are, I presume,' said Mrs Denfield, 'the young person in whose favour Mr Campbell spoke to me on Wednesday evening? Miss Morison, I believe, is your name?'

'Yes, ma'am,' said Clara.

'Pray, have you been accustomed to tuition? for I consider that a great point.'

Clara's distressed eyes glanced at the children, who were all eagerly listening, but whether Mrs Denfield thought that they would profit by the colloquy, or whether she thought it a good trial of the governess's patience to conduct her cross-examination before her future pupils, she did not take the hint, but looked impatient for an answer.

'I have never been in a situation yet, but I used to teach the little ones at school,' said Clara.

'An apprentice, I suppose,' said Mrs. Denfield.

'It was only because I liked it,' said Clara; 'I think there are no such things as school apprentices in Scotland.'

"Then you are Scotch; yes, I hear you have the accent very strong. Were you at a boarding-school or a day-school, Miss Morison?'

'I have been at both,' said Clara, 'and had instruction at home besides.'

'Are you acquainted with the routine of tuition? Could you give me any idea of how you would go through one day with these young folks of mine?'

'I cannot tell until I know what progress they have made. Probably your boys go to school, and as for the young ladies I must take each separately, as there is such a difference in their ages, and they cannot learn exactly the same lessons,' said Clara.

'I understood from Mr Campbell that you know a little Latin, Miss Morison; and if you could carry on James and Henry for a few months, to prepare them for a good school, I think it would be a good arrangement for all parties. What is the matter, Caroline?'

'Oh, ma,' said Caroline, who just now burst into the room. 'I wish you would come and speak to Louisa, she is so cross with Emily, and was just going to give her a slap, when I said I would run and tell you. And what do you think Sarah is doing, ma? She is scrubbing out your room with the same water she took to wash the passage; all her laziness to save her drawing more water from the well.'

'Servants are the plague of my life,' said Mrs Denfield. 'You will excuse me five minutes, Miss Morison. Put on your bonnets, my dears, and pick some grapes. I dare say Miss Morison would take a few this hot day if you dip them in cold water for a few minutes to cool them.'

When Mrs Denfield returned it was without her children, to Clara's great delight; she resumed her conversation without delay.

'Caroline, as you may see, is very sharp and observant; nothing escapes her, and as she tells me all that she sees, she prevents these girls from imposing upon me. I feel that under a mother's eye alone can daughters in particular be rightly brought up; and if we should happen to come to terms, Miss Morison, let it be on the distinct understanding that my authority is in no way delegated to you. You teach them such and such lessons, and report to me how well or ill they have been learned, and what their behaviour has been; for my children are of such an affectionate temper that they cannot bear anybody to find fault with them but me. And in the next place, Miss Morison, I wish you to tell me exactly what you can and cannot do. I beg that you will resort to no subterfuges, for children are acute observers, and if you lay claim to any knowledge or skill which you do not possess, you will completely lose their esteem whenever they find it out.'

'I can teach all the branches of an English education,' said Clara, 'and I understand French grammatically. I could give lessons in Latin for the first year or two, and I could instruct the young ladies in plain needlework.'

'No fancy work, knitting, or crochet?' asked Mrs Denfield.

'No, ma'am.'

'No music?'

'No, ma'am; I know only the notes.'

'Don't you draw at all?'

'No, ma'am.'

'Cannot you teach dancing?'

'Oh yes, at least I can dance well; my master always said I was his best pupil.'

'Was he a Frenchman?'

'Yes, ma'am.'

Mrs Denfield hesitated a little, and then said, 'May I ask your age?'

'Nineteen, ma'am.'

'In what vessel did you come out?'

'In the *Magnificent* — in the intermediate.'

'I have met a Mrs Hastie, just come from Scotland; I suppose a fellow-passenger of yours. May I enquire from her as to how you conducted yourself on board? Excuse my doing so, for in a colony like this one cannot be too careful.'

'Mrs Hastie knows nothing whatever about me, ma'am,' said Clara. 'We never spoke to the cabin passengers all the voyage. I have no reference except to Mr Campbell; my uncle did not even procure me certificates from the schools and masters I attended, for he thought that Mr and Mrs Campbell's interest would be sufficient to procure me the situation I wanted. Will you try me for a month, and see if I will not suit you?'

'Well,' said Mrs Denfield, 'with so few accomplishments, and no recommendations, I suppose you will be glad of a home. I cannot afford to give you a high salary.'

'I would come for twenty pounds a-year,' said Clara, anxious to bring the matter to some conclusion.

'Twenty pounds a-year! what an absurdly high salary for a nursery governess! If you had known anything of music I might have stretched a point, but I do not consider myself justified in offering you any more than fifteen.'

'That is very little,' said Clara; 'I do not see how a young lady can provide her dress and contingencies on such a small income.'

'I do not care for the young person who occupies the place of governess in my family dressing at all expensively. The plainer the better, provided she is clean and neat. Every governess I have had has assisted me with the family needle-work; and Miss Dobson, to whom I gave fifteen pounds a-year, used to dress two of the younger children every morning. She was no musician, certainly, but she drew nicely; I shall be grieved if Caroline's drawing is to be at an end: and she was very skilful in all kinds of fancy work. I cannot possibly offer you any higher salary, Miss Morison; it is for you to accept or decline it.'

Clara's colour went and came several times during this speech; she knew it would be a most uncomfortable situation, but yet she thought it right to take it; for, according to Mr Campbell's account, this was a fair specimen of colonial ladies, and no other employer might appear before her money was spent, and she was destitute. So she consented to take the salary of fifteen pounds a-year, board and washing (this last in moderation), for instructing Mrs Denfield's seven children.

Clara Morison: A Tale of South Australia during the Gold Fever (1854)

Home or away

IN *The Recollections of Geoffry Hamlyn* (1859), HENRY KINGSLEY (1830–76) GAVE AN IDYLLIC PICTURE OF A PASTORALIST'S LIFE IN AUSTRALIA, BUT STOPPED SHORT OF ENDORSING COLONIAL SCHOOLS.

'He must go to school, I am afraid,' said the Major, with a sigh; 'I can't bring my heart to part with him; but his mother has taught him all she knows, so I suppose he must go to school and fight, and get flogged, and come home with a pipe in his mouth, and an oath on his lips, with his education completed. I don't fancy his staying here among these convict servants when he is old enough to learn mischief.'

'He'll learn as much mischief at a colonial school, I expect,' said the Doctor, 'and more, too. All the evil he hears from these fellows will be like the water on a duck's back; whereas, if you send him to school in a town he'll learn a dozen vices he'll never hear of here. Get him a tutor.'

'That is easier said than done, Doctor. It is very hard to get a respectable tutor in the colony.'

'Here is one at your hand,' said the Doctor. 'Take me.'

'My dear friend,' said the Major, jumping up, 'I would not have dared to ask such a thing. If you would undertake him for a short time?'

'I will undertake the boy's education altogether. Potztausend, and why not! It will be a labour of love, and therefore the more thoroughly done. What shall he learn, now?'

'That I must leave to you.'

'A weighty responsibility,' said the Doctor. 'No Latin or Greek, I suppose? They will be no use to him here.'

'Well — no; I suppose not. But I should like him to learn his Latin grammar. You may depend upon it there's something in the Latin grammar.'

'What use has it been to you, Major?'

'Why, the least advantage it has been to me is to give me an insight into the construction of languages, which is some use. But while I was learning the Latin grammar, I learnt other things besides, of more use than the construction of any languages, living or dead. First, I learnt that there were certain things in this world that *must* be done. Next, that there were people in this world, of whom the Masters of Eton were a sample, whose orders must be obeyed without question. Third, I found that it was pleasanter in all ways to do one's duty than to leave it undone. And last, I found out how to bear a moderate amount of birching without any indecent outcry.'

'All very useful things,' said the Doctor. 'Teach a boy one thing well and you show him how to learn others. History, I suppose?'

'As much as you like, Doctor. His mother has taught him his catechism, and all that sort of thing, and she is the fit person, you know. With the exception of that and the Latin grammar, I trust everything to your discretion.'

'There is one thing I leave to you, Major, if you please, and that is corporal chastisement. I am not at all sure that I could bring myself to flog Sam, and, if I did, it would be very inefficiently done.'

'Oh, I'll undertake it,' said the Major, 'though I believe I shall have an easy task. He won't want much flogging.'

The Recollections of Geoffry Hamlyn (1975; FIRST PUBLISHED 1859)

Trash and vanity

LOUISA ANNE MEREDITH (1812–95), BORN IN ENGLAND, SETTLED IN TASMANIA WITH HER HUSBAND IN 1840. SHE WROTE AND ILLUSTRATED BOOKS ABOUT COLONIAL LIFE AND SOCIETY. IN THIS EXTRACT FROM A BOOK FOR CHILDREN, SHE STRESSES THE COLONIAL VIRTUES OF SELF-RELIANCE AND PLAIN LIVING.

'Do you really mean that Lina would roast meat, dress vegetables, and make puddings?' said Lucy, in a disdainful tone.

'I should be ashamed of her if she could not. I have always acted on the belief that my duty, as a mother of daughters, next to training them to be good, is to teach them to be useful.'

'But, dear Mrs Merton, surely young *ladies* ought *never* to go into the *kitchen!*' argued Mrs Bexley, with impressive emphasis.

'I should sincerely commiserate all such young ladies, if ever they became wives in these colonies, or even in England,' replied Mrs Merton, with quiet earnestness. 'No girl knows what vicissitudes may attend her lot in life. No human wisdom can assure to her unchequered affluence; and even should she enjoy such, it may not always command for her perfectly able and trained servants. So that in any case, even with the most secure and brilliant prospects, she ought to be skilled in all those duties which are truly and significantly summed up as "woman's work". Then, if rich, she can direct her household with independent judgment, and see that each member of it does justice to his or her branch of service. She will neither be unreasonably exacting, nor an ignorantly negligent mistress. Her house will be neat and orderly, her family comfortable and well served, and her servants diligent and cheerful.'

'*Hear, hear!* [said Mr Bexley]

'But Lucy, and the young ones too, *shall* know how to cook, and to do true woman's work, or, by George, they shall learn nothing else. A parcel of trash and vanity — that's what they learn now, like the rest of the girls. A smattering of languages — not one thoroughly understood. A tasteless squalling and strumming, in the name of music, that, though they're my own daughters, sets my teeth on edge. I don't believe one of them can make herself a frock, or me a shirt; but all over the house there's a lot of rubbishy "fancy-work" — as they call it, being devoid of either fancy or invention — that costs more time, money, and eyesight than would serve for mastering some useful trade or noble science. I'll stop it, as sure as my name's John Bexley [...] We are going to enter on a new system altogether. We shall see that a young lady is in no whit less ornamental because she is useful, and I trust it will not be very long ere we sit down to a dinner of Lucy's cooking; for, from this day forth, both she and Kate will add housewifery to their other lessons, and in turn act as their mother's disciples — apprentices — *aides-de-camp* — whatever title they like best, in every department of domestic arrangement. They cannot have a better teacher, that I know, and I hope they will endeavour to do her credit. But of this they may rest assured: unless they learn how to use a frying-pan, I'll lock up the piano; and if they don't very soon make me a shirt a-piece, with needles and fingers — *not machines* — I'll confiscate every scrap of fancy-work in the house.'

Tasmanian Friends & Foes, Feathered Furred and Finned: A Family Chronicle of Country Life, Natural History, and Veritable Adventure (1880)

Peaches and prayers

ALFRED HOWITT (1830–1908), EXPLORER, ANTHROPOLOGIST, MAG-
ISTRATE. TRAVELLING ON BEHALF OF THE CENTRAL BOARD FOR THE
PROTECTION OF ABORIGINES IN 1881, HE VISITED A MISSION SCHOOL
NEAR LAKE WELLINGTON IN GIPPSLAND, EASTERN VICTORIA, AND
WROTE AN ACCOUNT OF IT IN A LETTER TO HIS FAMILY.

We had a kind welcome from Mr Hageneur and his 'colleague'
and their wives and spent the afternoon seeing all that was to be
seen and eating peaches … The school … is a Rural School …
The writing of the children was wonderful … they added up
long sums and did division — They did grammar all about
nouns and pronouns etc. and I wondered if they understood it
all. Then the big bell began to sound and everyone trooped to
the church where they had a service of singing, some of the
scriptures read and prayers … Altogether I was pleased and felt
that good must really be done … the children are getting as
good an education as the bulk of the white children … I see no
difference in their capacity for learning, perhaps when they grow
older their minds will close up.

MARY HOWITT WALKER, *Come Wind, Come Weather: A Biography of
Alfred Howitt* (1971)

Lost in Wanneroo

AN ANONYMOUS CORRESPONDENT IN THE WEST AUSTRALIAN
Inquirer IN 1872 PLEADS FOR CHURCH AND STATE ACTION TO PROVIDE
A SCHOOL FOR THE CHILDREN OF WANNEROO.

Letter to the Editor.
Sir,
It is with deep and sincere regret, I am compelled to bring the
following to your notice, in the fervent hope that you will afford
it ventilation in your laudable journal. I happened recently to be

in the neighbourhood of Wanneroo, and not having been in that
direction for upwards of 14 years, when the district was sparsely
populated, I made up my mind to visit as many of the settlers as
it was possible for me to do without running the risk of losing
myself in the bush, to which I am not much accustomed. To be
concise, I visited about 14 families, the homes of which lay in
convenient proximity to the line of my travel. I was more than
surprised to learn from them that a face of a clergyman they have
not seen out there even when a death-bed summons required the
presence of a minister of religion. As for a Sunday gathering for
the worship of their Maker, such a circumstance has never been
known out there. Talk of a school or a place of worship for any
denomination, they answer it is far more certain to find the like
among the savages in the African deserts, with British missionaries supported by British funds, than in Wanneroo, 12 miles from
the Capital of Western Australia, a British Colony. The residents
of the neighbourhood positively informed me that the remaining
settlers in the district — four times their number (say about 60
families) are equally circumstanced.

Themselves at work all day, their poor children rambling about
the bush almost in a state of nudity, not many degrees removed
from their aboriginal companions, is indeed a painful reflection
for them during their hours of toil. Such a state of affairs is not
alone confined to the poorer classes, there being no school or
place for children of any [class] to resort to: they equally ramble
at large through the bush. Surely the heads of the various denominations in the metropolis should not allow such serious and palpable neglect, endangering the souls of so many of their fellow
creatures and all because of the want of a little exertion and union
on their part. I am aware that, with a little extraneous assistance,
they are sanguine they could erect a school house in such a convenient position that the greater majority of the children could
have easy and comfortable access to it, while its greater distance
from the few would only be about four miles. Of course, in so far

as promoting the measure they look to some Government aid in the shape of a teacher and his salary.

I think this a very praiseworthy and laudable object for the clergy, to unite in and promote, and I trust, for the sake of the poor, uninstructed little creatures now leading a semi-barbarous existance in this district, they will cheerfully undertake to carry it out [...]

I am, &c.,
Salus Populi.

MARIAN AVELING (ED.), *Westralian Voices* (1979)

Home visits

PUBLISHED AS THE WORK OF 'A RESIDENT', *Glimpses of Life in Victoria* IS THOUGHT TO HAVE BEEN WRITTEN BY **FRANCES KERR** (1833–?), WIFE OF JOHN HUNTER KERR (1821–74). IT INCLUDES ACCOUNTS OF VISITS TO MELBOURNE'S INSTITUTES FOR THE BLIND AND FOR THE DEAF AND DUMB IN 1871.

Blindness, from various causes, appears to be an affliction to which Australians are peculiarly liable. The scorching summer heat, the keen penetrating dust, the glare of bleached plains and dazzling sandhills, aided by carelessness and neglect, and frequently reacting upon constitutions predisposed to disease, all combine to render ophthalmia, in its various degrees of severity, very common, and often incurable. The Institution for the Blind is well worth a visit. It has been the aim of its promoters to conduct it as far as possible on liberal and un-sectarian principles, that none may be debarred from a participation in its benefits. All the inmates unite in daily prayer, but are permitted to attend their several churches on Sundays, if the means of transit thither can be afforded them. It is also the object of the Institution to give an education which may enable those who receive it to become in time partially or wholly able to maintain themselves.

The house, which is pleasantly situated near the St Kilda Park, is very large and well ventilated, with lofty spacious halls, and is provided with every appliance for convenience and cleanliness. Baths of unusual dimensions admit of the liberal use of cold water, and the care and attention paid to the poor neglected children has in many cases been rewarded by a complete recovery, which at first admission had seemed perfectly hopeless.

The children are trained to be as useful as possible in all household matters. The girls do the washing and mangling of the establishment, the boys the scouring and scrubbing, and all go about their tasks with wonderfully little awkwardness. Besides their lessons, they are taught useful arts, such as netting, knitting, matting, basket-making, etc. Most of them are very fond of reading, but the supply of literature in raised type is, owing to its expense, very small, being limited to the Bible and their primers. Books of various kinds are read aloud to them daily for a certain time, but the exercise is not universally appreciated, the sound of the reading voice appearing to be irksome to them. Like all blind people, these poor children develop a passionate love of music, for the gratification of which innocent taste benevolence has provided an organ, and several pianos, on which they are never weary of practising. The Committee, whose anxious endeavour it is to promote the true welfare of the inmates, are doubtful how far the cultivation of this talent may be conducive to the future happiness of the girls, who all belong to a humble sphere of life, yet it would seem a pity to restrict them in one of their few attainable pleasures.

On visiting the Institution, I was allowed to hear the musical performances, which were really very good. Coming unexpectedly into the large refectory with my conductor, a lady of the committee, we found a great sturdy boy, of about 15, seated at the piano, eagerly picking out chords and modulations, being evidently yet a novice in the art. He had just finished his allotted share of the scrubbing (it being a Saturday), and, his task done, had instantly taken possession of the much-loved instrument, with bare feet, and trousers still tucked up, from his work. The poor awkward fellow was quite absorbed in his occupation, and his sightless face looked perfectly tranquil and happy. A tall girl, one of the principal laundry-maids, and who possessed a sweet, clear voice, sat down, after a little pressing, to give us 'The dearest spot on earth to me,' which she sang prettily to her own accompaniment, which was true both as to time and tune. The most pleasing part of the performances was the choral singing of all the young inmates together, the effect of which was indescribably touching. The girls were ranged in rows on one side of the long hall, and the boys on the other. A small lad officiated ably as organist, and played the accompaniments to hymns and glees. The clear young voices, with their pure shrill tones, carolling out light and joyous strains, contrasted most pathetically with the disfigured faces and sightless eyes of the singers. Among the girls was one whose eyes were preternaturally open; hers was not a case of ophthalmia like the rest, but she was blind from her birth, and she would have been lovely, but for the awful vacancy of those rayless orbs, and the stony blankness they gave to her face.

The cheerfulness of the blind is proverbial, and among these children the same blessed gift seems to prevail extensively, as some indemnification for their privation. Everything is done here to render them happy as well as useful, and they are provided with ample play-grounds, good food, and good warm clothing. Every year they have a special holiday, in common with the children of the adjoining Deaf and Dumb Asylum, and are taken to some sea-side nook for a day's free exercise in the open air. Among the blind there are about twenty belonging to the Roman Catholic Church; and it is worth recording of the much abused race of cabmen, that certain among their number belonging to that church agree among each other to convey these children gratuitously to their chapel on Sunday mornings, the distance being beyond their walking powers.

The Deaf and Dumb are lodged in another large building in the neighbourhood of that devoted to the blind, the situations of both asylums being fine and open. This institution was commenced in August 1862, but the building in use at the present time was not erected till the year 1866, and has recently been enlarged by the addition of a new wing. It stands on six acres of ground, a part of which is used as a playground for the pupils, while the remainder has been carefully planted. The front of the house looks out upon broad gravel walks and grass and flower plots surrounding a fountain, while the rear of the garden is utilized for vegetable and fruit trees.

There are at present (1872) seventy-eight pupils in the institution, but there is sufficient accommodation to admit sixty of each sex. The dormitories are very spacious, and provided with excellent full-sized beds. In each is a small apartment for a teacher, and the whole house is lighted with gas.

The chief superintendent is himself deaf and dumb, but is a man of superior education. The appearance of the pupils is extremely pleasing, their faces radiant with health, and their eyes beaming with intelligence.

A visit to the large schoolroom, where these young creatures are collected learning their lessons in a silence which seems strange and unnatural, yet which leaves no trace of depression on their countenances, is very interesting. Here and there indeed may be seen a dull, heavy-looking face, but usually it is that of one who has been sent to the asylum when nearly grown up, and to whom the difficulties of learning are greatly enhanced by previous neglect.

Various signs are used to supplement the finger language, and the reading-lesson is also an object-lesson, the words to be mastered being drawn on a black board, and explained to the children by signs. The higher classes appear to be well advanced, their writing and ciphering are excellent, and they are capable of explaining by intelligible pantomime abstract terms, of which no drawn objects could convey the sense; such, for instance, as probable, improbable—pure, impure, etc. Several of the pupils show considerable talent for drawing, their style being bold and firm.

A few of their number are the children of parents who can afford to pay for their maintenance, but the majority are admitted free of charge. The boys and girls learn in the same schoolroom, and also dine together. They are taught various trades, and fitted to earn their own livelihood when they leave the institution.

The clothing provided for the inmates is all good of its kind, and has as little as possible the appearance of a charity uniform, the dress of the boys being a suit of plain coloured tweed, that of the girls warm shepherd's plaid dresses in winter, or prints in summer, with durable leghorn hats.

> *Glimpses of Life in Victoria by 'A Resident'* (1996; FIRST PUBLISHED
> 1876)

Waifs and strays

JOHN STANLEY JAMES (1843–96) CAME TO AUSTRALIA IN 1875. HIS
REPORTS ON HIGH AND LOW LIFE IN MELBOURNE WERE PUBLISHED IN
THE *Argus* IN 1876 AND REPRINTED IN *The Vagabond Papers* (1877). IN
THIS EXTRACT, HE VISITS THE GOSPEL-HALL STATE SCHOOL, OFF
LITTLE BOURKE STREET, MELBOURNE.

There has been so much talk lately about Ragged Schools and education, 'godless' and otherwise, that, the other day, I thought I would go and thoroughly inspect the workings of this institution, where endeavour is being made to reclaim, without the aid of the Churches, the little waifs of this city; so I solicited the services of my friend Mr Hill, the police court missionary, to introduce me without my object being known, I find that I am getting a very unenviable reputation amongst civil servants, and to obtain the truth I have to travel under the disguise of mediocre respectability, and not as a vagabond. Nature has

aided me in this endeavour, and no one could be more uncon-
scious of my identity than Mr Ellis, the teacher, who kindly
showed us everything, and volunteered the remark that 'if the
"Vagabond" was to come round here he'd get a fine study of
character.' We arrived at the school at two o'clock, and found
all voices joining in the chorus of 'Silver Threads,' the accompaniment being played by the young lady assistant, Miss
Hutton, on the harmonium ...There were about 100 girls and
boys present, of all ages, from three to fifteen years. The average
attendance is over 120, but on this day (Wednesday) many children were absent, selling in the market. Friday is another day on
which many children are kept away from school, sent gathering
wood, &c., by their guardians; and every afternoon a number
of boys leave at half-past two, to obtain the first instalment of
the *Herald*, which they sell in the streets. Partly for their sake the
school is opened in the afternoon half-an-hour earlier than the
usual time. The room is rather dingy and dirty, the only orna-
ments a few maps; but the children, seated on forms, sang
heartily and merrily, and appeared to thoroughly relish the
music. After 'Silver Threads' was finished, a boy of about twelve
was called out to sing the solo of the 'Little Crossing Sweep.'
His name was John Stanley. He had only one hand, but a magnificent voice, and would have made a good chorister. The
other children joined in the chorus with a will. Then some girls
sang 'Little Sister's Gone to Sleep' in a very affecting manner.
The music and singing were altogether good, and the children
seemed to enjoy them and to appreciate the sentiments of the
songs, and I cannot but think that they did them some good ...
The conclusion of the musical performance was the singing of
a verse in very 'pigeon' English by a little half-caste Chinese boy,
five years of age. He was well clothed in a knickerbocker suit,
and when Mr Ellis perched him on the desk he laughed and
crowed with joy, and no one would have thought that he was
the Ginx's baby of the establishment [...]

The Chinese children are, as a rule, the best dressed and cared for, and are decidedly the smartest. Their heathen parents appear to take pleasure in availing themselves of the Education Act, and send the children to school at a very early age. Here, *par exemple*, are the two Masters Hang Hai, aged four and six years respectively. The youngest has one of the finest heads I have seen for a long time, and is very precocious. When Miss Hutton takes charge of the junior class, containing about thirty children, and, giving a slate to each scholar, makes a series of figures on the blackboard, which they have to copy, Master Hang Hai commences displaying his skill by filling up his slate with a quantity of hieroglyphics, which he triumphantly shows to me. In return, he wishes to see what I have got in my note-book. Before I left I was on quite intimate terms with this young gentleman; when I returned to his class he saluted me with a friendly nod of recognition, and playfully shook Miss Hutton's cane at me. He had possessed himself of this instrument of tuition, and was banging the blackboard with it, evidently, in his own mind, 'bossing' the class — altogether a most humorous young customer.

MICHAEL CANNON (ED.), *The Vagabond Papers* (1983; FIRST PUB-
LISHED IN FIVE VOLUMES 1877–78)

Liberties unheard-of

RICHARD TWOPENY (1857–1915), JOURNALIST, BORN IN ENGLAND,
CAME TO AUSTRALIA IN 1876. HIS ACCOUNT OF AUSTRALIAN LIFE AND
CHARACTER FOCUSES ON THE PROCESS OF 'GROWING UP COLONIAL' IN
THE 1880S.

The Australian schoolgirl, with all her free-and-easy manner, and what the Misses Prunes and Prisms would call want of maidenly reserve, could teach your bread-and-butter miss a good many things which would be to her advantage. It is true that neither schoolmistresses nor governesses could often pass a

Cambridge examination, nor have they any very great desire for intellectual improvement. But the colonial girl is sharper at picking up what her mistress does know than the English one, and she has more of the boy's emulation. Whatever her station in life, she is bound to strum the piano; but in no country is a good pianoforte player more rare, or do you hear greater trash strummed in a drawing-room. Languages and the other accomplishments are either neglected or slurred over; but, on the other hand, nearly every colonial girl learns something of household work, and can cook some sort of a dinner, yea, and often cut out and make herself a dress. She is handy with her fingers, frank, but by no means necessarily fast in manner, good-natured and fond of every species of fun. If her accomplishments are not many, she sets little value on those she possesses, and never feels the want of, or wastes a regret, on any others.

Almost all girls go to school, but the home-training leads to little obedience or respect for their teachers, and the parental authority is constantly interposed to prevent well-deserved punishments. Accustomed to form judgments early and fearlessly, each girl measures her mistress by her own standard; and if she comes up to that standard, an *entente cordiale* is established, the basis whereof is the equality which each feels to subsist independent of their temporary relations [...]

The Australian schoolboy is indeed a 'caution.' With all the worst qualities of the English boy, he has but few of his redeeming points. His impudence verges on impertinence, and his total want of respect for everybody and everything passes all European understanding. His father and mother he considers good sort of folk, whom he will not go out of his way to displease; his schoolmaster often becomes, *ipso facto*, his worst enemy, in the never-ceasing war with whom all is fair, and obedience but the last resource. Able to ride almost as soon as he can walk, he is fond of all athletic sports; but it is not till leaving school that his athleticism becomes fully pronounced: thus reversing the order observed in England, where the great majority of the boys, who are cricket and football mad at school, more or less drop those pursuits as young men. He is too well fed and supplied with pocket-money ever to feel the need for theft, but it is difficult to get him to understand Dr. Arnold's views about lying and honour. Though not wanting in pluck, he lacks the wholesome experience of a few good lickings, and can easily pass his school-days without having a single fight. He is quarrelsome enough, but his quarrels rarely go farther than hard words and spiteful remarks. At learning he is apt, having the spirit of rivalry pretty strong in him.

In all but one or two schools classes are too much mixed to make a gentlemanly tone possible, and such little refinements as tidiness of dress are out of the question. When he is at home for the holidays, his mother tries to dig some manners into him (if she has any herself); but he has far too great a sense of the superiority of the rising generation to pay more attention to her than is exacted by the fear of punishment. Unfortunately, that punishment is very sparingly made use of; and when it is used, it takes a very lenient shape, public opinion being strongly against corporal punishment, however mild, and according to children a number of liberties undreamed of in the old country.

Town Life in Australia (1973; FIRST PUBLISHED 1883)

Pupil-teacher

MARY GILMORE (1865–1962), POET, WAS THE DAUGHTER OF AN ITINERANT CARPENTER. SHE HAD HER SCHOOLING IN VARIOUS NEW SOUTH WALES COUNTRY SCHOOLS, AND WAS AN UNCERTIFIED PUPIL-TEACHER WHEN SHE WAS TWELVE.

When I had learned my letters and could read 'Miss Jane Bond has a nice new doll,' Mrs Mackay sent for me to go and sit with her children and learn from their tutor. Under the tutor I began to write and make figures, and to say without knowing why it was so that two and two make four.

'Why do they make four and not five?' I wanted to know. I was told 'They do it because they do.'

The end of the lessons came soon, as, the building finished, we moved on. However, my father continued to keep me learning some sort of lessons, and by the time I was six my mother set me to teach my brothers. I taught them as my father had taught me — by analysis and comparison of form: A — like a tent with a stick across; B — like two D's, and so on. I got Hugh right on to Z; but John would not progress. I thought him terribly stupid. John was about three years old. I think we all thought ourselves nearly grown up [...]

When the family went on trek again I was left behind at Brooklyn to continue my education at the Brucedale school. Here I suddenly learned to write; not merely to make letters and spell words, but to express my own thoughts, and from then on, till I left that school, I spent my dinner hours at the slate in a fury of composition instead of going out to play. I was like something for whom the gates of the world had opened. I had wings. I could not help writing.

When I was about eight years of age the three elder of us were sent to Mr Pentland's Academy (usually called the Grammar School) at North Wagga Wagga. Mr Pentland at once set me to learning Greek, the only girl he thought worthy of the privilege; and as five minutes did me for my other lessons, I was put to teaching the other junior pupils in between whiles. My mother objected to my doing this, but my father wanted the Greek, and so I stayed on. Then the river floods came, the school was surrounded by the Murrumbidgee, and part of the place fell down [...]

When Mr Pentland's little Grammar School ceased to exist, we were sent across the river to the Wagga Wagga Public School on the sandhill above Gurwood Street, then under the headship of Peter Durie, with Miss Grace Annie Cameron Galloway as mistress of the girls' department. We walked three miles to school, and paid a shilling a week each for our education. Then while yet only twelve years old, I went to act as an uncertified pupil-teacher.

Old Days: Old Ways (1934)

The bush school

HENRY LAWSON (1867–1922), POET AND SHORT STORY WRITER, RECALLS HIS NEW SOUTH WALES STATE PRIMARY SCHOOL IN THE 1870S. 'MLISS' IS DERIVED FROM THE HEROINE OF BRET HARTE'S NOVELLA *M'liss* (1860).

Father and a few others petitioned for a provisional school at Pipeclay — it was Eurunderee now, the black name had been restored. Father built the school. It was of bark. I remembered the dimensions for a long time, but have forgotten them now; anyway it was a mere hut. It was furnished with odds and ends thrown out of the public school in Mudgee, when the public school got new desks, stools and things. Father made blackboards and easels and mended the rickety furniture. The books, slates and things were all second-hand and old.

A selector, an Irishman, named John Tierney, was selected as schoolmaster. He had served in some capacity in the Army in Africa, a paymaster or something. His strong points were penmanship, arithmetic, geography and the brogue; his weak ones were spelling, grammar and singing. He was six feet something and very gaunt. He spent some months 'training' in the public school in Mudgee, and had a skillion built on to the school, where he camped. I don't know whether he made his own bed, but his sister-in-law used to send his meals up to the school — one or other of us children used to carry them. I remember carrying a dinner of curried stew and rice, in a cloth between two plates, and a lot of the gravy leaked out. I suppose the dignity of Pipeclay wouldn't have stood his cooking for himself.

The Spencers went a couple of miles over the ridges at the back of Pipeclay to a slab and shingle public school on Old Pipeclay. Maybe their father thought they would get a better education. We went there later on — on account of a difference, I suppose, between our people and Tierney.

There were a good many Germans round; the majority of the farmers were Germans — all the successful ones were. There were a good few Irish, and the yellow and green had not faded yet. So there was fierce sectarian and international bitterness, on top of the usual narrow-minded, senseless, and purposeless little local feuds and quarrels; but there is no room for these things in this book.

The first day, one day in the first week at the Bark School, was a great day in my life, for I was given a copybook and pen and ink for the first time. The master believed in children leaving slate and pencil and commencing with pen and paper as early as possible. While setting me my first copy he told me not to go back and try to 'paint' the letters. I am following that rule in this book, with reference to sentences. Better to strike out than paint. We had learnt our A.B.C. — and about a Cat, a Bat, and a Fat Rat — somewhere in the dim past [...]

Then the trouble commenced. The master explained the hemispheres to us on the map, and doubled it back as far as he could to show us how they were intended to come together. We hadn't a globe. I thought the hemispheres should come round the other way; my idea was that the dome of the sky was part of the world and the whole world was shaped like half an orange, with the base for the earth, but I couldn't account for the other half. The master explained that the world was round. I thought it must have something to rest on, but I was willing to let that stand over for a while, and wanted the hill question cleared up. The master got an india-rubber ball and stuck a pin in it up to the head and told us that the highest mountain in the world would not have the ten thousandth (or somethingth) effect on the roundness of the earth that the head of that pin would on the roundness of the ball. That seemed satisfactory. He it was, I think, who tied a string to the neck of a stone ink-bottle and swung it round, to illustrate the power of gravitation and the course of the earth round the sun. And the string broke and the bottle went through a window-pane. But there was no string from the earth to the sun that we could see. Later on I got some vague ideas of astronomy, but could never realize boundless space or infinity. I can't now. That's the main thing that makes me believe in a supreme being. But infinity goes further than the supreme.

A favourite fad of the master's was that the school, being built of old material and standing on an exposed siding, might be blown down at any moment, and he trained the children to dive under the desks at a given signal so that they might have a chance of escaping the falling beams and rafters when the crash came. Most of us, I believe, were privately resolved to dive for the door at the first crack. These things pleased Father when he heard them, for he didn't build things to come down. When the new school was built, the Old Bark School was used by the master as a stable and may be standing still for all I know.

Our school books were published for use in the National Schools of Ireland, and the reading books dealt with Athlone and surrounding places, and little pauper boys and the lady at the great house. The geography said: 'The inhabitants of New Holland are amongst the lowest and most degraded to be found on the surface of the earth.' Also: 'When you go out to play at 1 o'clock the sun will be in the south part of the sky.' The master explained this, and we had to take his word for it — but then it was in the book. The geography also stated that in bad seasons the inhabitants of Norway made flour from the inner bark of a kind of tree — which used to make Father wild, for he was a Norwegian. Our name, of course, is Larsen by rights.

There was a Mliss in the school, and a reckless tomboy — a she-devil who chaffed the master and made his life a misery to him — and a bright boy, and a galoot (a hopeless dunce), a joker, and a sneak, and a sweet gentle affectionate girl, a couple of show scholars — model pupils the master called 'em — and one who was always in trouble and mischief and always late, and one who always wanted to fight, and the rest of them in between. The children of the Germans were Australians — and children are children all over the world. There was Cornelius Lyons, who rolled his r's like a cock dove and had a brogue which made even the master smile. And there was the obstinate boy, Johnny B —, who seemed insensible to physical pain. The master called him out one day: 'John B —, stand out!' Johnny stood out. 'Hold out your hand!' Johnny held out his hand, the master struck it, Johnny placed it behind his back and held out the other, the master struck that, and Johnny put that hand behind and held out the first; the master set his teeth, so did Jack — and so on for half a dozen strokes. Then suddenly the master threw down the cane, laid his hand on the boy's shoulder and spoke gently to him — and Jack broke down. Looking back, I don't think it was fair — Jack could have claimed a foul.

And there was Jim Bullock, whose 'eddication was finished' at the Old Bark School. 'Oh yes,' he said to me, years later, while giving me a lift in his dray, 'John Tierney finished me nicely.'

Amongst the scholars was a black gohanna. He lived in a dead hollow tree near the school, and was under the master's immediate protection. On summer days he'd lay along a beam over the girls' seats, and improve his mind a little, and doze a lot. The drone of the school seemed good for his nerves. They say a black gohanna haunted the tent I was born in, and I remember one in the house on the flat — I used to see the impression of his toes on the calico ceiling when he slithered along overhead. It may have been the same gohanna, and he might have been looking after me, but I had always a horror of reptiles.

COLIN RODERICK (ED.), *The Bush Undertaker and Other Stories* (1989; FIRST PUBLISHED 1970)

Whispers and whiskers

MARY FULLERTON (1868–1946), POET, BORN IN A BARK HUT NEAR
GLENMAGGIE, VICTORIA, PUBLISHED HER MEMORIES OF CHILDHOOD
IN *Bark House Days*.

I have sometimes wondered why they built the old schoolhouse
in that stretch of bush the settlers have still left in its primitive
state, because of its barrenness. Not a child of those who went
to it daily but had a fair walk to reach it. The settlement was a
selvage running along the river valley, skirting the hills that
hugged the valley in a kind of jostling embrace, as though trying to push it back to the water's edge. From this selvage of rich
farm land came the children that filled the forms of the old
schoolhouse. That is to say, old now; it was new then. A fine
place we thought it, roofed with the first galvanized iron that
had come to that district from the limitless world without, of
which Melbourne stood, to us, as the centre. We had never seen
galvanized iron before; we had known only bark as a covering
for rafters. The settlers, in their haste, and because of the difficulties of transport and the pressure of profitable work, had contented themselves with humble enough houses; a kind of superior mia-mia structure generally did service, though one remem-
bers that the early houses, crude as they were, were generally
comfortable […]

The day the school opened I remember well. It was a beautiful spring morning, and when we came over the hilltop that
gave us a sudden vision of the new building, our eyes were positively dazzled by the beauty and brightness of the roof flashing
in the sun. It was symbolic of the irradiation of learning on
ignorance; of knowledge on innocence. But it was too sudden,
our first introduction to that sight. Fortunately for our understanding, the processes of instruction within the school proved
to be of a more graduated and gradual nature. Our eyes ached
at the whirl of stars the sunlight made of that roof under which

we had been impatient to assemble, and we hung back. It seemed like going into the world, and we had not realized it. The boys pushed on promptly. 'Not a bad-looking place,' said Fred, patronizingly, to hide the thrill it had given him. Nearer, we saw a round chimney of black iron, and the walls outside painted like father's dray. No, not like father's dray, for that was red, but the dray was the only thing we had that wore a coat of paint. The walls of the school were white, or nearly so, and flashed at the addresses of the sun almost as brightly as did the roof that we lost sight of presently at closer approach. Inside, the building was cleaner than any school I have since seen, or ever think to see, unless I become an inspector of new buildings of the kind. It was white from the hands of the creator. It awed us, not that our homes were dirty — who so clean as the wives of the pioneers? But this was so new, so white.

I was one of the little ones, and had a place allotted me on a form when we were sorted out. I thought it lovely to sit in a row; we never sat so at home. Anyhow, to sit with strange little girls is much more interesting than to sit with one's sisters. The forms were one above the other; a gallery of them along one side of the school. The gallery was full of children all grown along the selvage of creek. Some of them I knew, some of them I did not know; there was not much visiting except among near neighbours.

At first I was too shy to notice my surroundings or my companions; then I began to look about me. The rest of the space, except where our hats and bags hung, was taken up by desks with ink-wells let in at regular intervals, and there were new slates lying in rows, and beautiful pencils with coloured paper pasted round them. We in the gallery had no slates and pencils; how I wished we had. There was a blackboard on an easel in front of us, which I found later was to be a kind of collective slate for the gallery; the teacher wrote on it, and we learned from it. In front of the scholars' desks was the teacher's, a wonderful piece of furniture I thought it. I nudged Claribel, next me, and whispered,

'See the chest of drawers'. I'd heard of chests of drawers, though we hadn't one. But though this had a long drawer under the lid that lifted up, we soon learned it wasn't what I'd thought it to be. The lid sloped, and the teacher wrote on the sloping part, sitting on a high stool. Later, I discovered that, besides paper and things of that kind which she kept in her desk, it was the receptacle for confiscated articles belonging to us children. I brought my favourite alley one day — we played at home with boy cousins, and had what are usually thought to be masculine tastes in games — to show Daisy Speary, who needed impressing, and that found its way into the teacher's desk. It was a week before I gained courage to ask for it, and then I didn't ask; it was Dick who did so. But Daisy was clumsy to let that alley drop, and roll as it did, and leap down the gallery steps, so that not even the most lenient teacher could ignore it. Dick asked for it when he was seeking recovery of his possum-skinning knife, which had been confiscated, too, when caught in the act of nicking his desk. For we were human children, and with aboriginal proclivities, sins or not, I cannot pretend to say. Know, then, that the virgin freshness of that dazzling interior — of the exterior, too — was before long transformed to a very work-a-day appearance. There were originally but carefully drawn maps on the walls, but soon, perhaps in a spirit of imitation, there were freehand maps in black miniature prodigally splashed about desks and floor, as well as more upon the walls than the Department vouched for. Nay, even the ceiling, I believe, shared the speckled condition of the rest, for there are such things as squirts where the objective is out of arms' reach.

Those who sat next me, and those around me, I gradually took stock of as that first day wore on. Everything was to be begun. The children had to be sorted; in the first place they were drafted according to size. It was the only plan till something of our accomplishments was known. Somewhat small for my age, I was first placed on a lower form of the gallery. That was tentative, till the next test was applied; information as to our ages was then sought. That sent me to a row higher up. Lastly, places for many of us were changed again, when the educational test was put. Some of the bigger ones came down, and some of the dots were given the importance of a seat at one of the desks. It was really an examination of our parents, as well as of us. Some of the parents had given their children a good start, while waiting for the erection of a school in the settlement. There were others of the parents who, through lack of time, thought, or educational capacity, had done nothing in the way of teaching their children. It was a painful hour for some of us; a triumphant time for others, that period of final winnowing.

I remember seeing, with amazement, Jim Speary, one of the brothers who had sawn the wonderful timber, pass from a higher desk to a lower one, amongst lads of seven or eight, to begin his A.B.C. His fluffy whiskers looked strangely out of place amongst the babies around him. His embarrassment would have touched the hearts of any but children. We read shame in it, and a tendency to rebellion, but, mean little primitives as we were, we were all a-grin.

Bark House Days (1964; FIRST PUBLISHED 1921)

The old bush school

John O'Brien was the pen-name of Patrick Joseph Hartigan (1879–1952), a Catholic priest who was for many years inspector of Catholic schools in the Goulburn diocese and parish priest at Narrandera, New South Wales.

'Tis a queer, old battered landmark that belongs to other years;
With the dog-leg fence around it, and its hat about its ears,
And the cow-bell in the gum-tree, and the bucket on the stool,
There's a motley host of memories round that old bush school —
With its seedy desks and benches, where at least I left a name

Carved in agricultural letters — 'twas my only bid for fame;
And the spider-haunted ceilings, and the rafters, firmly set,
Lined with darts of nibs and paper (doubtless sticking in them
     yet),
And the greasy slates and blackboards, where I oft was proved a
     fool
And a blur upon the scutcheon of the old bush school.

There I see the boots in order — ''lastic-sides' we used to wear —
With a pair of 'everlastin's' cracked and dusty here and there;
And we marched with great 'high action' — hands behind and
     eyes before —
While we murdered 'Swanee River' as we tramped around the
     floor.

Still the scholars pass before me with their freckled features
     grave,
And a nickname fitting better than the name their mothers
     gave;
Tousled hair and vacant faces, and their garments every one
Shabby heirlooms in the family, handed down from sire to son.
Ay, and mine were patched in places, and half-masted, as a
     rule —
They were fashionable trousers at the old bush school. [...]

Hard the cobbled road of knowledge to the feet of him who plods
After fragile fragments fallen from the workshop of the gods;
Long the quest, and ever thieving pass the pedlars o'er the hill
With the treasures in their bundles, but to leave us questing still.
Mystic fires horizons redden, but each crimson flash in turn
Only lights the empty places in the bracken and the fern;
So in after years I've proved it, spite of pedant, crank, and fool,
Very much the way I found it at the old bush school.

Around the Boree Log & Other Verses (1994; FIRST PUBLISHED 1921)

Voices from Aboriginal schools

A mission school manager, a teacher, and a mother give their views on the teaching of Aboriginal children in late nineteenth-century Victoria.

From the **Reverend C.W. Kramer**, manager of the mission school at Lake Ebeneezer Station, Lake Hindmarsh, 1 October 1879:

In reference to the complaint lodged by R. Stewart etc regarding the conduct of the teacher here, the Rev. T. Bogisch, I beg to say that, having carefully investigated the several charges brought against him by those men I find:

1. That there is no evidence of undue severity on the part of Mr Bogisch. Certainly the boy Johnnie received a flogging as a just punishment for raising an axe against Mr Bogisch and pulling him down by the beard. It may have been administered on the back as the part objected to by the blacks, but they object to any punishment. The fact of the boy having died some weeks ago accounts for the blacks complaining of a punishment administered more than two years since, for so they are in the habit of doing.

2. The charge of stone-throwing is not substantiated. They state that they saw a stone flying but did not see by whom it was thrown. Mr Bogisch is positive that he never threw a stone at the boys and believes it must have been thrown by one of the boys who will occasionally, when they think they are unobserved throw missiles such as small stones or lumps of earth at one another in a playful way, regardless of the consequences.

3. They have no means of forming an opinion as to whether the children get more flogging than learning at school beyond what they hear from the children and these will be sure to exaggerate every little slap they receive into a big flogging as they call it. Their tricks and naughtiness can of

course not always be winked at, if a proper discipline is to be upheld, but we act from the principle, that, if errors are to be made they had better be made on mercy's side seeing that we have to deal with a people who are fast dying out, and so the punishment we may have occasion to administer is always tempered with much mercy.

4. These men have no children of school age, while those parents whose children attend school have not brought any complaint against Mr Bogisch, who, I have reason to believe, is an efficient teacher and quite competent to conduct a school satisfactorily in every respect.

[...]

LETTER FROM TEACHER **D. R. MORRIS** AT LAKE TYERS TO THE SECRETARY, EDUCATION DEPARTMENT, 1 APRIL 1887:

I have the honour to acknowledge the receipt of the Program of Instruction just issued by the Department.

I desire briefly to lay before you the following considerations as regards its bearing on the school under my charge. To begin, I may premise the school is simply an aboriginal school connected with the Church of England Mission, nearly all pure blacks — one half-caste and four of European descent.

Their knowledge of English is extremely limited, and [they] are wholly dependent upon school for their knowledge of the language, being isolated from intercourse with any surrounding population — indeed there is none.

As a consequence their vocabulary is confined to the expression of their simplest wants. In class work every word not ordinarily used by them, allusion, or idiom, requires careful and repeated explanation, which would be clear to any English child. The aboriginal children have no homework — mostly living in Mia-mias or camps — their social condition precludes this: they are simply savages being brought under the first influences of civilisation. Parents [are] hunters — without any forethought or aspiration, other than the supply of their animal wants. Intellectually, their capacities are of the lowest type with hardly any power of abstraction or reasoning: this is the material we have to work upon: and by the Department we stand on precisely the same footing as the best State School in Victoria as regards the inspector's results and reports ...

... At last examination, the question of the new Program of Instruction was referred to, with the exceptional difficulties we had to contend with, and its unsuitability to a people such as these are who would be unable to comprehend it, and to whom it would not be of the slightest utility in their future lives as simply wandering aboriginals ...

[...]

LETTER FROM ABORIGINAL MOTHER **BESSY CAMERON** AND OTHERS TO THE SECRETARY, EDUCATION DEPARTMENT, 29 FEBRUARY 1891:

We the undersigned Aborigines at Ramahyuck most respectfully request that you will be so good to remove from our school as soon as you can the two ladies who have the charge of our school, as they demoralise our children so that we felt it our duty to take them from school, and shall not send them back until we get a properly trained and truthful teacher.

We need only one lady teacher, but no mischief makers, for it is no easy matter to bring up our children in the good way, but they receive bad examples and nasty words such as 'you horrible nasty creatures'.

We have requested Mr Hagenauer to call at your office, and to state things as they are, and what is needed. Please help us soon.

My Heart is Breaking (1993) AUSTRALIAN ARCHIVES & THE PUBLIC RECORD OFFICE OF VICTORIA

Choking on chalk

THEA ASTLEY (1925–) SET HER NOVEL OF RACE RELATIONS AND SMALL-TOWN PREJUDICE *A Kindness Cup* IN LATE NINETEENTH-CENTURY NORTH QUEENSLAND.

'In this noisome little colony,' Mr Dorahy replied mildly with more sweat than usual running down the edges of his weary hair, 'where masculinity is top dog, it seems to me that some occasional thought should be given, chivalrously you under-stand — *do* you understand? — to the sex that endures most of our nastiness.'

'You're mad,' Buckmaster said.

'You become that which you do.'

Mr Buckmaster allowed himself a tiny bleached smile. 'Any bloody teacher in this place would have to be mad.'

'I meant you,' Mr Dorahy said. The small scar of some long-forgotten protest whitened on his cheek. 'Would you want your son to become one of the mindless, insensitive, money-grubbing bulls you see around this town and that he gives every indication of aping?'

'I'll have you sacked, by Christ!' Pulling at his crotch. His cutaway donned for the occasion — running the bejesus out of a back-town schoolie — stank in the heat. Summer was crouch-ing all over the town.

'Please do,' Mr Dorahy said. 'I am so tired.'

But it did not, could not happen. Who else was there for a pittance in a provisional school slapped hard in the sweating sugar-grass north of the tropic?

I am single, Mr Dorahy told himself proceeding through the drudgeries of instruction. I am single and thirty-seven and in love with landscape. Even this. Other faces cut close to the heart. His assistants, say, who took the junior forms. Married and widowed Mrs Wylie gathering in the chickens for a spot of rote tables or spelling, beating it out in an unfinished shack at the boundary fence. Or Tom Willard with his combined primary forms and his brimstone lay-preaching on the Sabbath. Or himself as a gesture to culture, keeping on the bigger boys of his parish, for he was priestly enough to use that word, for a bit of elementary classics and a purging of Wordsworth. It all seemed useless, as foolish as trying to put Tintern Abbey into iambic hexameters. He had come with a zealot's earnestness, believing a place such as this might need him. And there was, after all, only loneliness: he was cut off from the pulse of the town, although, he insisted to himself rationalising furiously, he had been regularly to meetings of the Separation League and had blown only occasional cold air on their hot. He had drunk with the right men. He had kept his mouth closed. He had assumed nothing. And yet other faces, the wrong sort because they were black, had their own especial tug, the sad black flattened faces of the men working with long knives in the cane and their scabby children making games in the dust at the entrances and exits of towns. The entrances. The exits. Observe that, he cautioned himself […]

'Hands up,' Dorahy had said, 'the boys who have not prepared this prose.'

Eight hands were raised.

'All of you!' he marvelled. 'Not one! Well,' he said sadly, his snaggle teeth exposed in a disillusioned smile, 'you will have to be punished. Line up!'

He rooted in the corner press and took out a cane which he wiped down with his right hand, lingeringly assessing the shape and the pliancy of it. It was all parody. All burlesque. The boys wore half-grins as comic Dorahy passed down the line of them giving the lightest of sarcastic taps to each outstretched palm.

When he reached young Buckmaster he did not even bother with the tap. Ironically, dismissively, he brushed him to one side with the most offensive of negligent plays of the stick. The boy turned scarlet as the master moved on flicking parodically at the next two outflung hands, and his hate, which had been till then a nebulous affair, crystallised into the stubborn matter that he would bear vengefully through to his middle age.

Dorahy was unaware. Perhaps. Their enmity, though tacit, had long been sensed mutually.

The boys returned to their places and Dorahy, wearily, despairingly, took up his chalk and began scribbling the work upon the board. The grains of it, the choking whiteness of it, saturated his whole being, and the phlegm he coughed anguishedly at the beginning of each day was a purging more of the spirit than the lungs. His hands dusty with it, he wiped drily along the seams of his trousers, slapped till small clouds arose. Looking through the classroom window for a moment while the boys painfully took down his fair copy, he could feel that the whole landscape, right down to the seaward fence, was chalk. He sighed.

A Kindness Cup (1989; FIRST PUBLISHED 1974)

Ruffians now and then

RANDOLPH BEDFORD (1868–1941), NOVELIST AND NEWSPAPERMAN, HAD A STATE SCHOOL EDUCATION IN OUTER SUBURBAN SYDNEY.

My school had its place, while the state school was being built, in the Congregational church on Cook's River Road. There were large fig trees at the back of the church, and these were obscene with flying foxes in the fruit season. All summer the cicadas sang their songs to the sun. They were all sizes and colours, little black fellows, and green and yellow monsters, with rubies for eyes. I carried them in my pockets to school and my affection was fatal to many. Those who escaped death for the moment were the cicadas I had placed in a sun-ray on the desk, so that they should sing, and this produced beatings with a cane, very grievous to the buttocks of a small boy studying entomology at first hand. I was now definitely out of the boy-angel stage, having acquired a thirst for knowledge of anything and everything and become thereby mischievous. No more I recited 'Little Bobby Reed'. My mother had given up twisting my hair into a single fearful curl, shaped like a hippocampus, and teachers had decided that Angel-Face's palms and buttocks were no longer immune from the cane. I was growing up.

Being discovered for the third time in the possession of cicadas I was brutally beaten, and to mark my sense of the injustice, so lively that it banished fear and left me callous to pain, I in protest stamped all the way back to my desk. The enraged schoolmaster called me out again, flogged again, and I stamped all the way back to my seat, which I sat upon as lightly as I could.

He called me back again. He was transfigured by rage as he flogged me. I stamped back again and he flogged me again and again, until he threw down the cane and ran out. I stamped back again. I had beaten him, but I was so much a burning, living ache that I could not sit down and take my ease after stress. It was unjustly done in the first place. He had seen me inattentive to anything but the cicada, had walked up to my desk and caned me on the knuckles, recalling me to the facts of a hard world by the vicious bite of the unexpected cane. A little kindness to me then, and I belonged to him for life. But I had sulked after it and then had been called out to punishment by a mad man. Then it became my business to conquer him, or at least, not to be conquered; and I did it at the price of a burning, aching hide for the next few days, until my bruises established colouration, and so brought me ease, comparatively [...]

At the end of two years we left Fivedock. It was too far out of the city for my father's work. In those two years I had learned much from Mr Soutar, the headmaster, but had been taught very little of my own land. Australia I could not visualize from any teaching of school. The continent lay, a great sprawling body, without features of identification. We knew of the

Moonbi Range, and the Gourock Range, and of Hobart and Victoria and Fremantle, and Captain Cook; but of the Spaniards and the Dutchmen who had adventured before Cook, nothing. But we knew all about the Saxon Heptarchy and Boadicea, and could recite a long list of kings who didn't matter to us as much as the source and end of the lost rivers and of Central Australia's old inland sea.

The history of our own country was bowdlerized or ignored. Australia's first foundation was a convict settlement, established because there were scores of capital offences, now properly regarded as petty thefts, and muddled officialdom in England thought it cheaper to transport than to hang, especially as the American colonies had become the United States and were no more open to English felonry. Convict labour at the price of sustenance was commercialized, and the graft began with the contractors for transportation, who were paid for all the convicts embarked and not for the convicts delivered. So there was profit in 'letting them die'; and the voyages were terms of horror. All the facts were suppressed. Our 'history' became a laudation of the ruffians of the Rum Corps and their successors, the pure Merinos, and a generalization of all convicts as fiends incarnate.

Naught to Thirty-three (1976; FIRST PUBLISHED 1944)

Learning her place

The Getting of Wisdom BY HENRY HANDEL RICHARDSON (THE PSEUDONYM OF ETHEL FLORENCE RICHARDSON, 1870–1946), IS BASED ON THE AUTHOR'S SCHOOLDAYS AS A BOARDER AT THE PRESBYTERIAN LADIES COLLEGE, MELBOURNE, IN THE 1880s.

My dear mother

I sent you a postcard did you get it. I told you I got here all right and liked it very much. I could not write a long letter before I had no time and we are only alowed to write letters two evenings a week Tuesday and Friday. When we have done our lessons for next day we say please may I write now and Miss Chapman says have you done everything and if we say we have she says yes and if you sit at Miss Days table Miss Day says it. And sometimes we haven't but we say so. I sit up by Miss Chapman and she can see everything I do and at tea and dinner and breakfast I sit beside Mrs Gurley. Another girl in my class sits opposite and one sits beside me and we would rather sit somewhere else. I dont care for Mrs Gurley much she is very fat and never smiles and never listens to what you say unless she scolds you and I think Miss Chapman is afraid of her to. Miss Day is not afraid of anybody. I am in the first class. I am in the College and under that is the school. Only very little girls are in the school they go to bed at half past eight and do their lessons in the dining hall. I do mine in the study and go to bed with the big girls. They wear dresses down to the ground. Lilith Gordon is a girl in my class she is in my room to she is only as old as me and she wears stays and has a beautiful figgure. All the girls wear stays. Please send me some I have no waste. A governess sleeps in our room and she has no teeth. She takes them out every night and puts them in water when the light is out. Lilith Gordon and the other girl say goodnight to her after she has taken them off then she cant talk propperly and we want to hear her. I think she knows for she is very cross. I don't learn latin yet till I go into the second class my sums are very hard. For supper there is only bread and butter and water if we don't have cake and jam of our own. Please send me some strawberry jam and another cake. Tell Sarah there are three servants to wait at dinner they have white aprons and a cap on their heads. They say will you take beef miss

> *I remain*
> *your loving daughter*
> *Laura.*

Dear Pin

I am very busy I will write you a letter. You would not like being here I think you should always stop at home you will never get as far as long division. Mrs Gurley is an awful old beast all the girls call her that. You WOULD be frightened of her. In the afternoon after school we walk two and two and you ask a girl to walk with you and if you dont you have to walk with Miss Chapman. Miss Chapman and Miss Day walks behind and they watch to see you dont laugh at boys. Some girls write letters to them and say they will meet them up behind a tree in the corner of the garden a paling is lose and the boys put letters in. I think boys are silly but Maria Morell says they are tip top that means awfully jolly. She writes a letter to boys every week she takes it to church and drops it coming out and he picks it up and puts an answer through the fence. We put our letters on the mantlepiece in the dining hall and Mrs Gurley or Miss Chapman read the adress to see we dont write to boys. They are shut up she cant read the inside. I hope you dont cry so much at school no one cries. Now Miss Chapman says it is time to stop

> *I remain*
> *your afectionate sister*
> *Laura*

P.S.   I took the red lineing out of my hat.

Warrenega, Sunday

My dear Laura

We were very glad to get your letters which came this morning. Your postcard written the day after you arrived at the College told us little or nothing. However Godmother was good enough to write us an account of your arrival so that we were not quite without news of you. I hope you remembered to thank her for driving in all that way to meet you and take you to school which was very good of her. I am glad to hear you are settling down and feeling happy and I hope you will work hard and distinguish yourself so that I may be proud of you. But there are several things in your letters I do not like. Did you really think I shouldnt read what you wrote to Pin. You are a very foolish girl if you did. Pin the silly child tried to hide it away because she knew it would make me cross but I insisted on her showing it to me and I am ashamed of you for writing such nonsense to her. Maria Morell must be a very vulgar minded girl to use the expressions she does. I hope my little girl will try to only associate with nice minded girls. I didnt sent you to school to get nasty ideas put into your head but to learn your lessons well and get on. If you write such vulgar silly things again I shall complain to Mrs Gurley or Mr Strachey about the tone of the College and what goes on behind their backs. I think it is very rude of you too to call Mrs Gurley names. Also about the poor governess who has to wear false teeth. Wait till all your own teeth are gone and then see how you will like it. I do want you to have nice feelings and not grow rough and rude. There is evidently a very bad tone among some of the girls and you must be careful in choosing your friends. I am sorry to hear you are only in the lowest class. It would have pleased me better if you had got into the second but I always told you you were lazy about your sums — you can do them well enough if you like. You dont need stays. I have never worn them myself and I dont intend you to either. Your own muscles are quite strong enough to bear the weight of your back. Bread and water is not much of a supper for you to go to bed on. I will send you another cake soon and some jam and I hope you will share it with the other girls. Now try and be sensible and industrious and make nice friends and then I shant have to scold you

> *Your loving mother*
> *J.T.R.*

P.S.   Another thing in your letter I dont like. You say you tell your governess you have finished your lessons when you have not done so. That is telling an untruth and I hope you are not going to be led away by the examples of bad girls. I have always brought you children up to be straightforward and I am astonished at you beginning fibbing as soon as you get away from home. Fibbing soon leads to something worse.

P.P.S.   You must have written your letter in a great hurry for your spelling is anything but perfect. You are a very naughty girl to meddle with your hat. Pin has written a letter which I enclose though her spelling is worse than ever.

Daer Laura
mother says you are a very sily girl to rite such sily letters I think you are sily to I shood be fritened of Mrs Girly I dont want to go to Skool I wood rather stop with mother and be a cumfert to her I think it is nauty to drop letters in Cherch and verry sily to rite to Boys boys are so sily Sarah sends her luv she says she wood not ware a cap on her hed not for annything she says She wood just as soon ware a ring thrugh her nose.

> *I remain*
> *your luving sister*
> *Pin*

Dear mother

please please dont write to Mrs Gurley about the Tone in the College or not to Mr Strachey either. I will never be so silly again. I am sorry my letters were so silly I wont do it again. Please dont write to them about it. I dont go much with Maria Morell now I think she is vulger to. I know two nice girls now in my own class their names are Inez and Bertha they are very nice and not at all vulger. Maria Morell is fat and has a red face she is much older than me and I dont care for her now. Please dont write to Mrs Gurley I will never call her names again. I had to write my letter quickly because when I have done my lessons it is nearly time for supper. I am sorry my spelling was wrong I will take more pains next time I will learn hard and get on and soon I will be in the second class. I did not mean I said I had done my lessons when I had not done them the other girls say it and I think it is very wrong of them. Please dont write to Mrs Gurley I will try and be good and sensible and not do it again if you only wont write.

> *I remain*
> *your afectionate daughter*
> *Laura.*

P.S.   I can do my sums better now.

The Getting of Wisdom (1977; FIRST PUBLISHED 1910)

Discipline and punish

IN THIS EXTRACT FROM THE AUTOBIOGRAPHICAL NOVEL, *My Brilliant Career* (1901) BY **MILES FRANKLIN** (1879–1954), HER HEROINE, SYBYLLA MELVYN, STRUGGLES WITH REFRACTORY PUPILS AS A GOVERNESS TO A NEW SOUTH WALES FARMING FAMILY.

My predecessor, previous to her debut at Barney's Gap, had spent some time in a lunatic asylum, and being a curious character, allowed the children to do as they pleased, consequently they knew not what it meant to be ruled, and were very bold. They attempted no insubordination while their father was about the house, but when he was absent they gave me a dog's life, their mother sometimes smiling on their pranks, often lazily heedless of them, but never administering any form of correction.

If I walked away from the house to get rid of them, they would follow and hoot at me; and when I reproved them they informed me they were not going 'to knuckle under to old Melvyn's darter, the damnedest fool in the world, who's lost all his prawperty, and has to borry money off of pa.'

Did I shut myself in my room, they shoved sticks in the cracks and made grimaces at me. I knew the fallacy of appealing to their father, as they and their mother would tell falsehoods, and my word would not be taken in contradiction of theirs. I had experience of this, as the postmistress had complained of Jimmy, to be insulted by his father, who could see no imperfection in his children.

M'Swat was much away from home at that time. The drought necessitated the removal of some of his sheep, for which he had rented a place eighty miles coastwards. There he left them under the charge of a man, but he repaired thither frequently to inspect them. Sometimes he was away from home a fortnight at a stretch. Peter would be away at work all day, and the children took advantage of my defenceless position. Jimmy was the ringleader. I could easily have managed the others had he been removed. I would have thrashed him well at the start but for the letters I constantly received from home warning me against offence to the parents, and knew that to set my foot on the children's larrikinism would require measure that would gain their mother's ill-will at once. But when M'Swat left home for three weeks Jim got so bold that I resolved to take decisive steps towards subjugating him. I procured a switch — a very small one, as his mother had a great objection to corporal punishment — and when, as usual, he commenced to cheek me during lessons, I hit him on the coat-sleeve. The blow would not have brought tears from the eyes of a toddler, but this great calf emitted a wild yope, and opening his mouth let his saliva pour on to his slate. The others set up such blood-curdling yells in concert that I was a little disconcerted, but I determined not to give in. I delivered another tap, whereupon he squealed and roared so that he brought his mother to his rescue like a ton of bricks on stilts, a great fuss in her eyes which generally beamed with a cowful calm.

Seizing my arm she shook me like a rat, broke my harmless little stick in pieces, threw it in my face, and patting Jimmy on the shoulder, said:

'Poor man! She sharn't touch me Jimmy while I know. Sure you've got no sense. You'd had him dead if I hadn't come in.'

I walked straight to my room and shut myself in, and did not teach any more that afternoon. The children rattled on my doorhandle and jeered:

'She thought she'd hit me, but ma settled her. Old poor Melvyn's darter won't try no more of her airs on us.'

I pretended not to hear. What was I to do? There was no one to whom I could turn for help. M'Swat would believe the story of his family, and my mother would blame me. She would think I had been in fault because I hated the place.

Mrs M'Swat called me to tea, but I said I would not have any. I lay awake all night and got desperate. On the morrow I made up my mind to conquer or leave. I would stand no more. If, in all the wide world and the whole of life this was the only use for me, then I would die — take my own life if necessary.

Things progressed as usual next morning. I attended to my duties and marched my scholars into the schoolroom at the accustomed hour. There was no decided insubordination during the morning, but I felt Jimmy was waiting for an opportunity to defy me. It was a fearful day, possessed by a blasting wind laden with red dust from Riverina, which filled the air like a fog. The crockery ware became so hot in the kitchen that when taking it into the dining-room we had to handle it with cloths. During the dinner-hour I slipped away unnoticed to where some quince-trees were growing and procured a sharp rod, which I secreted among the flour-bags in the schoolroom. At half-past one I brought my scholars in and ordered them to their work with a confident air. Things went without a ripple until three o'clock, when the writing lesson began. Jimmy struck his pen on the bottom of the bottle every time he replenished it with ink.

'Jimmy,' I gently remonstrated, 'don't jab your pen like that — it will spoil it. There is no necessity to shove it right to the bottom.'

Jab, jab, went Jimmy's pen.

'Jimmy, did you hear me speak to you?'

Jab went the pen.

'James, I am speaking to you!'

Jab went the pen again.

'James,' I said sternly, 'I give you one more chance.'

He deliberately defied me by stabbing into the ink-bottle with increased vigour. Liza giggled triumphantly, and the little ones strove to emulate her. I calmly produced my switch and brought it smartly over the shoulders of my refractory pupil in a way that sent the dust in a cloud from his dirty coat, knocked the pen from his fingers, and upset the ink.

He acted as before — yelled ear-drum-breakingly, letting the saliva from his distended mouth run on his copy-book. His brothers and sisters also started to roar, but bringing the rod down on the table, I threatened to thrash every one of them if they so much as whimpered; and they were so dumbfounded that they sat silent in terrified surprise.

Jimmy continued to bawl. I hit him again.

'Cease instantly, sir.'

Through the cracks Mrs M'Swat could be seen approaching. Seeing her, Jimmy hollered anew. I expected her to attack me. She stood five feet nine inches, and weighed about sixteen stones; I measured five feet one inch, and turned the scale at eight stones — scarcely a fair match; but my spirit was aroused, and instead of feeling afraid, I rejoiced at the encounter which was imminent, and had difficulty to refrain from shouting 'Come on! I'm ready, physically and mentally, for you and a dozen others such.'

My curious ideas regarding human equality gave me confidence. My theory is that the cripple is equal to the giant, and the idiot to the genius. As, if on account of his want of strength the cripple is subservient to the giant, the latter, on account of that strength, is compelled to give in to the cripple. So with the dolt and the man of brain, so with Mrs M'Swat and me.

The fact of not only my own but my family's dependence on M'Swat sank into oblivion. I merely recognized that she was one human being and I another. Should I have been deferential to her by reason of her age and maternity, then from the vantage which this gave her, she should have been lenient to me on account of my chit-ship and inexperience. Thus we were equal.

Jimmy hollered with renewed energy to attract his mother, and I continued to rain blows across his shoulders. Mrs M'Swat approached to within a foot of the door, and then, as though changing her mind, retraced her steps and entered the hot low-roofed kitchen. I knew I had won, and felt disappointed that the conquest had been so easy. Jimmy, seeing he was worsted, ceased his uproar, cleaned his copy-book on his sleeve, and sheepishly went on with his writing.

Whether Mrs M'Swat saw she had been in fault the day before I know not; certain it is that the children ever after that obeyed me, and I heard no more of the matter; neither, as far as I could ascertain, did the 'ruction' reach the ears of M'Swat.

'How long, how long!' was my cry, as I walked out ankle-deep in the dust to see the sun, like a ball of blood, sink behind the hills on that February evening.

My Brilliant Career (1990; FIRST PUBLISHED 1901)

Nobody's truck

KATHARINE SUSANNAH PRICHARD (1883–1969), BEST KNOWN AS A
WEST AUSTRALIAN NOVELIST, HAD HER EARLY SCHOOLING IN 1890S
MELBOURNE.

I was eight years old when I went to school. I don't remember much about it, except trotting off on a rainy morning, and a small boy, who lived next door, saying: 'Girl, come under my umbrella.'

At the school, run by a gentle spinster, there was a large mulberry tree. The children were not supposed to climb it, or eat the mulberries when they were ripe. We did both, and when frocks and pants were stained with purple juice, faces and hands, also, it was no use denying our guilt. Parents protested but Miss Cox could do nothing about it.

The only thing I learnt at my first school was to play 'trains'. I had never played with other children, except my brothers, so was all eager excitement over this game. In 'trains', the little boys puffed about as engines, and the girls hung on behind them while the engines shunted and galloped wildly from one end of the garden to the other.

Then, one morning, two small boys started fighting as furiously as cockerels. Miss Cox rushed out from the schoolroom and put a stop to it.

'What's the matter?' she asked.

'Kattie's my truck,' sobbed the umbrella boy, with a bloody nose. 'And Artie says she's got to be his truck, 'cause she's his cousin.'

'You naughty little girl,' said Miss Cox. 'Why did you let the boys fight about it?'

Being anybody's truck has never appealed to me since — perhaps a survival of my dismay and discomfiture at being held responsible for this conflict.

Child of the Hurricane (1963)

A procession of governesses

DOROTHY GILBERT, ONE OF EIGHT CHILDREN, WAS EDUCATED BY A SERIES OF GOVERNESSES IN RURAL SOUTH AUSTRALIA IN THE 1890S.

Miss Molero had begun Joe's & my education with reading & pot-hooks, but when Kitty proved so very delicate all her time & care had to be devoted to her, while Emmie the latest arrival occupied Mother's attention, so our first Governess was installed, the daughter of old family friends, Miss Gussie Short, she was about sixteen, (I was barely six, Joe 7 & Bill 5). She was most impressively old with hair piled up on her head & long skirts. 'Miss Short' was with us for about a year, but I don't remember what we learnt so much as the games we played, indoor & out. I remember an instructive little book of multiplication tables & additions, a history primer with dates, & such interesting facts, as that 'Henry 1st never smiled again after his son William was drowned in the Channel'. 'King John lost his crown in the Wash' — To me 'the Wash' was the laundry basket in the bathroom & I always wondered about that crown '& died of eating green peaches & drinking sour ale', and the 'Duke of Clarence was drowned in a butt of Malmsey wine'.

Then came Miss Parker, she was with us for three years & under her we really did begin to learn the three Rs, also rudiments of Music & French. I can still picture her, fair sandy gold hair & pince nez, she left us to be married & became Mrs Malcolm Scott living in Adelaide, after a few years we lost touch. Then came a Miss Hotson for six months, more or less as a stop-gap while our parents were waiting for a Miss Dijou from Melbourne & Miss Hotson was waiting to become Mrs Formby & set up home in West. Australia. I don't remember much about her, except that she could run faster than anyone else I knew.

Miss Dijou was a slave driver more suited to a matriculation class, than a batch of children ranging from 6 to 11 years. However we certainly learnt under her, & her methods of language instruction were astonishingly modern, particularly French (she was of French Huguenot descent). We learnt the grammar of course, but also we walked about the room and sometimes garden saying 'I want', 'I see', 'I touch', etc, every conceivable article in every tense present, past, future, positive, negative and interrogative, till the construction of sentences, & the intricacies of regular & irregular verbs just tripped off ones tongue. In all this your Father had no part. When he was nine & I only four he went to live with a family at the Semaphore, the Rev. somebody Ward & Mrs Ward. Miss Molero had schooled him till then. They boarded & tutored boys from Tasmania in preparation for St Peters. Guy Wylie, & a boy named Bisdie were great heroes, also Heriot Hart, & Tom Coghlan, (Semaphore boys) went by day. There may have been others, but those were life-long family friends. Harry went on to school at ten, and at sixteen to Melbourne University so we really only knew him in holidays, & he generally brought one or more friends home with him.

After Miss Dijou came Miss Cohn about 1898 and she stayed with us for nine years, till Kitty & Emmie were ready for a final year at an Adelaide finishing school. We loved her dearly, she had a great gift for making learning interesting, and taught English, French, German, Latin, History, geography, music (piano) dancing & maths, not so successfully, but even so the boys all managed to get into their right classes for age groups as they each in turn went to school. Her salary for those 9 years was £100 ($200)! a year plus her return fare to Melbourne for the holidays. For much of the time she had me, Marjory, Tom, Kitty, Emmie & John, all at different stages of development. She lived & was loved as an accepted member of the family, sharing our recreations and friendships. She continued to teach for many years & eventually died at the great age of nearly 102.

'COUNTRY LIFE IN THE LATER NINETEENTH CENTURY: REMINISCENCES' (1973)

A little learning

THE LIFE STORY OF EUGÉNIE McNEIL (1886–1983), EDUCATED IN
NEW SOUTH WALES BY A SERIES OF GOVERNESSES, WAS PUT INTO
AUTOBIOGRAPHICAL FORM BY HER DAUGHTER EUGÉNIE CRAWFORD.

Mother was beginning to worry about our education. She'd
taught us our ABC and how to add and subtract, but she wasn't
very good at the latter herself. It was high time we stopped running wild and learned to read and write and a few accomplishments. She herself had received little schooling and done very
well, so she hadn't rebelled against the beliefs of her parents that
to be thought clever was almost as damaging to a girl's chances
as to be thought 'fast'. She wasn't planning to endanger our
future by any such handicap, but if we were to take our places
in society we needed a thin veneer of culture.

Visitors who came often to 'Auburn Park' included Frank
and Louis Fox. The latter died young, but his brother, later Sir
Frank, was a well-known journalist and as she did not wish us
to attend the small state school beside the pipeline, Mother
consulted him about her problem. The upshot of this was
that his sister, Florence, came to us for six months. The fourth
bedroom was turned into a schoolroom, we were bought slates
and horrid pencils that squeaked when we wrote on them, and
Miss Fox taught us our tables and to shape pot hooks and
hangars.

We liked Miss Fox. She smelled of cloves and played Puss-in-
the-Corner with us in the orchard, as well as teaching us a beautiful poem which began

> Big-bellied Ben
> Ate more meat than four score men;
> He ate the priest and all the people,
> He ate the church and then the steeple.

I don't think she taught us much else.

She was succeeded by Miss Reynolds, a Lady in Reduced Circumstances, who knew absolutely nothing about anything, but had very refined manners. She couldn't spell herself and laid the foundations of the chronic bad spelling from which I have suffered all my life. I was cunning enough to cultivate a small, cramped handwriting that I hoped disguised this weakness, because it was practically illegible. Fortunately my husband and daughter could spell, or I should have remained unable to communicate on paper for the rest of my life.

Miss Reynolds was genuinely fond of children, even other people's. She would have done much better to have lowered her status a little and sought employment as a nanny, for she had all the right patter for making a successful one. 'Children should be seen and not heard' or 'Early to bed, early to rise' were favourite maxims and at every meal we were admonished to 'Make a clean plate'.

This Lady in Reduced Circumstances was replaced by a tartar called Miss Fordyce. She was a great believer in Latin as the basis of learning, so we recited Latin verbs every day. She also believed in girls having a straight back and immediately persuaded Mother that Lydia, who was tall and inclined to stoop, needed a bracer. This was a sort of calico strait-jacket, into which she was buttoned every morning before breakfast to correct her faults of posture. Learning was taught by rote and every day, after our hair had been given a hundred strokes, we were marched round the schoolroom with volumes of *Chambers' Encyclopaedia* balanced on our heads, Lydia in her strait-jacket, while we recited 'Amo, Amas, Amat, Amamus, Amatis, Amant', and things like the Don, the Dneiper, the Dneister, the Volga, the Vistula, the Bug and Divorced, Beheaded, Died, Divorced, Beheaded, Survived, without a clue as to what these were or what possible purposes they served [...]

Our next governess, whose real name I don't remember, was a Frenchwoman, we called Mam'selle. She was enchanted to find the big pictures of Paris in the drawingroom, to hear our names and find we'd grown up on the fairytales of Perrault. I think she must have grown up on those of Jean-Jacques Rousseau, because she was full of romantic illusions about the simple life and called us her *belles sauvages*.

For a short time, she insisted on helping with the butter churn and handed us bread dipped in cream and sprinkled with sugar as a treat. Few country children acquainted with cows would even take milk in their tea, let alone eat a concoction like this. We were revolted, but thanked her politely and then hid it behind a big bush of cherry pie. To this day, I can't look on the beautiful purple flowers of the heliotrope without feeling my stomach turn over.

She was naïvely curious when she saw letters arrive from Monsieur Terrier, who had retired from Minchinbury and, like all good Frenchmen, returned to his native land — in this case to Dijon, in the Burgundy area.

We had now graduated from slates to exercise books and Mam'selle showed us how to ornament the headings of our compositions with flowers and birds and butterflies, all elaborately executed in coloured inks. Forty years have passed since I burned the last of these and I now regret it, because you can't imagine how beautiful were the grape vines that trailed down the margins nor the hours spent embellishing each page with pretty drawings. So beautifully, that there was little time left to write the compositions — an arrangement that suited both teacher and pupils.

After coming to grips with some of the less attractive aspects of our simple life, like The Outhouse and the shortage of water, Mam'selle remembered a bereaved aunt who needed her in an inner suburb and decided to leave us. It was an emotional farewell, because, with the unerring instinct of children for liking undeserving people, we'd grown fond of her. Strangely enough, I never remember her teaching us any French. But then, I don't remember her teaching us much else either.

A Bunyip Close Behind Me (1985; FIRST PUBLISHED 1972)

A thoroughly good home

IN THE CHILDREN'S NOVEL *Seven Little Australians* BY ETHEL TURNER (1870–1958), JUDY WOOLCOT IS BANISHED TO BOARDING SCHOOL IN THE BLUE MOUNTAINS, NEW SOUTH WALES.

There was a trunk standing in the hall, and a large, much-travelled portmanteau, and there were labels on them that said: 'Miss Helen Woolcot, The Misses Burton, Mount Victoria'.

In the nursery, breakfast was proceeding spasmodically. Meg's blue eyes were all red and swollen with crying, and she was still sniffing audibly as she poured out the coffee. Pip had his hands in his pockets and stood on the hearthrug, looking gloomily at a certain plate, and refusing breakfast altogether; the General was crashing his own mug and plate joyously together; and Bunty was eating bread and butter in stolid silence.

Judy, white-faced and dry-eyed, was sitting at the table, and Nell and Baby were clinging to either arm. All the three days between that black Thursday and this doleful morning, she had been obstinately uncaring. Her spirits had never seemed higher, her eyes brighter, her tongue sharper, than during that interval of days; and she had pretended to everyone, and her father, that she especially thought boarding school must be great fun, and that she should enjoy it immensely.

But this morning she had collapsed altogether. All the time before, her hot childish heart had been telling her that her father could not really be so cruel, that he did not really mean to send her away among strangers, away from dear, muddled old Misrule and all her sisters and brothers; he was only saying it to frighten her, she kept saying to herself, and she would show him she was not a chicken-hearted baby.

But on Saturday night, when she saw a trunk carried downstairs and filled with her things and labelled with her name, a cold hand seemed to close about her heart. Still, she said to herself, he was doing all this to make it seem more real.

But now it was morning, and she could disbelieve it no longer. Esther had come to her bedside and kissed her sorrowfully, her beautiful face troubled and tender. She had begged as she had never done before for a remission of poor Judy's sentence, but the Captain was adamant. It was she and she only who was always ringleader in everything; the others would behave when she was not there to incite them to mischief, and go she should. Besides, he said, it would be the making of her. It was an excellent school he had chosen for her; the ladies who kept it were kind, but very firm, and Judy was being ruined for want of a firm hand. Which, indeed, was in a measure true.

Judy sat bolt upright in bed at the sight of Esther's sorrowful face.

'It's no good, dear; there's no way out of it,' she said gently. 'But you'll go like a brave girl, won't you, Ju-Ju? You always were the sort to die game, as Pip says.'

Judy gulped down a great lump in her throat, and her poor little face grew white and drawn.

'It's all right, Essie. There, you go on down to breakfast,' she said, in a voice that only shook a little [...]

It was a wretched meal. The bell sounded for the downstairs breakfast, and Esther had to go. Everyone offered Judy everything on the table, and spoke gently and politely to her. She seemed to be apart from them, a person not to be lightly treated in the dignity of this great trouble. Her dress, too, was quite new — a neat blue serge fresh from the dressmaker's hands; her boots were blacked and bright, her stockings guiltless of ventilatory chasms. All this helped to make her a Judy quite different from the harum-scarum one of a few days back, who used to come to breakfast looking as if her clothes had been pitchforked upon her.

Baby addressed herself to her porridge for one minute, but the next her feelings overcame her, and, with a little wail, she rushed round the table to Judy, and hung on her arm sobbing. This destroyed the balance of the whole company. Nell got the other arm and swayed to and fro in an access of misery. Meg's tears rained down into her teacup; Pip dug his heel in the hearthrug, and wondered what was the matter with his eyes; and even Bunty's appetite for bread and butter diminished.

Judy sat there silent; she had pushed back her unused plate, and sat regarding it with an expression of utter despair on her young face. She looked like a miniature tragedy queen going to immediate execution.

Presently Bunty got off his chair, covered up his coffee with his saucer to keep the flies out, and solemnly left the room. In a minute he returned with a pickle bottle, containing an enormous green frog.

'You can have it to keep for your very own, Judy,' he said, in a tone of almost reckless sadness. 'It'll keep you amused, perhaps, at school.'

Self-sacrifice could go no further, for this frog was the darling of Bunty's heart.

This stimulated the others; everyone fetched some offering to lay at Judy's shrine for a keepsake. Meg brought a bracelet, plaited out of the hair of a defunct pet pony. Pip gave his three-bladed pocket-knife, Nell a pot of musk that she had watered and cherished for a year, Baby had a broken-nosed doll that was the Benjamin of her large family.

'Put them in the trunk, Meg — there's room on top, I think,' Judy said in a choking voice, and deeply touched by these gifts.

'Oh! and, Bunty dear, put a cork over the f — f — frog, will you? It might get lost, poor thing! in that b — b — big box.'

'All right,' said Bunty. 'You'll take c — c — care of it, w — won't you, Judy? Oh dear, oh — h — h! — boo — hoo!'

Then Esther came in, still troubled-looking.

'The dogcart is round,' she said. 'Are you ready, Ju, dearest? Dear little Judy! Be brave, little old woman.'

But Judy was white as death, and utterly limp. She suffered Esther to put her hat on, to help her into her new jacket, to put her gloves into her hand. She submitted to being kissed by the whole family, to be half-carried downstairs by Esther, to be kissed again by the girls, then by the two good-natured domestics, who, in spite of her peccadilloes, had a warm place in their hearts for her.

Esther and Pip lifted her into the dogcart, and she sat in a little, huddled-up way, looking down at the group on the veranda with eyes that were absolutely tragic in their utter despair.

Her father came out, buttoning his overcoat, and saw the look. 'What foolishness is this?' he said irascibly. 'Esther — great heavens! are you making a goose of yourself, too?' — there were great tears glistening in his wife's beautiful eyes. 'Upon my soul, one would think I was going to take the child to be hanged, or at least was going to leave her in a penitentiary.'

A great dry sob broke from Judy's white lips.

'If you'll let me stay, Father, I'll never do another thing to vex you; and you can thrash me instead, ever so hard.'

It was her last effort, her final hope, and she bit her poor quivering lip till it bled, while she waited for his answer.

'Let her stay — oh! do let her stay, we'll be good always,' came in a chorus from the veranda. And, 'Let her stay, John, *please*!' Esther called, in a tone as entreating as any of the children.

But the Captain sprang into the dogcart and seized the reins from Pat in a burst of anger.

'I think you're all demented!' he cried. 'She's going to a thoroughly good home, I've paid a quarter in advance already, and I can assure you good people I'm not going to waste it.'

He gave the horse a smart touch with the whip, and in a minute the dogcart had flashed out of the gate, and the small unhappy face was lost to sight.

Seven Little Australians (1994; FIRST PUBLISHED 1894)

Plaiting the future

LOUISE MACK (1870–1935), NOVELIST, BASED HER CHILDREN'S STORY *Teens* ON HER OWN EXPERIENCES AT SYDNEY GIRLS' HIGH SCHOOL.

Lennie plaited on to the end of her long, brown hair, then turned the ends up, and tied them tightly with a piece of black tape. Then she threw the plait over her shoulder, and looked sideways at it in the glass.

'I shall always wear a plait now,' she said.

'It would be horrid to have one's hair all hanging round one in the train.'

The others were all silent.

'I wonder what it will be like,' said Lennie, sitting on the edge of the bed, and looking at them. They hazarded no suggestions.

'There will be crowds and crowds of girls, of course. Heaps of nice ones; some nasty ones. I think I'll know at a glance which I shall like, and which I shall hate. And we'll all be sitting in a big room together, and we'll write our [examination] papers without being allowed to say one word. It will be awfully exciting.'

'You won't know one of them,' said Floss.

The element of the wet-blanket would keep creeping into the tones of the other three—the three who were not going up for an examination tomorrow.

'I dare say I will be introduced,' said Lennie.

'The headmistress told Mother she would look after me.' A tremendous sigh burst forth suddenly from nine-year-old Brenda.

'I *wisht* I were going,' she wailed. 'Oh, I *wisht* I were going.'

'Oh, it's lovely,' said Lennie, heartlessly. She had curled her round, black-stockinged legs up under her, and was crouched in a ball-like attitude on the bed.

'No more Miss Middleton! No more *Philosophe*! No more of those silly drawing-copies! No more writing essays, and getting no marks for them! It will be so heavenly to get marks, and to have girls to work against. And to beat them.'

Teens (1897)

The great escape

NORMAN LINDSAY (1879–1969), WRITER AND ARTIST, GREW UP IN THE GOLDFIELDS TOWN OF CRESWICK, VICTORIA, AND AFTER PERSISTENT ABSENTEEISM FROM THE STATE PRIMARY SCHOOL WENT ON TO THE CRESWICK GRAMMAR SCHOOL.

I had reached the fifth class; before me stretched a year's drudgery in the sixth before I was signed off the convict roll as having served full sentence; and rebellion arrived at crisis. In my mother's handwriting, I forged a formal statement that she was withdrawing me from the State and sending me to the Grammar School.

My mother wrote what was called the Italian hand, all spearpoints and angularities, as taught at the young ladies' seminaries of her youth. It was very easy to imitate, and its authenticity was not questioned by the headmaster, though the presentation of the note to him was a tense moment for me ... and for the last time I lugged my bag of books from that beastly, arid, dusty, frowsty brick barn, and went my way, thrilling with exultation. Almost it was worthwhile having been immured there for the major portion of my monage, for the ecstasy of that moment. Prison-camp escape literature has always had a special fascination for me, possibly derived from that moment.

From my small-boy days I had my system of wagging it well established. Its strategy was determined by old Mother Wright's corner cottage, situated half-way between our home and the school. From the home side, one could not be seen from the school, and from the school side, one was hidden from the home. On the school side was a small footbridge over the gutter, also essential to my strategy. If I left home with my bag of books just as the school bell gave its final dongs, all its wretched slaves and slave-drivers were in the classrooms by the time I reached the corner. Once round that, with an eye out for possible snoopers, I had only to kick my bag of books under the footbridge to be rid of the stigmata of an absconding scholar. Hopping the school fence, I crossed the playground to climb its opposite fence into a furze-patched space of common, and crossed that to the old culvert of a dried-up watercourse. When I dropped into that, I was below eye level, and could make a safe course to where it petered out at the Chinese camp and the old diggings.

There I was secure from all detection. No adults ever came there save a few old fossicking Chinamen, or a mad-hatter old digger, to wash out tailings of mullock for the bare chance of a few grains of gold overlooked by long-dead miners [...]

When it was wet and wintry, I had other bolt holes. Our loft was one, by connivance of the groom, always a dear friend of mine. To reach it, I had merely to turn in at the Wesleyan Church gate next door and go round the church to the back paddock, whence a small window in the back of our stable gave me entrance to the loft. A spyhole in the loft door allowed me to overlook our back premises, enhancing the charm of defying authority in the home by doing so under its very nose. Another wet weather lurking place was the small weatherboard shanty in the Grammar School grounds which was the habitat of old

Scotty Gibbs (old Poulter as a character in my fiction), save when rheumatics laid him up in the local hospital, which they invariably did in winter. Entrance to it was by burglarious approach at a small back window, screened by an overhanging fir-tree from the premises next the school. It was a frowsty little hovel, and very cold in winter, but happiness warmed me while I wrote my novel or practised pen and ink drawing, or lolled on old Scotty's bunk, reading Browning's lyrics—a pocket-sized edition of them lived in my pocket those days, and I can't pick them up today without savouring again the charm of those early readings, added to their enduring fascination.

For the rest, duplicity in the home merely required me to pick up my bag of books from under the footbridge any time after four o'clock and lump them home; and, of an evening, to be seen with textbooks and an open exercise on my bedroom table, as evidence of home lessons, while I read a novel or diverted myself otherwise.

My Mask (1970)

Food for thought

ADELAIDE-BORN SINGER AND SONGWRITER **PETER DAWSON** (1882–1961) HAD HIS EARLY SCHOOLING AT THE EAST ADELAIDE STATE PRIMARY SCHOOL AND THE PULTENEY STREET GRAMMAR SCHOOL.

The happiest days of my life, of course, were the school days, first of all at East Adelaide public school, and finally at Pulteney Street Grammar. Early school days were full of thrills, from stealing fruit out of people's gardens and off Chinamen's barrows, to swimming in all the holes of the Torrens, to say nothing of the days when we 'wagged' it. It was quite easy in those days to fill the school yard full of dogs by catching one, painting his tail with aniseed, and finishing up with at least a full pack. This helped the 'Lost and Found' column in the paper very much. At Pulteney street school one hot day, two boys and myself were sent by the old icecream man, Shaw, down Rundle street for a fresh can of icecream. This was too much for us. We sat down in Hindmarsh square and had a real feed, eventually going back to old Shaw with a much lighter tin than that with which we left the factory. Fortunately, Shaw did not notice the loss. He was so pleased that he gave us a real double icecream each, which we could not eat; so we asked him if we could change the icecream for a couple of jellies!

The games they used to get up to in the school must have been tantalising to the master. It was quite a common occurrence when the master had his back turned, for a handful of olives to be showered at his board; and, one day, an egg hit the board, the yolk of which rebounded and clung to his moustache. He rushed from the room, and immediately the boys began to shout and stamp. Dust rose until the room became befogged. Through the fog we saw the master standing in the door way, and all he said was, 'You little gentlemen.' That hurt us more than the cane.

'Guest Column', *The Adelaide Chronicle* (1933)

Stinks

W. J. Turner (1889–1946), expatriate, poet, drama and music critic, and literary editor of the London *Spectator*, was educated at Scotch College, Melbourne. His autobiographical novel, *Blow for Balloons*, gives an account of his schooldays when Scotch's science master was the eccentric Robert Morrison, younger brother of the Principal, Dr Alexander Morrison.

But the most obvious character among the masters was the doctor's slightly younger brother, the Vice-Principal, Robert Morrison, who was quite incapable of teaching anything and no doubt had therefore been allotted by his brother—in the righteous contempt of a classical scholar—the department of science. Even in those pre-Wellsian days there were a few maniacs who wished their sons to have a scientific education […]

When we entered the classroom we always saw with excited interest a long table between the blackboard and our desks, almost every inch of which was covered with miscellaneous objects—bottles of chemicals, test-tubes, beakers, Bunsen burners, magnets, phials of liquids, scales, rubber tubes, air-pumps and I don't know what. It reveals the nature of the Vice-Principal's teaching that at the end of years of attendance at Robert Morrison's science class—which may have been divided into 'elementary', 'intermediate' and 'advanced' in the school syllabus but which was invariably of the same nature year in year out—we had never learned even the names of the chemicals he used or what were the operations which he conducted with such deliberation and care that if they did not enlighten us they at least mystified and thrilled us. For if the subject of the teaching, whether for senior or for junior boys, was always the same *Unknown* nevertheless what happened during the course of the investigation of this *Unknown* was always totally unexpected. Robert Morrison was none of your pure abstract scientific thinkers, he was a Baconian, a strict empiricist, and nothing was ever spoken of by him in his class which he did not make happen or try to make happen before our eyes. In this lay part of his greatness, and of his greatness I don't think there was one among us who doubted. When we were all collected in the classroom at the proper hour Robert Morrison, a smaller and slighter man than his brother, wearing a rather shabby frock-coat, with none of his brother's this-world-liness, would glide behind the table and begin scribbling some figures in chalk on the blackboard which he would invariably wipe out with the duster he always held in his left hand. What the figures meant we hadn't the slightest idea and he never told us. He would then mutter unintelligibly in his beard and then perhaps light a Bunsen burner, which he might then immediately put out and returning to the blackboard with his duster still in his hand, scribble some more figures and wipe them out too. I may say that during these preliminaries all eyes were glued upon him as if fascinated; and fascinated we were, for absolute silence always reigned in his class and rowdiness or trouble of any kind had never been known to happen.

Sooner or later, after sentences more or less incoherent had been visibly addressed to us, he would open a bottle, light a Bunsen burner, sprinkle some powder on a metal disk, hold it over the burner and perhaps a marvellous cobalt light would dance momentarily in the air. Needless to say, in our complete ignorance, not having been told a word about anything that we could understand, not knowing what the powder was, what the Bunsen burner was (it was only years later that I learned even this), what the metal was, in this almost pre-alchemistic state of innocence the phenomena that Robert Morrison caused to appear were nothing but pure magic to us and his mutterings and unintelligible explanations had on us just the effect of a witch-doctor's incantations upon savages. After one such successful experiment there would be at least half a dozen failures. It was these alone which moved Robert Morrison to any flow of speech and what we then heard was something like this:

'Wha' now, what divil's got into the thing. Weel, weel, I shouldna ha' thocht it. Let me see now, I'll gi' 'em a bit of a surprise. Now this is $B_2F_6KL_{20}$ and that is $PQR_{14}F_5LMNO_{16}$. If this sounds compleecated remember water is only H_2O; weel, if you remember H_2O is just water then you needna be surprised at $PQR_{14}F_5LMNO_{16}$. It's a rare form, a lovely rare form of $PQ_7RF_6L_{14}$ and MNO_8. Wha' the devil won't the Bunsen burner burn?'

At this an excited boy might rashly call out: 'It's not lit, sir,' upon which Robert Morrison would say:

'Hoold your gab you unlettered divil. Now what can be the matter with this God-forsaken gob of a Bunsen burner? Niver trust any one named Bunsen. Weel, weel, niver mind we'll try something else. Noo this is $KP_{10}RS_{16}$ and we shall see what happens when it meets $RS_{14}KP_6$. This is a sort of chemical incest, boys, but you wouldna understand that. Niver mind, nothing happens. Noo then you see yon wee powder, it is $X_{14}Y_7Z_{21}$. It doosna do a thing itself but it's a catalytic and in its presence $RS_{14}KP_6$ and $KP_{10}RS_{16}$ combine to produce an entirely new thingamagig $KRS_{22}PS_{14}$ and P_{56}. Sich is a Berselius catalysis; it canna be explained but if ye wee ignorant bawbees were properly instructed in zoology ye would understand that it's what happens when an elephant and giraffe mate in the presence of another camel'—BANG!

At such a crucial moment in the Vice-Principal's chemical lecture one or other of the retorts which he had cooking was sure to explode to the immense satisfaction of the class. But nothing of this sort ever disconcerted Robert Morrison who seemed to be just as pleased when anything went wrong as when a demonstration was successful. Every now and then he would look at his watch to see how the hour and a half allotted to his class was going. Occasionally, when nothing would go right and he was in a particularly gloomy mood he would deliberately bring the lesson to a premature conclusion by emitting from some jar a vast quantity of sulphuretted hydrogen whereupon lifting the tails of his frock-coat and calling out 'Skedaddle noo!' he would be the first to fly from the room.

Blow for Balloons (1935)

Buttoned gloves

THE SCHOOL REPRESENTED IN *Picnic at Hanging Rock* IS CLYDE, A BOARDING SCHOOL FOR GIRLS AT WOODEND, NEAR MOUNT MACEDON, VICTORIA. THE PICNIC TAKES PLACE ON ST VALENTINE'S DAY 1900. JOAN LINDSAY (1896–1984) WAS A PUPIL AT CLYDE (THEN IN ST KILDA) SOME YEARS AFTER THE LATE COLONIAL PERIOD SHE CHOSE FOR HER FANTASY ABOUT THE DISAPPEARANCE OF A GROUP OF SCHOOLGIRLS FROM A HOLIDAY PICNIC.

Appleyard College was already, in the year nineteen hundred, an architectural anachronism in the Australian bush — a hopeless misfit in time and place. The clumsy two storey mansion was one of those elaborate houses that sprang up all over Australia like exotic fungi following the finding of gold. Why this particular stretch of flat sparsely wooded country, a few miles out of the village of Macedon crouching at the foot of the mount, had been selected as a suitable building site, nobody will ever know. The insignificant creek that meandered in a series of shallow pools down the slope at the rear of the ten acre property offered little inducement as a setting for an Italianate mansion; nor the occasional glimpses, through a screen of stringy-barked eucalyptus, of the misty summit of Mount Macedon rising up to the east on the opposite side of the road [...]

Whether the Headmistress of Appleyard College (as the local white elephant was at once re-christened in gold lettering on a handsome board at the big iron gates) had any previous experience in the educational field, was never divulged. It was unnecessary. With her high-piled greying pompadour and ample bosom, as rigidly controlled and disciplined as her private ambitions, the cameo portrait of her late husband flat on her respectable chest, the stately stranger looked precisely what the parents expected of an English Headmistress [...]

'Good morning, Mrs Appleyard,' chorused the curtseying half-circle drawn up before the hall door.

'Are we all present, Mademoiselle? Good. Well, young ladies, we are indeed fortunate in the weather for our picnic to Hanging Rock. I have instructed Mademoiselle that as the day is likely to be warm, you may remove your gloves after the drag has passed through Woodend [...] Have a pleasant day and try to behave yourselves in a manner to bring credit to the College. I shall expect you back, Miss McCraw and Mademoiselle, at about eight o'clock for a light supper' [...]

They were off; the College already out of sight except for the tower through the trees as they bowled along the level Melbourne-Bendigo road, vibrating with particles of fine red dust. 'Get up Sailor, you lazy brute ... Prince, Belmonte get back in your collars ...' For the first mile or two the scenery was familiar through the daily perambulation of the College croco- dile. The passengers knew only too well, without bothering to look out, how the scraggy stringy bark forest lined the road on either side, now and then opening out onto a lighter patch of cleared land. The Comptons' whitewashed cottage whose sprawling quince trees supplied the College with jellies and jams, the clump of wayside willows at which the governess in charge would invariably call a halt and head for home. It was the same on Longman's *Highroads of History*, where the class were forever turning back for recapitulation at the death of King George the Fourth before starting off again with Edward the Third next term ... Now the willows in rich summer green were gaily passed and a sense of adventure ahead took over as heads began to peer through the buttoned tarpaulin flaps of the drag. The road took a slight turn, there was a fresher green amongst the dun coloured foliage and now and then a stand of blue-black pines, a glimpse of Mount Macedon tufted as usual with fluffy white clouds above the southern slopes, where the romantic summer villas hinted at far off adult delights.

At Appleyard College silence was golden, written up in the corridors and often imposed. There was a delicious freedom about the swift steady motion of the drag and even in the warm dusty air blowing up in their faces that set the passengers chirping and chattering like budgerigars [...]

The morning grew steadily hotter. The sun bore down on the shiny black roof of the drag, now covered with fine red dust that seeped through the loosely buttoned curtains into eyes and hair. 'And this we do for pleasure,' Greta McCraw muttered from the shadows, 'so that we may shortly be at the mercy of venomous snakes and poisonous ants ... how foolish can human creatures be!' Useless, too, to open the book in her satchel with all this schoolgirl chatter in one's ears.

The road to Hanging Rock turns sharply away to the right a little way out of the township of Woodend. Here Mr Hussey pulled up outside the leading hotel to rest and water his horses before starting on the last lap of the drive. Already the heat inside the vehicle was oppressive and there was a wholesale peeling off of the obligatory gloves. 'Can't we take our hats off too, Mam'selle?' asked Irma whose ink-black curls were flowing out in a warm tide under the brim of her stiff school sailor. Mademoiselle smiled and looked across at Miss McCraw, sitting opposite, awake and vertical, but with closed eyes, two puce kid hands locked together on her lap. 'Certainly not. Because we are on an excursion, there is no necessity to look like a wagon load of gypsies.'

Picnic at Hanging Rock (1978; FIRST PUBLISHED 1967)

Free and easy

AUDREY, LADY TENNYSON (1854–1916), WIFE OF HALLAM, LORD TENNYSON, GOVERNOR OF SOUTH AUSTRALIA 1899–1902 AND LATER ACTING GOVERNOR-GENERAL, COMMENTS IN A LETTER TO HER MOTHER (18 NOVEMBER 1902) ON AUSTRALIAN PUBLIC SCHOOL STANDARDS.

Some of us & the boys went to the Annual Concert at the [Melbourne] Grammar School the other evening, which was a very creditable performance. I asked Mrs Blanche, the headmaster's wife — they are out from home — whether Mr Blanche considered the standard as high as at home and she said, 'Yes, nearly', but I do not think that is the general impression. The headmaster of the Wesleyan school here, who was at Rugby and Oxford & came out 12 years ago told me he rather dreaded the Australian boy as he heard they had no idea of discipline and was much surprised at the free & easy terms between boys & masters — but that you could do anything with the boys when once you gain their affection by *leading*. No Australian will be driven, they are much too independent; and he thought he had come round to think that the friendly feeling between master & boy — the boys talking to the masters & telling them everything as to each other — was better on the whole than the respectful distance kept up between masters & boys at home.

ALEXANDRA HASLUCK (ED.), *Audrey Tennyson's Vice-Regal Days 1899–1903* (1978)

High-powered youth

DAME MABEL BROOKES (1890–1975) SHARED A DAILY GOVERNESS WITH THE DAUGHTER OF THE LIEUTENANT-GOVERNOR, AT GOVERNMENT HOUSE, MELBOURNE, IN THE 1890S BEFORE 'RUNNING WILD' ON HER FATHER'S PROPERTY, THE BRIARS, ON THE MORNINGTON PENINSULA.

The life at Government House, as seen from a child's viewpoint, was of more regimentation, formality, and constant coming and going. Our room for lessons was next to that of the A.D.C.'s; the visitors and carriages and guards of honour passed our window. Lord Richard Nevill controlled the destiny of that corridor.

We walked sedately. At the foot of the terrace-steps we had a cubby-hole, a little square of dimness behind shrubs, where we set dolls and tea-cups and little chairs. We rouged our faces with geranium petals and played tea-parties and ladies. Years later when Queen Elizabeth set out from Government House, on her departure from Victoria in 1954, it so happened my childhood friend Beatrice Madden (now Beatrice Baillieu) and myself were together by the terrace-steps to see her leave. The years slipped away, and I mechanically glanced behind the bushes where once were the little chairs and dolls and two eager children, close on half a century back. There is something permanent in memory that transcends the flesh.

Father fixed his hopes on a brilliant academic daughter; but after a year or so I had a sudden blackout and was told 'no more lessons'. Then came a period of running wild at The Briars — no books, no regimentation, no music. The loneliness persisted, however; there were no other children. Dogs took their place — fox-terriers, collies, cattle-dogs, a French poodle and a Dandy Dinmont; horses—a pony that lay down disregarding the rider, a peaceful grey with barbed-wire scars; and in the paddocks more lessons to be absorbed, however unconsciously. Cows at sundown, milking, the business of the dairy, the killing of a snake, the taking of birds from the fruit nets, the harnessing of horses, the language of the bush (there was a black-tracker among the men); strange new learning. There was some evidence of the early days — a boomerang discovered in the creek; paths leading nowhere; tracks to a place which once had been a native camp, and broken bricks around a grass-covered kiln that spoke of grandfather's ambitions in home-building fifty years before. There were banks of maidenhair in the creek, with grandmother's herbs growing wild, coral fern higher up, solitude, birds and a million insects that created a chorus of gentle song. Later, Norman Hodges, son of a judge who was a friend of father's, took mother to task. 'Mabel is dull, plain, and reads too much,' he told her, and added: 'She has never yet been to a dance.' I was fourteen and it was the vogue of the flapper, the phonograph, the first Henley-on-Yarra, the Glaciarium, dances, motor trips in goggles and veils. Mother was startled but listened — a boy of seventeen can be uncompromising. The outcome was her permission for me to go to a flapper party at Homeden, the Hodges' home. More education — this time in fashion, in the kitchen-lancers, in boys, and in competition with other girls. The time was one of families with big houses, of ballrooms and of active young people to use them, and the generation that so soon went off to the 1914 war had the satisfaction of a high-powered youth.

Crowded Galleries (1956)

Child of the regiment

PAUL HASLUCK (1905–94) BEGAN HIS PROFESSIONAL LIFE AS A JOURNALIST. HE ENTERED POLITICS, SERVED AS A CABINET MINISTER SEVERAL TIMES IN LIBERAL GOVERNMENTS, AND WAS GOVERNOR-GENERAL OF AUSTRALIA FROM 1969 TO 1974. A CHILD OF SALVATION ARMY PARENTS, HE GREW UP IN WESTERN AUSTRALIA.

On the day I turned four years, 1 April 1909, I started day school at the Norwood State School, which was within an easy walk across an open recreation ground from where we lived in Beaufort Street. My hair had grown since I had been in hospital and my mother, following the fashion in nice homes of that day, had trained it in curls, which came down to my shoulders. She was immensely proud of my curls and, as my hair was naturally straight, she had reason to be as they were her own creation and her constant care was to keep the long tight curls in good shape by frequent setting in curling papers. She dressed me in what were known as tunic suits, with a rather full-skirted tunic which almost concealed the knee-length pants underneath. I was taken to school on my first day, beautifully dressed and beautifully curled and eager for learning, and left there. At playtime some jeering boys were around me taunting me. I stood with my back to the brick wall and said nothing but felt very sad inside because I had thought school was going to be wonderful and because they did not like me. For most of the time at that school the classroom was a refuge from the playground. Luckily we lived so near that I could run home at lunchtime and in the afternoon as soon as school was out without going into the playground. It was only the morning playtime that was an ordeal, standing by myself and wondering why they did not like me. Although my brother must have been at the school too, I cannot remember him being there. I do not remember a single friend or playmate from that school and in later years any state school with the same sort of standard building and gravelled yard and the same smell and the same feeling about it that Norwood had in 1909 still revives in me an agony of loneliness and that mixture of fear and shyness that was the commencement of my education.

Yet within a few months I was reading, trying to read everything in print from street signs to hymn books, reading far beyond my understanding of the meaning of words, for in those days we were taught by the phonetic method and learnt to read with more readiness than comprehension. My parents were immensely proud of my precocity and I used to be encouraged to show off in front of visitors by reading anything that was put in front of me.

Under my pleading my curls were shorn. My mother wept as she snipped off each curl with a large pair of scissors. One curl she kept, tied with ribbon at both ends, in a little cardboard box delicately scented from its original contents of cakes of soap and for years to come my curl was produced from time to time to be sighed over.

I was at Norwood School rather less than a year. Then my parents were again called by God. At a time when their health and their fortunes had improved and they had built their own small suburban home they decided to 'go back into the work'. Prayerfully they took a decision which meant that for the next thirteen years where I went and what I did and whom I met were wholly subject to my parents' committal of themselves to the service of God and, much more to the point, their subordination of themselves to the rules and regulations and the 'marching orders' of the Salvation Army. As a child of the regiment, I have no love for it. I grew to resent strongly the way the Army stopped me and my brothers and sisters from having the same life as other children. I grew to dislike the self-important authority of some of those who decided what should happen to us all, for some of them seemed much lesser people than my own parents. As I grew older I felt contempt for the way some second-rate person presumed to cover up his petty contrivances with the name of God. I started early to dislike this authoritarian organization.

The Salvation Army welcomed back my father by sending him to a succession of 'hard goes'. The first was North Fremantle which was in those days a slum. The officers lived in bad housing among those whom they were trying to help. We were at a poorer standard than I had previously known. Yet there are some happy memories, including my first venture into wrong-doing.

I went to the North Fremantle infants' school. I liked it. I found the first playmate I ever had in Ernie Martin, son of the postmaster. He was then revealed as 'a bad influence', for he led me into an enormity of evil.

Returning to school after one lunchtime, I was met by him and two other boys who told me that there was no school that afternoon. So we went down to the beach to paddle and romp in the mounds of fresh wet kelp. Those other urchins took off their clothes and splashed each other. I could not join in because although they were barefoot, I, as a respectable child, wore boots. They were button-up boots and I could not get them undone, and I could not undo the neck of the little galatea blouse I wore. So I had to romp less freely fully clad. It was fun. The fresh seaweed smelt good.

Next morning the truancy inspector and a big policeman came to the school. In those days truancy from day school was so common that the Education Department had a special staff to detect the offenders and run them to earth. The four of us, aged between five and six, were hauled off to the disgrace of a stern lecture by the policeman about the dreadful life of crime to which all this was leading. Our parents would be informed. I crept home at the end of the day to my first thrashing, a period of being prayed over with supplication to God that He might forgive me and help me to set a better example to little boys who had not had the advantages I had of a Christian upbringing and was sent to bed without any tea. This episode put into my mind my first doubts about justice, and a feeling that even when one is doing what other people think is wrong one can have a very happy afternoon.

Mucking About (1977)

Goodbye school!

MARY GRANT BRUCE (1878–1958) IS BEST KNOWN FOR THE CHILDREN'S SERIES KNOWN AS THE 'BILLABONG BOOKS'. HERE HER HEROINE, NORAH LINTON, IS SEEN THANKFULLY ENDING HER BOARDING SCHOOL DAYS AT A MELBOURNE CHURCH OF ENGLAND PRIVATE SCHOOL BEFORE RETURNING TO HER FATHER'S CATTLE STATION, BILLABONG, IN NORTHERN VICTORIA. THE PERIOD IS C. 1912.

The big hall was packed with visitors — proud parents, each supremely confident that 'our girl' was something quite beyond the average; big sisters, anxious to create the impression of being far removed from matters so juvenile as school; brothers, wearing the colours of different schools, and assuming great boredom. Then came Miss Winter, followed by church dignitaries and other notable people, including two members of Parliament, who behaved as though engrossed with affairs of State; whereat the infant classes arose and sang a roundelay with much gusto, and the business of the day began.

The Billabong contingent was not happy. It was uncomfortably crowded; its view was obstructed by immense erections of millinery on the heads of ladies immediately in front; frequently it was tickled on the back of the neck by similar erections belonging to ladies who leaned forward, from the rear, manoeuvring for a better vision of the proceedings. It was much embarrassed by the French play, acted by the senior class — the embarrassment being chiefly due to fear of laughing in the wrong place. Nor did lengthy recitations from Shakespeare appeal to it greatly, or a song by the red-haired girl, the said song being of the type known as an 'aria,' and ungallantly condemned by Jim as 'screamy enough to scare cockatoos with!' It brightened at a physical culture display, and applauded vigorously when a curly-haired mite essayed a recitation, broke down in the middle, and finished, not knowing whether or not to cry, until much cheered by the friendly clapping. The moment of the programme — for Billabong — came when Norah, very pale and unhappy, played a Chopin nocturne. Wally joined wildly in the succeeding applause, but Jim and his father sat up straight, endeavouring to appear unconcerned, but radiating pride. Norah did not dare to look at them until she was safely back in her place. Then she shot a glance at the two tall heads; and what she saw in their faces suddenly sent the blood leaping to her own.

Afterwards came the distribution of prizes — a matter which did not greatly concern Norah, whose scholastic achievements could scarcely be classed as other than ordinary.

However, she had carried off the music prize in her class — music being born within her, and, even in lessons, only a joy. She was still flushed with excitement when the long ceremony was at an end, and she was able to slip from the platform and find her way to the waiting trio — standing tall and stiff against the wall, while the crowd seethed in the body of the hall, and other book-laden daughters were reunited with parents as proud as David Linton.

'I'll look after that,' Jim said, with a masterful little gesture, possessing himself of Norah's prize. 'Well done, old chap!' He patted her head with brotherly emphasis.

'Proud to know you, ma'am,' said Wally, humbly. 'Norah, I was nearly asleep until you came on to play!'

'And quite asleep afterwards,' grinned Jim. 'Snored, Norah — I give you my word!'

'That's one I owe you!' said the maligned Mr Meadows, vengefully. 'I clapped until my horny hands were sore, Norah. Made a hideous noise!'

'Then there were two of us,' said Norah, laughing. 'I never knew old Chopin sounded so funny — catch me playing before a lot of people again! I was scared to look at old Herr Wendt. Probably he pulled out most of his remaining locks — I know I made at least three mistakes.'

'It sounded all right,' said her father, and smiled at her. 'Now, young woman, this is very nice, but one can have enough of it.' A wheat-trimmed hat brushed across his face, and he emerged in some confusion. 'How soon will you two girls be ready?'

'Must we change?'

'I sincerely trust not,' said Mr Linton, appalled at the thought of awaiting two feminine toilettes of a greater magnificence than was familiar to him with his daughter. 'Not if you have big coats — I've a motor outside. Your heavy luggage has gone, I believe' [...]

'Goodbye, Miss Winter. Merry Christmas!'

'Goodbye, Carrots, dear!' This to the red-haired singer, who accepted the greeting and the appellation cheerfully.

'Goodbye, young Norah. Behave yourself, if you can. But you can't!'

'Goodbye, Jean!'

'Goodbye, everyone. Mind you all come back!'

'Goodbye!'

'Merry Christmas!'

'Goodbye, school!' The note of utter thankfulness in Norah's voice brought a twinkle to Jim's eyes.

The motor chug-chugged on the path. Norah did not like motors — horses were infinitely better, in her opinion. But this one seemed a chariot of joy. They bundled in, pell-mell.

'Are you all right?' queried Mr Linton.

'I never was so all right in my life!' said Norah, fervently. The car slid away into the dusty haze of the white road.

Norah of Billabong (1992; FIRST PUBLISHED 1913)

The sound of malice

F. M. McGuire (1900–95), BORN FRANCES CHEADLE AT GLENELG, SOUTH AUSTRALIA, NOVELIST AND JOURNALIST, WENT TO A PRIVATE SCHOOL IN ADELAIDE.

I should have been happy at Miss Collison's school. I cannot recall any girl I disliked or quarrelled with; but hostility was there and I was aware of it, although I never discovered its source. That it was real, deliberate, and even organised was proved in an unmistakable way.

Once a term all the children who had piano lessons gave a concert which was held in one of the classrooms. There was no audience except the children themselves and one or two of the teachers. One after the other we went to the piano, made our carefully rehearsed curtsey and played the 'piece' we had practised for the occasion. Then we curtsied again and returned to our chairs. Each performer was applauded by the other children. Until it came to my turn. I returned to my chair amid a dead silence. After an astonished pause both teachers began to clap loudly and talk brightly. But the class continued to sit without moving.

Now, these children were ten or eleven years of age and to make a dozen or so children act in unison like that would take a quite extraordinary amount of persuasion or intimidation. The leader, she who had issued the orders, must have been one of their number. I am glad and proud to say that I did not show by the slightest sign that I was aware of anything out of the way. The Loutits of Orkney are said to have been 'as proud as the de'il', and this was one occasion when I was thankful that they had handed on a bit of their pride to me.

I have often thought about this incident since then. When children are jealous or dislike one of their number they generally resort to teasing or practical jokes. But what an unhappy little worm was eating at the heart of one of those children! She had taken time and care to persuade, drill, and organise her minions, and to see that by some means her orders were obeyed. This was no girlish prank, thought of and carried out as a lark. This was planned malevolence. I never found out who was responsible and I never spoke of it to anyone. I went on as usual, did lessons, joined in the games, took part in the school activities. But, with one exception, I never made a friend in that school. The exception was Mollie Barr Smith. She and I used to go riding together, and though our life-streams have carried us far apart and we have seen each other only rarely since then, some tenuous threads of affection have remained unbroken from those afternoons when we rode to Mylor or Longwood along roads bordered with flowering tea-tree, when the scent of the gum blossom hung on the warm air as the shadows grew long and the sleepy clop-clop of the horses' hooves brought us, tired and happy, home to tea.

Bright Morning: The Story of an Australian Family Before 1914 (1975)

Never made easy

ELLA SIMON (1902–81) WENT TO SCHOOL NEAR TAREE, NEW SOUTH WALES. THE FIRST ABORIGINAL WOMAN TO BECOME A JUSTICE OF THE PEACE, SHE PUBLISHED HER AUTOBIOGRAPHY, *Through My Eyes*, IN 1978.

Even at school I was never accepted as Aboriginal. They could see by my lighter skin that I was different to them. I had red hair and a freckled face.

That might be why some of my teachers and I were so close. And that didn't help to increase my popularity either! You know, I couldn't understand why I wasn't one thing or another. Whenever I went outside to play with some kiddies, there'd always be somebody there who came along and told me to get out of it and go back to where I belonged. I never knew where 'belong' meant, and neither did they, I suppose. They were just acting like all human beings do.

Some of them were very black and they'd try to get at me by saying I should have been over at Taree, at the whites' school. They would so often give me such a terrible time that sometimes I used to just go straight home and cry. My grandmother was always there to comfort me, though. She'd tell me I had to try to understand how they felt and forgive them. Oh, it was hard, I can tell you, especially when it got so bad that there were only a few kids who would play with me.

Some of the full-bloods came from Barrington where they used to live in their own environment and follow traditional ways. Yet I was always delighted when I'd be taken out into the bush with them. They used to show me all the plants and wild fruit you could eat and those you couldn't. Even today that information is valuable to me.

Anyway I might have been a bit too fat and big to beat them at running, but, mind you, I was good at skipping! Oh, yes. When we were having picnics I would always win the skipping contests. Funnily, all the kids would be barracking for me then. I remember there was a girl from Kempsey at one of our picnics and they put me up to skip against her and I beat her hollow. Oh, they were all with me on that occasion. But why I wasn't liked all that much, I would never know. It certainly wasn't because they were jealous of me for learning a bit quicker, because they didn't put any value on education anyway. We were all poor to some degree or other, and education was a luxury that not even their own parents thought much of.

The first school I went to was the first school at Purfleet. A missionary, Miss Oldrey, had been sent up from Sydney and they'd built her a house. She applied to the government for a school and got the return offer of '£10, all requisites and a teacher — *if* the Mission would erect a suitable building'. Well, the money was raised and the people built that school. It was mainly built by my own grandfather in 1904 with a Mr Belford from Glenthorne. In those days it doubled as a church on Sundays. My grandfather split the shingles for this place as well as our own home. He was a real craftsman when it came to those sorts of things. He even adzed all the timber for the floor and walls. It was no mean feat.

The school was originally just one big room with two windows and a door. Later a great big window was installed on one side and then, later still, a little extension added. The first teacher we had was Mr Williams. He came from locally — from the school at Taree. He used to drive out every day in his horse and sulky.

The paddocks around the school were still really rough with stumps and trees in Mr Williams' time. Now, a lot of children in those days used to come down from Gloucester to my grand-father's school, because it was the first Aboriginal school built in the whole area. They couldn't go to a local school. The law in New South Wales was that, if a 'European' parent objected, an Aboriginal couldn't go to that school. So we had to have our own schools and thanks to the Mission and our own hard work we got one at Purfleet. But, as a result, some of the children — the poor things — were actually just starting school at sixteen to eighteen years of age. Yes, they'd be sitting there in the first grades even at that age. Oh, it was funny then, but it is sad to think back on it nowadays. Anyway, on some days, Mr Williams would take the big boys outside and get them to dig up those stumps or cut down the trees. It must have been a blessed relief for them, even that. No doubt he did it on purpose precisely for that. It proved to be good in more ways than one, because the school finally got a really good playing area. So some good had come out of the poor things having to be there.

They got the stumps out by digging around them and then putting a lot of wood in the holes. Then they'd set it alight and burn the stumps out, you see. All night long there'd be boys hanging around the fires, having a high old time.

There were even some children who had to come from right out at Browns Hill, on the other side of Taree. Those kids had to make their own way to school and back each day past the local school that the law forbade them entry to! That's about three miles away. Occasionally one of them would stay with a local family and only go home weekends. I mention that because it's been said that Aborigines don't take to school much. That might be right in one way, but it was never made very easy for them either.

Through My Eyes (1995; FIRST PUBLISHED 1978)

Lock up your pupils

Dorothy Roysland (née Patey) grew up near the South Australian town of Renmark, on the Murray River.

When we first started school, we had to walk over four miles to Murtho Hills, cross logs over three running creeks, then climb the big hill. On top of the hill was a two-roomed schoolhouse made out of red pug. It always smelt funny first thing in the morning when we opened the doors: I think it was from the dampness. There wasn't much up on the hill except for a few dilapidated old stables and chaff-sheds, a small patch of grape-vines, and a few apricot and almond trees. There was also a big cement basin at the top of the incline and a chute leading away from it down the hill to the big boiler room of the pumping station. They would cart in the wood on horse-drawn vehicles and send it down the chute to fuel the irrigation pumps. Apart from these things the hill was barren, just red sandhills. When the wind blew everything was covered in red dust.

I was between five and six when I started school. All togeth-er there were only about eight children attending, including the St Clair children. Our teacher's name was Miss Tottie Hines, and she taught all of us, even though we were all different ages and grades, because there were so few of us. She was a very strict person. One morning, as we were all crossing the log at the first creek on the way to school, Miss Hines, who was walking with us, discovered that she had lost her purse. She thought she must have dropped it in the creek, and as Don St Clair was the only one among us who could swim, she had him diving in the icy cold water looking for it. He couldn't find it, so she became cranky and irritable with all of us. As soon as we reached the schoolhouse she sent me into the spare room and made me stand behind the door with my hands on my head. When it was time to go home she locked the door and left with all the other children. They were halfway back to Renmark before anyone remembered that I was still locked in the spare room, and they came back to let me out. Mother was worried that we were so late home, and I started to cry, but all Miss Hines said was that she had been so concerned about the loss of her purse that she had forgotten about me.

We only attended this school for a year. It was already in a very bad state of repair, and after a while it began to crack up so badly that it was no longer safe for us to be inside it. Today no one would ever know that a building used to stand there: all the clay sand from which it was made has disintegrated and mingled with the red earth all around.

A Pioneer Family on the Murray River (1977)

A perfect AMDG job

KATHLEEN FITZPATRICK (1905–90), HISTORIAN AND ACADEMIC, WAS SENT TO BOARD AT THE LORETO CONVENT, PORTLAND, VICTORIA, DURING WORLD WAR I.

Convents, in my day, were not child-oriented institutions; they were dedicated *Ad Majorum Dei Gloriam*. This was no mere form of words as in the Latin mottoes of many private schools, but quite literally true. AMDG was the heading I inscribed on every page of every exercise-book I used during my twelve years in convents. I write neatly and legibly to this day because the nuns insisted that blots and scratchings-out and 'm' that could be mistaken for 'n' were not for the greater but the lesser glory of God, and unsatisfactory writing had to be transcribed again and again until perfection was achieved. The same held good for the evenness of stitches in hemming and smooth invisibility in darning, even though it was not possible to inscribe AMDG all over our garments. Perfection was the standard and it was immutable.

But young children, engaged in the discovery of the world, are not perfectionists but empiricists, taking up this and casting that aside, leaving a trail of deformed or maimed objects in their wake. Therefore, according to the convent ethic of my time, they had to be forced to be perfect, just as Rousseau held that men must be forced to be free. The two principal methods used in the effort to make us perfect were routine, which acts like a soporific on individuality, forming habits strong enough to last a lifetime, and fear, which paralyses self-will and induces obedience.

The routine of life at Portland Convent was absolute and at first bore rather heavily on children such as us, who had always had a good deal of freedom and came from a home in which the element of unpredictability was a strongly marked feature of life. At Portland every minute of the day was planned and no time at all was allowed for that solitary, introspective mooching around to which I was then and still am prone. At first light we made our beds under supervision by a nun who applied the AMDG method to bed-making, pointing out that every valley must be exalted and the mountains and hills made plain. When we had undressed at night and folded our underclothes neatly on a chair, we were required to arrange our black stockings in a cross on top of the pile, thus dedicating our last action of the day to God.

At first there was a certain interest, soon dulled by repetition, in the novelty of the times at which we ate and some of the dishes. Breakfast was normal but there was no luncheon proper, only 'refection' served when classes ended at midday. Refection amazed us, as it consisted of thick chunks of dry bread and a glass of 'jam-water', a concoction made by adding a great deal of water to a very little plum jam. After refection we were taken for a walk or a swim or sometimes just told to play in the convent grounds. We were never for one minute unsupervised, but we were not taught how to play any games nor did we, as far as I remember, show much invention ourselves. All there was to do when told to play was to throw a ball about aimlessly and as I could neither throw nor catch I used to try to sneak off and hide, a manoeuvre always quickly detected and stopped, because nuns, unlike our absent-minded mother, had eyes in the backs of their heads. I remember on a bitter winter day begging, through my chattering teeth, to be allowed to go indoors and being told that children's health required fresh air and that as I was cold I must run about and run I had to, just to and fro, nowhere in particular, until the ringing of the school bell, at a quarter to three, put an end to the ordeal of outdoors recreation.

Hand-washing, stocking-straightening and hair-tidying followed, a joyous rush of preparation for the great event of the day — dinner, which, strangely, was served at three o'clock [...] The only decoration I recall in that bleak refectory was a framed notice in ecclesiastical lettering, which read — 'Do Not Eat With Your Eyes', an essay in wit which delighted me once I had grasped its import. We did not eat with our eyes and we did not grab, but pressed everything assiduously on others, and if offered something nice ourselves, did not take the largest or most succulent portion unless it happened to be the nearest one. It was considered unspeakably vulgar to eat dessert with a spoon and so that we should never succumb to this temptation only forks were provided. Once a nun gave us a lesson in how to eat jelly with a fork, but it was not very helpful because as the rules of the order did not permit her to eat with lay persons her jelly was imaginary and therefore much easier to manage than the genuine slithery article. We became adepts by necessity, learning that even stewed fruit with custard can be eaten with a fork if you hold fast to the correct technique of rationing the solid part and steeping each mouthful of it in all the liquid it will absorb. All round, indeed, we became elegant performers at the table under the constant surveillance of the nun on duty. Lay sisters, poor sainted maids-of-all-work, served the meal, while the nun proper circulated round the tables, watching, teaching and admonishing [...]

Porridge was — and is — nauseating to me, but at the convent it was served every morning. This led to the one and only challenge to authority I ever dared to attempt at Portland. I said that I could not eat porridge, that it made me sick and that, in short, I would not. The nun in charge received this ultimatum calmly, merely stating that I would not leave the table until I had eaten my porridge. So there I sat with the plate before me, while everyone else ate theirs and finished breakfast and said grace and went away, leaving me solitary in what seemed the enormous, empty refectory. And there I sat and sat on my bench of desolation before the plate of now revoltingly congealed porridge for what seemed to me like an eternity. After a discreet interval a nun appeared and opened negotiations. I would be released from the refectory if I ate my porridge, which would be reheated to make it more palatable. I was not made of the stuff of martyrs and to my eternal shame gave in and ate my beastly portion.

I was never forced to eat porridge again, but if you suppose that I had won a partial victory you are mistaken. I knew then, just as well as I know now, that I had suffered a major defeat. My being excused from porridge thereafter was merely an act of grace, an added humiliation of the conquered by the all-powerful conqueror, Authority. To authority the porridge itself was neither here nor there, as was demonstrated by my exemption from it. What was important was a conventual principle called Breaking the Will, familiar to all convent girls of my generation. The nuns thought it right to break wills in order to produce humble and contrite hearts: they most sincerely believed (and their whole lives bore witness to their belief) that it was to the greater glory of God that wills should be broken to perfect obedience to authority. After sixty years of brooding on the day my will was broken, my heart is neither humble nor contrite: I think it was a degrading experience and I resent it bitterly [..]

In all seasons we washed in cold water but once a week we had a hot bath on whatever night we were rostered for. I imagine that the convent had no hot water system and that the water for the hot baths was heated nightly in coppers. 'Utterly ridiculous,' Mother had said, on finding on the list of items Lorna and I must bring to the convent, the words 'bath robes'. From the specifications it was clear that these were not what we called dressing-gowns, for putting on before and after the bath, but just what the words said, bath robes, long-sleeved ample dresses right down to the ground, for wearing in the bath. At home we had long bathed ourselves, Mother attending only briefly to make sure we had not skipped the harder bits, but at Portland even the oldest girls, like Lorna, were bathed by one of the lay sisters. Each bath took a long time, because not only did the lay sister do a perfect, AMDG job, but in order not to offend against modesty, she folded back only a few inches of the bath robe at a time, washed and re-clothed the bare bit and began on another area. The same regard for modesty was shown in the dormitory where, although we had curtained cubicles, we were taught how to undress and dress without seeing any of our own flesh by making a kind of tent of night-dress or dress.

Protestant friends, when regaled with these details of convent life, have asked whether such attitudes towards our bodies did not make us prurient little beasts. No, I do not think so. Our view of the matter was that all adults were mad and nuns the maddest. We did not ask the nuns their reasons for giving us a bath in so laborious and inefficient a manner because, being children and therefore not mad ourselves, we knew that it was a waste of time to ask mad people reasonable questions. The same principle held good for the ban on what were called 'particular friendships', a curious term since friendship is, *per se*, particular: what was meant was making a favourite playmate or companion of any particular girl. No doubt it is necessary for nuns, in their sexually segregated communities, to guard against lesbianism. We, of course, had not the faintest idea of what they were guarding us from, nor did we have any curiosity about it: the rule against particular friendships was, in our opinion, only another instance of the madness of nuns.

What I remember as chiefly being stressed in our Portland curriculum was the correct way of doing things. Training was all, education (in the literal sense of bringing to light and developing individual character or talent) was nothing. What was in us, the nuns believed, was original sin and their duty was to drill it out of us by insisting that there was one and only one right way of doing everything and tolerating only that way. Sitting, for example, required the head to be up, shoulders back and down, feet side by side, heels and knees together, hands (unless usefully occupied) perfectly still and never engaged in hair-smoothing, ear-exploring or any other activity pertaining to the person. I can recognise a convent girl of my generation still by her posture and deportment. Slumping and sprawling were unladylike and anyway, impossible, because the only arm-chairs and sofas in the convent were in the parlour for visitors; for us there were only backless benches and stiff wooden chairs. An upright posture was further encouraged by a daily exercise of walking briskly round a room with blocks of wood balanced on our heads. Our speech had to be clear and our vowels correctly pronounced, and in the course of a year (for we did not return to Melbourne for the holidays) this became habitual, so that when Lorna and I at last reappeared at 'Hughenden' our young uncles, Ack and Len, pretended to be unable to understand a word we said because, they averred, our lingo was so lah-di-dah.

Solid Bluestone Foundations: Memories of an Australian Girlhood
(1986; FIRST PUBLISHED 1983)

Mountain romantics

MARY TURNER SHAW (1906–90), ARCHITECT AND HISTORIAN, WAS
A BOARDER AT CLYDE, ST KILDA, DURING WORLD WAR I AND LATER
WHEN THE SCHOOL MOVED TO WOODEND, NEAR MOUNT MACEDON.

The school was spread over a cluster of not over-large suburban
houses set among patches of threadbare lawn and asphalt, and
the boarders were divided among three of them. Lessons were
tolerable, for I was usually at or near the top of my class (and
complacent enough about it) while the evenings and weekends,
though unexciting, were comparatively relaxed. On Saturday
afternoons there were school matches or excursions to the
Brighton ladies' baths or the Violet Farm, on Sunday mornings
sedate 'crocodiles' to the adjoining Church of England and
Presbyterian churches and in idle hours we wrote letters, fed our
silkworms and knitted socks for soldiers. Many of the girls must
have had brothers or fathers at the war, but of this I remember
almost nothing. As my own brother and cousins were fortunate
survivors it was years before I understood the staggering proportion of lives lost.

When in 1919 our headmistress made the adventurous plunge
into buying the old mountain guest house and transhipping the
sixty-odd boarders up there life certainly assumed new dimensions, at least physically. At morning 'drill' on the terrace we took
in the magnificent view together with lungfuls of mountain air.
After school it was not too difficult to avoid some of the inevitable
games and then one could wander freely along the bush roads and
tracks within not very stringent bounds, and with permission and
in prescribed groups practically as far as one liked.

Punishments as such played little part in the school regime,
beyond the minor 'detentions' imposed occasionally by exasper-
ated class mistresses. A major misdemeanour led to the whole
school being assembled under the eloquent wrath of the headmistress, her address concluding with a raised hand and 'NO! I

don't want to know who did it; *they* know well enough. I don't want to hear any more about it. Simply, it must not occur again!' At the time it seemed to me unfair that all should suffer the sins of the few, and on occasion I longed to step forward and admit my guilt, missing the point that to be deprived of confession and absolution was punishment in itself.

I don't believe I loved our headmistress but I'm sure I feared her. She, rather than my non-church-going family, must have laid the foundation for the Presbyterian conscience my friends have complained of, and if ever I hear a great voice from the heavens it will probably be hers. I can't even say, as some of her other pupils have, that from her I learned to love English literature. My years in the upper forms were her last at the school and the classes she took in English and Scripture were all apt to end in similar discourses on the moral values we would need to face the 'Problems of Life' that lay in wait for us all. Bemusedly we wondered about these, and concluded they were most likely to concern love and marriage.

On our mountainside ours was a conventual community. With the single exception of one middle-aged widow who taught the piano, the staff were all spinsters. In the early years the scarcity of motor cars meant few if any weekend visitors and trips to the city for theatres, concerts or matches. When our drama class staged its exciting annual performance in the local hall, we did our swaggering but unconvincing best to impersonate male characters, and it was a notable landmark in my last year when a team of four boys from Melbourne Grammar School came up to debate against us.

Our weekends were relaxed and lively, especially those of the Saturday night 'entertainments' in the winter term devised by each of the four 'houses' into which we were grouped. Though no doubt intended to encourage youthful creative talent, the results of the highly secret planning, costuming and rehearsing more often echoed the romantic musical comedies of the day.

Romance, in fact, was the main preoccupation of most of our sixteen-year-old minds, certainly of my own. We grabbed our letters from the notice board, gloating over any public school crests on the back. Censorship of letters was not part of our regime and had it been imposed I doubt if any flights of erotic fancy would have been revealed. The important thing was to be the object of attention. It was a mark of distinction to be 'doing a line' with some public-school sporting hero and to nonchalantly disclose, days before a holiday dance, that one's programme was already full. Through that exciting evening the pairs sat out in cars in the tree-lined driveways and embraced with varying degrees of enthusiasm, the amorous gropings checked by convention at the frontier lines of the bodice and the garter. Only a rare rash schoolgirl might confess to an intimate crony that she had allowed these limits to be overreached. 'Virginity' was not a word in polite use but the importance of its preservation had been made clear to us all. A frequent maternal admonition was 'Don't make yourself cheap, dear.' The long periods of separation from the often pimply objects of desire may have encouraged romance rather than lust. Among older girls some dirty stories were always in circulation, but although with the realism of country children we understood them literally, imaginatively they occupied a different compartment of the mind.

Interfeminine attachments only slightly compensated for the segregation. Small girls were often known to be 'mad on' an older one and would run blushing to proffer gifts or services to the beloved, whose response was dignified acceptance and the practice of going to kiss the little one good night. I remember the real pangs of falling in love with a tall dark sparkling creature in an upper form. Rather than wear my heart on my sleeve I carried her snapshot in my bloomer leg (the usual repository for handkerchiefs and minor treasures) and when it dropped out inopportunely to be flushed away for ever, distress almost outweighed my sense of the ridiculous. By the time news of my devotion had seeped through to its object the spell was waning and when at last her friends propelled her into an embarrassed appearance at my bedside in a splutter of laughter, I was able to giggle too, and recovery was complete. Later there was an upper form classmate who took a line of her own. She was very plain with a long nose and narrow mouth but had a deep and beautiful voice. With this asset she set out quite openly to woo in masculine fashion one after another of the acknowledged beauties, mainly in clandestine visits after lights out. It was half in joke and half serious, the victims half derisive and half fascinated; behind her back she was called 'the Horse'. I am not sure now how explicit her advances were, and not one of those concerned is still alive to tell.

'Education of a Squatter's Daughter', Patricia Grimshaw & Lynne Strahan (eds), *The Half-Open Door* (1982)

Aboriginal hearts

Margaret Tucker, MBE (Lilardia) (1904–) was sent to mission schools on Aboriginal reserves near Deniliquin, New South Wales. When she was thirteen, the Aboriginal Protection Board took her from her mother and sent her to the Domestic Training Home for Aboriginal Girls at Cootamundra; from here she tried unsuccessfully to escape.

One day when we were at school I was thrilled because an older boy and I were the only ones to get the answer to a difficult sum. Mrs Hill praised us and as I am not brainy it really meant a lot to me. Between morning school and the lunch break, we heard the unmistakable sound of a motor car. Out where we were motor cars were very rare at that time, and although we were seething with curiosity, we did not dare to move from our desks. One or two ventured to ask if they could leave the room, but were not allowed. Our schoolmistress was called outside. She cautioned us not to move until she returned. Some of the boys got on the desks and took a peep through the window. They relayed to us what was going on outside. A policeman and a young man and Mr Hill were talking together. Mrs Hill came in for a minute, but did not take any notice of the few boys who she must surely have seen jumping down from the window. She seemed very upset. She called Eric Briggs and Osley McGee and spoke quietly to them. They left the school through the back door. I cannot remember everything that went on, but the next thing I do remember was that the policemen and Mr Hill came into the school. Mrs Hill seemed to be in a heated argument with her husband. She was very distressed.

The children were all standing (we always stood up when visitors came and the police were no exception). My sister May and another little girl, an orphan, started to cry. Then others. They may have heard the conversation. I was puzzled to know what they were crying for, until Mr Hill told all the children to leave the school, except myself and May and Myrtle Taylor, who was the same age as May (eleven years). Myrtle was an orphan reared by Mrs Maggie Briggs. She was very fair-skinned and pretty.

I had forgotten about Brungle and the gang of men representing the Aborigines Protection Board who had visited when we were staying there. But then it came to me in a rush! But I didn't believe for a moment that my mother would let us go. She would put a stop to it! All the children who had been dismissed must have run home and told their parents what was happening at school. When I looked out that schoolroom door, every Moonahculla Aboriginal mother — some with babies in arms — and a sprinkling of elderly men were standing in groups. Most of the younger men were away working on homesteads and sheep stations or farms. Then I started to cry. There were forty or fifty of our people standing silently grieving for us. They knew something treacherous was going on, something to break our way of life. They could not see ahead to the white man's world. We simply accepted the whites as a superior race. Around that particular part of Australia, I feel we were fortunate in having a kindly lot of white station owners.

Then suddenly that little group were all talking at once, some in the language, some in English, but all with a hopelessness, knowing they would not have the last say. Some looked very angry, others had tears running down their cheeks. Then Mr Hill demanded that we three girls leave immediately with the police. The Aboriginal women were very angry.

Mr Hill was in a situation he had never experienced before. He did not take into account that Aboriginal hearts could break down with despair and helplessness, the same as any other human hearts. Mrs Hill, the tears running down her cheeks, made a valiant attempt to prolong our stay. I did not realise she had sent our two radicals Eric and Osley to race the mile and a half to get our mother. I will never forget her for that. She stood her ground, against her husband, the police and the driver of the car. 'Well, they can't go without something to eat, and it is lunch time,' she said, in a determined way.

'No thank you Teacher, we are not hungry,' we said.

'All the same, you children are not going that long journey (first to Deniliquin, then many more miles to Finley, where we would catch the train to Cootamundra) without food,' she insisted.

She went out to her house at the side of the school, taking as long as she dared to prepare something to eat. Her husband, his face going purple, was looking at his watch every few minutes. At last she came in with a tray with glasses of milk and the kind of food we only got at Christmastime. We said we couldn't eat it — we were not hungry — but she coaxed us to drink the milk and eat something. Mr Hill couldn't stand it any longer and said a lot of time was being wasted, and that the police and the driver wanted to leave.

We started to cry again and most of our school mates and the mothers too, when our mother, like an angel, came through the schoolroom door. Little Myrtle's auntie rushed in too.

I thought: 'Everything will be right now. Mum won't let us go.'

Myrtle was grabbed up by her auntie. We had our arms round our mother, and refused to let go. She still had her apron on, and must have run the whole one and a half miles. She arrived just in time, due to the kindness of Mrs Hill. As we hung onto our mother she said fiercely, 'They are my children and they are not going away with you.'

The policemen, who no doubt was doing his duty, patted his handcuffs, which were in a leather case on his belt, and which May and I thought was a revolver.

'Mrs Clements,' he said, 'I'll have to use this if you do not let us take these children now.'

Thinking that policeman would shoot Mother, because she was trying to stop him, we screamed, 'We'll go with him Mum, we'll go.' I cannot forget any detail of that moment, it stands out as though it were yesterday. I cannot ever see kittens taken from their mother cat without remembering that scene. It is just on sixty years ago.

If Everyone Cared (1977)

Horrid mysteries

MARGARET, LADY STANLEY (1875–1967), WIFE OF THE GOVERNOR OF VICTORIA, IN A LETTER TO HER FAMILY IN ENGLAND, DESCRIBES HER SON'S DEPARTURE TO BOARD AT GEELONG GRAMMAR SCHOOL C. 1916.

It is a regular public school [...] and is very well run in every way, besides being in the healthiest of places. He will get splendid sun-bathing and cricket and football. The boys are very carefully chosen, whom they admit. The school he goes to now [Melbourne Grammar] is not having a very good effect on him

— rather slack discipline and not a good tone. Miss Curwen reported Edward to me when we were at Sorrento for using unsuitable language so I have made him sit down and write a list of all the bad and nasty words he had learnt at school. I sent him back several times and each time a few 'worser and worser' were added — but not a very bad list after all, the most offensive out of 20 words being good old Shakespearean or Biblical ones. I made him read the whole list out to me which caused him a good deal of shame, and then we solemnly burnt the paper. I don't feel very sure of myself coping with boys but I take immense trouble to try and teach E. to be fastidious rather than coarse — and I'm sure that all little boys go through a *dirtsy* little phase, and I cling to the hope that with a clean home and parents whom he loves (and is a little afraid of) he will come out all right. But beyond impressing E. to wash *everywhere* I find it difficult to get any farther [...]

He was very cheerful till the last, but his little face looked very white and small as it disappeared with the train and it was a struggle not to let the tears come. I took Adelaide and Pamela with me so I didn't have to turn away alone. It is a *horrible* moment, but I'm glad it is over for it had been hanging over me for weeks. One feels so worried, too, for fear one may not have done all that is possible to equip them for their new life. I was very doubtful in my mind as to what I should tell him. I know there are 'Horrid Mysteries' (*Northanger Abbey*, isn't it?) — little talks that mothers are supposed to have with their boys before they go to school — but I really never quite know what it is all about and I never like to ask! I believe there is too great a tendency to instruct children on subjects they cannot understand and which only excite their morbid curiosity and wonder. If they are properly looked after at school I don't believe there is any necessity to tell them things when they are so young.

ADELAIDE LUBBOCK, *People in Glass Houses: Growing Up at Government House* (1977)

A liberal education

MARTIN BOYD (1893–1972), NOVELIST, WAS A BOARDER AT TRINITY
GRAMMAR SCHOOL, KEW, JUST BEFORE WORLD WAR I.

When we moved to Yarra Glen the problem of my education became acute, and I was sent to Trinity Grammar School on Kew hill, about six miles from Melbourne. My parents chose this school, probably because the fees were less than at the larger schools, but also because of the character of the headmaster, George Merrick Long, afterwards Bishop of Bathurst and of Newcastle. They were indifferent to the fact that its status was less 'public school' than that of Melbourne and Geelong, now the Australian Eton, which also are called 'grammar schools' [...]

[Canon Long] was liberal, almost left, in his sympathies. There was no fagging, and there were not even compulsory games, in spite of which we beat all the schools of our size at cricket and football. He did not beat a boy if he thought reason would be effective. He drenched us in the sentiments of patriotism, and neither he nor his scholars were afflicted by any doubt that the British Empire was the most beneficent institution the world had yet seen, because it was the guardian and disseminator of the principle of freedom.

History was taught as the gradual evolution of the English people towards the state of individual liberty. The greatest heroes, Greek and English, were those who had resisted the tyrants. The implication of our headmaster's teaching was that now that particular struggle was over, and we were the inheritors of what had been gained by the death and agony of noble men. The days of corruption, tyranny, and misrule were far off, beyond the ocean and beyond the centuries. Our function was to build up the brave new world in our new country which was free of those dead evils. When he studied with us Wordsworth's sonnet on Milton, he read it as if only for its literary quality, as if no purifying influence could be needed for the fireside, the heroic wealth of hall and bower of present-day England [...]

From choice as well as obligation I soaked myself in the poetry of Tennyson. His cadences and those of Shakespeare formed the rhythms of my brain. I had read the whole of Shakespeare's works by the age of twelve. All the images awakened by my education were English and European. Tennyson filled my head with visions of English fields and gardens, but they were gardens where it was always afternoon. Round the sixth-form room were hung large photographs of Stratford-on-Avon and of famous cathedrals.

We were also, of course, taught the Christian religion. The headmaster wove its threads thickly into the historical pattern. Although he was High Church, it was the reformers whom he most admired. He caused us to believe that mankind, led by the Christian English-speaking peoples, was within sight of the final goal of its progress, and that with the nineteenth century, encouraged by the noble voices of Wordsworth, Arnold, and Tennyson, we had come round the last bend [...]

I was afraid when I went to school that I would be bullied and hurt, but I was greeted by a kindly matron, and put in a dormitory with half a dozen new boys nearly as nervous as myself. Our ideas of what school would be like had probably been formed by an extensive reading of *The Boy's Own Paper*, and *Chums*, augmented by books like *Tom Brown's Schooldays* and *The Hill*. We were all desperately anxious to behave in the correct public school fashion. If we had believed that this involved making incantations to Buddha or whipping ourselves with scorpions, we should have done these things. You can make a wretched, aspiring, vulnerable boy do anything if you tell him that it will bring him securely into identity with his species. We believed that it was correct to ask each other: 'What's your father?' and to have a fight. The result of this was that during a 'What's your father?' questionnaire in the dormitory, the boy who was the most hefty challenged me, who was the most frail, to a fight.

The next morning in the gymnasium with prefects keeping the ring, he began to batter my face. After the first round he asked if I had had enough, but although I loathed violence and saw no prospect of anything but more battering I believed it would be unthinkable to say 'Yes' so I submitted to a continuation of the process until the prefects with a deprecating smile stopped the fight. At Eton a hundred years ago two boys were kept fighting all day, sustained by brandy, until one of them died, so I was comparatively fortunate.

On another occasion in the dormitory, when we were still quite young, someone suggested that we should all get into the same bed. At first I thought this contact matey and agreeable, but as no one had any idea beyond propinquity, and as it soon became oppressive I gave a grunt of discomfort. The boy who had suggested it was deeply wounded in his *amour propre* and muttered: 'If you don't like it, why didn't you say so?' We fell apart and returned to our own beds. I was worried at having appeared prudish. This was the only sensual experiment I knew of at school. If we had been discovered we should have been expelled, and our subsequent lives spent under a cloud, though the incident had no more importance than if we had gone into a shop and bought a piece of indigestible pastry. As it was, two of those boys, including the one I offended, have their names on the Roll of Honour. They were killed at Gallipoli.

Day of My Delight (1965)

For England

BRIAN LEWIS (1906–91), ARCHITECT AND ACADEMIC, WAS AT WESLEY COLLEGE, MELBOURNE, DURING WORLD WAR I.

The team spirit of Wesley was produced by the daily assembly and assembly focused on the Head. From his central place on the dais he dominated all those hundreds of dots of faces which filled his hall — Adamson Hall.

From our second day at the Prep it was routine. After roll-call in the classroom we surged out of Middle I, out of the door under the little veranda, along the fence of the Prep ground beside the Back Turf, and past the physics lab. There were the wooden stairs up to the hall; into the hall we went, to the central rows of seats at the very front. Here sat the Prep under the eyes of the Head.

The hall filled, the boys like starlings returning to their roost, bickering and screeching until some group organized a war-cry for their form and other forms followed with theirs. It was noisy, but the sound gradually lessened until it got near to ten past nine. Sudden quiet fell as the Head walked through the door by the dais, the same one that we of the Prep used. He was on the dais, a short stocky man with a big jowled face, looking like a mastiff, but rather a bad-tempered one; his bright little eyes showed that he might bite. Yes, he did look like a dog with his short quick steps across the dais like a dog heading for a lamp-post.

Diffidently behind him walked Mr Nye, the chaplain, a humane and popular man who taught scripture and also Greek to the few wanting to study it. He had no trouble in keeping order by using reason. Both wore black academic gowns, the only time they were used in the school.

They sat down for a moment and then Mr Nye stood at the lectern and led off with the usual prayer, one of the best in the Anglican collection: 'Almighty and Everlasting God, who hast safely brought us to the beginning of this day; Defend us in the same with thy mighty power'. It passed over our heads as part of the daily routine, but perhaps some were unconsciously appreciative of the words. This had been the usual end of the chaplain's public religious duties for the day, but the war added something else:

More especially we pray for our own Australian brothers who are now facing their country's foes. In swift or lingering death be near them; if it be thy will, touch their wounds and make them whole again, and be to each and all their inspiration in the day of strife, teaching them patience in adversity, gentleness in the hour of victory and compassion for the fallen foe.

I don't know who composed that prayer — it could have been the Head, he was capable of writing lucidly and well, but if he had written it, it masked his real sentiments. The 'foe' to him were those born in Germany who now lived here. They were down, and the Head was the first to kick them. He had gone to some trouble to get himself elected to the University Council where he was one of the pack that yelped for the dismissal of all German-born members of staff; yet right through the war he stood by his old fellow-teacher, Otto Krome, and no one could have been more German than he. Germans to the Head were more obnoxious than masturbation or 'gels'.

From the end of April in 1916 the chaplain occasionally had another addition: 'On this day, so and so, an old boy of this college, died for the cause of freedom and righteousness in the world's war. May the memory of his sacrifice help each of us to make our lesser sacrifices for the good of others'. This really moved us; sometimes some boy snivelled at the name of his elder brother and sometimes the older boys remembered him at school [...]

I think one song in our songbook was the best patriotic verse of the war, more moving than anything by Rupert Brooke. It was 'For England', written by an old Scotch College boy, Corporal Burns. The first stanza began, 'The bugles of England were blowing o'er the sea'. The last verse:

Oh England, I heard the cry of those that died for thee,
Sounding like an organ-voice across the winter sea;

They lived and died for England, and gladly went their
way —
England, O England — how could *I* stay?

This was what we felt. It was an honour and a duty to go to fight
for England; not for Britain; not for the Empire nor for
Australia, but for England, and we were proud to be able to
help.

By the time we sang it, they had gone their way. Burns had been
killed on Gallipoli and Rupert Brooke had died on his way there.
There was no more verse of elated patriotism; patriotism was now
patient suffering and there was a different sort of writing.

Our War: Australia During World War I (1980)

My children want to learn

IN 1916, **JOHN KICKETT** CLAIMED THE RIGHT OF HIS CHILDREN TO BE
ADMITTED TO THE STATE SCHOOL AT QUAIRADING, WESTERN
AUSTRALIA. DESCRIBING HIMSELF AS A 'HALF-CASTE', HE SAID THAT HE
WAS LIVING LIKE A WHITE MAN, FARMING HIS OWN LAND. HIS PLEA
WAS REFUSED.

To Hon Mr. CôleBatch
Sir   I wish you would let me Know if there would be any
Objection my Children attendinging the State School at
Quairading   Some time-agoe there were a few of them going
Native Children and Some were not Clean so the Schools Board
put a stop to them   On My Part I have taken up 300 acres of
land am living on Same at Presant   My Children have not Been
to School yet   I have a two room hessian Place Put up   I am
living apart from my fellow members am mile away from
this town   I have Started Poultary Farming here and Pigs later
on   I have Been told By Mr. Millington M.L.C. to Send My
Children to the School I was thinking to write First to you see
what you got to Say   am living on My Block My Children

wants to learn Something I have Been to School ... This is my own hand writing am Pleased to write to you Probbley this is the only letter you ever got from an Half-Cast all My Children are Half-Cast   Am the only one got land here am Making a home of it living a honeste life [...]   Well Sir I cannot leave this home to goe any I must do the Best I can I am not goe roving about Same as the rest of Natives have been going on this long time loafing about I want to Bring My Children up the Best away

> *Sir do what you can*
> *for me am yours*
> *Trouley Severnt*
> *John Kickett*
> *Quairading*

+   Am Sending My Children Photo how I dress them

> *Mr. John Kickett,*
> *QUAIRADING.*

Sir,

I beg to acknowledge the receipt of your letter of the 11th September addressed to the Hon. Minister of Education. Permission cannot be given for your children to attend the Quairading School, but I understand that you can, if you choose, send them to the Carrolup Native Settlement for the sum of 4s. each per week. There the children would be properly fed, clothed, educated, and generally cared for. There is, moreover, a native school at Beverly — 30 miles from Quairading — at which your children could attend.

> *I have the honor to be,*
> *Sir,*
> *Your obedient servant,*
> *DIRECTOR OF EDUCATION.*

MARIAN AVELING (ED.), *Westralian Voices* (1979)

Everything in its place

HAL PORTER (1911–84), WRITER, RECEIVED HIS PRIMARY AND SEC-
ONDARY EDUCATION IN GOVERNMENT SCHOOLS IN BAIRNSDALE,
VICTORIA.

State School 754 is as architecturally solid, purposeful and comfortable as many schools built in Australia in the 1880s and
1890s. It is of red brick circumspectly enlivened by a geometric
fancy-work of primrose-coloured bricks, clinker bricks and lines
of black mortar. Its alp-steep, alp-high roof and false gables are
regularly inset with smaller ventilator-gables, attics for starlings
whose untidy nests protrude from the louvres, and whose baby-
ribbon-blue egg-shells are found in the school-ground caught
on the shores of the archipelagos of plantain and shepherd's
purse that litter the sea of gravel. Since each class-room has its
fire-place, on the shelf of which sit wheat growing in saucers of
damp cotton-wool, and pickle-jars decorated with shards of
broken china embedded in putty, there are many chimneys.
Above these shafts, of terra-cotta, and ornate, in the terra-cotta
manner, as Oscar Wilde's Tite Street house is, the bell-tower
soars up, pricks up its weather-vane, and trident lightning-con-
ductor, to overtop the elms and oaks and plane-trees and pep-
per-corns we are forbidden to climb. Higher than all is the red
gum, hundreds of years old, which stands, muscular, masculine
and primitive, at the edge of the several acres of playing-fields, a
pelt of couch grass and onion grass through which generations
of small soles have abraded deep, narrow, winding paths.

Inside the school, there is the smell of chloride of lime, chalkdust and cedar pencil-shavings. The white tongue-and-groove
ceilings seem miles up; the rows of hat-pegs and wash-hand-
basins in the tiled-floor cloakrooms seem endless (here there is the
smell of carbolic soap entwined with the P. and O. ship smell of
Brasso); the wide central corridor, lined with the indoor casement
windows and glass-panelled doors of the classrooms, symbolically

objectifies primary school life, for at the distant eastern end are the classrooms of the Babies at their sand-trays, paper-folding and uncertain singing; at the western end, peak of achievement, is the Sixth Grade singing 'Wind of the Western Sea' in three parts, diction momentarily refined and poetic — *wined* for *wind* — and voices still unbroken, and sexlessly melancholy.

Perhaps it is because I love Saturday and Sunday somewhat more than I love school, that Friday, the door opening on to them, seems the day of the week I recall most, the last hour of Friday afternoon, 3 p.m. to 4 p.m., summer.

Friday afternoon. Summer. Beneath the half-drawn blinds flows the faintly peppery scent from the miles of desiccated grass encircling the town. Outside, in the European trees, the cicadas, which have been unremittingly at their vast chorus since eleven in the morning, are running down like dentists' drills. Inside, the end-of-the-weekly tasks are done. The inkwells have been emptied and washed. The blackboard has been blacked. Teacher's strap is well-earned-resting until Monday when, once again, for the thousandth threatened time, no boy will have the foresight or the resin to rub resin on the palms of his hands. We all believe that, not only will this simple treatment protect us from pain but that it will shatter the strap into fragments as it strikes our palms. The class, twenty of us, drones contentedly with the droning blowflies — twenty of *them*. I drone, I listen to the droning, and watch myself and those others.

Heads weighed forward by foot-long curls or gushes of nitty hair, the pinafored girls inject stitches, with infinite ladylike languor, into soiled poly-angles of huckaback — huckaback bibs and comb-cases and nightdress bags and scissors-covers and sauce-bottle jackets. The girls' glass bangles tinkle as their soft, soft lips purse and part, purse and part over teeth smudged with mignonette-green. They had a bath last Saturday night; they will have a bath tomorrow night. Their hankies live about the elastic of their bloomer-legs, dirty mauve handkerchiefs into which they weep gently as overflowing cups when they lose their polka-dotted hair-ribbons, skipping-ropes with wooden handles ringed like Alice in Wonderland's stockings, little copper cable-bracelets with locks to which the keys are already long lost, and their hexagonal pencils, one end of which writes blue, the other red. Boys lose shanghais, bazookas, pen-knives, tops, water-pistols, tin soldiers, and the greenish glass marbles formerly stoppers in lemonade bottles. While the girls prick on at their huckaback, the boys — flannel-singleted, galatea-bloused, bare-footed, all of them uncircumcised, un-vocational-guidanced, un-medical-inspected, un-intelligence-tested — publicly 'model' on their modelling-boards plasticine ivy-geranium leaves and, under the desk, long skinny snakes, or small male sexual organs which they show each other in the curve of their grimy hands without looking at each other.

Teacher, sacrosanct on the platform, sits seemingly harmless, nearly human in posture and silence, but only to be trusted out of the corner of one's eye, at the table covered by its ink-blotted maroon serge cloth. What does he, in alpaca coat, winged collar, and boots with toes turned up like a London bobby's, or she, in pearl-buttoned voile blouse, and patent leather belt, write or dream or privately agonize about?

Matters not.

Huckaback, plakka, love letter, poem never to be published, lying letter to creditor, formless daydream, fretful vision of expected lustful satisfaction or foreseen loneliness, all in that schoolroom are earmarked. All occupy a set place in a scheme of rigid relationships. Nothing is equivocal. Boys dress as boys, girls dress as girls, teachers as teachers, and no one, least of all the teacher, suggests that any of one group should pretend to understand or magnanimously sympathize with any of another group, or should betray instinct and the facts, and, with democratic dishonesty or psychological pusillanimity, overlook the palpable differences in age, power, intelligence, position and class. It is still a world Victorian enough for one decisively and safely to know one's exact place.

To middle-aged (reactionary?) me this simmer-embalmed sense of safety, individuality and realism sums up State School 754, Bairnsdale, in the twenties of — it seems unbelievable — this century. Was it all, ultimately and really, a system giving a more accurate foretaste of Life than education tries too analytically to offer now?

The Watcher on the Cast-Iron Balcony (1985; FIRST PUBLISHED 1963)

Shades of the prison house

ALAN MOOREHEAD (1910–83), JOURNALIST, WAR CORRESPONDENT, AND BIOGRAPHER, WAS A DAY-BOY AT SCOTCH COLLEGE, MELBOURNE, FROM THE AGE OF SEVEN.

God knows I was never maltreated as a child; I was loved, and as the third child probably spoiled as well, and there had certainly been no horrendous, Dickensian background of wicked schoolmasters or unhappy family life. My school in Melbourne, Scotch College, was one of the best in the country, and yet later when I thought about it I found myself oppressed by sensations of frustration and despair.

I had been a most unsuccessful schoolboy, invariably at the bottom of my class and unable to get into any of the teams, but this hardly explains the sense of loathing — yes, positively loathing — that still overcomes me whenever I think of that place. I attended the school as a day-boy for ten years, and surely there must have been pleasant episodes in all that time. Yet all I can remember now is those meaningless morning prayers, the heat of those over-crowded classrooms through the long droning afternoon, those second-rate masters brought out from England with their harassed and defeated faces, those windy red-brick corridors with their clanging metal shutters, and the dead hand of suburbia over all. The bearded dominie who was the headmaster was, I believe, a kindly man and much loved, but to me he was an ogre and I still have a feeling of panic when I recall that awful voice, 'You boy. Come here.'

Clearly all this is very unfair, and indeed my sister, who is some years older than I am, has told me that I was a cheerful and happy little boy, and although I did not do very well at my lessons I was as bright as a button.

But I see a different picture. I see a small boy walking home in the late afternoon, and he has on his head a faded cloth cap with alternating stripes of cardinal, gold and blue radiating downward from a button at the top. The school badge attached to the front of this cap is an oval medallion, silver in colour, and it displays a seated, toga-clad figure whom I take to be some sort of a Greek god, probably the god of learning; he is reading a tablet and an oil lamp burns on a pedestal at his side; around this figure is the school motto: *Deo Patriae Litteris.* It is not a bad sort of badge, and I remember feeling disappointed a year or two later when they replaced the classical figure — was he too pagan? — by the burning bush of Moses. My sweater is red with gold and blue bands around the wrists and throat, the laces of my boots are criss-crossed between little metal stubs, and the leather satchel strapped to my shoulders contains my wooden pencil case and my hateful books. Nothing is new. My sweater is darned and so are my socks that are held up by black elastic garters. My boots need mending. The cardboard that supports the peak of my cap is broken and is beginning to show through the cloth, and that is because I have so many times rolled up the cap and shoved it into my trouser pockets or have used it to beat my companions when we have been playing or fighting.

Just now I am alone, and I am late getting back from school because I have once again been kept in for an extra hour as a punishment for doing my homework badly. I know that I will do my homework badly again tonight, and that I will be kept in again tomorrow, and that at the end of the term I will be, as usual, the boy with the lowest marks. I am not particularly lazy or defiant of authority; I simply cannot understand what the masters are saying or the symbols chalked on the blackboard or the words printed in the books. I do not like being at the bottom of the class. I hate it. It fills me with shame and resentment. There are other stupid boys in the class but somehow they manage to get by and most of them are bigger and faster on their feet than I am, and they find a place in the cricket teams in summer and the football team in winter — a thing I can never hope to do. And so I am a withdrawn and rather sullen little boy and I can see no hope of escape; the avenging master stands over me and the monotonous treadmill will go on and on forever.

Where is the truth? If my sister is right then I must have been a mighty self-pitier and self-deceiver. Either that, or I must have learned, even at that early age, the value of setting up a façade between myself and the world, an outward show of confidence that was designed, as a form of self-protection, to mask my weakness and uncertainty. Does a small boy ever really tell you what is going on in his inmost mind? Does he know himself? Perhaps at that stage I was unteachable and the school could never have helped me. It is hard to say. But whatever may be the truth of the matter I know that my memory of that long incarceration still persists and it is a memory that I wish I could forget.

Nor was my spiritual life in much better case. We all had to go to Sunday School when we were very young, and later on it was church every Sunday morning. Can there have been anything in the world so dreary as those Presbyterian services of the nineteen-twenties, anything so calculated to alienate a child from religion? The hard seats, the arid and interminable sermons, the thin, flat singing of the hymns, the woe-begone and accusing images in cheap stained glass and mass-produced plaster — it was all one long punishment, and my only moment of inspiration came when the doors were opened and I sighted sweet freedom in the sunshine outside. Then with a full heart I could give praise to God. My dislike of the church was such that it even survived a short period, just prior to my leaving school, when I was extremely devout, pouring out my prayers each night on bended knees, carrying my pocket-bible with me everywhere, pausing to close my eyes a dozen — twenty — times a day to ask a blessing. Even at the height of this fervour I would never willingly go to church; indeed, I resented the church even more because I felt that the utter dullness of the service would be an insult to my shining God.

A Late Education: Episodes in a Life (1970)

Sectarian passions

RUSSEL WARD (1914–95), HISTORIAN AND ACADEMIC, WAS A PUPIL AT THE QUEENSLAND CHURCH SCHOOL WHERE HIS FATHER WAS HEAD-MASTER.

The school in which we lived, Thornburgh College, had been founded at the beginning of 1919 by a sort of condominium, or pandemonium, as some irreverently said, of the Presbyterian and Methodist churches. At the same time a sister school for girls was begun in a proper, though unusually large, old house half a kilometre or so away along the almost dry creek bed. Here at Blackheath College the girls lived, but during school hours the more senior of them were taught in mixed classes with the boys at Thornburgh while their younger companions shared the same Blackheath classrooms with Thornburgh's small boys. I remember very little of what happened at Blackheath but much of the daily journeys to and from school. We enjoyed catching tadpoles in the stinking puddles along the creek-bed, and start-ling inoffensive horses grazing there with well-aimed glass alleys from our shanghais; but incomparably more effective in setting the adrenalin racing were our encounters with the Stango kids.

Then and there, just after the conscription troubles of the war to end wars, sectarian passions must have raged almost as furiously as they still do in Ulster. The Stango kids, we knew, were Catholics whose homeward path from their school crossed ours. So without understanding a syllable of the words, except for the delicate reference to defecation, we would taunt them by singing in unison:

> Red, white and blue:
> The Irish cockatoo,
> Sitting on a lamppost
> Doing Number Two!

or:

> Catholic, Catholic, go to hell:
> Protestant, Protestant, ring the bell!

To which the indomitable Stango kids would reply:

> Protestant hogs
> Born like dogs
> Out of a bucket of water!

Sometimes we would launch volleys of stones, goolies we called them, at each other, but in our case always from ambush; for we went in deadly fear of the Stango kids. It was not so much that we believed they were Catholic and probably Irish, as that we knew they were tougher than we privileged products of a private school. And in any case there was never any racism in my father's schools, however much it festered in other parts of the Australian community. Two of my best friends in the World were Luigi Bellario, son of an Italian sugar-cane farmer, and Jayasuria, child of an Indian ditto. Besides, when I happened to tell this tale to a Brisbane taxi-driver in 1984, he promised to remember me to his friend, George Stanger. With a name like that the senior 'Stango' kid was quite probably a Protestant of German descent.

Every Sunday morning the boarders of both schools marched to church in 'crocodiles'. To reduce occasions for sin as well as to treat the two parsons equitably, the boys endured alternately Presbyterian and Methodist sermons on those sabbath days when the girls suffered in the *other* church. The Presbyter was a long, lean, cadaverous person with a forgettable name like Sinclair: the Methodist minister a heavily moustached, black-haired, rather plump man known as Mr Bacon. We were far too young to have the faintest idea of what, if any, were the doctrinal differences between them; but we liked Mr Bacon better because his heaven and hell both seemed to be much jollier places than those preached by the stern Calvinist. Mr Bacon, unlike the early Christians described by Tacitus, clearly loved the human race. Far and wide in that remote bush world it was said of him that if you met five strangers sitting on a fence, or a stockyard rail, Bacon was sure to know three of them. Some years later when his beloved Thornburgh got into seemingly insoluble financial difficulties, he threw himself down a long-deserted mine shaft. In addition to sermons from these clerics, we attended an hour-long Bible class taken by my father every Sunday afternoon. I understood nothing of it, but my conviction of the importance of virtuous living was always strengthened by the *a priori* knowledge that Dad was himself a good, if stern, man.

He was also learned. He knew Latin, Greek, German and, it seemed in that down-to-earth pioneering world, everything else. Other teachers came to him with problems in Mathematics, History or Science and it was clear to us that even Mr Bacon deferred to his knowledge of the Bible. More surprisingly, because he did not give himself airs, he was accepted by even the most ignorant and unsophisticated people like the wealthy grazier, father of a boarder, who could write nothing at all except the signature to his own cheques.

A Radical Life: The Autobiography of Russel Ward (1988)

England their England

Kenneth Mackenzie (1913–55) based the autobiographical novel *The Young Desire It* on his own schooldays at Guildford Grammar School, Perth, and published it under the pseudonym 'Seaforth Mackenzie'.

This, thought Penworth, is a great Public School, run according to the English tradition; and it's no more English than the country itself is England. When I am about, their voices are polite and their manners are good — or if they're not I have to tell them so, and can punish them for their mistakes. When there's no one like me to make them self-conscious, what must happen? What must it be like among them?

And he realized that he had no more idea of their emotions and passions than they had of his. To him they were, and would always remain, crude, unchangeable young animals, who had never seen an English spring or an Oxford dusk; they were looking forward, but he looked back, for ever.

To them, he was a foreigner whose speech they happened to understand. They watched him as the men on their fathers' farms and stations watched any young English novice, hiding their smiles or not, as whatever courtesy they knew prompted them. The pure, cultured accent of his voice was always strange, even though they learnt to imitate it. They paid a high price in money for that accent, and for his knowledge of dead languages and their living tongue; he belonged to them, and to their successors — a necessary appurtenance; when they left the School to become, by passing through those dark gates, men, he would remain, and remain a teacher of young minds with a little brief and nominal authority over young bodies also. But he would remain as a stranger who talked of Home and meant that shape on their maps which they recognized as England, a place in which they believed, without imagery or emotion, and which few of them would ever see.

With the oldest boys, prefects and classical scholars of the Sixth, he had a rather better standing. He once confessed, when he was older and the School was not much more than a memory, that he felt, when among them, as if he had suddenly found himself back in his Oxford Common Room, among young graduates of his own age.

'My own age,' he repeated carefully. 'Not my own tastes, of course. But according to our standards at Home their general intelligence, and their worldly intelligence especially, were well above their years. Of course there were crudities. Of course. But they knew what they wanted from life, and you felt they were going to have their way. I thought at first it might be some contemporary characteristic, something to do with their generation, you know. But I realized — it's a sort of shock, even now — that after all their generation and mine were really the same. The difference was hemispheric: climate and culture and tradition. And then, of course, I smoked a pipe and drank whisky, which made me feel very much their senior. It was quite deceptive, all that. I don't even quite get it now. If I had read more Latin and Greek than they would ever hear of, that didn't concern them. But it did concern me. It was part of my manhood; they were young ruffians of boys. Yet — somehow — I never quite believed that. Couldn't.'

The Young Desire It (1963; FIRST PUBLISHED 1937)

Schoolroom with a view

Joan Colebrook, WRITER, HAD HER EARLY SCHOOLING IN THE 1920S IN A ONE-ROOM SCHOOLHOUSE, BUILT BY THE QUEENSLAND GOVERNMENT ON LAND ADJOINING HER FATHER'S PROPERTY IN THE ATHERTON TABLELAND OF NORTH QUEENSLAND.

It was after this very early time that a one-room schoolhouse was put up near the road to Malanda. Small and square, it was set up on stilts, so that the termites could not destroy the building too rapidly (and as a bonus, the pupils could play games underneath the building when it rained). The land on which the schoolhouse stood had either been given or sold to the Queensland government by my father, and was not far from the slight rise on which he had chosen to build the new house for his own family. So we looked across at it from our veranda, and could see that point on the horizon where the white skeletons of dying trees marked the place where the jungle cutters had temporarily ceased their work. On school days one could hear from our veranda the rhythmic nasal chanting of tables and spelling, and sometimes the sound of students singing such songs as 'Waltzing Matilda,' its meaning only half absorbed, but its chorus always shouted out with patriotic fervour.

My teacher had red hair and pale skin, and she would sometimes lift me up and stand me on one of the long wooden benches and have me read aloud parts of our first-grade book to the smaller children while she herself set tasks for the older pupils, or wrote sums on the blackboard, or even sat for a moment with her red head bent on her hands, as if she could scarcely bear any longer the confusion of so many children of different ages. Then we would guess that she had a headache, and when there was a pause in the lessons we younger ones would crowd around her with a certain inarticulate distress. Sometimes during the monsoon rains (which in this part of northern Australia enveloped the tablelands in moisture for three months of every year), some of the bigger pupils, who generally rode their ponies to school, bareback, and perhaps two or three to a pony, would not appear. So in that tin-roofed box of a place, even with the rain dripping onto the metal and drifting against the window, it would be quieter than usual, and the teacher would tell stories and let us go home early, because it had become so damp and mysterious, the mist creeping up and wrapping its long, eerie ribbons around the edges of the scrub.

This school was an integral part of our early lives. Among

other things, it acted as a screen through which were tested
aspects of our reality — through the school view we were forced
to look at the world in a more complex way. My first clear memory of the Aborigines, for instance, had come from an earlier
time, when — as a very small child and holding my father's hand
— I went into a dark part of the scrub where an Aboriginal family had built their gunyah under the jungle trees. It was an arched
shelter of rough boughs curved over into a semicircle and roofed
with the fronds of scrub palms. This was during the monsoon, I
remember, but the soft rain was deterred by the thick screen of
trees overhead. In front of the little shelter, a tiny fire smoldered,
sending up its smoke to drift across the dark faces that looked out
at us with a sense of infinite patience. There were the glowing
eyes of the old man, set in the hollows of his face beneath a fringe
of white hair, and the eyes of his two women, and of one or two
children, and the eyes of the half-dingo dogs — all those eyes,
dark and shining, and staring out at us from the heart of that passive, curling intimacy of bodies, as if they could not think why
we were there but accepted us all the same. My father must have
gone to offer them something — or perhaps to ask them to work
for him — but I only remember the sense of waiting, and their
staring at us as we stared at them. I remember also that I thought
them strange and beautiful, like something out of one of my
most treasured picture books. At school, however, a different
view had been propagated. To my simple thought that they were
beautiful and rather thin and fragile was added the theory that
they had no proper tools or clothing or cooking utensils and no
means of transportation, and that they were very lucky, therefore,
that we (white Australians) had come to teach them the importance of living properly.

Much of the knowledge attained at school was of that kind
— suggestive rather than concrete, but with the didactic power
of an organized idea. When we played games such as 'Oranges
and Lemons, the Bells of St Clement's,' or chanted (as we see-

sawed on the big planks from my father's timber mill placed there conveniently for us):

See saw, Margery Daw,
Jenny shall have a new master,
She shall have but a penny a day,
Because she can't work any faster ...

the words meant little, having come to us from so far across the seas. We did perhaps wonder why the one game should end with heads being cut off, and why the other should suggest such cruelty to children, but our speculation went no further than this. In the meantime, while we listened to the scanty outlines of our own history we were adjusting ourselves to pay tribute to the great virtues of the British. When we were told to put our shoulders back and march in line, or to stand silently and wait for the teacher to tell us what to do, the implicit understanding was that it was necessary to learn to obey — that we were in fact small soldiers of the great British Empire. Sometimes, as the harsh, bright light of the north pierced the aureole of jungle, or when the flat, slightly demonic laughter of the kookaburra disturbed the stillness, we were aware of a sensual difference in our state, but we could not grasp what that difference was. Already in the school of reality, where we learned how to handle horses and other animals, how to encourage crops to grow, and how to move with caution but without fear in country not yet tamed or completely understood, we accepted as well a purely exotic emotional world which harked back to disciplines worked out over centuries on a small, fertile, sea-surrounded island. These disciplines enfolded us still. They had been modified, of course, in various ways, having been transferred to Australia originally in those creaking ships which carried the convicts and the first settlers, and carried not only the spirit of an adventurous past but also the conflicting passions of an industrial society.

A House of Trees (1989; FIRST PUBLISHED 1988)

Ballet for bullies

ROBERT HELPMANN (1909–86), BALLET DANCER, CHOREOGRAPHER AND ACTOR, WAS AT PRINCE ALFRED'S, A PRIVATE SCHOOL FOR BOYS IN ADELAIDE.

Isolated by an incomprehension that could be sometimes openly hostile, the schoolboy Robert made a virtue of necessity. The more unpopular he felt himself to be, the more he made his presence felt. Used to being the centre of attention at home, he insisted upon it as his right at school, using his quick wits to attack as the best method of defence, his imagination to evade when punishment seemed imminent. An illustration of this was his manipulation of the initiation ceremony to which, like all new boys, he was subjected when sent to 'Prince's', one of Adelaide's two leading colleges.

His parents, though unconventional in matters theatrical, adhered to the traditions of their community. Sam Helpmann's son must go to college, not only to get an education but also to establish his place in the scheme of things. No doubt he harboured the illusion that a boys' school would 'knock the nonsense' out of his brilliant but intractable offspring. Boys have a habit of bullying each other into conformity, especially those taught to value conformity for its own sake. He reckoned without the ingenuity of his son. Robert's classmates had seen to it that he could anticipate each last detail of the ordeal of initiation ahead of the new boy. He used his dancer's training to confound his initiators.

Each boy, having been routinely ducked in a horse trough, was then commanded to lie down, turn over and get up again with a bottle balanced on his head. When the bottle fell off, as it inevitably did, punishment was meted out. Robert Helpmann decided that the bottle would not fall off. He practised his balancing act as assiduously as any dance routine. So well did he perfect it that the trick lasted a lifetime, to be given years later as a 'command performance' for Princess Margaret.

ELIZABETH SALTER, *Helpmann: The Authorised Biography of Sir Robert Helpmann, CBE* (1978)

Theatre of cruelty

MANNING CLARK (1915–91), HISTORIAN AND ACADEMIC, WON A SCHOLARSHIP TO MELBOURNE GRAMMAR SCHOOL AND WAS A BOARDER THERE FROM THE AGE OF TWELVE.

Lofty [the Headmaster, L. P. Franklin] planted an idea in my mind. 'Clark,' he said to me one afternoon when he was handing back our essays in Greek history, 'you can manage history. You can tell a story — only those who can tell a story should write history.' What he did not know and I did not know at the time was that the early years at Melbourne Grammar School had given me something to say later as a historian [...]

Melbourne Grammar School taught me a lesson about life, or rather to whom the world belongs. Years later I read the remark by a German author (was it Goethe?): '*Dem Mutigen gehort die Welt*' [The world belongs to the brave]. I was to have jokes about that later with my wife. I told her that Goethe must have meant 'the tough', even possibly 'the cunning' or 'the bullies'. I need a man of Goethe's stature to say that, but I cannot even tell my wife why this is so. There are still some things too painful to talk about to anyone.

Even now, sixty years afterwards, I stumble in my search for words in which to tell about the discovery. There were rumours of a coming ordeal: there were rumours about initiations. They would not be as savage as in previous years, rumour had it, because last year (1927) the son of a prominent Melbourne man suffered concussion when THEY, the members of the Long Dorm ('What's the Long Dorm?' I ask in alarm. 'You'll find out soon', was the reply, and so I did) rolled him down the stairs from the dormitory floor to the ground floor. The School, Lofty had said, would not stand for that sort of thing [...]

I wondered if Lofty knew initiations were still going on. I wondered if those men who wore a surplice of white linen every Sunday morning and every Sunday evening in the chapel, and read out those words about the 'lilies of the field' and having compassion on the 'least of the little ones', knew what was going on [...]

On the night when it first happened there was only terror. I remember we were told at tea one Friday night that we were to attend a meeting in a room where boarders sat and talked on rainy days. Eighty boys crowded into a room plunged in darkness except for one light over a table at the far end of the room. The members of the Long Dorm were standing around three sides of the table, their coats and ties off and their sleeves rolled up. Some of them were soaping the table to make the surface slippery, some of them were dipping pages of newspaper into a bucket of water and rolling the wet paper into balls the size of a croquet ball. At their end of the room, among the Long Dormers and the initiated from previous years, there was laughter. At our end, where the uninitiated were huddled together there was silence, as frightened eyes watched the preparations, or looked to each other for comfort and reassurance, only to discover that in such moments there is no solidarity, no fellowship between the victims, each victim being concerned with protecting his own skin. The members of the Long Dorm were the boys from whom the next batch of house prefects were chosen; they were on the first rung of the ladder of success in the school. I did not realise then the role of these young men as guardians of bourgeois society in Victoria. I saw them as bullies, as young men of whom I was scared. I had been scared before, but this, I discovered, was a super scare, like those early scares about annihilation, the scare on first confronting the men with the qualities, temperament and character of those who come to the top in every human society [...]

At the table they dance around me shouting 'Up, up, up' as I climb onto the table and duck to avoid the wet paper pellets thrown at me and the swishes with a roll of wet paper at my face. 'What's your name?' 'Clark', I reply, as they shout, 'He's scared, he's scared.' 'Yes, but what's your other name?' 'Manning', I reply in a shaky whisper. One of my tormentors — I can still see his face, and remember his name, and remember how he jerks his head like a golliwog, though 'Nuer', as he is called, is no clown — turns to the chorus of boys, and, miming an effeminate voice and making effeminate gestures with his hands, says, 'Our ickle Mann's quite a poet.' Gales of nervous laughter erupt from the spectators. When bullies hold the floor no one among the onlookers displays sympathy with their victim, no one dares call out, or may even want to call out 'Stop'. They want more, provided they are safe — and loud laughter is part of their insurance premium. The bully, not the victim, is what human beings are interested in.

I do not give them the satisfaction for which they hunger. I do not put on a counter show, like so many others, or treat it as a joke. I sing, and then lapse into sullen silence, while the paper cannon-balls burst on my face. Nuer sneers at me, 'See how you like this, "ickle Mann"', and he knocks my legs from under me, and I fall hard on the table, and have difficulty in standing up again because the soap has made it as slippery as ice; Nuer aborts all my efforts, as the others laugh at my impotence. The audience, too, find it funny. I wonder how long it will be possible to endure without giving them the satisfaction they crave. Insecurity from whatever cause is one of the states I cannot handle then and never will be able to handle. One among the pack of my tormentors takes pity on me, or maybe he is bored and wants to get on with the next act in the show — who can tell? He calls out, 'Break it up.' I am told to stand up, shake hands with Nuer just to show there is no intention to ostracise me from the pack.

I am now an initiated member of the pack. I step down from the table, and feverishly look into the eyes of those of my age, hoping for some sympathy, but they all look the other way.

The Puzzles of Childhood (1989)

Summer haunts

NANCY PHELAN (1913–), WRITER, ATTENDED MISS GRANT'S PRIVATE SCHOOL FOR GIRLS IN THE SYDNEY SUBURB OF MOSMAN.

The school was conducted downstairs in the old Grant house. In a corner of the lawn tennis-court facing the quiet street a notice said:

KILLARNEY

SCHOOL FOR GIRLS AND

KINDERGARTEN

At that time, Mosman had only Killarney and the Infants at the Public School. The Public School kids, we were told, were cheeky, common and verminous. We, they rightly claimed, were stuck-up.

Now that hard beginnings, rough schooling are so esteemed, my childhood appears pampered and effete. So much beauty surrounded me, so much sun and freedom, and I enjoyed it all so completely. I did not suffer at school; from the moment I entered Killarney gates at the age of five I was enslaved by the old house, its gardens and high-ceilinged rooms, its haunting atmosphere of grace and elegance.

Built perhaps in the 1880s, it stood in large grounds among fine trees. It was not beautiful, in the classic Georgian sense, but there was grandeur and dignity in its red-gravelled drive, square

Italianate tower, iron lace on the upstairs balconies, tiled verandas and French windows. Behind was a stable-yard with old red-brick stables and carriage-house. The two schoolrooms were large, lofty, with white marble mantelpieces. One room was papered tobacco-brown, the other bottle-green.

Whatever schooling I had at Killarney was subsidiary to the setting, the green lawns and tennis court, roses and jasmin-hung summer-house. As with the bay, it now seems to have always been summer, a world scented with pittosporum and garden flowers, of fine parched grass, plumbago hedges powdered with pale dust, of drowsiness and delicious struggle to keep awake in the dim shaded room while the heat pulsated outside and cicadas drummed in the camphor laurels.

Education, in any case, was not very complex. The Juniors, in the green room, had plasticine, raffia, cutting-out and pasting-in; the Big Girls, in the brown room, had sums and High Roads of History. You stayed at Killarney till you were ten, then went to Redlands or one of the Church of England Girls Grammar Schools. The little boys moved on rather earlier to Mosman Prep.

At one side of the house, part of the veranda had been enclosed for a cloak-room. Here we left hats and coats, entering the classrooms through the French windows. The front door and hall, Miss Grant's private section, were out of bounds.

I longed to explore this hall, large, dark and shiny, to sit there alone feeling the silence, smelling the scent of old polished furniture, strangely moved and disturbed in a way I could not understand by the vast staircase with carved posts and the stained-glass landing window filtering muted light. On the right was the heavy door of the drawingroom and a passage led off through a green baize door to stone-flagged kitchen quarters.

For the pupils, the hall, the drawingroom, the forbidden parts of the house were associated with illness, emergency, bad news, disaster. Only these qualified us for admittance; yet when, found to have chickenpox, I was isolated in the drawingroom until called for, my pleasure was overshadowed by shame and guilt.

'How *could* your mother have LET you come to school!' Miss Grant had said, shocked, so I felt it was all my fault; and when my mother arrived she too seemed to blame me because the spots had come out after I left home.

The only way to really enjoy the hall and drawingroom was to be an object of sympathy, the innocent victim of a fall or a bad cut with blood. At such times Miss Grant's mother came with basins of water and boracic acid and one was enclosed in soft compassionate murmurs. Once, being hit on the head by a swing, I was even taken upstairs to a gigantic bathroom with olive-green and white flowering tiles and enormous mahogany W.C.

Those who were old enough to stay at school all day ate their sandwiches in the garden, on benches by the plumbago hedge, beneath the camphor laurels or by the swings and bars, where after lunch one hung by the legs, full of jam sandwiches and water from the bubbler. The privileged Big Girls ate in the summer-house with latticed walls threaded with jasmine. This building became the setting for every garden proposal scene in every historical romance I read in my teens.

As the school prospered and grew, extra classrooms were made in the stables and coach-house. I longed to be old enough for this romantic world of white-washed arches, hand-made brick and courtyard pump where old Mrs Grant washed out with soap and water the mouths of pupils caught telling lies. I was incredulous when girls said their parents objected to their being taught in A Stable.

A Kingdom by the Sea (1990; FIRST PUBLISHED 1969)

Portrait of the artist

BERNARD SMITH (1916–), ART HISTORIAN AND ACADEMIC, BEGAN HIS WORKING LIFE AS A TEACHER IN A NEW SOUTH WALES COUNTRY SCHOOL. THIS EXTRACT COMES FROM HIS AUTOBIOGRAPHY, *The Boy Adeodatus: The Portrait of a Lucky Young Bastard*.

There it was at last. On a patch of rising ground, at the side of the road, as they crossed the creek before entering the forest. Murraguldrie provisional school, the small verandah looking vacantly into the bush.

'That's it,' said the mailman. 'That's where you'll do your time. Fred Reymer was there four years.' He stopped at the Thomas's mailbox and threw the canvas mailbag deftly into it. 'This is where you get out. Mrs Thomas will look after you real good if she likes you.'

Bernard stood on the side of the white granite road, deeply rutted and channelled by rain water. At the end of the track he could see a white weatherboard house behind the broken hedge of a small cottage garden. Coming up the track was a tall, gangling youth wheeling a barrow.

'G'day,' the boy said when he got there. 'You the new teacher?'

'Yes, that's right,' said Bernard. 'And what's your name?'

'Alan,' he said. 'Alan Thomas. Mum asked me to bring the barrow to put y'bags in. It's a bit dirty though.'

'Well, I've only got one port and it isn't very heavy,' Bernard said. 'I can manage, you don't have to carry my things.'

'Well, I brought the damn thing up,' he said, 'you may as well use it.'

So he let him have it. The weather was warm and he said so.

'It's nothin',' Alan said. 'Wait till summer comes. And it's pretty cold in winter. Where you from?'

'I'm from Sydney.'

'So you haven't lived in the country before?'

'Not in this kind of country, but I've just spent three months in North Queensland.'

'D'y' like walkin'?'

'Yes, I do.'

'Well, if y'like walkin' I'll take y' for a walk up that big hill.'

By this time they had reached the house. There were three dogs chained to their kennels at the back of the yard; a collie dog and two kelpies, barking.

'Mr Smith,' said Alan's mother, 'there's a room for yer here if you want it. but you don't have to stay if yer don't want to. I've just had the last teacher for four years; and it does make more work. You might like to stay with the Hennekers or the Camerons. There's no reason why I should have the teacher all the time.'

She showed him a small room at the side of the house, with a door leading to the front verandah. A large double bed had been made up, covered by a brightly coloured patchwork quilt. It took up most of the room. To one side, at the end, was a small dressing table holding an oil lamp; by the door a washingstand with a marble top, a basin and jug, and a tin soap dish with a piece of yellow soap. The window looked onto a small orchard. Outside the door, at the end of the verandah, was a large hawthorn bush, red with berries.

'It looks very comfortable,' he said.

'Well,' she said, 'just stay for a few days and tell me what yer think.'

He stayed for three years; and in the quiet forest began to read some sense and meaning into the confused riddle of his life.

'He says he likes walkin',' said Alan to his mother. 'So I think I'll take him up the trigsite and show him the country. He hasn't lived much in the country.'

'But he's come all the way from Sydney, Alan,' she said. 'He must be tired.'

'No, I'm not at all tired,' he said. 'I'd like a walk. I slept all the way to Cootamundra. I'm not a bit tired.'

They made straight across the orchard, through the home paddock and the flat to the foot of the big hill, Alan in front, setting a rattling pace and aiming straight for the sharpest scarp. As they began the ascent they twisted past big granite boulders and loose sand around rabbit burrows. It was becoming a strenuous pull.

'D'y' wanta rest?' Alan says, about a quarter of the way up.

'No, I'm okay,' says Bernard, puffing a bit. 'I'm fine.'

'It's a pretty good pull up,' Alan says, 'just here.'

He agreed that it was.

The lower slopes were covered with stands of yellow box, peppermint gum and black wattle, but as they got closer to the top of the big hill it became increasingly clear of timber, the green winter grass between the large boulders making a soft pad for their feet.

It certainly was a trigsite. The first really big hill you meet as you enter the hilly country on the road from Wagga Wagga to Tumbarumba after leaving the main southern highway south of Tarcutta. An outlying foothill of the Southern Alps. You could see in every direction. To the west the long flat lands of the Riverina; to the east the Southern Alps, already capped in snow, way down towards Victoria.

'I've never seen such a wide view anywhere,' he said to Alan. 'What a beautiful place.'

'Yeah,' said Alan. 'I suppose it is. Mum said she thought you were an artist or something like that. Sometimes I bring the dogs up here and we get a coupla rabbits.'

The Boy Adeodatus: The Portrait of a Lucky Young Bastard (1985; FIRST PUBLISHED 1984)

Bells, spires and doves

MEG STEWART (1948–) WROTE THE 'AUTOBIOGRAPHY' OF HER
MOTHER, MARGARET COEN, PAINTER, WHO WAS AT THE CONVENT OF
THE SACRED HEART, KINCOPPAL, SYDNEY, IN THE 1920S.

'Kincoppal' was written across the wrought-iron gate between
the big stone pillars at the entrance to the school. *Kincoppal* is
an Irish word meaning 'horse's head'; it referred to a craggy
sandstone formation that jutted out of the harbour at the bottom of the grounds.

A short, circular drive dotted with pink and white camellias
swung up to Kincoppal House and round so it was possible to
drive in and out without turning. In front of the house were
garden beds of thickly clustered rich blue, gold and purple pan-
sies tended by a whiskered old gardener named Mortice. The
nuns lived in Kincoppal House, the school itself was in another
building further down the hill.

Kincoppal House was two-storeyed and made of sandstone.
It had a heavy-brass knockered front door set back in a tiled
verandah that ran the width of the house. The front door
opened into a wide, high-ceilinged hallway. The chequered pattern on the verandah tiles outside changed to a star-shaped
design in the hall. On both sides of the hall were two rooms,
known as the parlours, which had wooden-shuttered French
doors leading onto the verandah. A cedar staircase led up to the
second storey, where the nuns slept. The upstairs windows were
also wooden-shuttered [...]

The school building was tall and narrow with about six storeys.
We stepped straight from the nuns' house into the school chapel.
Every morning we went to Mass in the chapel at half past seven.

After Mass we had breakfast in the refectory under the
chapel, built on another level of the hill as it dropped down to
the water. Because so many of the nuns were French, if we spoke
at all we had to speak in French at breakfast. Conversation as

such was not allowed at any meal. One girl sat behind a rostrum at the end of the refectory during the evening meal and read aloud. The school had an inexhaustible supply of novels to do with the torturing of English priests at the time of Henry VIII and Elizabeth I, the rack being their favourite torture instrument. They made grim reading and grim listening.

Above the chapel were a study and three big classrooms, and next floor up was the long dormitory, where we slept. There was another dormitory on the top floor which wasn't used much; we could see right out across the harbour to the Heads from there.

A long balcony ran the length of our dormitory. If we sneaked out on this in the evening we heard the lions roaring for their dinner across the harbour at the zoo. We could also hear the bells of St Marks chiming on the other side of Rushcutters Bay Park at Darling Point. Darling Point was an empty hillside except for the spire of St Mark breaking the skyline and a few houses among the gum trees.

Down some steps from the refectory was a huge recreation gym area. On wet days we amused ourselves in here. Trix played the piano for us. We danced the polka round the room to tunes like 'Ta Ra Ra Boom De Ay'.

The playroom opened onto a lawn with basketball and tennis courts. When I arrived at Kincoppal, I was fascinated to see girls with hoops, wooden balls and mallets, playing croquet on the lawn. How quaint and ladylike! I had thought croquet only existed in *Alice in Wonderland*.

The playing fields at Kincoppal were like a giant paddock, with a view stretching from Garden Island round the harbour to Rushcutters Bay. At the far edge of the paddock were two grassy inclines. They were too steep for mowing, so the grass stayed green and lush. In summer they were covered with long-stemmed orange and black ixia flowers, sometimes even rare, pale green ones. On Mondays after we had eaten our lunch and before we went back into class, an Italian organ grinder used to appear on these slopes. He placed a battered hat in front of him so that we could drop our pennies in and played the organ for us. Every Monday he churned out the same tune, 'Killarney'. Very occasionally, he treated us to 'Santa Lucia', but not often.

A gate at the slopes opened onto a winding path through bush. The path wound down cliffs twenty to thirty feet high to the harbour. The path was bumpy with twisted, twining, licheny roots of Moreton Bay fig trees and odd flame-coloured fallen flowers from the coral trees round the chooks' yard. The bush on the cliffs was full of wildflowers, native rosemary, lime-green banksias, pinky-mauve grevilleas, flat starry white flowers, native fuchsia and red honeysuckle from which we pulled the centres to suck the sweetness. Tongue orchids clung to the rocks. Over the years a freshwater spring seeping into the sandstone ledge at the bottom of the cliffs had hollowed out a natural rock pool like a bird bath.

A harbour swimming pool was fenced in for us and beside it was a bath house. Long-legged, black water birds perched on the white lattice roof. Seagulls and other water birds frequented all the grounds at Kincoppal, as well as pigeons and doves. The cooing of doves was a familiar background sound about the school. In summer we swam before early morning Mass. We had to get up at six and, wearing neck-to-knee swimming dresses (far too decorous to be called costumes), we walked silently in single file down to the pool. We were never allowed to talk when walking. It was a real privilege to go swimming. Anybody who misbehaved instantly lost her swimming privilege.

One feast day, a launch picked us up at the swimming pool and took us to a deserted island in the harbour for a picnic. Treats like this were what made Kincoppal so special and why I loved being there.

Autobiography of My Mother (1985)

Transplanted

In the novel *The Waves*, by **Virginia Woolf** (1882–1941), an Australian schoolboy at an English school refuses to demonstrate his shameful Australian accent.

'I will not conjugate the verb,' said Louis, 'until Bernard has said it. My father is a banker in Brisbane and I speak with an Australian accent. I will wait and copy Bernard. He is English. They are all English. Susan's father is a clergyman. Rhoda has no father. Bernard and Neville are the sons of gentlemen. Jinny lives with her grandmother in London. Now they suck their pens. Now they twist their copy-books, and, looking sideways at Miss Hudson, count the purple buttons on her bodice. Bernard has a chip in his hair. Susan has a red look in her eyes. Both are flushed. But I am pale; I am neat, and my knicker-bockers are drawn together by a belt with a brass snake. I know the lesson by heart. I know more than they will ever know. I know my cases and my genders. I could know everything in the world if I wished. But I do not wish to come to the top and say my lesson. My roots are threaded, like fibres in a flower-pot, round and round about the world. I do not wish to come to the top and live in the light of this great clock, yellow-faced, which ticks and ticks. Jinny and Susan, Bernard and Neville bind themselves into a thong with which to lash me. They laugh at my neatness, at my Australian accent. I will now try to imitate Bernard softly lisping Latin.'

The Waves (1931)

Transported

After enjoying comparative freedom at his first boarding school, Tudor House, in the southern highlands of New South Wales, novelist **Patrick White** (1912–90) was sent to the English public school, Cheltenham.

Ruth said while we were driving down to Cheltenham, 'This is the proudest day of my life.' When the gates of my expensive prison closed I lost confidence in my mother, and the Uncle James in me never forgave. What my father thought I can't be sure. An amiable, accommodating husband, he went along with what she wanted.

Cheltenham was a seed sown in an ambitious colonial mother's mind by the English head of a preparatory school in Australia. Though the man turned out to be what my parents considered a 'no-hoper', the damage was done. I started serving my four-year prison sentence.

Our days and nights in the house in which I was boarded revolved round the 'sweatroom' where we did our prep and led the little social life we enjoyed in an English public school. My first impression of this sweatroom was one of varnish and carbolic, together with the smell of radiators you could press against for warmth if you were lucky enough to have one alongside your desk. One wall was panelled with lockers. Smelling of emptiness and varnish at the start of term, the lockers developed a riper, more furtive personality, which asserted itself through gusts of musty fruitcake, tantalising whiffs of orange and chocolate, and the more passive presence of damp, mutilated textbooks. Secrets you kept in your locker became open ones, you suspected; the only safe place was your head, dreams the only refuge after we were locked in the dormitory at night.

They had to give us access to a lavatory in spite of the opportunities it offered. I spent half the night in it finishing prep for which there hadn't been time in the sweatroom, tormented by the mysteries of algebra and trig. Lulled by Virgil's *Eclogues* balanced on goose-pimpled thighs. Morning again: a quick slick-over, eyes and armpits, in the toshroom, before a final go at prep, and the lumpy porridge and bread-and-scrape we were served at breakfast. No wonder boys are at their cruellest at breakfast in a boarding school. Accents crop up: '… me dad from Bradford …' I was reminded of the deformity I carried round — my Australianness. I hardly dared open my mouth for fear of the toads which might tumble out, and the curled lips, cold eyes waiting to receive renewed evidence of what made me unacceptable to the British ruling class.

Any boy who had not thought about sex must soon have been made aware of it, such was the housemaster's obsession. Perhaps understandably. Shortly before my arrival the poor wretch had weathered a scandal when half his house had been expelled. He would burst into toshroom or gym hoping to catch us *in flagrante*. He was the tallest man I had seen. He smashed the light bulbs caning us. He promised to stamp out a 'morbid kink' on discovering my passion for Chekov, Ibsen, and Strindberg, and only stamped it deeper in. Never during my stay in his house did he uncover sex, though he must have disturbed fantasies in his forays through toshroom steam and the stench of sweat-sodden jerseys and mud-caked boots in a more puritanical gym. We were far too frightened, I think, and at least one of us found the climate uncongenial. Even in the more brazen days of my maturity, English sex shivered and plopped remorsefully like a gas fire on its way out. The strength of the game lay in the opening gambits.

When they considered I had settled down at my public school my family returned to Australia. The parting took place on a Swiss railway platform. At one point my mother withdrew with my sister, leaving my father to acquaint me, I began to sense, with the facts of life. Dusk was tingling with village lights and their refractions off snow as we plodded up and down in our felt boots, wordless banners of white mist ballooning out of our mouths. My heart was beating horribly, but at least it wasn't up to me to speak; the onus was on my unfortunate father. At last he accepted his duty. He warned me against the seats of public lavatories. We were both breathless with relief at the removal of a difficult situation. Only the light was nagging at me, the sounds of a train preparing to burrow through a Swiss landscape towards bleached grass, eroded creeks, and the wounding blows from butcherbirds' beaks. The wounds I suffered on the snow-bound platform were of a duller kind which promised suppuration. I was determined to keep my grief within the bounds of that manliness I was being taught to respect, when I would have liked to tear off the rabbitskin glove he was wearing and hold the sunburnt hand to my cheek. I did nothing. I didn't cry. I only throbbed as a windowful of faces slid away through the Swiss dark.

Kind friends escorted me back to resume my sentence at Cheltenham.

Would I have felt sentenced in Australia? The masochist in me might have seen to that. As it was, memory helped flesh out an English schoolboy's idyll: riding a pony bareback through girth-high tussock, stripping leeches from my body after a swim in a muddy creek, my solitary mooning through a forest of dripping sassafras towards the sound of the waterfall. My parents played no active part in this country of the mind. I clung to them as a lifeline. I wrote them each week a stilted childhood letter. I was a dutiful son, if not the kind they would have chosen, some doctor-grazier, cricketer-barrister, or my mother's version of a diplomat; we were all three guilty and innocent parties, suffering one of those betrayals by fate.

Flaws in the Glass: A Self-portrait (1981)

Coining a phrase

DONALD FRIEND (1915–89), PAINTER, WAS EDUCATED AT A SERIES OF PRIVATE SCHOOLS IN SYDNEY. THIS EPISODE COMES FROM HIS TIME AT CRANBROOK SCHOOL.

Donald was a brilliant scholar: maths, trigonometry, English, he breezed through. Latin, French and German he mastered with maddening ease. He was enormously talented at languages; later on, when he travelled and lived abroad, he spoke and wrote ten or twelve languages and dialects. It all seemed so easy for him and was infuriating for anyone plodding along behind him. His command of English was a joy in his writing, even though his precosity was awesome.

One day he was caught talking in class and told to write an essay as a punishment. I have the original which I quote in its entirety.

Essay on silence is golden

'Speech is silver, Silence is Golden.' How foolish are these words, and how impossible. Taken from a commercial point of view it is absurd, should this be so it would entirely displace all the monies of the world, and we would have to use sovereigns of lead or pewter. Masters would make themselves rich in a day by shouting and roaring like howling maniacs at the boys while the latter would be rolling in wealth by means of the quiet ways typical of boys of Cranbrook. I, for one, would take a small seat at the back of the classroom with Sharland and Cox and listen to the far-off roaring of Mr Scott or some other monster who had caught on to the above mentioned get-rich-quick scheme, with such quietness and patience that the gold would soon come in shapely haloes around my head. What is more, after taking a quiet day in the described manner, I would talk in my sleep, so as not to waste time. What with a week spent in this fashion I would have enough gold and silver to build a comfortable little cottage in the country where for the next month or so I would leisurely spend my time (having a generous mind) holding conversations with my friends Sharland and Cox (who have been gabbling wealth to the Bank authorities), and reward them for their appreciation of my wit by the shining silver of my elegant speech, and the rich gold of my well-timed and classical pauses. By this time we would all be very rich men, and I would take my favourite masters (such as the Major, Mr Palmer) into my golden residence in the country, I would also take my so dear friend Mr Scott to finish his now growing wealth in my shouting room (a sound-proof dungeon in my cellar), and also kindly provide him with Mice from the Rats' Hole (Harvey House) who, with their sticky fingers and chewing gum, would make excellent inspiration and a great encouragement for him to roar at. But, as I think I have mentioned before, this is entirely absurd.

D. Friend, 1928.

The original of this masterpiece was sent home to Mother with a stiff note demanding she should punish Donald for gross impertinence. Mother, enjoying his prose and admiring his nerve, showed it to various people with loving laughter. The outcome was that the essay was published in *Smith's Weekly* with a photo of Donald. And as *Smith's* was a paper not widely read by academics he got away with it. I think, however, that this among other things — his non-conformity to the rules and regulations of school life and the playing fields of Cranbrook — added up to his becoming a day-boy and finally leaving Cranbrook and going to Sydney Grammar School.

GWEN FRIEND, *My Brother Donald: A Memoir of Australian Artist Donald Friend* (1994)

Perfect uniform

Moira Lambert (1918–) was at school during the 1920s at the Brigidine Convent, Hawthorn, Victoria, which was then named Lyndale, later Kilmaire.

I started school officially at five years and some months (early 1924), coinciding with the opening of the new school buildings. The number of pupils had grown too large for the convent where I had started with Frank. An L-shaped building had been erected on the north and east sides, taking up some of the playground, which had been enormous. The schoolrooms were separated by folding doors. This building was later added to on the south side by two new schoolrooms, one housing a Botany lab.

A school photograph of Grades 1, 2 and 3 shows 29 children, 11 of whom were boys, with me at the end of the nine smallest children in the front row. I am clad in an incongruous round-necked tunic (made, no doubt, from a 'good piece of material') and squinting pale-eyed into the sun. Most of the girls were the privileged possessors of a rounded gold bracelet called, as I remember, a 'Nelly Stewart bangle'. I never dared even to ask for one as they were said to be pure gold.

I remember very little actual learning in my early school years though I still have my first school book — a slender volume called *The Austral Primers No. 1 First Steps at School*, published by Whitcombe & Tombs Ltd, Melbourne, and, regrettably, undated. It has copperplate letters gradually building up to single words, and pleasant little pictures of cats, rats, hats, mats, nests and eggs, leaves, houses, flags, dolls, footballs, ducks and boats. By the end of the year one had presumably to learn to spell and draw these, count to ten and write little sentences in copperplate.

I well remember the uniform — theoretically a navy-blue tunic with three pleats back and front, attached to a square, sleeveless yoke, white tobralco blouse and white socks (later black stockings), black shoes and black felt hat with hatband and metal badge. Vilely hot in summer. Then we branched out into navy fuji-silk, long-sleeved dresses with detachable white collars and cuffs and a cream straw hat for summer. These dresses had two narrow strips hanging from the shoulders, to be knotted as a tie in front. Our winter uniform remained almost the same throughout my school life. Much later, we had royal-blue 'Indian Head' (a sort of linen) tunics, pale-blue blouses, and fawn stockings, straw hats and gloves for summer. Blazers, hats and gloves were mandatory as soon as one moved outside the school. There were monitors on the gates to ensure that no one emerged in a state of undress.

When I first started school I played only with my brother and his boyfriends because I had never played with girls and didn't know any girls' games. Later I learnt to skip rope, and play games like 'Here were go gathering nuts in May', 'Oranges and Lemons', 'Drop the Hanky', 'Hidey', 'Chasey' and 'Statues'. The school grounds, even after the new school was built, were spacious, with barns near the back gate, clumps of peppercorn trees, a well, the ubiquitous mulberry tree, and plenty of finely gravelled playing space. The intrepid could sneak into the large front garden and climb up the creeping roses on the fence of the one asphalt tennis court to spy, unseen, on the seniors playing tennis; or you could find marvellous caves in the tall hedge of cypress trees which hid the large, circular central lawn from the front street.

At the age of six I was plain and shy. My hair remained curly until I went to school and it was put in one plait down my back, which straightened it. Nana used to put it in rags when I was going out anywhere — a painful process in which the hair was wound tightly upward round one half of a long strip of rag, and at scalp level the other half of the rag was wound downward over this sausage, and both were tied in a knot at the lower end. Then she would make 'spit curls' around my face which I would balefully brush away. When the plait was cut off I certainly didn't have the hairdo I admired — a square-cut bob with a fringe. Mine was parted on the side and held by a hairslide. I had disastrously crooked teeth, probably as a result of sucking my whole out-turned hand as a baby. Definitely an ugly duckling and sadly aware of it.

A Suburban Girl: Australia 1918–1948 (1990)

In loco parentis

JUNE EPSTEIN (1918–), WRITER AND MUSICIAN, WAS SENT TO A PRIVATE GIRLS' BOARDING SCHOOL IN PERTH AT THE AGE OF SIX.

I can never quite decide whether the benefits of boarding school — a sound musical training and rigorously enforced work habits — compensated in the long run for the emotional trauma of being wrenched at the age of six from a warm Jewish family and an adored mother to be set down among strangers. I look now at my own small grandchildren and cannot imagine how they would cope in such a situation. I think of small children throughout the ages trapped and emotionally starved in far worse circumstances (ours was a good school), and they possess my imagination as do all deprived children, so that I identify with them and constantly write about them.

We three little sisters were taken from home together in September 1924, undressed by strange women and put to bed in a row of small children. I was the youngest in the whole school. Next morning at breakfast my sister Eve sat, head bent, tears slowly running down her cheeks and dripping on her plate. Not a sound escaped from her lips; she was a proud child. Around the table a dozen small children, including my eldest sister, ate their porridge, peeping at Eve out of the corners of their eyes and exchanging meaning glances. It was forbidden to talk during meals. I didn't cry; the shock was too great.

Then the school routine absorbed us, teachers were kind, we made friends and settled down reasonably well. I was neither unhappy nor happy, living in an emotional limbo from which I sometimes think I have never completely emerged. The school, Girls' High School, was situated in Claremont, Western Australia, on a cliff overlooking the estuary of the Swan River. On one side of us was the boys' school, Christchurch Grammar, on the other was Judge Robert Burnside's house, Craig Muir, and his fruit trees, which occasionally a girl raided, a capital offence. Beyond that was the Methodist Ladies' College. The site was ideal, within reach of the city of Perth, set in green lawns with a breathtaking view of the river. On weekdays the lawns, flowers and trees overlooking the river were out of bounds, but I managed to creep round there every day for a private tryst with the water. It was never two days the same. Both Eve and I retained this special love for a river landscape; she now lives in a similar environment, and my family has a private retreat with the same kind of outlook.

During the weekends we were allowed to spread rugs on the grass and camp there with our books and friends. The Swan River was the scene of many exciting yacht races which we never tired of watching. Sometimes on a Sunday our parents came to take us out. Their visits were irregular and we never knew when to expect them. Hours dragged by while we waited impatiently at the top of the long drive until we were rewarded by the Maxwell chugging into sight, my mother's bright face and glorious smell as she put her arms around us, and the homemade goodies she brought.

On weekdays there was a blank period between school and the evening meal when a terrible loneliness possessed one's very soul. Daygirls were hugging their parents, foraging for things to eat, arguing with brothers and sisters, running to a friend's house to play, going to the shops for messages. After school, we ate a piece of bread and jam grudgingly issued by matron, and then, except for a brief music practice, wandered about like lost dogs. Nowhere to go, nothing to do [...]

The dormitory for the smallest boarders, where we were first housed, was ruled over by a white dragon. 'She was a wonderful asset to the school,' an ex-staff-member told me in after years. 'We always knew that no matter what happened in the rest of the school, Nursie's little ones would be well looked after. She was superb.' But she was the antithesis of my laughing, happy-go-lucky mother, and I was terrified of her. She stood immovably *in loco parentis*, the mother substitute in charge of our lives.

Nursie was the daughter of a famous English general. An ex-army nurse, she was a big woman, always dressed in creaking white uniform with a huge, rustling, spotless, stiff white headdress, too enormous to be designated a cap. Sometimes one sees such a headdress on stage in some flamboyant opera. Or in the streets of Paris, worn by religious sisters, but theirs have a softer aura. If Nursie slept and bathed like other people we could not imagine it. We knew that on her days off she went by bus to visit her son; she must have been the stranger we used to see in a toque and brown felt coat with a fur collar, over a maroon crepe dress with pin-tucked bodice.

As well as being responsible for the small children, Nursie looked after the health of all the boarders. The school also had a matron of whom we were slightly in awe, but she was quiet and harmless, and in the occasional clash between her authority and that of Nursie she didn't stand a chance. Nursie with her loud English voice and big dark piercing eyes stood no nonsense from anyone. She had her favourites and her *bêtes noires*. As she blew hot and cold there was no way of knowing into which category one might be at any given moment, and those little ones who were afraid of her tended to fawn. She was a strict disciplinarian and a fanatic about cleanliness. When we three sisters offended in some minor toilet routine she called us 'dirty little

Jews', until the headmistress heard about it and bravely checked her. There were five Jewish girls in the school and nobody else made issue of it except for being interested in our Jewish traditions. I think Nursie's mild anti-semitism was unthinking habit rather than malice, for with equal vigour she intoned her favourite epithets, *'Uncouth, uncultivated, uneducated* little *Australians!'* whenever any child offended her, which happened on all possible and some impossible occasions, most often during meals. She treated us all as if we were soldiers in an army camp threatened with all kinds of diseases, and established her routines accordingly.

Some of Nursie's more stringent practices had probably saved lives in the rough and ready conditions of wartime field hospitals — few soldiers would have dared to die under her ministrations. Or perhaps they were the result of her experiences with the devastating flu epidemic which claimed so many lives following the First World War. But for us little girls they were something to be dreaded.

One routine was the Gargle Parade. Every morning before breakfast the entire school lined up in the downstairs cloakroom where Nursie stood with an enormous jug of Condy's crystals, dissolved in a little water. A monitor stood beside her marking the roll so there could be no escape. Each girl was issued with a white enamel mug containing a centimetre or so of the repulsive purple liquid; we had to dilute it with water and gargle every drop, so there was a choice between a little at loathsome strength or a lot of a weaker consistency. This procedure was repeated before the evening meal. The seniors protested that their pretty white teeth were being discoloured, but nobody took any notice.

Another routine was Painting the Throat. At the first sign of a cough or a cold all the boarders had to line up open-mouthed. With a long-handled soft brush dipped in some aromatic mixture Nursie almost poked their tonsils down their throats — or so it felt. I was always terrified of swallowing the brush and choking.

Her passion for prophylaxis was evident also in the tiny sick-room. Here she kept under the bed a china potty full of brown phenyl and water. Before treating no matter how minor a cut or splinter she rinsed her hands in the evil-looking liquid, and for years I believed the same article was used for more natural purposes. Her primitive methods were effective, for we never once had the epidemics common in other boarding schools.

Once a week she washed our hair with strong yellow laundry soap. I still recall the sensation of those energetic fingers digging into my scalp, leaving it sore for several hours. She rinsed by sloshing buckets of gaspingly cold water over our heads, and when our hair was dry it gleamed like silk.

Woman with Two Hats: An Autobiography (1988)

Floyd's flock

GEORGE TURNER (1916–), AUTHOR, WAS A CHORISTER IN THE CHOIR SCHOOL OF ST PAUL'S CATHEDRAL, MELBOURNE, WHOSE DIRECTOR WAS DR A. E. FLOYD.

Doctor Alfred Floyd, Organist and Choirmaster, an English musician of talent who had chosen to make his home in Australia, was an extraordinary personality, one of those 'unforgettable characters' of whom you later realize you have learned nothing deep or revealing. He was birdlike, short and spare, thrusting his head in a quest for worms of wisdom, leaning his body after with hands behind, so that in talking he pecked at words while cocking a bright, expectant eye.

He was temperamental, enraged by incompetence, often blindingly and sometimes brilliantly insulting, and most understanding of the young and lost. He refused to treat us new boys as learners fumbling a study of musical elements while around us younger but more experienced lads moved easily among the mysteries. When things became difficult he gave a brief lesson to the entire choir, never singling out our ignorance. He knew what many a teacher never learns, that a child will accept a dressing down with the proper display of submission (tears if required — there is always a modicum of role-playing) but will not soon forgive humiliation before others. The only recognition of our novice state was that we did not sing in a cathedral service until he was satisfied with our progress.

How he monitored progress puzzled me greatly; that he could detect the tone of each individual voice among two dozen was inconceivable. There had to be a knack to it. 'Knack' was a word in much use for explaining away the inexplicable abilities of others — such as a discriminating ear.

His system worked — for everybody but me. At the end of four years I had not mastered the groupings of accidentals called key signatures, and could read music about as well as demotic Greek. Thirty years later, in a chance meeting, I confessed to him that I had dissembled ignorance to the end, and to my acute discomfort he took excessive blame for it, as though some carelessness of his had doomed me to life in a condition of musical insensibility.

I loved the music — lots of Mozart, Handel, Bach, Brahms, Purcell, Mendelssohn — and was able to memorize anthems, psalms, magnificats and the rest in a single rehearsal, even to exactness of initial attack at the proper point in the introduction. That I got away with it is hard to credit, but so it happened. This opacity to musical elements has left my appreciation almost wholly sensual; intellectual and technical content I glimpse rather than grasp. So, after soaking in the music of the eighteenth and nineteenth centuries it took me many years to grope towards Ravel, Stravinsky, Janacek, Britten. Composers like Bartok and Ives remain purveyors of alien sound, but the huge repertoire accessible to me is more than I will assimilate in what's left of a lifetime.

My voice was no more than FAQ but I was filled with the joy of singing, however mediocre the noise. There was almost unendurable joy in the whispering mystery of 'God So Loved the World', the rocking near-waltz of 'For He Shall Feed His Flock', the exultant yell of Stainer's operettaish 'Fling Wide the Gates' or, during Nativity recitals, the down-dropping melody of a dozen boys representing angel voices high up in the lantern gallery. It was a joy that had nothing to do with religion and everything to do with psychological release. It was the same tension that strained and choked in peaks of enthralment in books or the spectacles of the screen — with this difference, that as singer I was *creating* the joy.

If I could recover anything at all of those years I might choose the return of that ability to respond totally in unspeakable rapture and wonderment. It recedes with time, thinned by repetition and familiarity, dulled by intellection, flattened by critical dissection.

Eight services a week brought me no closer to God. I doubt that I ever consciously listened to a sermon (*Magnet* and *Gem* were then the choirboy's undercover reading matter; what curiosa they hide under their cassocks today boggles the imagination). The other boys were similarly unengaged. Any amusement would do to pass the time of the service, from the spreading grin of the overweight tenor in the cantoris stalls at the Psalm verse 'All ye who are fat upon Earth have eaten and multiplied' to the occasion of young Heriot's breaking the rowdiest fart that ever racketed through that hall of echoes and reduced our two dozen charmless souls to aching, silent hysteria.

Charmless indeed. As a group we existed in a state of internecine feud, taking instant sides on any matter or, when open warfare applied, gathering in a righteous group about some unfortunate convicted of social error, to shred him with the cruelty of birds at a wounded fellow. Heaven help (but it never did) the victim betrayed by incautious word or deed! The only semblance of fair play rested in the certainty of each one sooner or later enduring his turn in the psychological stocks.

Over this loutishness lay the screen of our voices: if we learned little else, we learned to speak well. Doctor Floyd insisted on fine diction; we were given dramatic words to sing and the words should be heard. So when he corrected our pronunciation it was his Wykehamist accent that we absorbed, and very Wykehamist it was; it took me thirty years to lose the accent I learned from him.

In the Heart or in the Head: An Essay in Time Travel (1984)

Passionfruit and persimmons

JOAN AIREY WENT TO THE SALT CREEK STATE SCHOOL IN RURAL SOUTH AUSTRALIA IN THE 1930S AND SUNDAY SCHOOL IN THE SALT CREEK HALL, ON THE PORT AUGUSTA ROAD.

We were sixteen and a half miles from Cowell and one and a half miles from the Salt Creek Hall and Salt Creek School. They were situated one each side of the Port Augusta Road. The Hall was corrugated iron with a supper room attached, also iron tank and underground tank. We had church, Sunday school, dances, birthday parties, pre-election speeches, polling booths and concerts in the Hall. There was a piano and organ and stools lined up around the sides of it. It was unlined and unceiled until 1940, and photos of soldiers from the 1914–1918 war graced the walls. There was a cupboard with 'Wunderlich' doors on it to keep the hymn books, collection plates, etc. in. Mrs V. was usually pianist for the dances and sat on a 'bentwood' chair playing hour after hour such tunes as 'My Bonny lies over the Ocean', 'When it's Springtime in the Rockies' and 'Little Brown Jug'. She received no remuneration. She would be relieved at supper by Mr B., a quietly spoken bachelor who played his button accordeon for the dances. There were no heating facilities and a big stump fire always blazed about half a chain away. The men like Dad always yarned around the fire and watched the four-gallon buckets of water coming up to the boil to make the tea and coffee with. Mum helped the other ladies with the supper and washing up.

The Sunday school was run by Mr F. and was non-denominational. We had our anniversaries there with morning service, dinner, and afternoon service. It was here that I learnt about 'Doing things unto the Lord and not unto men'. Mrs F's eldest daughter was our organist. We were Church of England, and were in a minority, but for a time we had services conducted by the Bush Brotherhood (I think it was the Bush Brotherhood, but there is no one I can ask for sure). They were young single Englishmen. They had to be single, as they got so little money that they couldn't be otherwise. Eventually the Church of England ceased coming to our little Hall and we were supposed to go to Cowell, but of course could not afford to go. We then went to the Methodist services, but Mum always read the Collect, Epistle and Gospel from the book of Common Prayer on the appointed day. Dad was Church of England too, but played no part in it […]

The school, like the Hall, had gum trees planted around it. The original school was made of pug and pine, and up on the gable had the inscription scratched in the cement 'Established 1902'. (It may have been 1903.) In the mid 1930s a shelter shed was added, and in December 1938, Sir George Ritchie opened a new weather-board Government school in the same grounds. There were also pepper trees in the school ground, and we would have seats in them, also play houses. We played hide and seek and plum duff, and we had to make our own fun as there was no money for the sporting equipment such as is spent on school children today. We did not lack exercise, as we walked to school and home again, five days a week. We were cautioned against riding with strangers. The children that drove horses and jinkers to school got 'conveyance money' from the Education Department. School went in at 9.15 a.m. and finished at 3.40 p.m. The first quarter of an hour was spent on weather observation, drill, and 'showing hands'. Depending on what grade one was in, one filled in charts of the wind, the cloud, and whether it was a dull day or bright day. Once a week we 'did' the 'shadow pole'. Our lessons were spelling, composition, dictation, arithmetic, mental, geometry, mensuration, geography, history (English and Australian both), grammar (never English), reading, silent reading, poetry, singing (a big percentage, including me, were tone deaf) nature study, free-hand and pastel drawing, transcription and copy-book writing and manual. In our big cupboard, we had a library with some of the 'Wonder Books' and Mary Grant Bruce books and others. Also in the cupboard were our home-made sewing boxes. We did not have much instruction in sewing until 1939 when we got a sewing teacher, a local woman who came on her bike to teach us. As I was always fond of fancy work I just lazy-daisied and chain-stitched away to my heart's content.

We did all our writing in cursive, no printing at all. When I started school, 1931, there were about eight children and the number fluctuated at times and when I left in 1939 there were over twenty. We had a lady teacher when it was a 'small' school, and a man when it became larger. Our school had four windows and two doors and a huge fireplace. We had no axe so we would have big logs burning all day and would push them further in as they burnt out. We took our dinner to school in our 'dinner-time' and in summer we would have a very unappetising dinner, but that was the least of a country child's worries. In the school grounds stood our three-compartment lavatories (never toilet in those days). They were pit system like every other lavatory in the district, and, like the modern songster, we often had a 'red back on the toilet seat'. Ashes or soil would be 'put down' the toilets to keep our 'hygiene high' as the saying goes. We had a stern school inspector who came once or twice a year. His nice grey tourer with his water bag on the running board would pull up and we would be all petrified. In the late 1930s we were visited by a more jovial type of man, and I realised the 'Inspectors' were not the problem that I had always found them [...]

Our school drinking water would also be quite hot as that fierce sun shone down on the tank in those hot days when one's feet blistered no matter how good a condition one's boots were in. The water was often a bit straw coloured too, as the mallee trees dropped their dead leaves into the school's spouts. Our school, like most homes in the district, did not boast of a thermometer, but it used to get hot, and one would stick to one's desk. Our school, also like every home in the district, did boast of some home-made furniture made from petrol cases [...]

Until our teacher went to Adelaide for her holiday and brought back some passion fruit and persimmons, I had never even heard of such fruit. We had the passion fruit for nature study one day and sampled them, and the persimmons sat around for a week for study and tasting next week. Some children did not wear boots to school, and some got 'free books', and Mum dared us to ever comment (pass remarks Mum always said) on the situation.

'Rural Life Between the Wars' (1975)

Pains and penalties

Graham McInnes (1912–70) came to Australia with his novelist mother Angela Thirkell, his brother and stepfather in 1920. His first school in Australia was Hutchins School, Hobart.

Though I attended Hutchins School only for a single term, it is graven on my memory with all the force of 'the first school'. In England I had attended the co-educational and vaguely progressive Froebel Educational Institute in West Kensington where Roger de Coverley and eurythmics mingled with stiff instruction in Latin, Arithmetic, conversational French and the geomorphology of the Pennine Chain. But Hutchins was a *real* school. We stayed for lunch and the smell of Irish Stew still has the power, equalled only by that of Proust's *madeleine*, to induce almost total recall.

Hutchins was not only the oldest school in Tasmania but one of the oldest in Australia, having been founded in 1846 when Tasmania was still Van Diemen's Land. Dad and his elder brother Winston had attended it in the early 1900s. Its Horatian motto, *Vivit post funera virtus* (which I construed, owing to the separation of the words on the school cap badge, as 'He stays at his post by virtue of the funeral'), expressed to the full the zeal of the mid-nineteenth century middle class evangelical whereby one consecrated one's life to the purchase of a big tombstone to impress the neighbours. The motto was forcibly brought home within the first few days at Hutchins. As a new boy, and what's more a new boy with a 'Pommy' accent, I was put through the third degree about personality, tastes, antecedents and basic right to exist. At one point I was questioned on the voyage out from England. Where did I embark? 'Why, at Devonport.' There was a howl of derisive unbelief. He doesn't come from England at all! He's a fake! Grab his cap! A kind friend pointed out that there was a Devonport in Tasmania.

'My Devonport's older than yours.'

'It is not.'

'Yours was called after mine.'

'You're a liar.'

I swung at the tormentor with my left fist and followed it up with a smart right-cross with the school cap. The boy staggered backward and blood began to trickle down his cheek. In my fury I had forgotten the heavy enamel school badge held to the front of my cap with two safety pins. A low menacing growl came from the boys as they closed in. 'Coward! Hit a fellow with his cap badge.' 'Why don't you pick someone your own size, Pommy?' Hands grabbed at my grey sweater, someone kicked me in the shins and I was clearly headed for a good beating up when a master strode into the midst of the churning group.

'Now boys, what's all this? All right now, one at a time.'

When the case had been put to him by both protagonists he said to the other boy. 'Bramwell you're a fool. Go and spend ten minutes with the atlas,' and to me, 'Don't be so free with your fists or you'll end up in the detention room. Now both of you apologize and don't let's hear any more about it.' The apologies were subsequently cemented by a truce offering at the tuck shop, but neither Bramwell nor I ever really grew to like each other. *Vivit post funera virtus.*

The foundation was generally C. of E. and the Headmaster, the Rev. C.C. Thorold, was a sharp-nosed cleric with a blue chin and a dog collar. Form IIb was presided over by Mr Muscamp, a jolly young man in his early twenties whom the class held in admiration because he could twiddle his ears. He used to say, with bland sincerity, that this was the way to keep warm. As it was the June term when the mercury in Hobart dropped to the twenties and we cracked the ice on the enamel pitcher in our little cubicle at 405 Elizabeth Street, this was obviously an accomplishment to be acquired without delay. On frosty mornings when we assembled in the bicycle shed before going to prayers, many was the sweater-clad boy, his hand pocketed against the numbing cold, his breath coming in frosty puffs, but on his face a look of intense concentration as he tried hard to twiddle his ears. The grounding received at Froebel, together with, I must assume, some native talent, quickly procured me a promotion and after that Mr Muscamp became only a dim figure flitting across the playground, or heard from the school lavatory during break playing Sidney Baynes' waltz *Destiny* on a faintly off-key piano.

Under the new form master, the going was tougher. Mr Tennent had a large tobacco-stained moustache and was a disciplinarian. He caned on the spot, and with extreme savagery any boy who light-heartedly presumed to test the severe bounds which he imposed upon us. A boy who put calcium carbide in an ink-well was given a foot rule over his knuckles in the presence of us all. I can still hear the dreadful crackling in my mind's ear. Boys who could not manage the fourth declension were given a hundred lines, to be done after school, and woe indeed to the boy who endeavoured to shorten the task by the skilful wielding of three pens in one hand. He was held up to Mr Tennent's ridicule, more fierce and rancorous even than his sumptuary punishments. 'Now here's a boy that's taken a short cut. You know what happens when you take a short cut? And you miss your way? Because you've been too clever by half? You get behind, boys. You come out from your short cut with brambles and burrs sticking to your backside. And where are your companions that took the long way round? They're up ahead. And you're not.' Then turning with a fierce swish of his gown, 'And you're not either Davis.' Pause. 'Five hundred lines! You can stay after school two nights to do them.' Readers who crave an extension of similar memories are referred to the stories of Talbot Baines Reed which adorned the pages of the *Boys Own Paper* in the earlier years of this century. The pains and penalties meted out in *The Fifth Form at St Dominic's* and *My Friend Smith* had crossed the seas with inexorable finality, and faithfully reproduced themselves 'down under'.

The Road to Gundagai (1985; FIRST PUBLISHED 1965)

The sin of lunchlessness

THIS EXTRACT FROM 'THE OLD SCHOOL', A SHORT STORY BY CHRISTINA STEAD (1902–83), IS SET IN A SYDNEY PRIMARY SCHOOL.

[Maidie] was sitting there one morning hunched more than usual because of her dress. Someone was reading the lesson, 'A man in a land where lions are found was once out late in the day far from home' (a phrase I have never forgotten), but the little girls' interest was glued to a topic right at home and they interrupted the fascinating lion story (I remember that the man hid in a hole under the cliff and the lion leaped right over him into the gulf), to remark to the teacher that Maidie was wearing a new dress made out of a sheet. 'No, it's a flour bag, her mother hasn't got any sheets.' This was a serious argument without malice. 'Mrs Taylor, she shouldn't come to school in a dress made out of a sheet' — craning, inspecting, deciding. They had been simmering with this news, waiting for the moment to let it out. Before school, she had pulled away from their inquisitive puzzled fingers and eyes, little sparrows pecking at the odd-feathered one, her large opaque black eyes on them and then away — with what feeling? Even in the lines that morning, they, the good, had been disorderly, fluttering. And now, when the bright haired woman settled them all, they told her she had been obeyed. Maidie had only stayed away the last time because she had no dress to wear. Now she had a dress, 'It's made out of a sheet.' 'Flour bags?' 'No, it's a sheet.' The teacher, curious, went right up to Maidie's desk and studied the dress.

It was soft old thick cotton, made in fashion, with a deep yoke, long sleeves into wristbands, several inch wide pleats into a waistband, tucks and a wide hem to let down. It was white and remained white, though certain marks (which had made them say flour bags) had faded with washing.

Maidie never had any lunch. During the lunch recess she sat by herself at the far end of the wooden seats which ran round under the high brick walls. The rest of the girls in groups in the noonday shade of the buildings occasionally glanced her way, during a lull in their busy colloquies, condemning her for her misery, some, perhaps, curious about her life. If a newcomer, a wandering casual, not yet incorporated socially or perhaps even kind-hearted, approached her, the playground leaders at once dispatched a messenger, 'You musn't talk to her: she hasn't any lunch,' and some other parts of the indictment might be added, if the wanderer hesitated.

Some hungry children ate their lunches in snatches under the desks during school hours and had none left when noonday came. Some of these grasshoppers cast eyes on their friends' lunches and even begged; but they got little if anything. They too had the sin of lunchlessness, though it was understood they were more weak than sinning. Was it one of those who in the morning poached another's lunch? In the middle of the morning Dorothy (a sweet little girl who was not an informant) found her lunch gone. 'The thief — the thief' a word they liked to shrill and who could it be? Yes, Maidie it might be — but for some reason the informants had grown a little careful […]

She listened at her desk, motionless: she sat in the shed or playground. At last, the lunchless one, Maidie wept, but no one pitied her. They sang the midday song, 'Home to dinner, home to dinner, hear the bell, hear the bell, bacon and potatoes …' etc. Dorothy lived too far away to go home and the teacher gave her money for the IXL shop.

It is a hard cruel knot that has gathered in the shade at the top of the yard, looking over their shoulders fiercely at the girl in the white dress, a bundle of submission in the sun sometimes shaking her black basin-crop which she scratches ('she has nits') and glancing mildly round her: perhaps she is shortsighted. 'Thieves oughtn't to be allowed in school,' and they bring into their talk the reformatory, these pink and blue girls, whispering secrets, boasting and harsh; and yet all are afraid. The reformatory for Maidie, there with coarse dishes, coarse clothes, sleeping on sacking or planks, there children are flogged, though it serves them right, there is the cat o'nine tails, there they are put into cells alone, there are iron bars on the windows and if they escape the police catch them. The little girls in pink and blue know the names of the jails — Long Bay, Parramatta, Bathurst. Where do the charming little balls of fluff, their mothers' happiness, gather this awful lore? Mrs Taylor, the teacher, comes round the corner of the infants' building where Maidie sits in the midday sun, close to the side gate leading into the headmaster's dark snug cottage. Mrs Taylor speaks,

'Are you hungry, Maidie?'

'Yes.'

'Have you any lunch?'

'No.'

'Don't you ever bring any lunch?'

'No.'

'Come and have lunch with me.'

She takes her by the hand. They go round the corner towards the infants' building where the teacher has her packet lunch, done up in a white damask serviette, on her desk.

The teacher does not acquire merit by this action. How set back the informants are now! 'She oughtn't to do it!' Yes, morality has got a black eye. The teacher has fallen from grace. 'She shouldn't give her lunch when she never brings any.' What Mrs Taylor does will henceforth be debated with less than latitude: she has sided with the luckless, rebuffed the righteous. I was there. I was never able to make up my mind about things; and so it is still there, clear to me, the ever burning question of good and bad which (to be fair to the informants) so greatly occupied their minds. I always thought it strange that adults do not notice how profoundly little children are engrossed and stirred by moral debate. They are all the time sharpening their awareness of the lines and frontiers.

Ocean of Story (1985)

The inspector calls

BETTY WARE, NÉE GORMAN, GRAZIER (1924–), HAD HER EARLY
EDUCATION WITH HER FOUR BROTHERS IN A 'ONE FAMILY' STATE PRI-
MARY SCHOOL ON HER FATHER'S PROPERTY IN SOUTH-WESTERN NEW
SOUTH WALES.

I don't suppose we were unique in having our primary education at a school made up entirely of our own family members,
but it must have been unusual. In 1926 my father bought
'Meilman', a station property in south western New South
Wales, on the Murray River. A year later he moved his family
there: his wife and their five children — the eldest was nearly
seven and the youngest a six months' old baby. As well there
were his two younger brothers, then unmarried, and a young
English nanny called Sabina.

Conditions on this remote property left a lot to be desired,
especially from my mother's point of view. No hot water, no
refrigeration, no electricity. The household appliances were
primitive: a large copper for washing clothes, a mangle and a flat
iron. Lighting was achieved with candles, kerosene lamps, and a
rather fearsome petrol contrivance equipped with mantles and a
reputation for exploding unless approached with great trepida-
tion. There was plenty of wood for heating. There was a large
centre fire stove in the kitchen, and a wood-burning bath heater
was installed, also a coolgardie safe for cooling meat, milk, butter etc. In later years, a strange box-like thing appeared, under
which a flame lit by kerosene somehow contrived to cool the
box's contents. This was surprisingly effective, except that when
the weather reached heatwave conditions it 'defrosted', causing
sour milk, runny butter and great consternation.

However, the greatest drawback to existence on 'Meilman'
was undoubtedly the isolation. On the property of 42,000
acres, the homestead was ten miles from the main road between
Balranald and Euston. Mail was delivered once a week to our

gate, and the ten-mile drive to collect it was over a track which at best was full of potholes, and at worst could be impassable because of rain. The nearest town — a very small one — was Euston, some 24 miles away. It did have a primary school, but there was no question of our going there: even the one way journey, in our still handsome but ageing Austin tourer, would have taken half the school morning. In fact we would have needed a full-time driver to get us there and back. As for boarding school, we were too young and it would have cost more than we could afford.

Correspondence school from the NSW Education Department was one way out of the difficulty. This consisted of weekly exercises, which with the aid of a supervisor, mostly the mother, were filled in and sent away to be corrected and returned duly rewarded with elephant stamps and stars. We used this scheme for a few years but then the Depression intervened, with a major drought. Wool prices dropped disastrously and we could not afford household help — Sabina returned to England and was not replaced. This left my mother with all the cooking, washing and housework for a household of nine. She made bread, and did all the dairy work, after we children had milked the cows, and she managed to establish a garden, under great difficulties. She couldn't supervise our lessons as well. So, enter the Governess.

We had three governesses, first a Miss Douglas, then her sister. I think each of them lasted only a year. It must have been a strange isolated life for them. I remember encouraging the third governess, Miss Maloney, to get on a horse. She was probably terrified. Her exclamation of 'Jesus, Mary and Joseph!' shocked me, as I thought she was swearing, but it must have been a prayer for help.

Then came a new deal. Probably it was an inspiration of my father's. It was discovered that five children of school age were entitled to a school subsidy from the NSW Education Department. A new teacher, Miss Kelly, was engaged and part of our verandah-sleepout became an official classroom, with a big table, a blackboard and impressive quantities of Education Department chalk. At the beginning of the first year, 1932, my eldest brother Kevin would have been eleven and the youngest, Adrian was four and a half. Adrian mightn't have done much schoolwork but he made up the necessary quota. We went to school promptly at 9 a.m., having brought in the cows and done our milking duties; and we kept classroom hours fairly regularly. There were exceptions. We regarded it as our God-given right to leave our places at the table whenever a paddlesteamer came up the Murray, past the homestead. We would watch it solemnly, give it a ritual wave, and go back to our sums. I remember what rage and resentment I felt when for some misdemeanour — I forget what — we were forbidden to go out and watch the riverboat passing. It was a terrible injustice.

On the whole, Miss Kelly was quite indulgent and we liked her well enough, though of course we thought her bossy. She was out rabbiting one day with us when the Inspector called. What's more, she was dressed in rather terrible old trousers — this was long before women wore slacks. Our parents were away for some reason, and the Inspector made the obvious joke: 'When the cat's away, the mice will play'. Adrian refused to take the joke: 'We haven't got a cat', he said, deadpan. Miss Kelly must have been embarrassed when the Inspector wanted to check our progress in singing. Five musically challenged Gormans made an attempt at 'Cockles and Mussels' which would have pained the Inspector as well as the teacher.

We all learned to read early. The older ones were taught first by our grandmother and aunt who spent a winter with us one year. Then Granny used to send parcels of books — usually pretty solid reading. But we were so hungry for books that we made our way through things like *The Last of the Mohicans* and *The Cloister and the Hearth* very early — maybe at nine or ten. We were given Scott and Dickens and *Lamb's Tales from*

Shakespeare. No comics: we didn't know that comics existed, and we'd never heard of Buffalo Bill. When we were desperate for reading matter we would read the store catalogues: anything in print was prized. At night we played card games: anything from Slow Donkey and Old Maid to Euchre, in which Dad would join in.

We didn't come across other children. We went to Euston very rarely — once a month at most — and to Melbourne perhaps once a year. There was no point in going to Euston: we didn't shop in today's sense. Stores were bought twice a year: chests of tea, bags of flour, and for the children a five-pound tin of boiled lollies as a bonus. When the river was negotiable, they would be delivered by the paddlesteamer *Marion*; but when the water level dropped we would have to get the provisions by road from Euston, which was much less convenient. Newspapers came once a week to the mail-gate and were collected there.

It was understood that if times got better we would go to boarding school in Melbourne, where our grandmother lived, but we were in mortal terror of the alternative which was to go to Hay High School and be 'boarded out' in the town. From there we would have gone home for a weekend perhaps once a month.

When Miss Kelly's regime ended, about 1936, and the older boys went to board at Xavier in Melbourne, they were academically well prepared, but in some ways they felt as if they had come from Mars. They hadn't played football, or any team games, and 'school spirit' was an alien concept. They didn't know any swear words — my father being rather strict with any men on the place. Even the shearing shed wasn't as enlightening as might have been expected, so that the vocabulary of city boys was a revelation.

Our two young uncles were a strong influence in making sure we didn't show off. Any skiting would earn a comment like: 'Let me know when you're raffling yourself: I might buy a ticket'. We didn't have much idea of competing in lessons or games, though once we sent a map of Africa to the Balranald Agricultural Show and won a certificate of some kind for that. There was an exam at the end of Sixth Grade called Primary Final which we had to sit in Euston. There's a family belief that we all did extraordinarily well. At any rate we all passed without any trouble. Having negotiated that hurdle, we could have left school. But somehow or other, boarding school fees were managed, and we ended the Robinsoe Crusoe existence of 'Meilman' with its one-family primary school.

Unpublished memoir (1996)

Cold comfort

Dick Roughsey (Goobalathaldin) (1924–85), artist and writer, describes his schooling at a Presbyterian mission school in North Queensland.

All the big trouble after the killing of Reverend Hall had frightened our people. They now knew that the white man was too strong and they would have to follow his ways. Another missionary, Reverend Wilson, and his wife came to replace the Halls. They built a school and dormitory and persuaded the people to bring their children in to live in the dormitories and go to school.

I can still remember the day my parents took me in to the mission. I must have been seven or eight then and although I didn't really understand, I sensed that some great change was to take place in my life, and I was afraid. I remember sitting on my father's shoulders and crying as we set out on the long day's walk into the mission.

I was terrified by the large buildings of the mission, but even more so by all the people in strange clothes, both black and white, who seemed to be too interested in me. My parents stayed a few days, probably to let me get used to the place. Then one morning I stood wailing under the dormitory, held back only by the enclosing wire netting, while my parents, also crying, vanished into the bush on the way back home.

I soon settled down there however, and we lived a happy life in the dormitory and school. I had been given the name of Dick. I had three mates, Percy, Dan and Douglas. They were about my own age and we formed a little gang for defence against the other boys, grownups and missionaries.

Reverend Wilson believed in discipline. We learned the Bible scriptures off by heart, and we could recite many hymns. If a boy was caught stealing another's clothes, or fruit and vegetables from the garden, he got a good hiding. The boy to be punished was laid face-down on a table and held by four men while he was belted on the bare bottom about fifteen times with a piece of rubber from an old car inner tube. I can still remember the blisters on my bottom.

It was a hard life. We were turned out of bed, a blanket on the floor, at about 6 o'clock every morning. A bucket of cold water served as an alarm clock. We then had to carry more water and wash out the dormitory. This was necessary as small bush boys are used to just chucking out their water as they sleep. We then hung our blankets out to dry in the sun and lined up to be given our breakfast jobs. Before each meal we had to do some work to earn it. This usually involved carrying firewood, gardening and other jobs about the mission.

After breakfast we joined the girls and the mission staff in a short church service before beginning school for the day. Our main teacher was Mrs Wilson, and she kept us hard at work on our slates all day, writing, doing sums and learning to read. She was a very good teacher and kind. I never forgot her and many years later when I went to Brisbane for my first big art show, I went to where she is now living to see her. She knew me at once and even my tribal name, Goobalathaldin.

We probably looked forward to school holidays even more than white children. In those days most of our parents still lived out in the bush on their own countries; only a few stayed about the mission. When holiday time approached the bush people came in to get the children, to stay a few days around the mission to meet relatives and friends, and then take us for a holiday in the bush. How good it was to throw away clothes and run about playing and helping our old folks to gather food. Then we'd sit round the fires at night, listening to the old stories, and we'd wake later to hear the rhythm of the clap-sticks and the men chanting corroboree songs.

Moon and Rainbow (1995; FIRST PUBLISHED 1971)

Empire in the sun

DONALD HORNE (1921–), WRITER, ACADEMIC, AND SOCIAL HISTORI-
AN, WENT TO THE STATE PRIMARY SCHOOL IN MUSWELLBROOK, NEW
SOUTH WALES.

As well as being Australians we were also British, first-class citizens of the Empire, and at school this was what we were most taught to admire. One of the themes of the history curriculum was 'The growth of an empire based on liberty'. In this growth the campaigns of Clive and Wolfe, the Indian Mutiny and the Boer War led up to the climax of the Great War, in which the imperial dominions joined the mother country in fighting for freedom. A large part of the geography curriculum was given over to the theme of 'Australia and the Empire'. Jute in India, huskies in Canada, geysers in New Zealand, springboks in South Africa, rickshaws in Singapore. We learned the names of the British naval stations, the principal sea routes that linked them, the names of the great imperial cities, and we learned nothing about the rest of the world. That came later — in the newspapers, when, nation by nation, year by year, the rest of the world demanded that we pay attention to it.

On Empire Day we would assemble in the school playground, clattering the tin mugs we were taking to the picnic. Arranged in classes, we would stand easy while some of the children gave Empire Day speeches. We stood to attention while Dad conducted us in singing patriotic airs, and then we would march to the Strand picture show, where we were joined by the boys and girls of the convent. Here we would sing 'Land of Hope and Glory', 'Rule Britannia', 'Three Cheers for the Red, White and Blue' and 'Advance Australia Fair', a song between each speech. When the three Protestant clergymen and the headmaster spoke to us they would suggest that the empire held together only because of some particular moral virtue. To the Presbyterian minister it was truthfulness; to the Methodist minister, the belief that if a thing was worth doing it was worth doing well; to the headmaster, love and good feeling; to the rector, unswerving loyalty and devotion in our sacred duties to King, God and Country. The rector would also tell us the story of the Indian prince who poured his tea into a saucer and blew on it when he visited Queen Victoria at Windsor and how, to put him at his ease, the Queen then poured *her* tea into a saucer and blew on it too, thus showing that the empire was a commonwealth of peoples. We sang 'God Save the King', then the convent children marched off to their picnic and we marched off to ours — sandwiches, jellies and lemonade provided by the Parents' and Citizens' Association.

The Education of Young Donald (1967)

A foreign country

GEOFFREY DUTTON (1922–), WRITER, WAS SENT FROM HIS SOUTH AUSTRALIAN COUNTRY HOME TO SCHOOL AT GEELONG GRAMMAR SCHOOL AT CORIO, VICTORIA.

Everything around Geelong was totally foreign to me. I had spent my country life on red soil, among hills and thousands of old gum trees. Here the soil was a dirty grey, there were windbreaks of cypresses, not the slender green flames around the front lawn, but flattened, stunted trees with their boughs growing into each other, in themselves a promise of bitter winds. There were hardly any gum trees, and they stuck up straight like posts. The landscape was flat without any sheltering hills, and the houses were built of wood and the churches of a black, prison-like stone mysteriously called bluestone. Being the time of the Depression, most of the wooden houses had not been painted for years, and this made them look even more dismal.

The school itself was built of a glaring brick; I had never seen large brick buildings before, except for the Hamilton Church. They stood in a semi-circle overlooking football and cricket ovals, more cypresses, and the lagoon, a dreary inlet in the smelly bay, where there was a rickety wooden construction, the school baths, fifty yards square. The wooden piles were encrusted with big mussels; if you were pushed off the walkways, a favourite sport, you were liable to receive deep gashes down your legs or backside from the razor edges of the mussels. No bathers were worn in the baths, so you were particularly vulnerable.

Beyond the powdery dust of the cypress windbreaks, and the paddocks of grey grass and boxthorn with its bitter smell, were the industrial areas of Geelong, an oil refinery, a whisky distillery, the Ford works.

It was a prison, without locks or bars, but from which there was no escape. Every now and then a boy would run away, but he would always be brought back, looking sheepish, to be caned before being cast back into the mob.

The Headmaster of the Junior School, Mr Jennings, inspired instant distrust in me. Although almost totally ignorant of strangers in authority, I sensed immediately from his slippery smile and the few grey hairs separately greased down over the dome of his head, that he was not to be trusted. I was to learn that he was very popular with parents, and hated by the boys.

When we were at our first assembly, he gave us some invaluable advice about our lives at Geelong Grammar Junior School. On Sundays we wore Eton collars, huge stiffly starched affairs that sat down to our shoulders; they were, mysteriously, called 'bomb-proofs'. Inside the collar, and down our chests, was a light-blue tie — 'Light blue for purity, boys'. We were told that we would be good sailors as long as Captain Will Power was on the bridge. We were told never to do anything that we would not do in front of our sisters; I thought this would give me plenty of latitude, not knowing, of course, what he really meant.

At tea in the dining hall I was appalled to find that a boy was rostered to stand behind Jennings' chair and scratch his head with a quill. Fortunately I was never one of the favoured boys elected for this disgusting duty.

We had been shown our beds in the dormitory, and the rug each boy had brought as part of his equipment was folded on the blanket, giving the bed a vestige of individuality. Lights were put out early in our dormitory. On the first night my resolve that all these mysterious happenings must be borne without complaint was shattered as I began to be aware that strangled sobs were emerging from most of the beds. In no time I was sobbing too, at the same time as thinking it was ridiculous and not at all what my mother would expect of a lucky boy sent to this lovely school.

We were put down for a rest after lunch in the dorm, and some ingenious boy demonstrated that by tying the tassels of our rugs to the curved metal ends of the beds a private tent could be made. This was most consoling. A chance to be alone was one thing never available at boarding school.

This pleasure did not last long. One day we heard someone burst in the door and then Jennings' voice shouting 'You horrible little boys, you beastly boys', as he rushed along tearing down our rug tents. I had no idea what we were supposed to be doing that was beastly or why he was so worked up, but there were no more rug tents in the dorm [...]

One day at general assembly Jenno gives us a lecture about buying and selling, about things he calls commerce and industry. 'Your fathers,' he says, 'are graziers and lawyers, surgeons and captains of industry.' I haven't got a father, but I put down 'Grazier' all the same; definitely not 'Farmer'. 'Now all these things are bound together by commerce and industry, by selling what you have to sell, whether it's wool or skills, and other people paying for it. Profit is what makes the world go round. It's called capitalism. Don't be taken in by evil people like communists who don't like capitalism. Capitalism is the best system because it is based on the profit motive.'

My friend Bob shoots up his hand. Bob is skinny, with a face like a frog and big round glasses, and his own way of looking at things, though he can hardly see the school tower without his glasses. He is also a very good long-distance runner, but I don't hold this against him. I like Bob. 'Sir,' says Bob, 'what about the Depression?' 'A very good point, boy,' says Jenno. 'But it would take far too long to explain just now.' Bob grins at me.

Jenno goes on to explain that he is launching something called The Industrial Scheme. Instead of going to the tuckshop to buy whatever you want you'll buy it off another person. You have to have a licence to sell whatever you want to, and if you do anything wrong you are imprisoned for half an hour in the telephone box. You can also perform services for other people, such as cleaning their bikes or polishing their shoes, and charge a fee for it, like a surgeon or a lawyer.

But the aim of the whole show is to teach us about commerce and industry, not to make a profit. Bob gives me a nudge in the ribs.

Bob suggests we go into the shoe-polishing business. We don't have to buy brushes or polish because we already have them, and if we look like running out of polish Bob'll get his parents to send over some more. We'll charge a penny a pair of shoes, and it'll be all profit.

So we make a big sign, 'Shoes polished. One penny a pair', and sit in the back corridor where all the kids run out to their bikes, but no one wants to pay a penny to have their shoes polished, when all you need do is give them a rub with your hanky before Inspection. (In Inspection we all line up, the housemaster goes along the row saying to each boy 'Hands. Thumbs. Palms'. If they're dirty you get detention. He also looks at your shoes.)

We give the shoe-cleaning business away and set up in the Marmite and Cheese business. We make a new sign: 'Purveyors of Marmite and Cheese to the Gentry. Under Vice-Regal Patronage'. Jenno is not sure about this sign. We get all the marmite and cheese free from home in food parcels, so we make lots of profit, fifty-five bob in the winter term, but we don't tell Jenno how much we've made.

Out in the Open: An Autobiography (1994)

Station kids

EVELYN CRAWFORD (1928–) HAD HER SCHOOLING IN THE TOWNSHIP OF YANTABULLA, QUEENSLAND, IN THE 1930S. WITH OTHER ABORIGINAL CHILDREN, SHE SHARED LESSONS WITH WHITE CHILDREN FROM THE TOWN AND NEARBY STATIONS.

None of the children in that tiny township of Yantabulla had ever been to school. The children of the station owners had governesses, and when we were near the homestead we would sit at the edge of the verandah and listen. No one hunted us away, but we didn't share the lessons. So the dads in the place must have decided to ask the government to send a teacher and they all got together and built a bush school, and a bush school it sure was! It was just a big shed, with beefwood uprights at the corners, and long beefwood beams to support the roof. The walls were filled in with wired bundles of canegrass, solid up to about six feet, then there was a gap about three feet high all round to let in the light, and then the roof — more bundles of canegrass. We couldn't see out unless we got up on the desks, or put our toes in the wire and climbed up the side like spiders. The floor was just red sand. Later on they built a proper schoolroom with a wooden floor and a tin roof, but we still used the canegrass shed when it was really hot.

The long desks — long enough for five or six kids — were split beefwood logs with split pine planks for seats. You know how splintery pine is, so you could say there was one schoolful of kids who didn't wriggle in their seats. We learnt the hard way — a splinter in your *thithee* (bum) hurts more coming out than going in! The teacher's desk and even her chair was split timber, but I don't know if it was as splintery as our seats. Anyway, she had long petticoats and skirts, and she didn't wriggle.

The men cut the tops out of square five-gallon petrol tins, painted them inside and out, and the teacher had them piled two, four high, on their sides with the mouths open. That was her 'filing cabinet' where she had all her stuff.

The blackboard was on a three-legged easel made from bush timber, with holes bored through to take the pegs the board rested on. There was another homemade table where she kept things like book pencils, slate pencils, rubbers and chalk, and where we stacked our slates. We used slates and squeaky slate pencils most of the time, and cleaned our slates with tiny pieces of rag tied on bits of string nailed to the desk all along, swingin' there all the time.

We had one special book with our name on it and we used to do sums in that book, or a bit of dictation, or our best writing. It was a very special day when we worked in our book. We used little bits of pencil stuck in a tin holder. The teacher cut pencils in four to make them go round. They were red pencils, but they wrote black. She sharpened them with a pocket knife Granny Mallyer cadged from Grandfather. He used to keep it sharp for her.

There were forty-two kids in that little school, but I don't ever remember seeing forty-two there all in one day. There'd always be ten or twelve missing. Aboriginal kids didn't have to attend school in those days. If they came along the teacher taught 'em, if they didn't, well, that was it. It must have been real hard on the teacher. If their mums and dads understood what school was they'd send the kids most days. My mother and father could read and write pretty good for blackfellers at that time so me and Gladys went to school most days. It wasn't only that kids stayed home to play. Whenever dads got work on stations any big distance away, they took their whole family with them. No one would ever say to a kid's Granny or Aunty, 'We'll leave so-and-so with you so he can go to school.' Being with your family was the most important thing.

In our little school there were Aboriginal kids and white kids from the town and the nearby stations. There wasn't any calling names like 'black kids' or 'white kids'. If you were born on a station or lived there you were 'station kids' and if you lived in town you were 'town kids', black and white alike. All of us had to call all grownups Mister, Missus, Uncle, Aunty, Granny, Grandfather, whatever was respectful, even if they weren't our real Uncle or Granny. We had real good times together and got into mischief together — just kids.

Over My Tracks (1993)

Australian gothic

Dorothy Hewett (1923–), poet and playwright, went to state primary and secondary schools in Perth before moving to an Anglican convent, Perth College.

Perth in 1936 is an innocent little city, not much bigger than a large country town, lost in time and distance, floating like a mirage on the banks of the Swan River. We live in a middle-class suburban street south of the river, lined with lopped-off plane trees, in a hideous, dark, liver brick bungalow I immediately christen 'The Castle of Despair'. I have never known such misery. School is a nightmare. I stand in the girls' playground, under the pines, watching the other kids play … French and English, fly, knucklebones, marbles, skipping games, passball … I don't know any of them and am too shy and awkward to join in. Many years later I will go back and see my eldest son, a wan, lost little figure, standing under those same pines in the boys' playground, hiding behind the trunks just as I did, suffering the identical horrors of the different child who doesn't fit in. I will long to be transformed by that little bottle labelled 'Drink me' into a twelve-year-old again, so that we can share our terror and our loneliness. But instead I turn and go home, knowing there is nothing I can do to help him. At least he never has to suffer the ignominy of being taken out of the 'scholarship class' and put in with the 'dummies', because he can't do arithmetic. He becomes a Doctor of Pure Mathematics. I get two out of twenty for mental arithmetic, even in the dummies' class.

Every morning my hair is pulled and twisted into two curls with tight rubber bands and I suck the ends obsessively. My mother tells a story of a girl who sucked her hair and had to be operated on and a huge hairball removed from her stomach, so I suck my handkerchiefs into holes instead.

I have to wear long, black, narrow college shoes that pinch

my feet unbearably. I have gone barefoot all my life, but the feet that were horny and tough, that could walk over rocks and stubble and hot sand, are now as soft as any 'townie's'. My legs ache with what the grown-ups call 'growing pains' and when I stick my burning college shoes out into the school aisle, the teacher trips over them and I get into trouble. There is a girl who pinches and sticks pen nibs into me, and another who has 'things' in her hair that crawl out and across her forehead before my fascinated stare. When it's composition or spelling or dictation, I move up to the top of the class; when it's anything to do with the hated sums, I plummet to the bottom, which means I always end up somewhere in the middle, just over the border from the real dumdums or those who refuse, out of some wild principle of revolt and despair, to learn anything at all. But Mr Lewis, the miniature teacher with the bright red face and sandy hair, likes me, so I am nicknamed 'teacher's pet'.

There is a vicious fight in the school playground between two girls. One of them is the bad girl of the class, with narrow eyes and twisted mouth. I'm horrified and without thinking I run between them, my face white and my eyes blazing. They are rolling over and over on the gravel, biting, kicking, screaming, pulling out each other's hair. I wrench them apart.

'Stop it, stop it. You should be ashamed,' and, miraculously, they stop. The bad girl is amazed. She grins crookedly. 'What's up with you?' she says, and after that, if there is ever any trouble, she always defends me.

Malcolm McAuley, tall and handsome, with a larrikin's lopsided grin, smiles at me. When I come to school one morning there are signs written in chalk all over the girls' shed ... MM LOVES DH. I try to rub the chalk off the weatherboard walls and pretend to despise him, but I watch him with a secret glow and suffer when he gets the cane [...]

At High School I'm not much happier. I can't do French or Algebra or Geometry. I have to sit in the classroom for a whole week with a sign round my neck because I can't remember the French verbs.

Miss Bonus — blonde bun, horn-rimmed glasses, pale, hand-knitted suits — says: 'Stand up, Dorothy Hewett. Are you a moron when it comes to Maths?' I bite my lips, struggling against tears, but they drip down my face and she looks ashamed.

I love the English lessons. When we do *The Merchant of Venice* I play Shylock, creeping crookbacked between the desks, hissing: 'Signor Antonio, many a time and oft/On the Rialto you have rated me …'

I borrow Miss Bonus's bathers to play the Amazonian female lead in the school play. The other teachers seem astounded at the transformation. I hear them discussing me as I dress for the opening night: 'What a lovely little figure she's got, and so mature for a thirteen-year-old.' I am filling out. I have breasts, a small neat waist and swelling hips. I take off all my clothes and stare at myself in the cheval mirror. There is a soft fuzz growing between my legs and I don't like the look of it. My grandmother, dressmaking, with her mouth full of pins, says: 'She's got a sway back. She needs a little pad in her lower spine.'

I've learnt to play French and English, and fly and knuckle-bones, but at lunch time I often sneak away to the old graveyard behind the school and sit amongst the gravestones writing poetry in my English exercise book. At school assembly we sing 'God of our fathers, known of old/Lord of our far-flung battle line/Beneath whose awful hand we hold/Dominion over palm and pine', or 'Bring me my bow of burning gold'. I look up at the names of famous women engraved in gold letters around the Assembly Hall … Boadicea, Florence Nightingale, Madame Curie, Queen Elizabeth, Elizabeth Barrett Browning … and my voice soars out under the stained-glass windows. Some day, I think, with absolute certainty, my name will be up there [...]

My parents visit the school, worried about my tears in bed at night. 'She's not suited to a state school,' says Miss Bonus, a snob at heart. 'Send her to college, where she'll fit in. She's so sensitive.' So I am enrolled in the Business Course at Perth College in a white middy blouse, a gored navy-blue skirt, a panama hat and the black stockings of my dreams, to learn typing, shorthand and book-keeping.

Wild Card: An Autobiography 1923–1958 (1990)

The cave of empire

CHRISTOPHER KOCH (1932–), NOVELIST, WAS BORN IN HOBART, TASMANIA, AND HAD HIS EARLY SCHOOLING AT CLEMES COLLEGE, WHICH MERGED WITH THE FRIENDS' SCHOOL IN 1945.

Like many another child of the Empire in the thirties, I had been named after Christopher Robin; *When We Were Very Young* had been read to me when I was three. My brother and I had Dickens read to us when we were seven and nine years old, and Oliver Twist and Pip and Little Nell and Mr Bumble were famous figures we might some day meet: our parents and relatives spoke of them as though they were real, and I can still see my mother pursing her lips over Uriah Heep. 'Give us a child until the age of seven.' It wasn't the Jesuits who had us until that age, it was Christopher Robin, Buckingham Palace, Little Pig Robinson, Mr Toad, Sherlock Holmes, and a school called Clemes College. Our teachers made us keep scrapbooks on the doings of 'the little princesses', Elizabeth and Margaret Rose. What chance did we have?

Clemes College was a decaying private school where our father and his brother had gone, housed in a musing nineteenth-century building with french windows leading from the kindergarten room onto an antique sandstone terrace, surrounded by English gardens in which stone urns gathered English moss. It was run by old, vague, white-moustached Mr Clemes, who was English, and by a staff of English maiden ladies who smiled a lot but who displayed sadistic tendencies, setting about us with rulers, and watching with gleaming eyes as big boys tortured smaller ones in the playground. These ladies read us *Alice in Wonderland* and *The Jungle Book*, and pointing to a globe of the world in the corner of the classroom, showed us how red was the dominant colour on the map, a pattern ending at the bottom with the little red shield of Tasmania. We were left in no doubt of what we were and where we were; being Australians was secondary, and at the top of the map, in the south of that dragon-shaped island we had never seen, the great web of London waited for us to come to it [...]

Our seasons were the seasons of my English story books. Snow fell in our midwinters, which were the winters of *Boy's Own Paper* and *The House at Pooh Corner*. I walked to school through London fogs. On the day that World War II broke out, the old English ladies who taught us at Clemes College were in tears. They explained to Grade Two the danger England was in, and my father's godmother thundered out 'There'll Always be an England' on the piano. We played German bombers in the playground, until we were made to play English bombers. Only Nobby Clark (now the Director of the National Institute of Dramatic Art) showed the misguided force of character to remain a German bomber, until he was shot down in flames. I had joined the English bombers with cowardly haste, desperately hoping to cover up my German name. I would fail.

The society that had produced us, so far away from what it saw as the centre of civilisation, made us rather like the prisoners in Plato's cave.

Crossing the Gap (1987)

Kindergarten Bus

RHYLL MCMASTER (1947–) WAS BORN IN BRISBANE. MANY OF HER
POEMS RECALL SCENES AND EVENTS OF CHILDHOOD AND SCHOOL LIFE.

I am four years old and still trustful,
but dragging slightly
on my mother's tight, impatient hand.
At the deep stone cutting I see
the bus that rides to away.
The driver is dark blue, gleeful and shiny.
He laughs at my whines.
My mother condones
his terrible eccentricity,
his tic-toc glance, his wooden neck.
Her head glides past the window sections,
gaily waving/blank/turned abrupt.
My screams are not enough
to stop this little murder.

Have I heard her right?
She's not coming with me.
The ladies in their corset dresses frown and fiddle;
they are in fine shopping fettle.
They sit solidly like Mrs Noddies;
they could be dead, they are staring
so straight ahead.

The bus drives out the back of all protection
to a dropping-off place
where there will be a glaring bin with a bent lid
in the middle of a white space.

Flying the Coop: New & Selected Poems 1972–1994 (1994)

School rulers

BRUCE STEELE (1931–), ACADEMIC AND MUSICIAN, WRITES OF HIS
EXPERIENCE AT A SMALL PRIVATE SCHOOL IN SUBURBAN MELBOURNE
(1938–42).

Aged six I went from kindergarten to Hyrncastre Preparatory
School for Boys run by the spinster ladies the Misses Hotchin —
Miss Elsie and Miss Ethel. They were strict Methodists, dressed
almost always in black. The elder, Miss Elsie (always Miss
Hotchin to us) was tall and thin and pale, and subject to fits of
lassitude and occasional deep shock at the misdemeanours of her
charges: 'Erraahhhh!' she used to gasp. The younger, Miss Ethel,
was shorter, plumper, red-faced, peppery and impatient. She wore
glinting glasses on her hooked nose. A practised wielder of the
school ruler, she could inflict stinging vocal as well as physical
rebukes upon the ignorant and the backslider. One always sensed
her distasteful enjoyment in the application of ruler to hands or
legs — never posteriors, interestingly enough. That was reserved
for the men at my next school — also interestingly enough.

The curriculum was standard and thorough — reading, writing, spelling, arithmetic, tables, elementary French and, in my
last year, at age nine/ten, Latin. This was all in keeping with the
school motto: '*Labor vincit*' — 'work conquers' — as the Misses
H never tired of reminding us. The Weber and Rice Physical
Culture Institute sent a man in white once a week for a different kind of work-out. I have a medal from them celebrating my
one apparently successful lapse into sport. And of course religion. Every day began with a hymn, a reading from the Bible
and prayer. Hymns appropriate for tiny persons like 'Rock of
Ages ...', 'Will your anchor hold in the storms of life?', 'Hold
the Fort for I am coming, Jesus signals still! Wave the answer
back to Heaven, "By thy grace we will!"', 'Joyful, joyful will that
meeting be, When from sin our hearts are all set free ...' — the
reference was to heaven (and reunion with those who had gone

before), but as my father always seemed to be at meetings of a fairly dull kind, I had problems with that one. Miss Ethel belted them out on the old piano; we had to learn all the words by heart, and, in one of their own favourite expressions, 'Woe betide the boy ...' who did not remember them! There was always a lot of 'Woe betide ...' so that the avoidance of woe was a daily preoccupation for some.

Lessons proper began with the recitation of 'Ten Spelling' and 'Ten Mental'. Which means that ten words must be memorised from a little brown spelling book: I remember particularly the section on diseases like 'diarrhoea, croup, quinsy, etc.' and to this day know the meaning of only the first; mental was short for mental arithmetic: addition subtraction etc. to be done at speed in the head. If you were lit upon to answer and couldn't, there was again a return to 'Woe betide ...' Parsing of words and analysis of sentences came early, so that by age eight one knew a preposition or an interjection if one met one. Almost every lesson was punctuated with epigrams: 'A verse from the Bible fits in here boys. What is it?' 'As a man soweth that shall he also reap, Miss Hotchin?' 'Very good Billy!' Billy M. always got these things right and was in any case 'teacher's pet'. Get it wrong and you risked a woe-betide and a ruler.

Other bits of wisdom found their way into lessons too: 'Use or lose, boys! Always remember that.' This was usually taken to apply to our brains, but analogies with wasted muscles and other sad cases were always on hand to drive the lesson home. Smuttier-minded boys, however, found other applications for the adage. 'And, boys — remember the two saddest words in the English Language ... what are they?' '"Too late," Miss Hotchin.' 'Yes,' rolling her eyes to heaven, 'Too Late!!' That one was usually celebrated with a rendering of the hymn 'Jesus of Nazareth passeth by' — last verse sung solemnly '... has passed by!' Some poor devil missed out (on being cured of something?) because he didn't seize the moment for a miracle. But perhaps my favourite hymn was 'Yield not to temptation, For yielding is sin ... Fight manfully onward, Dark passions subdue ... ' The young mind was intrigued by 'dark passions'; they certainly sounded exciting. If school was a continuously exciting moral dilemma, the classroom was stimulating moral drama.

We were, however, copiously and generously read to: the Billabong books, 'Little Lord Fauntleroy,' 'What Katy Did' and 'What Katy Did at School' but NOT 'What Katy Did Next' because, it was explained, she got married, the silly girl, and that was not appropriate reading for boys. The British Empire could do no wrong and nothing Japanese was to be brought to school: 'It's all imitation and rubbish!' In fact, while you could request your pencil to be sharpened at any time, Japanese pencils (especially after 1941) were not only knocked back, but reviled at the same time. Once a boy added to his request, 'It's the Japanese one, Miss Ethel.' The reply was 'Then you know perfectly well that I will not sharpen it. Tell your mother to get you another!' Parents were honoured by appropriate memorised verses for their days: 'Always at your beck and call/Mother!', one began; 'Only a Dad with a tired face/Coming home from the Market Place. Little of worldly wealth he brings,/But as he comes, he always sings'. The long deceased Hotchin parents were frequently extolled as models: Father (in answer to a request for permission to do something — probably enjoyable): 'What did your Mother say?' 'She said "No."' 'Then that is my answer too!' What a weak-willed twit! We were never told what happened if he were asked first — perhaps a revealing insight into the Hotchin family.

Toilet-training was rigorous too. Only one boy at a time in the loo — an outer slate-slab-against-the-wall job for the obvious and beyond that, for more serious business, a sanctum known as the 'inner lavatory.' You were encouraged not to ask permission to perform either activity during class. Queues at playtime were therefore long; they were also carefully policed. If the call was urgent your request might be met but only after public cross-questioning. Once a boy had used excessive amounts of paper which blocked the system; now there was none on site. Consequently a request had to be made for permission to use 'the inner lavatory' at such times, whereupon one was handed but two sheets! It always reminded me of the High Priest entering the Holy of Holies only once a year. The result of your efforts was scrutinised before Miss H or Miss E herself pulled the chain. Other matters of hygiene were looked to. 'When you take a new handkerchief, always hold one corner and shake the folds out before putting it into your pocket. Then you will always CATCH your sneeze. And catching the sneeze is both polite and hygienic.' This instruction always came with a graphic demonstration of the right and wrong ways of dealing with a sneeze and the blowing of the nose — one nostril at a time or risk bursting your eardrums! If you felt a cold coming on, you must 'gargle' the throat and 'douche' the nose with salt water. Demonstrations of this ritual were offered also. We occasionally overheard the real thing as we walked up the drive to the school past the Hotchin bathroom. Grotesque sounds of gargling and douching were heard. Later at assembly we would be told: 'I had a cold this morning boys, but I fought it off!' The sounds of battle were truly epic.

There were lighter moments. During one Friday afternoon reading session, the great Miss Ethel was treating us to a rendition of 'Casabianca': 'The boy stood on the burning deck/Whence all but he had fled ...' — an affecting tale. It nevertheless produced sniggers in a certain quarter of the room. Miss E. laid down the book, gazed balefully at the offender and said (I think this is verbatim): 'Why are you sniggering? Do you know a wicked parody of this?' I was dimly aware of what a parody might mean in literary terms, but there was no mistaking the import of the question. Gary D., a dill, naively said: 'Yes M'ss Ethel.' 'Very well,' she replied, 'you will come outside and repeat it to me!' Another example of confession being good for the soul I suppose (and titillating for the confessor, too, no doubt!). People were constantly being exhorted to confess to all sorts of things. A speculative hush fell while the two went outside. They returned a few moments later. Gary, fittingly tearful, sat down; Miss Ethel made her throat-tearing disgust noise 'Uch!' and Miss Elsie gasped orgasmically 'A-a-a-a-hhh!' as, 'St Teresa in Ecstasy'-like, she rolled her eyes to Heaven. (These reactions — peculiar to the Hotchin sisters — are difficult to simulate.) 'Don't any of you ever ask him to repeat it!' added Miss Ethel. Well, I mean! At dismissal there was such a rush to Gary in the cloak-room that revelation was only just prevented by the maddened sisters. So we had to wait a little longer till we reached the safety of the street. For the record, the forbidden item ran: 'The boy stood on the burning deck/In nothing but his shirt./The flames came licking up his leg,/And burnt his little squirt!' We all fell about in hysterics!

One needed to be wary of the surveillance system, however. The sisters had ears and eyes everywhere. Playing in the sandpit very early in my career, I was led to remark 'Golly! something or other.' In total ignorance, I had overstepped the verbal boundaries — whether of decency or blasphemy I know not to this day — but penalties were applied in the form of lines, 50 or 100 of them to the tune of 'I must not ...' whatever it was. Woe-betide the boy who 'swore'! — 'Golly'?

'HOTCHIN'S HOTHOUSE', FROM AN UNPUBLISHED MEMOIR (1996)

I spy

BARBARA HANRAHAN (1930–91) GREW UP IN ADELAIDE. HER MEMORIES OF KINDERGARTEN AND SCHOOLDAYS ARE REFLECTED IN THE AUTOBIOGRAPHICAL NOVEL, *The Scent of Eucalyptus*.

The Kindergarten was named after the Governor's Lady. It was hidden in the back streets of Thebarton, coming dangerously close to the terraced houses of Hindmarsh and Brompton; dangerously near the maze that was Bowden — tucked behind the zig-zag railway that separated it from the upper class homes of North Adelaide, with their sandstone walls topped by plumbago and grape-vines and broken glass.

I was far from pretty blue plumbago as I walked with my grandmother through a world of concrete and cement, brick and asphalt, macadam and corrugated iron. Even the gardens looked sickly and grimed with dirt — Rose Street seemed far away.

The bulk of gas-works loomed over everything; its scent was everywhere. It drifted through Bowden from First to Seventeenth Street; merged with the reek of the tannery by the river; mingled with the fumes that crept from the Southwark Brewery. Gas soaked the walls of houses, turned the sunlight sour, clung to my skirts, settled in my hair.

There was a Salvation Army citadel where people marched with flags and brass trumpets on Sunday. There were yards of sand and gravel and scrap metal; advertisements for Ipana Toothpaste, Woodroofe's Lemonade, Amgoorie Tea. There was the Kindergarten with its drive lined with Norfolk Island pines.

I was quite happy the first morning until my grandmother led me to a strange lady who was the headmistress. She gave me flowers to arrange, and when I looked up from their redness Nan was gone. Abandoned — I cried. Yet, in the afternoon when she came to claim me at the gate, I was taken unawares. I had almost forgotten her.

I became a number, a name, a picture in the Kindergarten's files. The antiseptic fingers of a doctor probed and poked me. I was stood upon a pair of scales and weighed and measured; taken into a room where I was photographed without my clothes.

There was a lavatory with a row of cubicles and washbasins. I liked to sit and see how long I could pee for, listening to the other dribbles and tinkles and gurgles about me. I was happiest when I was a spy, a *voyeur*, an eavesdropper. I thought it strange to hear the boys' voices outside — how funny it would be if the wall wasn't there.

After lunch we rested. Best friends went next to each other — clasped hands and giggled before they fell asleep.

I came home and at night I could not sleep for thinking of the next day. Each morning the excitement mark on my cheek tingled, burned red.

We finger-painted, grew wheat in saucers, cut chains of figures with blunt-end scissors. We shook dewdrops onto our tongues, hunted for lucky clovers, found daisies in the lawn. We frightened ourselves on the slippery-dip, flew through the air on chains, calmed ourselves on the swing.

There was a sinister wooden tower that I watched others climb. There were books with buttoned covers and felt pages. There were dressing-up clothes, and I longed for the black and white Pierrot; the ones who climbed the tower got it first.

(I dream of the Kindergarten children still: Joan Stott, born on my birthday, who wet her pants at the Botanic Gardens; Betty and Joan Smith — the Twinnies, whom you couldn't tell apart; monkey-face Stanley Oliver, whose sister pulled out her hair; Brucey Neighbour, who lived in a house with a hedge dotted in berries I put in a matchbox; Daphne Ring, whose dress was embroidered with egg.)

Daphne became my friend. She had a skin disease that made her hands look like snakeskin gloves. One day we hid from the teacher in a cement pipe; pretended we were moths in a cocoon, rabbits in a burrow. Daphne scratched her hands, made a storm of snowflakes; she told me her father killed chickens, and the dead skin merged to feathers and I smelt blood.

I was amoral, secretive, devious: stole a milk-jug cover of net and beads; picked up other people's hankies and gave them to Reece to boil [...]

We got ready for the Christmas play. I was the tallest so I was the Angel. I wore a sheet, crêpe paper wings, and waved a star. Mary was a show-off in royal-blue.

On the last day there was a Fête with lucky dips, toffee apples, and a flute band. My grandmother and the mothers made dolls for the Christmas tree; I chose the one Joan Stott's mother made and Nan was hurt and wouldn't speak. There was a concert, and I watched a girl like Shirley Temple do the tap-dance.

I had to say goodbye to the Norfolk pines, the lavatory, the black and white Pierrot; to Miss Trembath and the headmistress. Even to some of the children, for not everyone was going to the Infant School at the end of Rose Street.

For some there is the convent beside the Queen of Angels' Church and a blazer with badges and a lily on the pocket.

The Scent of Eucalyptus (1985; FIRST PUBLISHED 1973)

We know who we are

CHESTER EAGLE (1933–) WROTE OF HIS MELBOURNE GRAMMAR SCHOOL EXPERIENCES IN *Play Together, Dark Blue Twenty.*

Picture the scene. The walls are lined with premiership photos going deep into the nineteenth century. Athletes, cricketers, footballers and oarsmen, they stare from frames, capped, moustached, wearing knee length trousers which shorten as the years progress. They're in blazers with wild hair, hair watered, hair brilliantined. Their coaches sit sternly between captain and vice captain or stand in the back row. In 1931 Grammar took out the four premierships and the photos of that year are in one frame which hangs above the fireplace. Parents and grandparents of the present school look down on maids rushing trays to prefects, before whom empty plates are stacked. They serve. On weekends, when there's less pressure, boys in the middle may get their dinner first. At other times, seniors take their plates, then pass indifferently towards the middle. If one side of the table has an uneven number, a voice in the process of breaking may cry, 'Hey! What about me!' The prefect will say, 'You belong to the other end.'

Power's clustered, and may be arbitrarily employed, but most of the time there's security in our hierarchical system. We know who we are, and if we're exposed to others, they also are exposed to us. We know each other's sounds and habits. We've nicknames for each other of brutal aptness. Yet night after night, in our blue suits, we push into dinner, with masters at the centre table. A hundred and twenty boys stand at their benches. Fred Jarrett, School House master, grunts; it's his call for silence. '*Benedictus, benedicat, per Iesum Christum, Dominum nostrum,*' he says. We sit. The prefects on duty produce their rolls, calling names at speed. We answer 'Sir!' The meal won't be served till the rolls are finished, so the prefects hurry, answers coming two or three names behind the call.

'Baillieu, Bodinnar, Brown,' says the prefect, and they answer 'Sir!' right down to 'Whitehead, Wiseman, Withers.' Missing a roll call is serious. Boys arriving late are greeted by Fred's 'See me after.' They're caned, or gated. When the senior roll's completed, Perry, the junior boarding house, is called. Their voices come out too loudly, or in falsetto. There is general merriment when someone's voice goes wrong, though we dare not, in the presence of the masters, squeal as we would if the same vocal accident occurred in the shower room. Fred glares in the direction of any exuberance. The serious business of eating has to start, and we're our own enforcers.

There are few leisurely moments in our cycle. Between the end of classes at 3.30 and dinner at 6, some of us would like to read, and others to explore the city, but sport's compulsory. Boarders turn out four times a week, cadets consuming the remaining afternoon. Even the day boys have to turn out twice a week, getting their names marked off or they too will face schoolboy justice. This is meted out in the boarders' shower room because it's an echoing cavern and the amplified sound of a caning finds its way into the quad, warning slackers to beware.

Six of the best, touch your toes! *Whack, whack, whack!* [...]

We wonder why so few of Australia's test cricketers have been Grammar men; there's a feeling of naked energy in the cruder suburbs, and greater exposure to fashion. Things we wouldn't dream of are spawned there. Standing in the queue for a film, on a Saturday night, we're disgusted by children with mohawk haircuts rushing past us to the ticket box. How dare they? And for that matter, why let them in? We're vindicated when the manager leads them out, clutching their grubby sleeves. Back to Footscray, we think, where you belong.

We're not teenagers, we're boys becoming men.

We laugh loudly, showing off our balls. We jostle, doing the same. Our bodies are changing before each other's eyes. We know what everyone's like inside their suits. When we hear someone chuckle in the night, we know what he's doing. Most of us wait for our morning erections to go down before we shower, but some are more flagrant. Swollen skin at the tips of our penises means we've been masturbating. When we sit warmly in classrooms, our trousers bulge. We can cope with it in each other, but if it happens in a tram, it's awful. We dry our shorts, socks and jockstraps in the boiler room, a smelly turret beside the upstairs locker room. On cold nights we go in there to warm ourselves. There's a weak globe just above head height, but mostly we gather in the gloom, pressed against this heat source while from the many pipes dangles the gear we need dried out. Boys rush in to finger their socks and jockstraps, taking them if they're dry. Others stay; it's a democratic little cave where ridicule's less frequent than elsewhere, because to be there is to be out of sight.

Play Together, Dark Blue Twenty (1986)

Doing OK

RUBY LANGFORD GINIBI (1934–), WRITER, WAS BORN IN CORAKI, NEW SOUTH WALES, AT BOX RIDGE MISSION. SHE WENT TO HIGH SCHOOL AT CASINO, NEW SOUTH WALES, BUT LEFT AT 15 TO TRAIN AS A CLOTHING MACHINIST IN SYDNEY.

At Casino High there were only about twelve Koori kids, the rest — a few hundred — were white. We were doing OK though; we were doing all right. We were class captain and sports captain, we ran the fastest, wrote the longest stories, and Beatrice Hogan was dux of fifth year. Lismore and Grafton didn't like to see us arriving with our hockey sticks.

Tiger McGee told us about the old sailor who stopped the wedding guest with his glittering eye and we chanted:

Water, water, everywhere,
And all the boards did shrink
Water, water, everywhere,
Nor any drop to drink.

But the poem I liked best was about a churchyard in England (Gray's 'Elegy') and for some reason I memorised this part:

Full many a gem of purest ray serene
The dark unfathom'd caves of ocean bear
Full many a flower is born to blush unseen
And waste its sweetness on the desert air.

In class I always said this part the loudest and Tiger McGee always gave me a strange look.

At lunchtime I went to the Assembly Hall and messed around on a German-made piano called a Wurlitzer. I started with 'Twinkle Twinkle' and progressed to 'Believe Me if all Those Endearing Young Charms'. Tiger McGee came in one day and showed me how to do the bass, then he told me the correct fingering for the scales. We started up a class band, clarinet, violin, saxophone and piano. I learnt to read music enough to follow easy tunes [...]

In October the fifth year students started coming in to practise for the Debutantes' Ball, and the man who was organising them asked me to play waltzes for them. The night of the Ball came and I went with Olga Olive and the Hogan girls. It was being held in the Casino Memorial Hall. When we arrived there were balloons and flowers and streamers everywhere and a red carpet ran from the stage down the centre of the hall for all the debutantes to walk on after they were presented to the Lord Mayor. I watched and they danced and everything went well, but then I was sent for by the organiser to go up on the stage.

I had no idea what was going on. I waited in the wings while he was talking over the mike, and he suddenly said, 'I'd like to thank our little pianist Ruby Anderson for playing for our practice sessions,' and he called me out on to the stage. People began to applaud. I walked out with my head down, said thankyou and started to leave. The organiser grabbed my arm and made me walk right down the red carpet. I got about a third of the way and then I ran for it.

At the end of my second year Dad came to pick me up at school. He told me I had a stepbrother, he and Mum Joyce had a new baby called Dennis. The baby was blond and blue-eyed, so now we had a real mix. I told him about the flower in the desert air, the hockey games, playing waltzes for the debutantes, how I ran down the red carpet, how I met the eel, how I trained my memory.

He took me up to the headmaster's office and told me to wait on the bench outside. I heard Dad asking him about my progress, and then Mr Rubenach's voice saying he wanted me to go on to third year and do my Intermediate Certificate. Dad said he didn't know about that. Mr Rubenach said I should then go on to teachers' college, the reasons being I was a class captain and school prefect and had come first in my class again.

I sat on the bench, my head buzzing. Every teacher I'd ever seen was white. I tried to imagine black kids being taught by black teachers, then I tried to imagine white kids with black teachers.

'Why not?' Mr Rubenach was saying. 'She's made very good progress, and there's no reason to think she won't continue. The Aborigines' Protection Board would put her through College — '

'No thanks,' my father said in a dry voice, 'if she wants to go to teachers' college she'll get there under her own steam and not through the help of the Aborigines' Protection Board.'

They said some more in quiet voices and then Dad came out and took my arm. He was a very proud man. He looked like a big detective — he always wore a hat and a large gaberdine overcoat. He shook the headmaster's hand and told me to do the same.

Out on the street, he asked if I'd heard what they said.

'Most of it.'

'I don't know about third year. You decide about that. But I'm not having any protection board put you through college. All the protection they've done so far is take people from their land and split up families.'

He marched ahead of me to the bus stop, but in a while his mood changed. He was a man who rarely smiled but when he did his whole face lit up, and now he was hugging me and saying he was proud I'd done so well.

Don't take your love to town (1989; FIRST PUBLISHED 1988)

Class conflicts

JILL KER CONWAY (1934–), HISTORIAN AND EDUCATIONIST, SPENT HER CHILDHOOD AT HER FATHER'S PROPERTY, COORAIN, IN WESTERN NEW SOUTH WALES. IN SYDNEY, SHE WENT FIRST TO A STATE SCHOOL BUT WAS SOON TRANSFERRED BY HER MOTHER TO THE PRIVATE SCHOOL FOR GIRLS, ABBOTSLEIGH.

The first day of school in February was hot, 105 degrees. The school, a brick building with an iron roof, was like a furnace, and its inhabitants, teachers and students, wilted as the day wore on. I hated it from the moment I walked in the door. I was a snob, and I knew the accents of the teachers and most of the students were wrong by the exacting standards we'd had drummed into us at home. Worse still was the unruly behavior of everyone of every age. Boys pulled my hair when I refused to answer questions I took as rude or impudent; girls stuck out their tongues and used bad language. Teachers lost their tempers and caned pupils in front of the class. Few books were opened as the staff waged a losing battle to establish order. Recess and lunchtime were purgatorial. Crowds, or so it seemed to me, of jeering boys and a few girls gathered around to taunt me about my accent. 'Stuck up, ain't you,' they yelled, as I faced them in stubborn silence.

They were right. Now I was in a more diverse social universe than I had known at Coorain. I had no idea how to behave or what the rules were for managing social boundaries. I had been friends, one could say special friends, with Shorty, or with Ron Kelly, but that was in a simple world where we each knew our respective places. Here, I knew only that the old rules could not possibly apply. Everyone around me spoke broad Australian, a kind of speech my parents' discipline had ruthlessly eliminated. My interrogators could unquestionably be described by that word my mother used as a blanket condemnation of lower-class people, customs, and forms of behavior. They were 'common.' My encounter was a classic confrontation for the Australia of my generation. I, the carefully respectable copier of British manners, was being called to raucous and high-spirited account by the more vital and unquestionably authentic Australian popular culture. I was too uncertain to cope. I faced them in silence till the bell rang and we returned to the pandemonium of the unruly classroom.

After school, the same group assembled to escort me home to the accompaniment of catcalls and vivid commentaries on my parentage. I knew these city children could not outlast someone who was used to walking ten or twelve miles a day behind a herd of sheep, so our comic crocodile set out. I, stalking in front in frozen indignation, my attendant chorus gradually wilting as I led them along hot pavements and across streets where the heat had begun to melt the tarmac. After the last one had tired and dropped away, I made my way home where my mother was ostentatiously doing nothing in the front garden, on the watch for my arrival.

We had our afternoon tea in blissful silence. Finally she asked me how the day had gone. 'It was all right,' I said, determined not to complain. She studied my face thoughtfully. 'You don't have to go back,' she said. 'I made a mistake. That's not the right school for you.' Years later, I asked how she guessed what my day had been like. 'I didn't have to ask,' she said. 'You were a child whose face was always alight with curiosity. When you came home that day, your face was closed. I knew you wouldn't learn anything there.'

In fact, had I persevered I would have learned a great deal, though little of it from the harassed and overworked teachers in the ill-equipped classrooms. I'd have been obliged to come to terms with the Australian class system, and to see my family's world from the irreverent and often hilarious perspective of the Australian working class. It would have been invaluable knowledge, and my vision of Australia would have been the better for it. It was to take me another fifteen years to see the world from my own Australian perspective, rather than from the British definition taught to my kind of colonial. On the other hand, had I learned that earthy irreverence in my schooldays, it would have ruled out the appreciation of high culture in any form. My mother had no training for that appreciation, but she knew instinctively to seek it for her children. She did not reflect much about the underlying conflicts in Australian culture. She was simply determined that I would be brought up to abhor anything 'common,' and that, despite her financial worries, I would have the best education available in the Australia she knew.

The Road from Coorain (1992; FIRST PUBLISHED 1989)

The spelling prize

GWEN HARWOOD (1920–95), POET, GREW UP IN QUEENSLAND, BUT SPENT MOST OF HER LATER LIFE IN TASMANIA.

Every Child's Book of Animal Stories
To compete, we stood on the wooden forms
that seated four in discomfort.
When you missed your word, you sat down
and wrote it out twenty times.
At last only two were left:
Ella and I, who had sailed
past *ghost, nymph, scheme, flight, nephew,*
the shoals of o-u-g-h
and I before e, stood waiting
for the final word, Whoever
put her hand up first when Sir
announced it, could try to spell it.
A pause, while Sir went outside.
Some of the girls started hissing,
'Give Ella a chance. Let her win.'

Through the window I saw the playground
bare as a fowlyard, the ditch
in a paddock beyond where frogs
lived out whatever their life was
before the big boys impaled them
on wooden skewers, a glint
from a roof in the middle distance
that was Ella's home. I had been there

the week before, when my grandmother went
to take their baby, the ninth,
my brother's old shawl. Ella coaxed me
to a ramshackle tinroofed shed
where her father was killing a bull calf.
A velvety fan of blood
opened out on the concrete floor
as one of her brothers pumped the forelegs:
'You do this to empty the heart.'

The father severed the head, and set it
aside on a bench where the eyes, still trusting,
looked back at what had become
of the world. It was not the sight
of the entrails, the deepening crimson
of blood that sent me crying
across the yard, but the calf's eyes watching
knife, whetstone, carcase, the hand that fed.

Ella followed, 'I'll show you my toys.'
In that house where nobody owned
a corner, a space they might call their own,
she kept two old dolls in a showbox.
Below me the whispers continued:
'Let Ella win the prize.'
Why, now, does memory brood
on Sir's return, and the moment

when he put down his cane and smoothed
his hair grease-tight on his skull
and snapped out the last word: MYSTIC,
a word never found in our Readers.
My innocent hand flew up.
Sheer reflex, but still, I knew it,
and knew I could slip in a k
or an I for a y and lose,

but did not, and sixty years
can't change it; I stand in the playground
and the pale dust stirs as my friends
of the hour before yell 'Skite!'
and 'Showoff!' and 'Think you're clever!'
They gather round Ella, who turns
one hurt look from her red-rimmed eyes
at my coveted, worthless prize.

Bone Scan (1988)

Badgers and wombats

Nan Chauncy (1900–70) published a series of novels for children with settings in remote, rural Tasmania. In this extract, her central character, Badge, is sent to a Hobart school where his cousin Sam is already a pupil.

Jumping from the lorry last, Badge dodged his cousins and plodded reluctantly to school on his own. Sam would not walk with him after he met his friends, and Bron's kind, pitying looks were more than he could stand today.

He wanted to turn things over, to try to understand why he must leave the bush he knew and loved for this rum sort of world. At the Farm, Aunt Florrie laughed at him because he had never slept in a bed standing up on legs before, nor seen a window with glass panes, nor even turned a tap for water from a tank, instead of dipping it up from a pool in a bucket [...]

Then there was school, worse and more noisy than the Farm.

It was one big room with a veranda outside for hanging coats on rows of pegs. It was dark inside, for the windows were high and small, and the air was smelly. The desks were all the same size, whatever children sat at them, so that the younger ones had their feet dangling in mid air and complained that their legs went to sleep.

No one seemed to like the teacher, Miss Ironwick, who was old and whose cottage had windows so that she could spy on them during playtime. Badge had stopped trying to please her. Sometimes the smells and the noise made him so muddled and stupid that he gaped open-mouthed instead of answering to his new name of *Brian,* and Sam was more ashamed of him than ever.

Sam had been friendly enough at first, telling everyone his cousin lived away in the bush and had never seen a dog or a cat, or even a telegraph pole, and the boys were interested and friendly.

But one day he climbed the old pear-tree in the yard and heard Sam, who hadn't seen him, telling his holiday adventure, the time Dad had taken them all to Devils' Hill after a lost cow. Dad was scarcely mentioned, however — it was all how clever Sam had been, galloping about on horseback and throwing ropes over the horns of wild beasts. Sheer amazement kept Badge dumb till he heard Sam say: 'But for me finding the track of that flaming cow — '

'Sam! — you never!' cried Badge, descending at his feet. 'That was Bron!'

From that moment they were all against him. As soon as he appeared at school someone would yell: 'Hullo, Badge — have you seen a *man*? — have you seen a *house*? — have you seen *yourself*?' And they seemed to like Sam more than ever, though he was the one who had told the lies.

Of course there were fights, with Bron chewing her lip in anguish for him; and once he made Sam's nose bleed. The teacher saw through her window and warned Badge she wasn't having rough boys from the bush fighting in *her* school, and if she had any *more* trouble with him ...

So, instead of learning, he withdrew into stupidity as a snail into its shell, and dreamed through the days of nothing but home.

Turning all this over in his mind, Badge still couldn't see what good school was doing him.

'Hey, Badge!' called Sam, all smiles as he ran up. 'It's early yet; let's go round by the Swamp.'

It seemed Sam had changed again; he wanted to be cobbers. He even gave advice about how to keep on the right side of teacher, but Badge only shook his head. 'I give it a fair go and I doan like school, Sam.'

Said Sam, reasonably enough, 'Well, who cares if you like it or not? You got to attend; you might as well learn something. What about if school don't like *you*, Badge?'

'Aw ...' he considered this, 'but I give her no trouble, do I?'

'You always look asleep; you never show an interest. Shove a hand up — *say* something to show you listen, that's what she likes.'

They were at the marshy, reedy place where there were frogs. It seemed that's what Sam had come for, but he couldn't find one. 'We'll be late,' said Sam, 'give us the one you caught? I don't want it for long. You can have it back.'

'When?' asked Badge, parting with the little brownish fellow with great reluctance. 'Before school's out?'

'Oh, yes,' Sam called. 'Come on!'

Could he grudge the frog in payment for Sam's friendship?

The day went better: others, beside Sam, were friendly. Thinking over Sam's advice, Badge decided to attend more keenly. For his reward something was read out about native animals: this was really interesting and Badge was all ears. Kangaroos, native cats, Tasmanian devils, wombats ... smiling broadly, his hand shot suddenly in the air and waved round wildly, asking to be noticed. The teacher stopped and stared.

'Please, Miss, that bit you read about that badger — '

'What *badger*?'

'Aw, we call 'em "badgers" out our way. The *wombat*. Well what it says is all wrong!' He failed to hear the deathly hush and went on eagerly. 'The book says the pouch opens like a kangaroo's — well, it never! It's at the back, so the mother can run through the bush without hurting her baby ... see?'

He stopped. A titter grew to a roar round him, a gale of laughter encouraged by the teacher's grim smile. At last she raised a hand and said with biting sarcasm, 'Dear me! So the dullest boy in the room, who knows nothing, though he is twelve years old, presumes to correct the printed books, does he?' *And so on.*

The Roaring 40 (1963)

Austral-ee-yah!

The Merry-Go-Round in the Sea, A NOVEL BY **RANDOLPH STOW** (**1935–**), IS SET IN GERALDTON, WESTERN AUSTRALIA, DURING WORLD WAR II.

The morning was fresh and cool, the floor was cool under the boy's bare feet. None of the boys wore shoes to school. Wearing shoes was sissy.

The school was old, with new bits added. The hall was funny, one side of it was the outside wall of the old stone schoolhouse, and the classroom doors opened on to the hall like doors opening into the street. The classroom doors had fanlights above them, like the front doors of old houses.

The headmaster was talking, he was talking about the war. Then the piano struck up, and the children began singing. This morning the song was *Australia Australia Australeeyah*. On another morning it would be *Advance Australia Fair* or *Waltzing Matilda*. The boy sang hesitantly, unsure of the words.

There is a land where summer skies
Are gleaming with a thousand eyes ...

A thousand eyes. Was that right? It sounded a bit scaring. And the other children, evidently, were uncertain. The singing lagged behind the piano, then burst out at the end in a confident shout.

Australia! Au-australia! Austral-ee-yah!

The assembly was dismissed, the children marched to the classrooms. The boy beside Rob was Tommy Johnson. He was a blacknigger and had a great gobbet of pale snot on his upper lip.

Rob did not mind the blackniggers, some of the older ones he rather admired. But his mother was furious because Nan was sitting next to a blacknigger in school. 'They're dirty,' said his mother. 'They all have bugs in their hair.'

It was funny about blackniggers. They were Australian. They were more Australian than Rob was, and he was fifth generation. And yet somehow they were not Australian. His world was not one world.

Some people sent their children to the convent to keep them away from blackniggers. These people were despised. The State school kids hung over the fence as the convent kids passed, chanting:

Convent dogs
Jump like frogs
In and out the wa-a-ater.

Rob chanted with them. He was a Protestant, and his world was not one world.

He sat in class beside Graham Martin, who was a white boy and lived in the next street to the Corams. The classroom smelled of chalkdust and children and the sour ink that was brought round in earthenware bottles. It was a different smell from the smell that school had had before he went away, when he had been in First Bubs. In First Bubs the smell had been of biscuits and oranges for play-lunch, mouldering bean-bags and paint-boxes and crayons. The desks had been different too, with green cloth bags on the backs of the seats for putting things in. These desks were wrought-iron and shiny wood, carved with people's names.

He sucked a new pen-nib and dipped it in the inkwell and sucked it again. It tasted metallic. His copybook was open in front of him. In laborious copperplate he began to copy.

What have I done for you,
England, my England?

The Merry-Go-Round in the Sea (1979; FIRST PUBLISHED 1965)

Aux armes, citoyennes

MARY STEELE (1930–), AUTHOR OF A NUMBER OF CHILDREN'S BOOKS, WAS AT THE QUEENS CHURCH OF ENGLAND GIRLS' GRAMMAR SCHOOL, BALLARAT, VICTORIA, DURING WORLD WAR II. THIS EXTRACT COMES FROM AN AUTOBIOGRAPHICAL WORK IN PROGRESS ABOUT HER BALLARAT CHILDHOOD.

At school, Current Affairs became a new and solemn subject. Sixth-formers equipped with large maps and a long pointer addressed school assemblies on the progress of events in Europe. We learnt about the Siegfried Line and the Maginot Line, those fortifications along opposing sides of the German–French border. The Maginot Line we were assured was impregnable and as the 'phoney war' drifted eerily on to 1940, we joined in singing the Allied taunt, 'We're going to hang out our washing on the Siegfried Line,/Have you any dirty washing, Mother dear?' But as Hitler began his wildfire conquest of Europe and the bombing of Britain, we stopped singing this song. We listened to the news and watched the newspaper maps, with threatening black arrows pincering their way towards Dunkirk and Paris. The Maginot Line was forgotten.

Early in 1940 we were set to learn 'La Marseillaise' at school so that we could sing it in assembly, as though to give fresh heart to the crumbling French armies. At our age this was a stern introduction to a foreign tongue — but 'L'étandard sanglant est levé' is certainly a more stirring notion than *la plume de ma tante*, and there was something irresistible about 'Aux armes, citoyens! Formez vos bataillons!', so we committed this resounding battle-cry to memory along with its thrilling tune and sang it with gusto, but even at nine years old I felt sad at the futility of it all. The French armies did not respond to our call and Hitler marched in to Paris. Later on, the hymn 'God the all-terrible, King who ordainest...', with its Czarist associations, was added to our morning repertoire, this time in support of our (non-Czarist) Russian allies — and with rather more success.

On the maps the black arrows and pincers began to reach into the Mediterranean, over Greece and Crete and Libya and across North Africa, and towards Russia. The shapes of Europe and the Mediterranean became very familiar and, as the conflict spread, my knowledge of the world grew with it. The war was a vast and living geography lesson, filled with action and drama. The missionary world of Greenland's icy mountains and India's coral strand was gradually replaced by a litany of names with a rhythm and mystique of their own — Benghazi and Bardia, Sidi Barrani and Mersa Matruh, Tobruk and El Alamein. There seemed to be no sign of 'Afric's sunny fountains' in the Western Desert.

As impressionable children we were absorbing the stuff of history and geography without realising it. Our heroes and villains were not football stars or pop singers but massive figures of destiny. Their features stared forth at us from the swap cards in sweet packets — the sombre, determined faces of Churchill, Roosevelt, de Gaulle and General Smuts, of Monty and Wavell and Mountbatten — all associated in my memory with the taste of licorice. I became adept at drawing caricatures of Hitler, Goering, Himmler and Mussolini, or pictures of aerial dogfights filled with plummeting, smoking Messerschmidts and triumphant, soaring Spitfires. Union Jacks and Swastikas adorned our blotters and Battleships and Cruisers was a favourite game under the desk.

Slit trenches were dug in one corner of the school hockey field; the grass grew unchecked all around and for some time we played no games on that arena. Hanging beside our desks we each had a kitbag containing emergency rations (raisins or chocolate) and spare clothing. Around our necks we wore corks or rubbers on strings, to bite on when the bombs began to fall. When instructions about these requirements were first handed down to us in assembly, the Headmistress read out the list of kit-bag contents then pounced on me and asked me to repeat it for the benefit of all (and, no doubt, to see if I had been listening). This was a more trying experience than she guessed, for as I stammered through the list I was acutely aware of one item which had to be named, come what may. Stupidly, I put it off until last, by which time the tension in the hall was electric. I came to the end, turned crimson, and croaked, 'And a spare pair of bloomers, too', at which the entire school collapsed.

During the following months our kitbags were inspected at intervals; nearly always, of course, the emergency rations had been eaten. Air-raid drill was sprung on us at intervals and when the whistle blew everyone lined up in a double file down the long corridor. The smallest girl in the school — who happened to be my sister Elizabeth — was paired off with the Head Prefect, and in this way the little ones were in the care of the biggest. Being in the middle of things, our class was left to look after itself as we marched — 'in an *orderly* fashion, girls!' — out to the trenches, trailing our kitbags and losing items of under-wear on the way. We each had an appointed place in the trench, and Margaret and I found ourselves in a soggy corner which had very early sprung a leak. We considered this rather an advantage.

Jenks had been sent to Melbourne to attend an ARP course and when she returned she was put in charge of these day-time arrangements and also of the precautions in the boarding house. The school was only a short distance from a power station, which made it vulnerable to air attack. Larks carried out the mammoth task of making blackout curtains for the boarding house, while Jenks instructed the girls and house staff in air-raid drill. The night shelter was the old cellar under Manifold House. The boarders went to bed with their emergency kitbags beside them and their slippers turned upside down on the floor in case of flying glass. The girls were forbidden to run when/if the siren went.

At a fairly low level, we children did our bit for the war effort. We saved up pennies for sixpenny War Savings Stamps, which were stuck on a card until there were enough (forty) to convert into a War Savings Certificate. At school we were taught to knit strange khaki garments to send to 'the boys' at the front. At our incompetent level in Form 1 we were confined to long narrow strips called 'garters', done appropriately in garter stitch, although the older girls were let loose on socks and balaclavas. Several times after school, Margaret and I visited a friend of Mother's to learn how to make camouflage nets which was a much more sensational operation than knitting, with much quicker results.

From my point of view, austerity had some undeniable advantages. I belonged to the first wave of twelve-year-olds who were exempted from wearing regulation lisle stockings at school. This was comparable to being saved from a fate worse than death, and scenes of jubilation took place when we were told in assembly that we could wear brown sockettes. As it happened, mother decided to knit our socks and the toes of mine were always finished off in another colour — blue or yellow — to save breaking into a further ball of brown wool. Coloured toes caused me acute embarrassment in the cloakroom, but anything was better than being encased in thick stockings and suspender belts.

'BESIDE THE LAKE, BENEATH THE TREES: A BALLARAT CHILDHOOD'
(1996)

Les enfants du paradis

GAVIN SOUTER (1929–), WRITER AND HISTORIAN, WAS A BOARDER AT THE SCOTS COLLEGE, WARWICK, IN SOUTHERN QUEENSLAND, DURING WORLD WAR II.

On warm nights we sometimes left our beds in the earliest hours of the morning, carried our bikes down across the paddocks, joined the road at a safe distance from school, and rode into town. One night we rode the full length of the deserted main street, took off all our clothes, tied them to the racks of our bikes, and did the return journey stark naked. Another time we climbed the fence around the town baths and went for a swim. Stimulated though we were by these excursions, especially by the hazardous return to school, when we half expected to find our light on, there was really not much one could do in Warwick between 3 a.m. and 4 a.m. After the novelty had worn off, we abandoned the practice.

Breaking bounds in daylight was a more attractive proposition. As Senior students we were expected to study after school hours and on Saturday mornings and Sunday afternoons. At such times it was an easy matter to slip under the back fence and walk unobserved through the bush that bordered the northern bank of the Condamine. On midsummer afternoons we sometimes walked to a rock ledge about six feet above the river, which at that point was still in the early stages of its circuitous journey to join the Balonne, the Culgoa, the Darling and finally, after more than a thousand miles, the Murray River in South Australia. We stripped, swam around noisily, and then dried off on the rocks like lizards. On the other side of the river, beyond a line of willows, a few cattle grazed at their leisure, and in the distance Warwick seemed little busier than at 3 a.m. Sometimes we studied, but more often we simply lay in the sun and talked — about the war ('Did you see that picture of Musso and his girlfriend hanging upside down?'), about sex ('They reckon a real orgasm feels like a flock of pigeons flying out of your arse'), about the school and about the Senior examination which lay in wait for us at the end of the year.

As the Senior came closer I took to going off on my own with textbooks, either into the bush if the weather was good, or into one of the deserted Army hospital buildings beside the school. The Army had left some traces of its tenancy. In my silent reconnoitrings in search of suitable places to study I found old copies of *Salt*, rusty forceps and a few rising-sun hat badges. There were New South Wales and Victorian serial numbers pencilled on the walls, and declarations that Foo had been on the premises. As I slipped unseen from ward to ward I tried to imagine what the hospital had been like two or three years before: Atebrin-jaundiced men under grey blankets, Army nurses and VADs going their merciful rounds, and white-masked surgeons performing miracles of plastic surgery on torn flesh and shattered bone. The real thing may have been quite different, but that was my version of it.

Sitting in a corner of one of the wards now empty of everything except a steel sink, I spent long hours memorizing passages of nineteenth century English poetry. The set poets were Wordsworth, Coleridge, Byron, Shelley, Keats, Tennyson, Browning and Arnold. My response to them was sensory and conventional, but at least I did respond. The images which stayed in my mind were nearly all romantic, supernatural, or to do with remote and unfamiliar landscapes. From Tennyson: 'Far on the ringing plains of windy Troy'. From Keats: 'The owl, for all his feathers, was a-cold;/The hare limped trembling through the frozen grass,/And silent was the flock in woolly fold.' From Coleridge: 'Where Alph, the sacred river ran,/Through caverns measureless to man/Down to a sunless sea'.

The only poem that appealed to me in more than a sensual way was Wordsworth's *Intimations of Immortality from Recollections of Early Childhood*. I was interested in his speculation about the gradual fading of the glory and the dream, though I was not persuaded that these dwindling commodities came originally from heaven.

> There was a time when meadow, grove and stream,
> The earth and every common sight,
> To me did seem
> Apparelled in celestial light …
> Heaven lies about us in our infancy!
> Shades of the prison-house begin to close
> Upon the growing Boy … […]

I could vouch for the celestial light, wherever it flowed from. I had seen it reflected by clouds in the sky, by Nestles wrappers in the gutter, by mauve wisteria and ivory rock lily, by dragonflies among the reeds of the Macleay River and coral cod in the fish trap at Kangaroo Island. And I still saw it almost every day in the yellow wattle behind the school, the pink berries on the pepper trees, and the uncanny red of poinsettia flowers. If shades of the prison-house were beginning to close, I had not noticed them.

The Idle Hill of Summer (1972)

Reading MND in Form 4B

PETER PORTER (1929–), POET, WAS A BOARDER AT BRISBANE CHURCH OF ENGLAND GRAMMAR SCHOOL AND LATER AT TOOWOOMBA GRAMMAR SCHOOL DURING WORLD WAR II.

> Miss Manning rules us middle-class children
> Whose fathers can't afford the better schools
> With blue, small, crow-tracked, cruel eyes.
> *Philomel with melody* — a refrain
> Summoning the nightingale, the brown bird
> Which bruits the Northern Hemisphere with bells —
> It could not live a summer in this heat

Queen Titania, unaware of Oberon,
Is sleeping on a bank. Her fairy watch
Sings over her a lullaby,
The warm snakes hatch out in her dream.
Miss Manning is too fat for love,
We cannot imagine her like Miss Holden
Booking for weekends at the seaside
With officers on leave. This is not Athens
Or the woods of Warwickshire,
Lordly the democratic sun
Rides the gross and southerly glass.
Miss Manning sets the homework. Thirty boys
Leave the bard to tire on his morning wing;
Out on their asphalt the teams for Saturday
Wait, annunciations in purple ink,
Torments in locker rooms, nothing to hope for
But sleep, the reasonable view of magic.
We do not understand Shakespearean objects
Who must work and play: that gold stems from the sky:
It poisons 1942. To be young is to be in Hell,
Miss Manning will insulate us from this genius,
Rock the ground whereon these sleepers be.

Elsewhere there is war, here
It is early in an old morning, there is pollen
In the air, eucalyptus slipping past
The chalk and dusters — new feelings
In the oldest continent, a northern race
Living in the south. It is late indeed:
Jack shall have Jill, all shall be well,
Long past long standing eternity,
Eastern Standard Time.

Collected Poems (1984; FIRST PUBLISHED 1983)

From Kew to Chattanooga

Shirley Hazzard (1931–), novelist, set some early scenes of *The Transit of Venus* in New South Wales during the first months of the war in the Pacific.

The school was moving to a country house, where the invading Japanese would hardly penetrate. Grace was too little to be saved by such methods, Caro would go alone. Caro would try out the fugitive state; if it came up to snuff, Grace might later be included.

Caro was installed one afternoon at the foot of the Blue Mountains. On the plain below, gum trees straggled back towards Sydney, bark was strewn like torn paper. The littlest children cried, but the parents would visit them in a fortnight if the petrol held up and the Japs did not arrive. There was also an ancient train as far as Penrith, a weatherboard town with telegraph poles and the sort of picture-house where you could hear the rain.

Grace waved out the car window: jealous, guilty, and safe.

It was Sunday. After sago pudding, they sang 'Abide with Me,' and Caro went out on the upstairs veranda. Fast falls the eventide. The darkness deepened in silence more desolate for the squawk of a bird they had been shown in illustrations. Incredulous response cracked in Caroline Bell's own throat. Smells of dry ground, of eucalyptus and a small herd of cows gave the sense of time suspended, or slowed to a pace in which her own acceleration must absurdly spin to no purpose. The only tremor in dim foothills was the vapour of a train on its way up to Katoomba. It was insignificance that Dora had taught them to abhor, and if ever there was to be insignificance it was here. The measure of seclusion was that Penrith had become a goal. Caro took herself in her own tender embrace, enclosing all that was left of the known. Caro was inland.

She had crouched into the angle formed by the balustrade and one of the high supports of the veranda. Bougainvillea was trained on the uprights; and a round plaque, cool as china, impressed her cheek. There were insects in the thorny vines, there was the scuttle of some animal in the garden below. Dora would have confirmed that death is not the worst.

In a room with six beds, all subsequently cried themselves to sleep. In the morning, Caro saw that the medallion on the balcony was blue and white, and Catholic. On of the girls told her, 'Miss Holster says it's a Dellarobbier.'

The house was at once seen to be peculiar. There was a lot to look at. It was owned by the Doctor, who was not a doctor at all but an architect; and Italian, even if on our side. He had withdrawn to a smaller building alongside — servants' quarters was a phrase that came readily enough to them from books, or from the old stone houses built by convicts. The Doctor wore a short white cotton jacket and a little white pointed beard and, although not lame, carried a stick. According to Miss Holster, he had seen through Mussolini from the word Go.

The house had 1928 in Roman numbers on the porch; or portico. For its construction, coloured marbles and blond travertine had spent months at sea, fireplaces and ceilings had been dismantled outside Parma, where the ham and violets came from. And whole pavements of flowered tiles uprooted and rebedded. The dining-room was said to be elliptical. All the doors, even for bathrooms, were double, with panels of painted flowers, and paired handles pleasant to waggle until they dropped off. There were velvet bell-pulls, intended for maids, that fell into disrepair from incessant tugging. There was also the day Joan Brinstead broke an inkpot on the white marble mantel in the music room and ammonia only made it worse. Miss Holster had a canopy over her bed; but could not say why lemon trees should be potted rather than in the ground.

These rooms enclosed loveliness — something memorable, true as literature. Events might take place, occasions, though not during the blight of their own occupancy. At evening the rooms shone, knowing and tender.

In a forbidden paddock below the house, a wire fence surrounded tents, tin buildings, and thirty or forty short men grotesquely military in uniforms dyed the colour of wine. The Doctor's countrymen had come to the ends of the earth to find him, for the men who dug his fields and gathered his fruit were Italian prisoners of war. At dusk they led in the cows before being themselves led behind the wire. The Doctor could be seen in the mornings moving among them, white beard, white jacket, white panama: once more the master. They learned that, like a baby, he slept in the afternoons. They had seen, or caught, one of the prisoners kissing his hand.

From the fields, or behind the wire, the prisoners waved to the schoolgirls, who never waved back. Never. It was a point of honour [...]

One morning a girl whose father had been in America for Munitions came to school with nibless pens that wrote both red and blue, pencils with lights attached, a machine that would emboss a name — one's own for preference — and pencil sharpeners in clear celluloid. And much else of a similar cast. Set out on a classroom table, these silenced even Miss Holster. The girls leaned over, picking up this and that: Can I turn it on, how do you work it, I can't get it to go back again. No one could say these objects were ugly, even the crayon with the shiny red flower, for they were spread on the varnished table like flints from an age unborn, or evidence of life on Mars. A judgment on their attractiveness did not arise: their power was conclusive, and did not appeal for praise.

It was the first encounter with calculated uselessness. No one had ever wasted anything. Even the Lalique on Aunt Edie's sideboard, or Mum's Balibuntl, were utterly functional by contrast, serving an evident cause of adornment, performing the necessary, recognized role of an extravagance. The natural accoutrements of their lives were now seen to have been essentials — serviceable, workaday — in contrast to these hard, high-coloured, unblinking objects that announced, though brittle enough, the indestructibility of infinite repetition.

Having felt no lack, the girls could experience no envy. They would have to be conditioned to a new acquisitiveness. Even Dora would have to adjust her methods to contend with such imperviousness.

Never did they dream fingering those toys and even being, in a rather grown-up way, amused by them, that they were handling fateful signals of the future. The trinkets were assembled with collective meaning, like exhibits in a crime, or like explosives no expert could defuse. Invention was the mother of necessity. It was not long after this that the girls began to wave their unformed hips and to chant about Chattanooga and the San Fernando Valley. Sang, from the antipodes, about being down in Havana and down Mexico way. Down was no longer down to Kew. The power of Kew was passing like an empire.

The Transit of Venus (1981; FIRST PUBLISHED 1980)

War games

THIS SCENE FROM *Cloudstreet* BY WEST AUSTRALIAN NOVELIST TIM WINTON (1960–) IS SET IN PERTH AFTER WORLD WAR II.

School just gave Quick Lamb the pip. He was too slow to get things right the first time and too impatient to force himself to learn. For a while he was an army cadet, a soldier under the command of mathematics teachers who exchanged the steel rule for the brass ended baton and who liked the sound of both on a set of knuckles. In the cadets Quick learnt to shoot and also to crap with the aid of one square of shiny paper. He loved the khaki serge of battledress and the smell of nugget in the webbing, and he loved to shoot because he was good at it. He could see a long way, pick things in the distance that others couldn't, and the two hundred yard target seemed close to him, only a barrel length away. In the end, even Quick knew the only reason the school kept him on at all was to win rifle trophies for it. Sometimes, after a shoot, he'd see the whole world through a V. There was only ever one teacher Quick Lamb could talk with, but he was the sort of man who winced when you brought up your shoot scores, or rolled his eyes when you spoke warmly of a Bren gun. His name was Krasnostein and he had a limp. He taught history and he liked to have the class in an uproar of debate and discussion. He had the sort of dandruff that found its way into your books and papers and his teeth were like burnt mallee stumps. When he breathed on you, there was no telling how you'd behave.

Quick almost never spoke in class discussions. He could never get out what he wanted to say in time. Mostly he felt breathless and confused, sometimes furious with Mr Krasnostein who baited them all about the Anzacs and the Empire. Yet there was laughter allowed, even out-spokenness. After one class Krasnostein kept Quick behind. Itching with dread, Quick stood by the little man's desk.

You have lovely handwriting, Mr Lamb, but I'm afraid your essay is anything but lovely.

Sorry, sir.

The teacher sucked his moustache and smiled. You must remember that the *West Australian* and the *Western Mail* are not final authorities on history. Nor is what you hear over the back fence. Do you know any Japanese people?

No, sir.

No, I thought not. They really are more than just combustible material, Lamb. Do you know any Jews?

No.

Well you do now.

Quick looked him up and about. He felt his chin fall.

Here, Lamb, take these and read them over the weekend. If you'd like to change your essay afterwards let me know.

Quick went out lightheaded and he didn't even glance at the two bundles until he got home. In his room he opened the crumpled old magazine, a *New Yorker* from 1945. The whole thing seemed to be about Hiroshima, which he'd mentioned in his own essay. Between pages were loose photographs of what looked like burnt logs or furniture, but when he looked close he saw the features of people. He put it down and picked up the small pamphlet. It was called *Belsen: a record*. He picked it up without thought. Inside were long lists, and photographs of great piles of ... of great piles [...]

Now he sat with pictures on his lap that were beyond sadness and misery. This was evil, like Mr Bootluck the minister used to go on about at the Church of Christ. Here were all those words like sin and corruption and damnation [...]

Mr Krasnostein was not at school on Monday. In his place they had a strapping blonde man called Miller who looked like a wheat farmer. His eyes were the colour of gas and he read to them from the *Yearbook, 1942*. Mr Krasnostein never returned. Quick kept the magazine and the little stapled book in his bag, tucking them inside the loose skirting board in his room when he got home. As he came out onto the landing he saw Rose Pickles by the window at the head of the stairs, and it struck him that her silhouette was just like something out of Belsen. He'd noticed she was getting thinner every week, and now, as she turned, her eyes stood out in her head enough to make him feel repulsed. Somehow it struck him as sickheaded for a pretty girl to starve herself like that.

Oh, it's you, she said.

Quick said nothing at all. He was too choked up with disgust. He went down the stairs four at a time. He'd quit school — that's what he'd do.

Cloudstreet (1996; FIRST PUBLISHED 1991)

Bulby Brush boy

Les Murray (1938–), poet, walked seven kilometres to his bush school at Bulby Brush, New South Wales, in the 1940s.

Close in around the school were the first pine trees I ever saw, and I still associate the smell of pines with Bulby Brush school. We also had silky oaks, which I've loved ever since. The last thing you did before you walked up the slope to school was to jump over the gully. It was hard to do — you could only just get there — but it was a matter of pride you didn't walk around.

We used to jump over fences. We'd race to jump over a gate and the fellow who came last would say, 'It's all right, I'm last, but I'll be first in heaven.' We were all soaked in the bible. We talked about bible stories on the way to school as part of our normal conversation: 'You remember when Samson went up against the other blokes …' We never had a word of it at school. There was just the visit of a minister, maybe once a year.

We had an air-raid trench provided for us in case the Japanese air force came over the hills and decided to take this strategically important school. There were sixteen kids when I started and fourteen or thirteen when I left. About six kids could sit at a desk. Two people dipped into a common inkwell. When you started mucking around, sooner or later the ink ended up down the front of your trousers. Every time it landed in the same place, soaking down the front of your trousers.

At the front of the room was the teacher's table. There was a library, a three-by-three shelf, which I devoured. I can still remember the books on it. There was Mawson's journal of his travels in the Antarctic, a great big tome, and I fell upon it. The teacher knowing I was only nine years old said, 'Oh, that would be too advanced for you'. I said, 'Can I borrow it anyway, Sir?' I devoured it, thought it was wonderful, and still remember chunks of it […]

The teachers sent from the city belonged to something like the official culture of Australia, and the official culture didn't exist in the small-farming bush. We were always despised as Dad and Dave, and all that. But it was an utterly different culture. It was the culture of hard-working peoples, based on music and storytelling. It was entirely oral, and heroic and ancient. It had nothing to do with city culture. If teachers couldn't step across the cultures, then they were isolated, the poor souls.

HANK NELSON, *With Its Hat About Its Ears* (1990; FIRST PUBLISHED 1989)

Crone zone

BARRY HUMPHRIES (1934–), WRITER AND ACTOR, IS BEST KNOWN FOR HIS DAME EDNA EVERAGE STAGE PERSONA AND FOR OTHER ONE-MAN STAGE SHOWS. IN HIS AUTOBIOGRAPHY *More Please* HE DESCRIBES HIS CHILDHOOD IN THE MELBOURNE SUBURB OF CAMBERWELL, WHERE HE BEGAN HIS EDUCATION AT MRS FLINT'S KINDERGARTEN.

Mrs Flint was my very first teacher. I have thought of changing her name in case some litigious descendant recognizes his venerated great-grandmother. But I can find no better name for her than her real name; grey quartzy sharp-edged hard. She ran a small kindergarten in her own grey pebble-dashed Californian bungalow down the hill from our place, and her two best rooms, the lounge and dining-room, to the right of her dark hallway, had been turned into a classroom for local tots. Edna, my first and favourite nanny, would escort me every morning down the steep pavement of Marlborough Avenue until after several twists and turns and carefully crossed, sparsely motored roads we arrived at Mrs Flint's front gate, already jammed with tricycles and mothers. Mrs Flint, wearing a large apron to keep the chalk off her faded if flocculous print dress, stood on the front step screwing her face into what she imagined to be a friendly and motherly grimace as she welcomed her little pupils and reassured departing parents. She was a good actress, this old battle-axe, for the mothers all went home fondly believing that their littlies were in wonderful hands in spite of the panic-stricken screams that most of Mrs Flint's pupils emitted as soon as they realized that they had been abandoned to her care. No sooner had the last mother gone and the drone of the last parental sedan faded up Orrong Crescent than Mrs Flint's true mineral nature asserted itself. Once she was alone with her infant charges the ingratiating smile of the kindly old widow who adored children quickly faded and she would swing around from her blackboard and exhibit to the class a very different and frightening countenance on which rage, spite and ignorance jostled for supremacy.

It always took a long time for the crying to stop at Mrs Flint's kindergarten. One little girl called Jocelyn cried all the time and no amount of cajolery could stop her. In the end Mrs Flint put her out to graze in the back yard where, still bawling, she executed endless circuits on her trike. Inside we sat at miniature tables on stools enamelled cherry-red, one of the most popular hues of the late thirties. Because the classroom occupied Mrs Flint's lounge and dining room there were a few of her more substantial pieces of furniture — a Genoa-velvet couch, a bookcase and a Jacobean-style dining table with matching sideboard — shoved against the wall to make room for our small chairs and tables. Mrs Flint made it very clear that if anyone so much as laid a curious finger on one of her trumpery treacle-coloured sticks they would be put out in the yard with the eternally blubbering Jocelyn.

Mrs Flint was no great reader; except for the *Pears Cyclopaedia*, a couple of Ethel M. Dells and a Netta Muskett, her bookshelves accommodated faded family snaps and gewgaws which she called her 'ordiments'. However, every morning, seated in one of her deeper fawn-and-russet Genoa-velvet lounge chairs, with her dress hitched up so we could see her surgical stockings, she read us a story. Her favourite was Hansel and

Gretel and even the least imaginative child found a painful empathy with this tale and its themes of parental abandonment and persecution by a cannibalistic crone.

There was a mid-morning break and we all filed out the back to our trikes and lugubriously circled Mrs Flint's prickly lawn. When I first saw Doré's engraving of convicts dismally revolving in their bleak exercise yard, I had only to imagine them with gaily painted Cyclops tricycles and scooters between their shanks to be grimly reminded of playtime at Mrs Flint's.

More Please (1992)

Happy little Vegemites

BARRY OAKLEY (1931–), NOVELIST AND PLAYWRIGHT, WENT TO CHRISTIAN BROTHERS' COLLEGE, ST KILDA, MELBOURNE, IN THE 1940S.

On a hot day in February 1943, with sandwiches and a lemon tart in my lunchbag and butterflies in the gut, I propped my Malvern Star in the bike-shed, made my way through the shouting kids in the quadrangle, and joined the line outside Room 21. First Year they called it, as if the kid's stuff of the Three R's was over and the real business of education about to start. We acted tough, pushed and shoved, banged the lids of our desks, but I for one didn't like the look of it. Those beam balances down the back in glass cases! So many new books, alarming subjects! I recognized the crude drawings of Flinders Street Station and Australian Rules football in *Livre de Français*, but I couldn't make head or tail of the stories, with their fenetres, garcons and plumes. *Latin for Today* showed Horatius Holding the Bridge and Mucius Scaevola thrusting his fist into burning coals, but it too was in code. Algebra, Geometry, General Science: we were like migrants in a strange country, and for the first time we had lay teachers as well as the Brothers to shepherd us through.

The first of these, a Mr Taylor, with an old sports coat that came almost to his knees, inspected us frowning and humped over, as though he'd just come out of a cave. He carried the *Argus* in one pocket and a meat pie in the other. He'd set us some sums to do, turn his back, whip out his dentures and give them a polish, nibble his food, peep at the paper, tell himself a couple of private jokes, smile, mutter, then come back to earth. 'Righto, you chaps. Come out all those unsteady.' He'd say this every few minutes, and no one would ever move — but soon he did, for after barely three weeks he was gone.

That left Mr Hooker to carry most of the burden, but he didn't mind. He was tall and rawboned, with a skin dried to pemmican from years of biking it eight miles each way every day, a whistle for the fine weather and a sou'wester for the wet. He rode slow and straight-backed, an irascible Quixote with mackintosh for armour, pipe for lance, and forty little Sanchos struggling to keep up.

'This boy has Vegemite in his sandwiches,' he rasps, his pipe poking the classroom-heavy air. 'This boy is helping the enemy. You didn't know that, did you, boy? If you want to help the Seventh Day Adventists, go on. Eat your Kornies. Tuck into your Vegemite. You just go right ahead.' Whenever he grew vehement the fine drops of spittle flew, and a fleck of it struck me down in the fourth row, baptising me into the realities behind the scenes. We were big kids now, and this was not information to be told to everybody.

It never occurred to us to question all our strange new subjects, because we'd never at any time expected school to be relevant to our lives. School was a good giggle, a furtive windbreak, a fast swap of the stamps. Discipline was strict but we bent school our way, linking it with our world through innumerable secret wires. Science meant the chance to make Hydrogen Sulphide; French became a secret code

School to us had nothing to do with education. It was an imposition we'd come to accept, a hundred-mile obstacle race where you jumped, climbed, swerved, ducked, your eyes fixed only on the weekends. Each year the rules got harder, but it was basically pretty much the same. Either you learned them and kept on moving, or you slipped back slowly and died.

That was one of the funny things about school. Like the stage, it's an image of life: life accelerated, life concentrated, life more formidable. Life's a contest, but only at school do they number you 1–40 at the end of each year. Life's hard, but school's worse. Fail and fall at school and it's a public thing, a slow-motion nightmare up there in front of the mob, a hundred eyes enjoying every turn of the screw before you can creep back into the safety of the herd. School's the kind of test that belongs to the end of life, not the beginning.

Already the strong showed out, and the weak had gone to the wall. When Brother Conroy leaves the room for a minute, McEvoy lights up a cigarette, Kennedy does some fast gorilla-thumps on his chest, Adams belches, Cleary sings a song, but the rest of us meekly go on with our work. We were the mediocre middle, the vast unindividuated mass, with boy-heroes to worship and weaklings to despise. Like Smith, who whimpered after getting the cuts, and Henry, who vomited in class and condemned himself to eating his lunch alone for years.

At 12 noon a halt was called to the battle for power, and the Angelus prayer was said. The nearby churchbell tolled, the heavy-handed peasants down their tools. The prayer starts, everyone on edge because for weeks the genuflection contest has been running. When Brother Conroy intoned 'The word was made flesh and dwelt amongst us', we would all go down on one knee, and the prize went to the one who dared to stay down the longest. The winner was Sugar O'Brien who rose pious and flamingo-unsteady from one bony leg, the entire prayer over —

into a leather fusillade from Conroy's strap, carried gunman-handy in a hip pocket of his shabby black habit [...]

Say Christianity to the Asian and he'll think of Western imperialism; say it to the old college boy and he'll recall May Altars, three Hail Marys and the baptism of leather. For ten years we lived in constant threat of it ...The meaning of Extreme Unction. The gerund, the dative case, simultaneous equations. 'You don't know, boy? Hold it out then, and take it like a man.' One day, even God rebelled. When the foolhardy Gunson ventured, 'But surely, sir, a mixed marriage isn't always evil?' Brother Conroy blackened, stamped his foot hard, the floor trembled, and the picture of the handsome Christ above the blackboard fell down on his head.

Nineteen forty three was the year of the New Order in our school, as well as in embattled Europe. We got a new principal, our first taste of the professional educator. No more relievo, kick-to-kick or games of territory with the penknife. We sat quiet and gloomy over our lunches, as College boys should. Caps were put straight and pulled down hard over the eyes, and Herb, the travelling ice-block salesman, waddled off slowly in his grey dustcoat, never to be heard of again. 'You're all here in my big book,' said the new man, Brother Fogarty, with a smile that wasn't friendly. 'You, McEvoy, you're here, yes, under L for Larrikin — and you, Adams, under U for Undesirable — for selling *Heralds* in your school cap.'

Scribbling in the Dark (1985)

Matzoh for lunch

MORRIS LURIE (1938–), NOVELIST, BORN IN MELBOURNE, WRITES IN HIS AUTOBIOGRAPHY *Whole Life* ABOUT THE DOUBLE DISPLACEMENT HE FELT IN HIS JEWISH SCHOOL AND IN HIS STATE SCHOOL.

In *shul* it's crowded and everyone steps on you and pushes you and they've got a smell like inside your mouth when you wake up in the morning and hairs in their noses and the horrible sound when they sniff and it's always the same and it takes forever and there's nothing to do except pretend.

I don't want to go.

I have to.

And it's not only *shul*, there's *Talmud Torah* every day which I hate and Sundays too, and then there's *Yom Kippur* and *Rosh Hashonnah* and *Purim* and *Pesach* and —

What if I don't go?

What if I just don't go?

What if I refuse?

I have to.

God is behind the door where I can't see, and in the wardrobe until I open it, and under the bed, and behind my head, always, an old man with fierce eyes and an old fashioned long white beard, no matter how fast I turn.

(God is smarter than just ordinary invisible.)

It's a Jewish holiday.

I don't have to go to school.

(Everyone knows. You don't even have to bring a note.)

I'm one of the Jewish kids.

When it's *Pesach* we've all got *matzoh* for our school lunch. Mum makes me an allie bag out of a *matzoh mel* bag. You can still see the writing even when it's been washed, the Jewish Star of David.

Everyone knows you're Jewish.

Jew.

Jewboy.

Yid.

Graham Warren bashes me when he gets an Indian headdress for Christmas, him and his brother and other kids playing with all their new stuff out in the street that Father Christmas brought them, bows and arrows, genuine leather chaps.

'I didn't say anything!'

'Well, wha'cha lookin' at?'

The Chosen People.

Jews are smarter.

All the smart kids in school are Jewish.

You don't have to believe it.

It's a simple fact [...]

'*Er veiss gornicht!*' says the inspector.

He knows nothing!

It's true.

I can't translate.

I can't read properly.

I don't even know how to recite the whole alphabet by heart.

I don't care.

I'm glad.

I hate it.

I don't want all that rubbish inside my head.

That's not the real world.

Whole Life (1987)

A double life

AMIRAH INGLIS (1926–), WRITER, ARRIVED IN MELBOURNE FROM
POLAND WHEN SHE WAS TWO YEARS OLD. AS AMIRAH GUST (THE
ANGLICISED VERSION OF HER FAMILY NAME) SHE WAS EDUCATED AT
PRINCES HILL PRIMARY SCHOOL, ELWOOD CENTRAL STATE SCHOOL,
AND MACROBERTSON GIRLS' HIGH SCHOOL.

There had never been any question of my going to a 'church' or
'public' school, both because my parents believed in State education and in equality for all children, and because they thought
that Jews had no place going to 'church' schools. They had been
brought up in a country where 'the Church', which meant the
Roman Catholic Church, was more bitterly anti-semitic than
the State; they had been kept shut in their family homes on

Good Friday to avoid being beaten up by pious and ignorant church-goers avenging themselves for the death of Jesus. Their Polish experiences had so eaten into their souls that they never quite believed that Christianity in Australia was not Christianity in Poland. This left them with no stomach for 'church' schools of any denomination, nor for any religion.

But for me, Jessie and Joan and Elwood Central complicated even more the puzzle of religion. It was impossible to ignore at school, since the Christian message was taken for granted as the standard, the aim, the good to which we all aspired. Our school provided religious instruction every Tuesday morning and we had either publicly to opt out, or to go along. The Jews, the few Catholics who did not go to the parish school, and those Protestants who did not approve of the form of instruction came along with notes to say that they were not to attend. Every Tuesday morning we used to spend first period playing 'Puss in the Corner' in the smelly shelter sheds. We were not allowed to come to school after first period, I suppose, because the roll had already been called, or for some other bureaucratic reason, or perhaps because the Education Department feared that privilege would create a sudden increase in the number of Catholics or Jews. Anyway, there we were: Adele Segal, Betty Phillips, Margery Berman, Norma Phillips, Amirah Gust and the Catholics and sectaries whose names I have forgotten. All the others had been sent along with notes from their parents saying that they had *religious* reasons for abstaining. My parents thought that this would be hypocritical for us, since we were not religious, so I was sent to school with a note saying that we didn't believe in any religion.

I had to agree with this in principle but it did seem a bit much when on Yom Kippur (the Day of Atonement) every other Jewish kid was allowed to stay home from school but I was sent along.

'Can't I stay home today?' I would beg, thinking of a day spent mucking about and reading.

'Do you believe in God? Are you going to fast? NO! Then why should you have a holiday? That's dishonest!'

I suppose it was. So off I went. But I took secret revenge on their probity in my last year. First period and I put up my hand. 'Please, Miss Egan, I can't write today.'

'Oh,' enquired the concerned but stern Miss Egan. 'Why not?'

'It's a very special Jewish holiday and I'm not allowed to write,' I proclaimed.

'Would you like to go home?' she asked. She was too kind, I suppose, to ask me why I had bothered to come at all and not suspicious enough, or perhaps as it was now 1939 she may have heard about the Jews and their troubles in Europe and hesitated to add to them in Elwood.

'No thank you. I can stay in the class, but I can't write,' I answered solemnly. And stay I did for part of the time, until someone decided that a non-writing pupil might as well be sent out into the little garden in the front, where I spent the rest of Yom Kippur reading until school was let out.

I was never made to feel uncomfortable by this mark of difference. No one treated us badly for not going to religious instruction. As I remember, we were never jeered at or commented on when we came into class each week after it was over. At school, religious instruction was something everyone had to endure; perhaps we were considered lucky.

The Europeanness, the Jewishness perhaps, of my parents began to embarrass me more and more as I approached the end of my years at Elwood Central, although it was never commented on and I was treated by my school mates as an equal. My mother used to talk to me on the tram as we rode into the city and, each time the tram stopped, she went on talking, her accented voice and her moving hands making us both painfully conspicuous in a tram full of women who sat, it seemed to me, with their hands folded neatly in their laps, expressionlessly staring at us. This was the time of the first arrival of the 'reffos' — Austrian and German refugees from Nazi anti-semitism, in particular refugees from the horrors of the 'Crystal Night' at the end of 1938 when, after a Jewish boy shot a Nazi diplomat in Paris, Nazi supporters burned synagogues and smashed shops, and 'mediaeval atrocities' all over Europe were reported in our daily newspapers. To Australians these refugees were alien-looking people: they wore long overcoats and carried brief-cases; they talked in outlandish foreign languages; some waved their hands when they talked; and, what was worse, they did it all on Melbourne trams, with the *men* paying their fares from small *purses!*

I wish that I could say now that my reactions to them were quite pure, that I welcomed them with open arms and uncritically as the first victims of a policy that would end in unbelievable horror. But I can't say that I did. The Commonwealth Government disliked them; the President of the Victorian Jewish Advisory Board issued a press statement saying that it was not in the best interests of the Jewish community already here to face a large influx of Jewish refugees. I felt embarrassed by them.

I was one of them, but I knew how my fellow pupils spoke of them and I heard 'Why can't they speak English?' 'Why can't they speak more softly?' 'Look at those overcoats!' and I didn't answer back. And instead of talking on to my mother during the deadly silence of the tram stops, *I* would fall silent, look out the window, wish she'd behave like everyone else, and offend her by my coolness.

Amirah: An Un-Australian Childhood (1989; FIRST PUBLISHED 1983)

Theatre of the absurd

ANDREW RIEMER (1936–), WRITER AND ACADEMIC, CAME TO AUSTRALIA FROM BUDAPEST IN 1947. KNOWING NO ENGLISH, HE STARTED SCHOOL AT HURLSTON PARK PRIMARY SCHOOL IN SUBURBAN SYDNEY.

I cannot adequately describe the sense of total desolation that descended on me during those first days. I can state my condition: I understood almost nothing of what went on around me—none of the instructions the teacher seemed to be giving; nor the significance of the map he unrolled in order to explain something; nor the radio broadcast to which we had to listen. These things may be stated; but I find it impossible to convey the experience of living in a state of almost total incomprehension, of being cast into a group governed by elaborate rules and mechanisms which you cannot comprehend. I was surrounded by a world where things happened, where things were done, where certain actions had consequences, without possessing any ability to discover what was expected of me. What was the strange chant that the class took up at one point? Why did one of the boys get called out to the front to receive a couple of whacks with a stick? What was the point of the teacher's joke that sent the whole class into gales of laughter? Of course there was some trickle of understanding: I realised that the chanting had something to do with numbers; I knew that the boy got whacked because he had been making a great deal of noise. The joke, on the other hand, remained totally incomprehensible – like the many migrants and aliens, I was beginning already to nurture a healthy crop of paranoia: was I the butt of that joke? [...]

I was treated with sympathy and a degree of kindness, apart from one or two roughnecks who jeered at me and mocked my prissy ways. People were well-meaning but bemused; they did not know what to do with me. They had been called on to deal with a kind of deaf-mute in striped socks. Their solution to the problem I posed was, in the circumstances, understandable, though at the time it produced much distress and anxiety. I remained in that limbo for a couple of weeks, growing increasingly isolated behind a wall of incomprehension. At least the bright socks had been retired and my road to assimilation had begun. My parents had mustered enough precious clothing-coupons to buy the thick woollen shorts and other heavy gear children wore in that humid, stifling autumn.

Finally, a note addressed to my parents was handed to me one day. At home, with the aid of a dictionary, we deciphered its message: I was to be transferred to a 'Special Class', which everyone at the school, teachers and pupils alike, always referred to as the Idiots' Class. It consisted of a group of thirty or so children of widely varying ages and uniformly abysmal intellectual capacities who were sequestered in it until they reached school-leaving age. What became of them afterwards was, clearly, no concern of the authorities.

My classmates were a collection of largely amiable children, most of them far too handicapped and individual in their freakishness to be conscious of my difference. Several had obviously insisted on wearing clothes as idiosyncratic as mine had been during my first days at school. In retrospect I see them as an oasis of individuality in that undifferentiated, conformist world. They were able to evade the iron rules of convention because, in a sense, they were beyond the bounds of social norms, just as I, in my alienness, fell outside such confines.

Their eccentricities and disabilities revealed themselves in spectacular ways. One large girl spent most of the day sitting impassively at her desk without the least trace of a response or reaction to anything that went on around her, except when an attempt was made to teach us arithmetic. That brought her to life with a dazzling and vivacious display of mental-arithmetic skills. She was a virtuoso in reeling off answers to complicated sums in a clear, high-pitched voice wholly devoid of inflection

— or so I got to learn in my last weeks in that class, when I had
achieved a degree of understanding. One small boy would occasionally suffer convulsions; people rushed to place a solid object
between his teeth once he started writhing and wriggling. A
great hulk of a boy who sat next to me — his name was Clive
— dribbled constantly from his gaping mouth. Another child
threw up at least once a week. Others proved incapable of con-
trolling their bladders; a squeal would, from time to time, go up
in the classroom: 'Sir, Neil's wet himself again!'

This chaotic world was supervised by a particularly clapped-
out old man. He was even more decrepit and moth-eaten than
the other teachers at the school, all of whom had obviously
stayed on during the war years, getting older and older, more
and more passive, incompetent and irresponsible, refusing to
move aside for the hastily trained ex-servicemen who were clam-
ouring for the right to be employed. The old teacher's attempts
to suppress the frequent bouts of anarchy that periodically
shook the classroom were purely ceremonial. The scene was
Dickensian in its exaggerated grotesquerie. The teacher — I
have long forgotten his name — would threaten the most dire
and bloodcurdling of punishments if we didn't cut it out this
moment, immediately. No-one paid any attention because
many, like myself at first, did not understand much of what he
was saying. He would wait with resignation for that mysterious
moment when, as if by common consent, the uproar ceased,
and the class was again seated quietly at its desks as models of
exemplary behaviour. In those brief periods of truce, he would
make an attempt to instruct us.

His pedagogic ambitions were, quite understandably, modest.
He tried from time to time to teach us to chant the simpler tables,
but only the silent girl was able to master their intricacies. He
made occasional attempts to teach us how to spell some of the
words in the thin, grey-covered primers in use at the time, or to
get us to read in chorus a page from *The School Magazine*. None

of his attempts met with much success; most of our days were taken up with various manual tasks — endlessly marbling sheets of paper, producing miles of French-knitting and hundreds of pom-poms in brightly coloured wool. We enjoyed that hugely; these were always the happiest and most peaceful of times. Sometimes we made simple wooden figures by gluing clothes pegs together, or coloured in crudely stencilled shapes on sheets of yellowing paper. From time to time he tried to teach us a few songs: 'Ho-ro my nut brown maiden' and 'The Maori's Lament'. Occasionally he would give up, staring vacantly through the grimy windows of the classroom at the powerlines outside, until the rising tide of anarchy made him leap to his feet to threaten us with the most fearful thrashings, which he never carried out.

I should probably feel resentment for my seven or eight months' confinement in that Idiots' Class. I have always found it hard, however, to whip up much anger. When I descended on that unsuspecting and unprepared school, which had never experienced anyone as exotic as I was in their eyes, they did, I suppose, the best they could for me. In contemporary Australia there are structures designed to help migrant children learn English and to adjust to their new environment and to alleviate, if that is possible, the anguish and distress most of them experience. Indeed, there are institutions designed specifically to encourage them to retain their native language and culture. Such things were undreamt of in 1947 when people like my parents and I represented the first trickle of non-English-speaking migrants to have reached the country for many years. What else could that decrepit and probably ill-funded institution have done with me? It was, after all, a small suburban school catering for families of no great educational ambition or sophistication, whose children would all leave school as soon as possible to work in factories or to marry at a pathetically early age to become careworn, prematurely aged grandmothers in their early thirties. I was for them no different from the incompetents who were marooned in that class, colouring-in and French-knitting their lives away, because I lacked, as they did, the skills on which the social and economic system was based.

My physical appearance alone excited the curiosity of the people in that school. Otherwise they remained detached and uninterested; no-one showed any inclination to ask about the world I had left — even if I had been able to tell them about it at all coherently. They could not conceive that I was a refugee from Venice and the Midget Theatre, from nights at the opera, and from the arcane social rituals of prewar Central Europe. Such things were meaningless for them. My membership of the Special Class was merely a formal acknowledgement of the general predicament my parents and I faced — handicapped and disadvantaged through our inability to communicate, lacking those skills of language that provide the grounds for a community's existence and self-definition. The Australia of 1947 could not have found tolerable the babel of tongues envisaged by the more idealistic contemporary advocates of multiculturalism.

Inside Outside: Life Between Two Worlds (1992)

Public Library, Melbourne

BRUCE DAWE (1930–), POET, WAS BORN IN GEELONG, VICTORIA, AND NOW LIVES IN QUEENSLAND.

Three kids came sandshoe-quiet through the door
crowding together defensively against
The multiple ambush of Argus-eyed belief
Aimed at them from every tiered wall.
Go easy, kids, here sleep your history's parents
Coffined in vellum, decently laid out,
But ruling from their dry octavo tombs.
Give over grinning, boys, and stand up straight,

Respect your elders, park that chewing-gum:
Ancestor-worship is our mutual mineral
Deep in the blood and never to be shed.

Pull down your baseball caps, spin on your heels,
Let the door close softly behind you with a sigh;
A frail balloon of merriment eludes its hinge
Ascending gently to the glass-domed sky.

No Fixed Address: Poems (1962)

The tyranny of niceness

MARY ROSE LIVERANI (1939–), WRITER, BORN IN GLASGOW, CAME
TO AUSTRALIA AT THE AGE OF THIRTEEN, AND WENT TO SCHOOL IN
WOLLONGONG, NEW SOUTH WALES.

'Sorry about interrupting you, Mrs Mahon,' the Deputy said,
drawing me behind him into the classroom. 'I've got a new wee
girlie for you. A lass from Glasgow.' He turned to the faces
above the desks. 'Good morning, one bee.'

His name, it seemed, was Mr Whittle, and the name must be
used when saluting him. Miss and Sir were no longer acceptable
titles. If you said: excuse me, Miss, you would hear giggles and
if the lady were married she would react indignantly: MRS
Brown, if you please.

'This is Mary Lavery. She's from Scotland.' Evidently he felt
it necessary to locate Glasgow. 'She's probably feeling very
strange.' This was an effort of imagination I wasn't often to
encounter at school. The Deputy squeezed my arm. 'How long
have you been out, lass?'

'A week, sir.'

'Uh huh. Well, you'll find this class a particularly nice lot
of boys and girls who'll be only too pleased to help you settle
in. You'll be an Aussie before you can say Robert Burns.' This

statement contained a number of horrific assumptions that weren't immediately apparent to me, though it didn't take too long to work them out.

First, niceness is a virtue preceding all others. To be nice is better than being stimulating, or analytical or witty. You must always say 'How are you', or 'How are you going', nicely, but without expecting an answer. If some fool starts to tell you how he is, keep smiling but walk off and leave him with his jaw dropping, or keep smiling and stare at his right ear lobe. Then he will dry up and smile nicely, asking you how you are.

Second, people always want to settle, like old hulks settling into the mud. People don't crave drama or excitement or uncertainty. Make sure they set hard.

Third, people always want to be Australian.

If you aren't you can get by with a particular note of apology.

'I'm not yet, but I'm doing my best.'

The Deputy, his warm welcome at an end, spied me out a seat and directed me to it.

'There you are. There's a seat beside Wendy. She's a bit of a yakker, so don't let yourself be tempted.'

The girl he was portraying giggled and cooed:

'Oh, Mr Whittle, that's defamation of character. I'm as dumb as a mummy.'

All the class laughed at this, and the Deputy smiled benignly.

'Well, there's someone awfully like you, sitting in your seat, who never takes a breath.'

He looked across at the teacher, for support.

'Isn't that right, Mrs Mahon?'

It was, evidently. I sat down amid the confusion of laughter and noisy chat that erupted suddenly in the room, and the Deputy left. Another rule: seek out humour in the banal or you will be isolated from the fellowship of laughter.

'That will do, one bee.' The teacher was tightening her mouth. Little lines sprouted from her top lip. The Deputy had gone, leaving not one reverberation of his wit. 'We must get this prose finished or there will be no time for revision before the exams.'

During the lesson, Wendy began a non-stop monologue to which I responded with nods of the head. So you're Scottish. I'm English, from Kent. We came out in 1950. Have you done French? She's a real drip, Mrs Mahon. Always tired. All the teachers are, except Mr Whittle. He teaches maths. I'm going to a private school next year. Mum and Dad think this school's too rough. We have sport every Wednesday. That's today. It's compulsory. Do you like sport? You can choose between swimming, softball and tennis. I play tennis. Of course you wouldn't have your costume here. Swimmers, the Australians call them. So you'll probably have to play softball. How did you do at school in Scotland? Are you any good at French?

I was trying to remember the word for mourning. I'd seen it somewhere.

'Oh, all right,' I whispered. Was she never going to shut up? *Le deuil*, that was it. This passage was from *Jean Christophe*.

'Right, class, get on with it.' Mrs Mahon dropped her chalk into the groove under the board and moved sideways to her desk. 'If you don't get it finished before the bell goes, you can finish it for homework.'

'Aw geez, you're tough,' someone groaned.

Colloquial language and familiarity of tone are permissible when speaking to the teacher. A formal mode of approach will only make him ill at ease and he will avoid your eye. He might even think you are being insolent. You are not to exalt him. He doesn't think he is worth it. To obey him will be enough. It will establish the difference between you.

I couldn't remember the French for some words, so I left blanks and concentrated on the verb endings. When I lifted my head, I saw the teacher watching me. Blast. I've caught her eye. Now she's coming to examine my work. She's got a queer hair style. Flat to the head. I really hate that, especially when it's grey. Dreary. And those loose little curls all round the bottom. Pin curls, not very well formed, and straight bits poking out. Wonder why she wears such a low necked dress when her skin's all shrivelled at the front?

The teacher wrote in the missing words for me and dangled her pen above each verb like a divining rod, seeking out the wrong inflections. Apparently satisfied there were none, she ticked the passage and initialled it. Then, in an embarrassingly loud voice that got the attention of the whole class, she said: 'Very good, girlie. I can see we won't have any problems with you.'

You don't see much then, do you?

Wendy stiffened beside me. Her whisper, despite its softness, was softly disapproving.

'Are you a brain or something?'

It sounded like: Are you a Catholic?

Careful. 'Heavens, no. I've read some of the book that passage is from.'

'What! In French?'

Her whisper vanished in a squeak.

'Well, actually, our teacher read to us.'

How is she taking it?

'Aw, you were lucky, then?'

Ah that was it. Luck, luck. I grinned with relief. 'Yes, I was, wasn't I?'

The Winter Sparrows: Growing Up in Scotland and Australia (1977; FIRST PUBLISHED 1975)

Role play

JILL ROE (1940–), HISTORIAN AND ACADEMIC, WAS AT YALLUNDA
FLAT PRIMARY SCHOOL ON SOUTH AUSTRALIA'S EYRE PENINSULA IN
THE 1940S.

In the schoolroom girls were tops and in the yard boys ran
things. Parents would lament that their boys were so unscholar-
ly, and how they would regret it in later life, but the fact was that
they were there to become small farmers, they wanted to be
nothing but small farmers, and what we did in recess and at
lunch time was play farms.

We played farms endlessly. The game was called 'little'. It was
an exact replica of what was going on in the farms of the community. And the boys ran that area of our lives.

The boys weren't particularly interested in academic work.
All through my rural education the girls were scrupulous, interested, quiet and good. The boys were troublesome. At best they
didn't have too many ink blots on their books and were quiet
until allowed to get on with the real business of sport and farms.

'Little' was quite imaginative. Everything that came to hand
was used to reproduce the farming season and life. Pine cones in
various stages were used for sheep, cattle and horses. Other bits
and pieces scattered around were used to make roads and buildings. Paddocks were laid out. A good size farm at Yallunda Flat
school was five feet by ten. Everything that went on there was
supposed to reflect what went on in the wider society. The land
was scratched into furrows. When it rained the land was turned
over again. After harvest there was burning-off in the surrounding stubble, and attempts were made to burn-off in the school.
I blush to say that I managed to set the school yard on fire.
Fortunately it didn't go too far because stinkweed, which covered half the yard, is evergreen and unburnable. But everyone
had to come and put it out.

The game was nomadic. Weeks would go by then someone would see better land down the yard, and slowly we would all shift. At times we would play other games. But the ruling game was 'little'.

HANK NELSON, *With Its Hat About Its Ears* (1990; FIRST PUBLISHED 1989)

Mad habits

GERMAINE GREER (1939–), AUTHOR OF THE INFLUENTIAL FEMINIST WORK *The Female Eunuch*, WAS BORN IN MELBOURNE AND EDUCATED AT STAR OF THE SEA CONVENT, GARDENVALE.

At the time, the Star of the Sea Convent seemed to me a very big, forbidding, grey Gothic building with a tarmac yard like a prisoners' exercise yard. Of course when I went back there seventeen years later it was just a little place, a sweet, little school.

I remember all the nuns vividly. There was Sister Raymond who taught me about art. She had big round bosoms and big round hips and she loved art even though she'd never seen any. She'd never seen anything. Yet she used to stand there pointing to these pictures saying: 'Look at it, it's beautiful! Oh, look it's really beautiful!' I sometimes wonder what it would be like if I took her with me round Europe and said: 'You remember, you taught me about Chartres. Well this is Chartres and this is what it looks like.' And Durham. Every time I go there I can hear that voice saying: Look! It's beautiful!

Then there was Sister Cyril who taught us French and who was very frail and rather sensual and feminine. When men came into the room to do things like mend the window catch she used to practically writhe herself into conniptions. We decided she was a pretty sad case.

There was Sister Philip who taught us Chemistry and who I remember because I hit her with a softball straight into the front of her coif, which crumpled it and knocked her flat. I remember everyone. Sister Michael who taught me German and who had a face that looked as if it had been scrubbed hard with steel wool. And Sister Attracta, who taught us singing. I'll always remember Sister Attracta. she really did wonders with us. I sang three or four times a week in a madrigal choir. We sang Masses, we sang operetta, we sang everything. I'm still singing the same things, thirty-five years later.

I especially remember Sister Eymard who tried to teach me the philosophical proofs of the existence of God, and thereby destroyed my faith completely because she didn't know them. Rather, she did know them but they weren't valid. She was always in a hurry — the sort of nun who would go through a room rearranging all the furniture with her habit. There was one room in the convent where we were never allowed to go — the parlour — unless it was very important. For some reason I was waiting in there one day when I heard an enormous crash outside in the corridor. I opened the door and peeped out and there was Sister Eymard on her back having skidded on the drugget down the middle of the corridor. All I know was that I was not to go and pick her up; I was to shut the door very quietly and just go back and sit on the horsehair sofa until somebody came. Poor Sister Eymard. In the end she got run over, probably because she was charging across the road without looking.

I think one of the reasons why I was never properly domesticated is because I was actually socialised by a gang of mad women in flapping habits. I'm more like them than I am like my mother. I owe them more in a way because they loved me more and they worked harder on me than my mother did. They really loved us. I realise that now, although I didn't realise it at the time.

They were very excited to have such a clever little girl in the school and anything I did was all right with them. I was forgiven within two seconds because I'd say something funny or clever.

They brought out the best in me and it needn't have been brought out, it could have stayed right where it was. I could have married a stock-broker and settled into a life of three cars and a carport. They made that impossible because I was hungry for something else — spiritual values. Just not their spiritual values.

I was always in trouble but I always came bouncing back for more. The nuns used to say I took correction beautifully, but then they gave correction beautifully. Having been a teacher myself it was the orderliness of the school that impressed me most. The calm, and the fact that we were disciplined in soft voices. The worse trouble you were in, the softer the voice. They'd deliver this rabbit killer punch in a soft, soft voice. If you were being really rambunctious and a pain in the neck you'd be asked to leave the room. You'd be standing outside the room, thinking: Oh God, it was pretty boring in there, but it's much more boring out here. Every time, along would come Reverend Mother, the silent padding presence in the corridor. She'd come silently down the corridor just looking for someone like me and say: 'Well Germaine? What's the trouble?' And I'd say: 'Oh, I said I didn't think Communism was the work of the devil.' And she'd say 'Oh, Germaine, you could be a great saint or a great sinner. The choice is entirely up to you.' I'd be thinking: 'great sinner, great sinner!'

I think all girls' schools are fairly hysterical institutions. I'm very fond of women in groups. I want to see women being happier in their groups and less apologetic for them. I like the way women laugh without self-consciousness when there are no men around. If you go into a pub you won't hear women rolling on the floor with laughter. You'll hear the polite responses to men's jokes. You won't hear too many jokes by women either, because they're watching someone else's performance. When you're within convent walls or college walls then the women's innate creativity has to come out. So, we were uproarious and the nuns were uproarious too. They were all droll and mad in their particular ways. They didn't conform to any stereotype, they were all different.

JACKIE BENNETT & ROSEMARY FORGAN (EDS), *There's Something About a Convent Girl* (1992; FIRST PUBLISHED 1991)

Formulae for life

JACK WATERFORD (1952–), EDITOR OF THE *Canberra Times*, WRITES OF HIS NEW SOUTH WALES COUNTRY SCHOOLING AND HIS CATHOLIC BOARDING SCHOOL IN THE 1950S.

We lived 30 miles out of town, on a road three miles in from the main boundary. Our mailbox was a 44-gallon drum with one end opened, and the routine of the mailman was that he would come down the road, dropping off mailbags at each box, go to the next town, have a jar or two, then go back picking up mailbags from the boxes as he went. Each mail would contain a week's correspondence lessons.

I would ride out to the mailbox with the mailbag, its key and a pencil, and when the mailman came, open up the week's lessons, sit astride the 44-gallon drum and do them. One had to cheat a bit. I always copied out the dictations, making a deliberate error or two. When it was done — an hour or two's work — it would go back into the envelope, and, the job done, that was my week at school. The best days of my life.

Within a couple of years, I had two sisters also on correspondence. My mother became somewhat more conscientious, even trying to set up a school room in our house. One dread year, she hired a governess from Sydney to supervise us. We were horrid to her, though the local lads for miles round were not; I do not think we ever had so many visitors in our life.

When I was nine my mother threw in the towel, and my sisters and I went off to school by bus each day. At the local town I discovered myself miles ahead of many of my classmates in the amassment of trivial historical facts, and miles behind in things like sums. I fell madly in love with the girl sitting next to me and let her copy my examination papers: we seemed to take it in turn coming first and second. But I was miserably unhappy with the travelling, the dust and the teasing from kids on the bus. So I was sent off to boarding school, and that was where I acquired almost all of my formal education.

It is conventional for people to say such experiences were miserable — mine was not a bit, though I made at least a few teachers' lives miserable and, by the end, was regarded as a 'bad attitude' case. I had marvellous, professional and dedicated teachers who loved learning and who loved their kids, even if, by modern day standards, their ideas of instilling knowledge were at times heavily on the prescriptive and, more than occasionally, on the disciplinary side. They were almost entirely members of Catholic religious orders, but I do not believe for a second that the dedication, quality or idealism of teachers in other school systems was lower. Indeed, teachers in government schools were probably better qualified. But we were all united by common curricula [...]

The school I went to was noted for the ferocity of its discipline, though most of it was focused on having us where we were supposed to be at particular times, rather than on mis-shaping our impressionable minds. Our Latin teacher believed that conjugations and declensions could be drummed in at one end or the other, and declared that he did not care much which. One of the maths teachers taught my classmates and me formulae by belting the backs of our fingers with a ruler, saying as he did it things like 'How many times do I have to tell you, Jack, that $(a + b)^2 = a^2 + 2ab + b^2$'. I can still remember most of my formulae, and occasionally even use them.

Otherwise, we could more or less say what we liked in the classroom and had, I think, rather more academic freedom than most kids of our age at the time. The signal breach of clear freedom that I recall was when I was in Year 12, and an English teacher, a young English honours graduate with a passion for Gerard Manley Hopkins, began declaiming *The Windhover*. Out of the corner of his eye he saw me talking and rounded on me; 'What's that you said, Waterford?' 'Nothing, Brother.' 'I saw you talking. What did you say? Out with it.' I said, 'Well, it looks like Father Hopkins has been on the altar wine again, doesn't it?' I was flogged for that, but it was worth it.

'THE BEST DAYS OF MY LIFE' (1992)

I know where I'm going

GRAHAM LITTLE (1939   ), WRITER AND ACADEMIC, ATTENDED THIR-TEEN SCHOOLS IN THREE COUNTRIES. THE LAST OF THESE WAS MELBOURNE HIGH SCHOOL.

Melbourne High was built like a castle. Its corridors echoed with the feet of boys on parquet-flooring and stone steps. It had high ceilings and a tower that housed two libraries reached by a spiralling staircase. The Hall held a thousand, and was lined with honour boards listing School Captains, Senior Scholarships and Exhibition Winners, but mostly the Old Boy toll in two World Wars. In fact, something obscure to me called 'Legacy' and/or 'RSL' seemed to pervade the school, a psycho-logical companion for the rotten-egg gas that escaped from the chemistry room. Brigadier Langley wept when assembly speak-ers touched on military days, while Bill Woodfull, who followed him as Principal, glared steely-eyed disapproval if a speaker made any reference to his own Bodyline heroism. There were R.I. speakers on Tuesdays: I was impressed by a high church Englishman who mocked the agnostics by giving the Latin equivalent, 'ignoramuses'. John Robinson from Campaigners for Christ, looking and talking like Jim Cairns, hinted at a cer-tain Bad Habit, a hint we were nervous about taking in case we would betray our wickedness by knowledge of the sin. It was from the same platform that I was introduced to the convenient phrase 'in the Southern hemisphere' — as in, 'The best/biggest State school …'

Teachers (not 'masters' now) spoke an approachable language. One called us to order with 'Fair crack o' the whip' and we ourselves made obscene play, actress to bishop, with the goldrush phrase 'Put it away, Mr X, or we'll all have our throats cut'. I abandoned French, embarrassed by the oral work, failed Leaving British History (factory acts, not the War of the Roses) to my patriotic chagrin, and took up Geography as my required 'science'. There I sat next to a boy with a pointed nose and jug ears who collected climates in a contraption he kept in his backyard. Every morning he would give me and my friend who was President of the Railway Club a world run-down: Addis Ababa's precipitation, the Yukon's record freeze, and on-and-on. He never got a Herbertson classification wrong. Another boy rivalled him, jumping up from his seat and going to the blackboard to correct an amazingly long-suffering teacher. As he returned to the back row this extrovert was applauded by a boy in dark glasses and a leather jacket who looked like Elvis Presley and won the Exhibition. These were Rock Around the Clock days, when Morris Lurie drew cartoons in the school paper and the English teacher's private copy of *Barchester Towers* after he'd 'slipped out for a minute', and of Peter Oyston's pained-Pole theatrical beginnings; of another actor, a teacher, called David Niven; of the boy who played Lady Bracknell in the school play turning up in *Truth*. And of two teachers who sent us postcards from their shared long-service leave in Greece, whose names were Dear and Cocks […]

I did time at every type of school. In Ireland there was rural school, Public Elementary and Dames'. In England, besides the high-toned lay Catholic St Anthony's, I went to one of those private schools run by disillusioned Anglican clergy for hopeful parents in the lower-middle class; I had two days at Freddie Titmus's old Grammar School in London, a bit longer at a Secondary Modern in Kent. I've been on both sides of every fence: Irish/English, private/state, Catholic/Protestant, even soccer schools vs. rugger schools; and of course boys-only and co-ed — in fact, there were even two terms of futile violin lessons, going twice a week, at a girls-only convent. I toddled, walked, cycled, rode buses and trolley-buses, trams and trains, and at the end pursued the pleasures of Melbourne High from Mornington, leaving at 6, arriving home at 7, the day dark at both ends but the journey worth it to keep my tally at thirteen […]

The threat of the Real World never seemed so great at Melbourne High, though 1199 boys and 39 teachers — I excuse 'Tappy' Larsen, the music teacher — knew exactly where they were going. The school was virtually a route-march to examination success. I topped English and did miserably at everything else. I founded the Social Services club, supervised by a temporary teacher who was tall with Mandrake hair and a doctorate in Law from Prague. He was the most tortured man I'd ever met, sweating in profuse droplets and whipping into a now extinct pub in Elizabeth Street as soon as our little band of do-gooders descended from the tram opposite the Public Library on our way to stack urine-smelling mattresses for the Brotherhood. I was deeply involved in the Inter-School Christian Fellowship and sang hymns in the Physics classroom with boys who would do medicine, preparing like Liddel in *Chariots of Fire* to join the China Inland Mission. My big moment was when I managed to convert — for a week — the most enviably sex-experienced boy in the form (his girl had probably missed a period). I was shiny-eyed at the fifty-year celebrations, and prickle-backed because a MacRob girl behind me on the bleachers rested her legs against my shoulders. In fact the tantalising presence of a sister school is a tempting solution to the single-sex or co-ed question —

benignly tantalising because, as we ground out our 'Men of Harlech' and 'Honour The Work', we were excited to know that hidden on the balcony behind us they were appraising us, waiting their moment for 'Nymphs and Shepherds' and thinking of Saturday night.

Black Rock, with untended edges to the roads, sand on the footpath, milk-bars with galvanised iron roofs and paint-blistered verandah posts, reminded me of holidays in Ireland where we rented a gypsy caravan fixed among the sand-dunes. In Richmond, St Kilda and Prahran (which took a long time to learn to spell) I discovered the sleep-out. I was shocked and envious. In Northern Ireland the Protestant upwardly-mobile did not live in 'Irish cottages'; I thought my school-mates must be very poor, and of course in 1954 and 1955 families in the inner suburbs probably were. The great thing was how intimate it all was, school and the world: aiming for your matric and listening to the radio when you got home, going down to St Kilda, cap in your back pocket, or to the MCG when you were supposed to be training for the annual marathon. All my English schools seemed to want to be boarding schools. Here teachers came and went in the latest powder-blue Holdens. One boy came to school on a Vespa, pausing to re-arrange his Brilliantined hair before making a splendid entrance. School was reassuringly ordinary, not monastic, not cruel-to-be-kind. We ate Noon pies and vanilla slices ('snot-blocks') at lunchtime, standing next to the incinerator contented in our deep talk as we looked into the factory yards behind the school. Cadet parades, largely composed of third-formers, barely interrupted us as we recited Browning ('My Last Duchess') and weighed into Hardy, especially the Christians.

I did not know it but all the time we were on the Top State School's escalator to matric success and a blitz on first year 'Uni'. There the escalator suddenly stopped and Melbourne High boys were thrown off in such numbers as to inspire academic research for years to come. British History that year, following the turn-about colonialism of the time, was Australian History: First Fleet, Hume and Hovell, Gold Rushes, Marvellous Melbourne, Bank Collapse, Harvester Judgement. It engaged me much less than Brahms in Mus. App., an oasis of sound in a school day. But I felt sympathy for the teacher, whose notorious colleague spoonfed his class with notes and went to football pie nights and sat on the Examination Board. I got a first in this very non-Tudor history, achieved by rote learning most of Clark's *Select Documents in Australian History*. This volume attracted my attention, initially as it were, by a printing error on the dust jacket: the title page clearly read C.M.H. but the jacket, print-ed in its thousands, had C.H.M. If the Real World could make mistakes like that — I was an early reader, you may recall — then perhaps I could work my way through it after all.

My last school slid away from me in the amber gloom of South Yarra railway station, after our sixth-form dinner. I had to wait alone for the Frankston train, not minding having to walk the six miles on to Mornington. Exam results came out in January, but you couldn't live on a Commonwealth Scholarship. In February I started at Mayne Nickless, promising myself I'd do Dutch at Taylor's on Wednesday nights and get into Arts. I tallied work sheets and made up the monthly accounts, worked the branch (three-line) telephone switchboard and toured the workshop to take the mechanics' lunch-orders. Two of them reminded me of the Da Silvas — giants who'd just fled Hungary and didn't know whether to complain that the meat pies were hot and the apple pies cold, or vice versa. I even did some typ-ing, feeling inexplicably hurt when the boss endorsed one letter: 'Excuse terrible typewriting — regular girl away'.

'THE HAPPIEST DAYS OF YOUR LIFE' (1987)

Y-Cough

JAN OWEN (1940–) IS AN ADELAIDE POET WHO HAS WRITTEN EVOCA-
TIVELY ABOUT CHILDHOOD, TIME, AND MEMORY.

Sir was hooked on Y-Cough,
there wasn't a doubt —
empties in three spare lockers,
quick nips out,
specially in Maths,
and not a cough for months.
The boys all liked him though:
when Hughes or Sincock
whooped and choked
on Sir's return,
high above it all,
he'd hand out
Bonnington's Irish Moss,
a sparkling smile,
and fifty lines.

Blackberry Season (1993)

The hidden curriculum

ROSALEEN LOVE (1940–), WRITER, RECALLS LIFE AT IPSWICH
CENTRAL SCHOOL FOR GIRLS AND HOW, IN 1951, CLASSROOM ACTIVI-
TIES TOOK ON A LIFE AND MEANING OF THEIR OWN, REMOTE FROM
THE INTENTIONS OF THE QUEENSLAND EDUCATION DEPARTMENT.

My Grade Five teacher was a drug addict. Each day she'd come
into the classroom, look at us all, shudder, and take out a Bex.
She'd unwrap the paper with care, jiggle the powder into a corner and raise it to her lips. She'd swallow it dry. She was into the
hard stuff.

She blamed the girls in Grade Five for her ferocious headaches. Gaunt, mad-eyed Miss Wilson, she terrified us all.

I look back on primary school as a time of horror. When I was eight my family moved from Sydney to Ipswich, and I left the safe haven of the progressive Sydney system for a system stuck somewhere half a century behind. There were some good teachers despite everything, but Miss Wilson was not one of them. She hated us all. She hated the slow learners for being 'stubborn' and she hated the bright kids because they were too smart by half and consequently 'stuck up'.

She was particularly hard on Elizabeth. Elizabeth would never learn her seven times table, no matter how often she was whacked for her stubbornness. Elizabeth knew it. Elizabeth wasn't stupid. Elizabeth was made to sit in the front row, so she could be more easily thumped for getting things wrong.

The smart kids sat in the back row. We spent our days reading under the desk.

Years later, Bex was banned. It contained phenacetin which often caused serious kidney damage leading to death. Miss Wilson was caught in the vicious cycle of dependence. She took Bex to relieve the headache which in turn was caused by the powders. Miss Wilson gave us a daily lesson in drug education long before the topic was placed on the formal curriculum.

One day Coca Cola went on sale in Ipswich, for the very first time. We were as excited about the event as our children would be about the day the first man walked on the moon. On that great day, Miss Wilson fronted up to Grade Five with an open bottle of Coke in her hand. She took out her usual Bex and swallowed it.

Everyone knew if you had a Bex and drank a Coke you got hopelessly drunk. It was true. It was the talk of the schoolyard.

What was she thinking, Miss Wilson, as she looked out over her class that hot afternoon and saw all those bright attentive faces? Didn't she know that Bex and Coca Cola made an explosive mix? Didn't she care? What did she make of Elizabeth, her eyes alert and shining, following every move of the Coke bottle, every grain of the Bex as it slid into the open mouth?

We were waiting for Miss Wilson to get legless. We waited all afternoon in high anticipation. But Miss Wilson didn't fall over, dead drunk. It was a terrible disappointment. The story wasn't true. We learned the power and the futility of wishful thinking. We learned of the unreliable nature of urban myths.

Miss Wilson did one good thing for me, though I hated her for it at the time. There was a tacit understanding that the girls in the back row could read under the desk as long as they didn't get caught.

One day I got caught.

'Rubbish!' cried Miss Wilson as she pounced. She threw my Enid Blyton magazine down on her desk.

I never saw that magazine again.

I'd read half-way through a story. It probably was rubbish, but I liked it. Whatever happened next? How did that story end? I spent all my time for weeks afterwards, thinking it through, first with one ending, then another.

I was a ten year old post-modernist junkie in search of her closure fix. The desire has never left me.

Unpublished manuscript (1996)

Portrait of the critic as a young man

Robert Hughes (1938–), art critic and historian, was a boarder at the Sydney Jesuit school, St Ignatius, Riverview.

'Would it not be a good idea, ah, Robert,' Father Wallace asked me one day, 'if you were to put your poetical abilities to the, ah, service of your school? We do not, as you know, have a school song.' It was my first commission, but I declined it, and joined a Catholic Action group instead: once a fortnight, I preached to an audience of apathetic lovers and hostile Baptists in a Sydney park.

The Jesuits were appeased, but suspicious. 'Robert's intellectual interest in the truths of Catholic doctrine is admirable but does not seem supported by simple Faith,' one of them noted on my end of year report, perceptively enough, 'I suggest a prayerful reading of the *Imitation of Christ*.' Father Jones was more sanguine. He plied me with tomes on Roman and Greek history, with economic theory, with Maritain's *Creative Intuition in Art and Poetry*, made me captain of the school debating team. Father Wallace, who taught the English Honours class, commenced, as if initiating a novice into the Eleusinian mysteries, to pull out books and hand them to me: *For Whom The Bell Tolls* (I went later to ask him what this metaphor about the earth moving meant, and, painfully and scrupulously, he told me), Kant's *Critique of Pure Reason* (of which I understood not a syllable), and, daringly, an anthology of James Joyce. I left Joyce on a bench beside the pingpong table in First Division. When I got back it had gone. That night, there was a summons to the study-hall. Father Drury, a lean Savonarola with glittering pince-nez, an exponent of *Kraft durch Freuds*, addressed us:

'Boys, today I have made a disgusting discovery. One of the boys in this Division is a reader of pornographic literature. Filth! Filth! I will not expose him to the humiliation of naming him in public, though he deserves it; I shall merely advise him to come to my study at 10 p.m. this evening.'

'Ah,' I thought, and dismissed the matter from my mind. Someone had been caught with a copy of *Man Junior* in his locker. It happened all the time. That and cigarettes. I went to bed.

At 10.5, Father Drury stalked into the dormitory and stood at the foot of my bed. We looked at one another. Father Drury said nothing. 'Goodnight, Father,' I said.

'Is that all you have to say?'

I could think of nothing else.

'I have been waiting for you, son,' said Father Drury, 'for exactly five minutes.'

'Oh?' I said, feeling stupid.

'I am not disposed to this,' Drury snapped. 'Come to my study at once.' I scrambled into my dressing-gown and shuffled after him.

Father Drury closed the door of his study, an ominous gesture, and sat down, steepling his fingers. I remained standing. 'Presumably,' he said silkily, 'you are under the impression, Hughes, because of the powers of your intellect, which are greater than those of the Fathers at this school and indeed superior to the wisdom of the Church, that you have the right to defy authority and corrupt your fellow pupils. Am I correct?'

A fearsome thought occurred to me. *My God, he thinks it was me that stuffed young Darcy.* 'I don't follow you, Father,' I said shakily.

'Indeed? Have you nothing to say?'

'Well, if you'd tell me what this is about — '

'It is about literature, Robert, literature. Your reading habits.' He opened a drawer and produced Father Wallace's copy of *The Essential James Joyce*. 'I take it that you recognize this?'

Relief flooded me. 'Oh, yes, that, it belongs to — '

'I am not concerned with its owner, Robert, the object of my enquiry is to determine how you could bring yourself to import this — filth! — into the school and then have the effrontery to leave it on a bench. Before I punish you, I should like to *know*.'

'Father Wallace lent it to me.'

'You are a liar, Robert. You have lied to me frequently in the past. I now propose to teach you that nothing is gained by lying.'

'Ask Father Wallace.'

'Father Wallace is now in bed.'

'Well ring him or something, Father, I mean, honest — ' I began to babble. Pornography, six on the bum.

Father Drury looked at me. A crinkle of doubt appeared in his forehead. 'Wait outside.' He reached for the telephone. I glued my ear to the door but could hear nothing. At last the door opened. 'Get back to bed, Hughes,' Father Drury snapped.

'Can I take the book, Father?'

'You may not. I will return it to Father Wallace myself. You are obviously irresponsible.'

He did so. The next day, Father Wallace summoned me. 'I think,' he said, clearing his throat grumpily, 'that you had best regard Father Drury's behaviour as proper under the circumstances. You haven't left that copy of *Sweeney Agonistes* lying around, have you? Thank God. Don't. You may go.'

'Flying the black mamba' (1969)

Bravura passage

Clive James (1939–), writer, critic, and television presenter, grew up in Sydney and finished his secondary education at Sydney Technical High School.

My clever lip won me whatever popularity was coming to me at the time, so that I was able to go on finding myself welcome, or not unwelcome, among Griffiths' surfing parties and the school YMCA team that competed annually for the Pepsi-Cola Shield. Indeed among the latter crew I at last found myself a measure of sporting stardom, since the vaulting I had so painfully learned at Boys' Brigade was something of an advance on anything the other Centurions (that was the name of our team) could improvise uninstructed. My feet-through and flying angel-roll on the long box were instrumental in bringing the Pepsi-Cola Shield home to Sydney Technical High — a fact duly announced at school assembly. It didn't sound much of an achievement (and in fact was even less of an achievement than it sounded, since the teams we had defeated looked like pages from a Unesco pamphlet about the ravages of vitamin deficiency) but it was something. I also managed, at the eleventh hour, to be chosen for Grade football. It was only Third Grade, which consisted mainly of rejects from Second Grade, but you were given a fifth-hand jersey to wear and travelled about, meeting similarly decrepit sides from other schools. My position was five-eighth: what in Britain would be called a stand-off half. I had just enough speed and agility to tempt myself into trouble, but not enough of either to get out of it. My short career was effectively finished in a game against Manly, whose two enormous breakaways, like the clashing rocks of mythology, hit me from different directions while I was wondering what to do with the ball. Semi-conscious and feeling like an old car after it has been compressed into a block of scrap metal, I scored against my own side on the subsequent move and thus acquired the tag 'Wrong Way' James.

But at least I was able to have 'Third Grade Football 1956' embroidered in blue silk under the school badge on the breast pocket of my maroon blazer. Senior boys were encouraged thus to emblazon their achievements. My paltry single line of glory looked insignificant enough on its own and ludicrous beside the listed battle honours of the true sporting stars, which extended below their pockets on to the blazer itself. 'First Grade Football 1954. First Grade Football 1955. First Grade Football 1956. CHS Swimming 1952. CHS Swimming 1953 …' My lost companion Carnaby had a block of blue print on his blazer that looked, from a distance, like a page of heroic couplets. As for the Captain of the School, Leslie Halyard, it was lucky he was seven feet tall, since his credits went on and on like the titles of an epic movie.

The blazer was an important item of equipment. I bought mine after I was elected one of the school's eighteen prefects. I came in at number seventeen on the poll, one ahead of the school bell-ringer. Without the Third Grade football credit I never would have made it, and would thus never have enjoyed the heady privilege of supervising detention or of booking other boys for running in the playground. Admission to the rank of prefect was my sole latter-day school success. In other respects I might as well not have come to school at all. Indeed most of my clothes looked as if they had already left. By this time young men's fashions were reflecting the influence of *Rock Around the Clock* and *Don't Knock the Rock*. Another influence was the lingering impact of the bodgie era which had occupied the immediately preceding years. The bodgies had favoured a drape-shape rather like the British Teddy-boys, with shoes the size of Volkswagens and a heavily built-up hairstyle razored square across the neck. The American tennis manager Jack Kramer also played an important part in shaping our appearance, even though his palpable influence was confined to the apex of the head. His flat-top haircut was faithfully reflected by what occurred on top of our own craniums, where each hair rose vertically to the level of a single, imaginary horizontal plane and then stopped dead. Even Halyard, normally conservative in his attire, turned up one day with the top of his head looking as if it had been put through a band saw. Griffiths set up a barber shop in the prefects' room and gave us his skilled attention, checking the results with a tee-square. Well greased with Brylcreem, the side panels of our haircuts were left to grow long and be swept back with an octagonal, many-spiked plastic rake which looked like the inside of an Iron Maiden for butterflies. At the back, above the straight-as-a-die bottom line, a muted duck's arse effect occurred, further echoing the just-vanished bodgie ideal and directly presaging the incoming cultural onslaught of *77 Sunset Strip*, among the first programmes to be shown on Australian television.

Continuing to read downwards, we come to the drape-shape jacket. The emphasis was on heavily padded shoulders and a waistless taper towards a hem line on the lower thighs. Cut to my personal specifications, the drape of my own jacket was so tastefully judged that you had to look for several seconds before noticing how a supernumerary set of shoulders, sloping at a steeper angle, started where the real ones ended. Shirt and ties were something assertive from a shop near Museum station called Scottish Tailoring, the pink, cerise or Mitchell Blue shirt flecked with white and the multi-banded iridescent slub tie cut square at the bottom like a decapitated coral snake. Scottish Tailoring also supplied the peg-top bottle green slacks with the 14-inch cuffs and the personalised fobs. Socks were usually chosen in some contrasting colour to the shirt. I favoured mauve socks myself, since they interposed an arresting bravura passage between the bottle green cuffs and the quilt-top ox-blood shoes with the half-inch-thick crepe soles. Moving, the shoes made a noise like cow pats at the moment of impact. Stationary, they allowed their occupant to lean over at any angle. You will understand that I am describing a representative outfit for day wear. In the evening I dressed up.

Unreliable Memoirs (1980)

Boys who don't pivot

Novelist **DAVID MALOUF** (1934–) grew up in Brisbane, which is the setting for his semi-autobiographical novel *Johnno*.

Moss's Dancing Academy was a gloomy, refined establishment in the basement of an insurance building, where boys and girls of the better schools (non-Catholic) learned dancing, made innocent or not so innocent assignations, and planned the week's social round of barbecues, coming-out dances, end-of-term hops, tennis parties, swimming parties, picnics, and Sunday excursions to the coast. Moss's was eminently respectable and stiflingly genteel. We learned the quickstep, the jazz waltz, the Pride of Erin, the Gipsy Tap — and as a gesture towards the late forties, the Samba, whose respectability was guaranteed by its being the favourite modern dance of Princess Margaret. Tall, bland-faced, utterly unsexy, Mr Moss's 'ladies' were to be seen each week pushing new boys a good head shorter than themselves round the boraxed floor while Victor Silvester oozed sweetly from a radiogram. Those of us who had graduated danced with *real* girls (Test of Manhood) who sat in rows along the wall opposite and waited demurely to be asked. At a clap of Mr Moss's plump, hairy hands, we crossed the floor in a mob, some of us actually *sliding*, and did not actually grab the girls, which was barbarous ('Barbarous' Mr Moss would shout above the melee), but surged and jostled around the most popular of them, insisting breathlessly: 'Excuse me — I was here first! — could I have the pleasure? — get lost! — would you care to dance?' If the young lady said: 'No thank you, I think I'll sit this one out', you asked someone else (never of course anyone close enough to see that she hadn't been your first choice), or slouched off crestfallen to the boys' side of the room, where a group of the shy, the rejected, the frankly uninterested would be gathered around the Coke-box, engaged in a noisy argument about motorbikes or the selection of a team [...]

Test of Manhood ...

I had fallen heavily in my last year for a Somerville House girl called Roseanne Staples, who wore nylon stockings that shifted their lights like mother of pearl and was a G.P.S. diving champion. All one Wednesday at Moss's, and again the next, we danced dreamily under the rafters and I took her afterwards for mint juleps or malteds at the Pig 'n Whistle, a milk bar at the top of town that had been a favourite pick-up place for American soldiers and retained something of its wartime glamour and notoriety. It was regarded as daring and I was out to impress. When the waitress, who looked as if she might remember the place in the old days, slid our milk-shakes down the glass-topped counter, she winked in the direction of the innocent Roseanne and whispered: 'There y'are love. That'll put lead in yer pencil.' I could hardly wait for the week to pass. But on the third Wednesday, as we went whirling across the floor in what seemed to be a most accomplished manner, Roseanne, with a casualness that astonishes me even today, it was so low-keyed, so undramatic, pronounced the words that put an end to our affair, pfft! just like that, and changed the course of my life. Looking straight over my shoulder, in the most neutral tones: 'If there's one thing I can't stand,' said Roseanne Staples, slowly, 'it's boys who don't pivot.'

I was thunderstruck. The pivot — that little side-step and pass at the corner of the floor that I had never quite got the knack of, it seemed so silly, hardly worth worrying about. I smiled wanly and guided her through the rest of the set, closing my eyes and swallowing hard as we approached the corners and wishing Moss's was triangular. *Four* corners was suddenly more than I could bear. Back safe among the boys I waited for something less subtle, like a Gipsy Tap.

So much then for the test of manhood. There were things they hadn't warned us of, pitfalls in the corners of rooms, girls who would expect you to pivot and perform God knows what prodigies. There was also the Cold War, the Cobalt Bomb, premarital intercourse, the death of God — it was a battlefield, as the headmaster had warned us, and I thought with envy of all those old boys whose names were picked out in gold on the honour-boards, lying safe in some corner of a foreign field that would be forever Wynnum or Coorparoo. Ours was to be a quiet generation. It was the little tests that would break us (not forgetting the wives and mothers) and there was no one to help us through.

Johnno (1976; FIRST PUBLISHED 1975)

After the ball

This extract from **Faith Richmond**'s *Remembrance* depicts the annual ordeal of the school social at a Canberra high school in the 1950s.

I know what I'll be wearing to the school social on Saturday. My mother is finishing my outfit. It's the first dance I'll ever have been to. It will be held in the Albert Hall, not far from Parliament and about half an hour's walk up Acton Road till you turn the corner. On the right a bus route highway takes you to the hall. On the left is the avenue of poplars which leads to the new bridge over the Molonglo. I've had a vision in my head for weeks as the dance draws nearer. I see myself stepping from the bus and walking up the path and into the ballroom. I imagine my horror if a boy approaches me across the shiny floor for a dance. And the equal horror of one *not* asking while my class-mates titter and nudge each other and look me up and down because I'm the only one sitting. I know why I'd be the one wall-flower there that night. It's because of my dress.

My mother sits in a deck chair in the side garden. Her screen is positioned to catch the sun, its back section pressed against the prunus tree. Above us is the harsh blue autumn dome of the sky. I can smell the pine tree nearby. I look down the garden and across the Acton flats. One small patch below is bright with yellow broom and over beyond the cricket pitch and pavilion there's a knot of children who wait their turn in a game of rounders. Occasional snatches of their shouting drift up to our garden. My mother whispers as she counts the stitches for the new mittens:

'Fifteen, sixteen, seventeen — that should do.'

She cocks her head to judge:

'No, perhaps a couple more to be safe — *there*.'

I look up at her brown face with its young lines starting round the eyes. She sees me looking and smiles. A questioning smile — as warm as the sun on her knee when I touch it to thank her. My fingers are clenched in my other hand which rests on the grass. I can't tell her. The dress is so pretty. It's taken her weeks to complete. The background is white knitting with pink and blue stylised snow-crystals in a Fair Isle pattern across the chest and round the shoulders. The colours are repeated on the cuffs and round the bottom of the skirt which comes inches below my knees. White knitted socks almost meet the skirt and the Fair Isle snow crystals form a band around their tops. I was able to stop her knitting a cap to match by saying that it would mess my hair for the social. The other girls are wearing flared viyella to just above the knee with full sleeves and coffee coloured lace at the wrist. Some are allowed to borrow their mothers' stockings for the evening and just a touch of lipstick. I heard them talking and felt sick. I want to tell her how beautiful the dress is. How hard I know she's worked. I'd like her to understand how different I'll feel from all the others. I fantasize that we sit casually together and talk almost as equals. I describe my classmates' outfits. She doesn't knit or sew or read, but gives me her exclusive attention.

But such are the delicate, rigid bonds and balances between my mother and me, formed so very long ago and strengthened by my dependency, love and fear, that the possibility of a dialogue like that is just a chimera. I watch her knit the first row. Pink, blue and white strands fall from her wrists across her serge skirt and cling to the thick darned stockings she wears. She lifts her work to show me. The pattern is just starting to develop:

'Look! The beginning of the snow crystals!'

There's a touching innocence about her that's difficult to describe and I grieve inwardly both for myself and for her.

On Saturday evening my sister starts readying herself at six o'clock. I can't swallow my food. I look across the dining table at her shining face. At half past seven she tells me I look nice but she doesn't meet my eyes. To my surprise she even dabs my nose for me with her pink powder.

We walk together in the dark to the end of Acton Road then take the short bus trip to the Albert Hall. There are lights outside and all around it, suffusing the bushes and the trees nearby. I think it looks like Hollywood. My legs and feet are suddenly very heavy. We walk up the long path to the stone lions at the step, passing stiff rose bushes in a formal garden. Girls with glossy curled hair flock round the entrance talking and laughing with nervous anticipation. They twirl around to order showing off their new skirts and laugh self-deprecatingly at their friends' compliments. It's cold enough that their breath comes out in whispers of steam. The boys watch from the sides of their eyes. They press down their scented hair with anxious palms and suck their musk life-savers. The teachers look different all dressed up as we've never seen them before — some minus their glasses.

Inside, the polished floors yawn ahead of me as I look for someone from my class. Lights thirty feet overhead are bright clusters. They illuminate the elaborate cornices. I can see in an ante-room long tables with white ironed cloths and jugs of soft drink at regular intervals. A group of boys scuffles through the door from outside. One of them is pushed ahead by his guffawing friends and sprawls — sliding across the shiny boards on the seat of his pants. The hall starts to fill gradually. Boys one side, girls the other. They pretend not to look across. One boy whistles softly as a senior student strolls through the door in her mother's high heels. I feel everyone's eyes on my legs and school shoes. I look for the toilets in a panic and can't see them. If I could just go somewhere — anywhere — till the ballroom is full and I'm not so conspicuous. Two girls from my year approach me:

'Did your mother make your outfit? It's so pretty.'

They're really trying. But somehow I feel worse — like an object of pity instead of ridicule as I'd expected. As casually as I can manage, I retrace my steps to the front door. Mr Ricks, my science teacher, smiles my way:

'Enjoying yourself?'

I think even *he* is looking me up and down. I barely meet his eyes:

'Yes thank you, but I'm trying to find someone — they might be outside.'

The bus back to Acton Road comes after ten minutes. I walk home slowly to take up time. Mr Carver's light is on in his bungalow. The dog in the house on the other side barks just once when I tread on a stick. There's a rectangle of light on the grass at the kitchen window. I look inside. My father is sitting at the table with his head in his hands. My mother stands near him pouring from the teapot. Her mouth moves and I can hear occasional words. They're talking about the university. As she leaves the room with the tray, the light swings slightly with the movement of her passing and the fridge in the dark corner is momentarily lit by its swaying spill. My father remains there. After some moments his chest heaves in a sigh and he puts his palms on the table, elbows up like a frog, rises slowly and leaves the room.

My mother looks up alarmed when I arrive in the sitting room doorway. Her finger marks her place:

'What on earth are you doing home? It's only just after nine.'

I cross to the fire and stretch my frozen hands out, almost touching the flames:

'Didn't I tell you? They send the first year students home early.'

Remembrance (1989; FIRST PUBLISHED 1988)

Cotton and chiffon

HELEN GARNER (1942–), NOVELIST, WAS HEAD PREFECT AT THE PRI-
VATE GIRLS' SCHOOL, THE HERMITAGE, GEELONG, VICTORIA.

In 1960 I believed that all Jews and homosexuals lived in New
York. I was eighteen years old, dux of a provincial church girls'
school. To my eternal shame I was dumb enough to let them
railroad me into being head prefect: I was a miserable, lonely
boss's stooge. I hit a tennis ball against a brick wall and despite
my elevated status was always picked last in sporting sides.

I did not read the paper. I did not know what the word 'politics' meant, and none of my teachers saw fit to enlighten me. I
was foxed by the faultless aplomb of our sixth-form English
teacher who declared, as we pored mystified over Byron, that
'*sensuous* means *of the senses*: but *sensual* is a bad, bad word.' I
didn't know anything.

Our headmistress, who frightened me, spoke at assemblies
(after the doors to the recessed altar had been trundled shut)
about the goodness of the Lord. 'Think of it!' she cried. 'He
made grass and trees green for the resting of our eyes. Imagine
our discomfort, had He made them red.' This Valkyrie also
informed us from the dais that people with backhand writing
were untrustworthy. My mother wrote backhand and was of a
transparent truthfulness.

In the gloomy dining room smelling of floor wax and nean-
derthal sausages, we fifth and sixth-formers gave one dance a
year. I was a frump, a breastless creature barely past puberty with
hair that wouldn't curl up at the bottom, who blushed in agony
when addressed by man or beast, who was clad stiffly in cotton
while others floated divinely in chiffon with the coveted shoe-
string straps.

Before the event the headmistress summoned us into the
assembly room with its gold-littered honour boards (I always
scanned them for Norah Linton, Saint Norah of Billabong, but

stopped each time, incredulous, at someone called Daintry Gillett) and inspected us for *commonness*.

She dragged me out to the front in my square-necked, high-necked, frump-necked, flat-necked horrible cotton dress with wattle flowers printed on it, my ugly white shoes whose sand-shoe polish was already showing cracks. 'Now why can't every-one be like Helen? Modest and plain.'

> 'At Nine Darling Street', *True Stories: Selected Non-Fiction* (1996)

Melbourne millefeuilles

John Funder (1940–), medical research scientist, writes of his time at two Jesuit schools, St Patrick's College, East Melbourne, and Xavier College, Kew.

In 1949 I was in fifth grade, my last year at the parish primary school, where Bubs to third grade was the province of Sr Edwardine, and fourth to sixth of Sr Augustine. Sr Edwardine was pink, cheery, and nineteen in 1946, the year we both began at St Benedict's. Sr Augustine was vastly old — probably almost fifty — and of very uncertain temper, channelled into pro-longed and vigorous shaking of those found wanting. Sr Edwardine taught us how to do drop-kicks, and once confided to me how much she was looking forward to boiling an egg, gift of some chook-raising parent, for her lunch.

That year the sixth grade class at St Pat's in East Melbourne was by all accounts formidable. They had cut their teeth on a young Jesuit scholastic, and then dispensed with three short order lay teachers. Some genius then employed Mr McConville, retired Warrant Officer from the Royal Australian Engineers, grey dustcoat, medium build. Within a term all was serene, with the sixth grade on track for the long metamorphosis into priests, public servants and professionals for middle-class Melbourne.

In 1950 Father McAreavey taught us Religious Knowledge, and the now cruising Mr McConville everything else — English and Arithmetic, History and Geography. Prodigious feats of memorisation were encouraged: three of us learned seventy-two eight line stanzas of Macaulay 'Lars Porsena of Clusium, by the nine gods he swore…'; note the cultural imperialism of the lower case 'g'. What might best be described as smartarserie was not encouraged: as the only hand up to answer Mr McConville's 'Who knows what a Ghurka is?' the answer 'It's a little green thing that grows on a cucumber bush' brought six cuts, leather strap across open palm.

First Year (alias Form 1, or seventh grade) meant different teachers for different subjects, and a whole new world view — algebra, geometry and trigonometry, Latin and French, as well as everything else. English grammar text was from M. Alderton Pink, Master of Arts, Part 1: not just main clauses and parsing and stuff like that, but the difference between purpose and consequence, and so on. Pedagogically medieval, and stifling all our creative burgeoning: on the other hand, a dollar for every time I've inserted 'although' for 'however' in manuscripts from students and postdocs would be a nice little earner. Inflation-proof, too.

French and Latin were taught by the Rector, known as Bullfrog, in an uncompromisingly simple way: start at one corner of the classroom, teacher's strap raised, student's hand out. 'Mensa' he would say, and then you would continue, down to the ablative singular. We also learnt timing: premature withdrawal of the hand (? cuttus interruptus) would bring an amphibian smile, and 'mensae', gentle invitation to plurals as well. Your neighbour would then get dominus, the middle order all the complexities of the third declension, and so on. Some of us learnt Latin, and others took their cuts; either way, I can think of no more powerful introduction to an attitude of life-long anti-authoritarianism.

We were also introduced to subtlety, in various ways. We learned it as a group, memorably with Fr Fitzgibbon, who professed to be able to tell the time by looking at the position of the sun in the sky. Afternoon recess was from 2.45 p.m. to 2.50 p.m.: on cold, grey, overcast Melbourne winter afternoons we would approach him. 'Tell us the time, Father, please Father, go on, etc.' He'd twinkle, gaze at the sky, purse his lips and then pronounce 'It's jist after a quarter of thray'. Someone with a wristwatch would then pronounce him correct to within a minute. He knew we knew, and we knew he knew we knew, and as a liturgy it provided enormous enjoyment and comfort to all involved.

In Second Year I cringed with embarrassment at the announcement that I was moving from St Pat's to Xavier, and knocked down the Archbishop. St Pat's, founded in 1845, was the original Jesuit school, in the cathedral grounds; Xavier, four miles away on a hill in Kew, had taken over from St Pat's as 'the Catholic Public School' around the turn of the century. The ostensible reason for transfer was that at Xavier I could do Greek; the announcing (lay) teacher knew, and I knew, and the class knew that I knew and he knew, that Xavier and St Pat's occupied different levels in Melbourne's millefeuille society in the fifties.

Archbishop Daniel Mannix was a Maynooth man, leader of the anti-conscription movement in World War I, over six feet tall with a mane of silver hair, fit from his daily walk into the Cathedral from Raheen in Kew. On Mondays, because the bread was stale, I'd be given sixpence for lunch, two meat pies, from the local shop in Victoria Parade. Even at that age keenly interested in food, I devised an episodic stratagem to ensure early access: at 12.25 p.m. or so, hand up, miming acute lower abdominal discomfort. 'Sir, sir please sir, I've got to go.' And so I went, and, miraculously relieved, barrelled up Lansdowne Street, head down, little legs pumping. Around the corner, straight into Dr Mannix, sitting him down, knocking his top hat off, me spinning into the gutter where I lay paralysed by the

dawning enormity of what I had done. He laughed uproarious-
ly, dusted himself off, patted my head and gave me two shillings.
Manna from heaven, meat pies for the rest of the week. Except,
of course, vegetable pasties on Friday.

Xavier was bigger, much bigger, with nearly all the 1953 intake
into Sub-Intermediate from the two prep schools, Burke Hall and
Kostka. This brought a bloom of new friends, from among the
hothouse flowers that comprised the Greek class, Sub-Inter A; my
friends then, such as survive, are among my closest friends today.
There was the novelty of boarders — city kids from pubs, from
interstate or overseas; country kids from Victoria and the
Riverina. The latter were a curious mix of droll and feral, and
commonly got as good as they gave. 'That, O'Connell, is a book.'
'I know, sir, but I don't need to know all that stuff: I'm going back
onto the land.' 'What as, O'Connell, what as: manure?'

Where school spirit at St Pat's had been a sort of resigned
pride, at Xavier it was noisier. The Head of the River was rowed
then on the Barwon at Geelong, despite there being four
Melbourne schools to two in Geelong, presumably to discour-
age recent Old Boys from too close an involvement over the
Friday and Saturday, the Friday night in particular. In 1959 the
pantheon was opened up to another five schools, introducing
further complexity into the maturing millefeuille: well I remember, as a university student, wicked Melbourne Grammar boys
taunting their new peers from Haileybury 'Give us a "haitch"...'

I also thought I should support the footballers of the first
XVIII in their opening match of 1953, against Geelong Grammar
down at Corio, imagining that I would be one of dozens if not
hundreds. Not so: twenty burly footballers, one lantern-jawed
coach, one rotund twelve-year-old. I changed ends every quarter,
sang, 'Hoorick, hoorah, hoorick, hoorick, Xavier, Xavier, Yah yah
yah etc.' happily to myself and the discomfiture of the Geelong
goal umpire, Clyde Packer, elder brother of the more famous
Kerry, and was allowed to give out the orange segments at three-

quarter time. The eighteen-year-old behemoths were mystified but not rejecting, and I was as happy as a sandboy.

Sub-Inter was also *The Gondoliers*, with an all-male cast; for me double jeopardy in terms of cross-dressing: singing contadine, costumed gondolieri. The following year I was judged sufficiently unprepossessing to play Katisha in *The Mikado*, but ultimately banished to the chorus for always singing the soprano line in quartets. After being hit on various bodily parts by eight consecutive balls in an under-14 house match, the umpire helpless with laughter and unable to pronounce leg-before-wicket, I retired hurt and took up tennis. Football was better, but being short and stately my progress was from the under 14Cs to the under 15Ds to the under 16Es to captain of the sixths, finally singing gondolieri.

Most of our teachers were Jesuits — Fr Owens for Latin and Greek, essentially all the way through to two years Matric (Year 12); Fr O'Mahony, ex RAAF, and then Fr Walmsley Smith, in another life an engineer, for Maths; Fr Fitzpatrick for Physics and Chemistry. Gerry Owens was elliptical, elusive, and thrived on the dozen or so in his Greek classes each year. In my second year Matric Wal Smith, at his suggestion, coached me for two hours after school each Thursday, 2.45 p.m. to 4.45 p.m., using early 1940s Cambridge entrance papers, and savouring a packet of 10 Craven As, lighting one off another until they were all gone. Our English teacher was the poet Joe O'Dwyer, whose classes were bravura exercises in finely controlled mayhem; extraordinarily stimulating, rarely about English, ghost of M. Alderton Pink finally laid to rest.

As always, we were dedicated to testing the limits. The school motto was 'Sursum Corda' (Lift up your hearts), which doubled as the name of the school paper. A slight broadening of the vowels could turn it into 'Sursum Cauda' (Lift up your arse); if you got it just right, you would get a sharp look from Gerry Owens. Given the full New Zealand treatment, glottal stop going on no roof to your mouth, you could actually leave the hearer quite unsure of whether he heard 'heart' or 'arse' in the English version.

From the eyrie of forty years on, I believe I was lucky enough to receive a superb education, but as a scientist I don't have control. We had the basics drummed into us, but with humour and matter-of-factness; we were invited to consider, to criticise, and most importantly to wonder. In a loose sense Xavier took the sons of lawyers and doctors and accountants, and turned them into judges and professors and politicians. The Jesuits conveyed a lot more by example than by precept. What they conveyed was a love of learning, a spirit of collegiality, and — most importantly — that we never have all the answers.

UNPUBLISHED MEMOIR (1996)

School without rules

PENELOPE NELSON (1943–), WRITER, WAS AT FRENSHAM, A GIRLS' BOARDING SCHOOL AT MITTAGONG, NEW SOUTH WALES.

'Just been up on Eight. All them idle rich.'

That was the comment of a Central Station railway worker on the squealing, embracing, greeting at fifty paces and panicking that went on in the half hour before the Southern Highlands Express left its platform.

'Got your hockey stick, darling?'

'How about a kiss for Daddy?'

'Give my love to Angie!'

'Bags I get the window seat!'

'Be a honey and pop down and get me a packet of butterscotch, Mum?'

'My God! What have you done to your hair?'

It was the first Tuesday in June 1954. I was eleven. Micky was in Hollywood. My father and I bade each other farewell, quietly by the standards of Platform Eight, and leaving me with Carole

Money, a slightly older girl whom I had known for years, he departed just before the train chugged out. That was a relief because the emotional pitch of some of the mothers was shrill and unsettling. It would not have taken much to start me crying.

In our carriage all eyes were on a beautiful fourteen-year-old who had had her hair cut in a short, feathery style known as an urchin cut. With dark eyes and an animated personality, she was making a dramatic story of her transformation. 'I just sat down and said to him, "Take it *all* off, I'm sick to death of it."'

'But it was so lovely and thick and wavy when it was long.'

'Suits you though, it's nice and glossy, and you've got the profile for it.'

'You look just like Leslie Caron.'

'It looks divine, Sal,' someone said, confirming something I'd heard: Frensham girls used the word *divine* frequently.

After the subject of Sally's new hairstyle had been exhausted — some time before the train reached Strathfield — one of the others asked Carole who the new girl was. She introduced me to the other occupants of the carriage. The girl with the urchin cut was Sally Spurgeon. The pleasantness of Carole's friends, who were all two or three years ahead of me, took the edge off my nervousness, at least for the time being.

Nothing could really have prepared me for the sight of thirty-two unmade beds on an open verandah. No window panes! Fresh air was one thing, but surely in winter term this was ridiculous. 'What happens when it rains?' I asked. Someone explained that in the worst weather canvas blinds could be rolled down. The rest of the accommodation was also very basic — a small wooden changing cubicle with a cupboard and some drawers; showers without shower curtains. And what were these lists of who was to do which chores and who could wash their hair mid-week? Wasn't Frensham supposed to be a school without rules?

I was in North Wing and Gilly wasn't. Nor was Carole. I found myself essentially alone. Somehow or other I got through the day, tagging around with one person or another, until late afternoon. By 6.25 when the dinner bell rang it was cold and dark. Various new acquaintances, struggling into suspenders, lisle stockings, twinsets, tartan skirts and brown cloaks, said, 'There's the bell,' before vanishing into the night. For dinner, we wore our ordinary clothes instead of the brown uniform. I'd just put on my own suspender belt, twinset and pleated skirt. I did not yet know about the compulsory false collar that completed the outfit. (I had two twinsets, a jumper, a dress and two skirts and was naive enough to think that added up to a lot of clothes.) I stumbled down the three ill-lit staircases, went out on to the pebble path, and dashed in the dark towards the dining room. Or rather, in the direction in which I hoped to find the dining room. At last I saw some lighted steps and rushed up them, flustered, sure I would be reprimanded in front of three hundred strangers for being late.

Disaster! It was not the dining room. It was some kind of private room. The principal, Miss Bryant, came out on to the steps, saw that a new girl had lost her way and even remembered my name. 'It's vey vey confusing, isn't it, Penny?' she asked, before redirecting me to my left and telling me no one would be too concerned about my being late on my first night. I need only explain to the 'end' of my table, whichever sixth former it happened to be, about not being able to find the right building in the dark.

Vey vey confusing, I repeated to myself as I scurried on towards the lights and the voices, grateful for her kindness and a little awed by her English accent.

Apart from my dismay at the institutional appearance of North, many of my early impressions of the school were favourable. There were half as many girls as at Kambala and at least ten times as much space. The school felt free and friendly. No lining up. No saluting the flag. No glove inspections. Amazingly, no marks! In theory, the school favoured co-operation, not competition. Workbooks were marked with As, Bs and Cs, and personal comments, but never with numbers.

Every morning we had prayers in the hall, usually led by Miss Bryant. There was always a huge bowl of fresh flowers on the stage behind her. Blossom sprigs seven feet tall were not unusual. The singing was excellent: I found out why when we toiled through practices of any new hymn.

Best of all, there was no sense that every pupil had to be supervised at every minute of the day. During free periods we could read in the grounds, talk to one another, or — my old vice — listen to the radio.

Being new, I had to sleep on the row near the open windows, with my head away from the wall, the two least popular options. I discovered there was a knack to surviving in the semi-open. You made the bed with your own eiderdown wedged between the two army blankets provided by the school. You filled a hot water bottle with the hottest water possible, and put on your bedsocks. Then you burrowed into a sleeping bag made from a sewn-together blanket, and wriggled in between the sheets, under the eiderdown and army blankets. On really cold nights, you jammed the pillow over your face. With any luck, you then fell asleep before the hot water bottle lost its warmth.

Penny Dreadful (1995)

Bush High

JANETTE TURNER HOSPITAL (1942–), NOVELIST, SEES THE TRANSITION FROM HER BRISBANE PRIMARY SCHOOL TO HIGH SCHOOL IN 1957 AS A TURNING POINT IN HER LIFE.

It is one thing to recognise happiness in retrospect and another more vibrant thing altogether to recognise it while you hold it in your cupped hands. The second kind never becomes retrospective; it remains forever accessible, a permanent present-tense glow. That is what the four golden years at Mitchelton High School were, and are, for me. Here is one sharp and objective measure of difference: when I was in primary school, I used to pray each night, quite fervently, that I would die before I woke. It was the only solution I could think of (though the radical powerlessness of outcast children breeds remarkable creative adaptations and inner forms of strength).

And then, on the day after Australia Day 1957, by some miracle of demography and civic zoning, I was catapulted into a parallel universe, a different catchment area. Virtually no one else from my primary school went to Mitchelton High, so I arrived without labels or baggage or stigma. And suddenly I couldn't wait to get up each morning, couldn't wait to get to the railway station, couldn't wait to join the throng which thickened with each mile of the train journey, couldn't wait to talk and argue and laugh with them on the mile-long walk at the other end, from Mitchelton Station to the school.

Some groups bond organically and some don't, and anthropologists, psychologists, social scientists have all brought scholarly attention to bear on the issue of why bonding does, or doesn't, occur. Certainly it occurred with our class, which began its existence as Form 4A1 in 1957 and which matriculated as Form 6A and wrote the State Senior Exam in 1960.

There was, I think, something of the cohesiveness of pioneer settlements about us. Our school, which we entered in the second year of its existence, was quite literally carved out of the wilderness. There were just two buildings on stilts in a small clearing, and the bush pressed in so closely on all sides that lunch-time duty for teachers included first-aid routines for the removal of leeches and ticks. The dense rainforests of Cedar Creek Falls and Mount Glorious were no more than a longish bike ride away. In fact, there were members of our class who lived right in the rain forest, and to whose farms we others would subsequently cycle for weekend hiking and camping.

'Bush High' was the dismissive term used by the established city schools (Girls' Grammar, Boys' Grammar, Churchie,

Brisbane State High, etc.) because Mitchelton High and Kedron High (where the rest of my primary school went) were the first upstarts beyond the circle of Brisbane's old Ivy League, as it were. What protected us in our charmed lives was that we were too isolated at the densely forested fringe of the city, too ignorant, too blithely unaware of social strata to be offended or to feel inferior. We were all blue-collar kids but kids from families who (because of the Depression and the war) had a reverence for higher learning.

It was, and continues to be, one of the supreme values of the Queensland Department of Education, that the best and worst teachers are democratically distributed all over the state. Perhaps it was just the luck of the draw but we had a striking contingent of dedicated and innovative teachers — and it is part of the ongoing pleasure of my 'Mitchie High' years that those teachers who are still living are personal friends. I don't see all of them every year but we stay in touch, write letters, make telephone calls, have dinners together in Brisbane, on the south coast, in north Queensland … wherever Queensland Department of Education scattering, or retirement, has taken them.

They are all of them, dead and living, still dear to me, but I want to pay special tribute to Mary Messer, now in Townsville, who taught me English and Latin; and to Elizabeth Sharpe, now in Southport, who taught me French.

Elizabeth Sharpe seemed to us wonderfully exotic and cosmopolitan. Though she had grown up in a working-class Brisbane suburb, like the rest of us, she had actually lived in Paris as an au pair girl and was fluent in French. She smelled deliciously of the Left Bank and Montmartre and the Jardin du Luxembourg. The very thought that it was conceivable that someone who grew up in Brisbane could just take off and move to Paris … well, it opened tantalising doors in our minds […]

It was also, I suppose, the luck of the draw that the little band of 40 who matriculated together from Form 6A in 1960 were so evenly matched academically, and so eagerly and non-rancorously competitive. In any case we drove each other on to prodigious work and achievement levels. By the time we reached university, when we first actually became aware that in establishment eyes it was academic and social nothingness to have come from Bush High, we could be privately amused by the knowledge. Academically, at Queensland Uni, none of us had any trouble outperforming the private school students. A quite disproportionate number of our small group has achieved statewide, national and international distinction in our different fields — though it is not this fact which is of primary significance for me.

What I cherish most is the rich and permanent bonding, especially of the smaller group within the group, of those of us who rode the train together every day, and walked up the long hill together. I have written in a recent short story that we were 'part of a multi-celled Us-thing' (I owe this image to Les Murray's brilliant poem about cows at milking time); that we were not Other to each other, but were organically and Significantly Us. I can't think of a better way to explain it.

'TURNING POINTS' (1994)

Command performance

Tony Maniaty (1949–), writer, was at Ithaca Creek State Primary School, Queensland, in the 1950s.

Day one, first day. Is this the real start that I've spent six years waiting for? In my head I'm already composing a pretentious little essay for my memoirs: 'It was hot and muggy that January day in 1955. My world shrank at the moment I walked through the archaic iron gates of the Ithaca Creek State School, and with a tilt of the eyes, caught in a single glance all that was ugly in this brick edifice. I must have razed that building a thousand times in my dreams, but every morning it remained — pompous and British, as if that mattered to a half-Greek boy ...'

The reality: Mum brings out the Box Brownie, that simple and great recorder of our lives. I'm wearing a pressed shirt and shorts and new leather shoes — and with my knapsack on my back, and hair slicked down, I'm ready to take on the world. Only later do they tell me the truth, that I'm expected to go through this charade for another twelve years.

I'll return to this spot thirty years later — surrounded by skate boards and trail bikes — and have my photo taken with a $2000 camera, but it won't look nearly as good. And back in 1933, my mother stood here to begin *her* brief education; the school photo in 1938 shows a quiet and confident girl in a blazer, surrounded by children posing as young adults. Maybe the looming war focused their energies. Look at us, they say — preparing for the great unknown of war, the struggle.

'Was it chance that brought me here to Ithaca,' I'll write in my memoirs, 'or just plain luck ...' I take my place on a long pine bench, open my Grade 1 spelling book and start chanting: is i-s, me m-e, it i-t, go g-o, up u-p, at a-t, by b-y ...

Later a man arrives with a *real* camera: a real monster on legs. We're positioned class by class in one corner of the schoolyard, in front of the great neo-classical facade that in reality is only twenty years old. They built it in the Depression, to soak up jobs. Since we're Grade 1A, we're the first: they line us up, girls in the first two rows and boys at the back. We look taller but of course we're standing on timber benches [...]

'What sort of life will I *really* have?' I wonder, staring at [the teacher] Mrs Windsor. She's got the same name as the Queen, a mysterious figure who's always in our Queens-land lives, and rides around on a horse. You see her face everywhere: on money, at the post office, and — most important of all — in the *Women's Weekly* magazine. She's got two children, Charles and Anne. One day Charles will be the King of England and Australia and half the world — which, let's face it, is pretty hard to beat. They're almost perfect, Mrs Windsor says, unlike us.

When the new Queen came to Australia last year, every schoolkid in Brisbane got dragged out to the Exhibition Grounds in the steaming sun, just to see her. 'Everyone likes flattery,' said Matthew Arnold, 'and when it comes to Royalty you should lay it on with a trowel.' They sure did; before she arrived in her maroon Land Rover, they organised it like a military operation, although the kids were just kids: seven and eight and nine years old. Each school had an allotted position, and then a plane flew over and took a photo very quickly before anyone moved and they put it on the front page of the *Courier Mail*. The next morning all of Queensland woke up and over their cornflakes saw OUR QUEEN made up of a hundred thousand schoolkids dressed in white at the main oval, all on the verge of fainting. There were another million in black who'd already fainted deliberately to make up the dark background. Our school got a big mention. It was reported that the kids from Ithaca Creek were standing on a part of the first letter E of the word QUEEN. They didn't say exactly where.

All Over the Shop (1993)

Beating About the Bush

PRINCE CHARLES (1948–) SPENT A FEW MONTHS AWAY FROM HIS SCOTTISH PUBLIC SCHOOL, GORDONSTOUN, IN 1966, TO ATTEND TIMBERTOP, THE BRANCH OF GEELONG GRAMMAR SCHOOL SITUATED IN THE FOOTHILLS OF THE AUSTRALIAN ALPS IN NORTH-EASTERN VICTORIA.

A popular cry seems to be that Timbertop is very similar to Gordonstoun. This is not strictly true, although it may seem so at first sight. From what I make of it, Timbertop is very individual. All the boys are virtually the same age, 14–15; there are no prefects and the masters do all the work that boys might otherwise do in a school. This way I think there is much more contact between masters and boys as everyone is placed in the same sort of situation. Almost everyone, masters and boys, enjoy themselves up here and don't look forward to the restrictions of the main school when they go back. Most of the boys seem to expect hours of free time, but in fact there's very little and one never seems to stop running here and there for one minute of the day, from 7.30 a.m. breakfast — and no morning run, though there's worse to follow — until the lights go out at 9.15 p.m., having had tea at the unearthly hour of 5.30 p.m. If you have just done a cross-country at 4.45 p.m. and arrived back at 5.15 p.m., it's difficult to persuade your stomach to accept food!

Before I left England in January someone wrote to me saying he hoped I had time to do other things besides chopping down trees. There is a lot of wood-chopping done here, but I'm afraid it's very essential as the boys' boilers have to be stoked with logs and the kitchen uses a huge number. The first week I was here I was made to go out and chop up logs on a hillside in boiling hot weather. I could hardly see my hands for blisters after that! Each afternoon after classes, which end at 3 o'clock, there are jobs which are rather equivalent to P.W., but involve chopping and splitting wood, feeding the pigs, cleaning out fly-traps (which are revolting glass bowls seething with flies and very ancient meat), or picking up bits of paper round the School. After these jobs a cross-country is usually required twice a week, along a path through the bush. When the weather is hot and there is a lot of dust it is very unpleasant, but I believe it makes you reasonably fit to go on expeditions over the week-ends.

Expeditions are a main feature of Timbertop and they take place every week-end, which is very different from Gordonstoun. After a pull up Mt Timbertop, which rises behind the School, on the first Sunday, there were three more compulsory week-end expeditions to prepare one for going out for longer periods in the bush. All the mountains in the area are very thickly wooded, with equally thick undergrowth down below. When you are walking through the bush you can't see anything except gum-tree upon gum-tree, which tends to become rather monotonous after a time. When choosing a camp-site you have to be very careful where you put your tent as a certain kind of gum-tree sheds its branches without warning. Apart from that you virtually have to inspect every inch of ground you hope to put your tent on in case there are any ants or other ghastly creatures. There is one species of ant called Bull Ants which are three-quarters of an inch long or more and they bite like mad! Some boys manage to walk fantastic distances over a week-end of four days or less, and do 130 or even 200 miles. The furthest I've been is 60–70 miles in three days, climbing about five peaks on the way. At the campsite the cooking is done on an open fire in a trench. You have to be very careful during hot weather that you don't start a bush fire, and at the beginning of this term there was a total fire ban in force, so that you ate all the tinned food cold.

In between all these diversions work has to fit in somewhere. In fact, the weeks just seem to be a useful means of filling up the gaps between the week-ends, which come round very quickly. Obviously work cannot be taken quite as seriously as in an

ordinary school, but there are classes all morning after Chapel at
8.45 and there is a two-hour prep period in the evening.

There is no organised sport in the form of field games, but
each Wednesday there is either a tug o' war between the boys'
units, or houses, or, if it's hot, there is swimming, or perhaps
someone is feeling sufficiently cruel to organise a race that
involves carrying half a tree for a certain distance. I almost convinced one or two Australians outside the School that we rustled
kangaroos at Timbertop and that we performed this art by
creeping up on them from behind, grabbing them by the tail
and flicking them over onto their backs, where you had them at
your mercy.

The School is situated in the foothills of the Dividing Range
and all the buildings are extraordinarily well hidden from view
as there are gum-trees everywhere. The boys live in units, or
bungalow-type buildings, of which there are nine, holding fifteen boys a piece. The Chapel is in the centre and is in the shape
of a continuous steep roof that reaches to ground level. Behind
the altar there is a huge window that looks out onto a series of
ridges receding into the distance. When I arrived here everything was very dry and brown, but now it is all green since early
rains came. I have been out to several farms in the area and have
watched some shearing being done. I was asked to try my hand
at it, but, of course, made rather a mess of it, and left a somewhat shredded sheep. Everyone asks how Australia compares
with England, which is a very difficult question, as there isn't
really a comparison. The mountains are so different from
England because there are no ordered fields, but rolling hills
covered in grass and with gum-trees dotted about everywhere. I
came over here expecting boiling hot weather all the time, but
one soon discovers one's error, and it can certainly become very
cold, especially during winter, while it's the summer term at
Gordonstoun.

Gordonstoun Record, 1966

Cave dweller

PETER CONRAD (1948–), NOW TUTOR IN ENGLISH AT CHRIST CHURCH, OXFORD, WAS CHOSEN WHEN A SCHOOLBOY IN HOBART TO PLAY THE PART OF BRICK IN THE FILM VERSION OF NAN CHAUNCY'S *They Found a Cave*.

The film [*They Found a Cave*] did away with the book's discreet ideological designs on Tasmania. It made its own propaganda, which was touristic. It advertised Tasmania's scenery, as we processed through country towns in our dray or scampered through orchards. I had one emblematic little scene in which I reached up for an apple — polished in advance by the props lady — and bit a chunk out of it, unable even then to wait for Eve to take the initiative [...]

To me, this trailer for Tasmania didn't matter. I had my own private scenario. The film wasn't about settling down to a practical accommodation with reality, as Nan Chauncy had counselled; it was about contradicting that reality, or stepping out of it into the fourth dimension of licence: art. Nan Chauncy's characters were English children learning to love Tasmania. I was a Tasmanian child already discontentedly in love with the idea of England (or perhaps, less specifically, with anywhere which was elsewhere). The film wrote a fantasy of mine into truth: the children are said to be disoriented, as their train fumes into the station in the bush, because they're 'used to living in a big city like London'. Since we were all internees of Hobart's northern suburbs, that introduction had a dreadful irony; but the film allowed us to pretend that our existences were otherwise. The locations too, though near where we lived, were changed when we assumed our false identities in front of them. A tumbledown farmhouse off the Huon road, reached across a bridge of rickety planks, was chosen as Jandie's farmstead. The impoverished farmer, his depressed wife and their squalling babies stood aside as we briefly occupied their domain and transformed it into the happy valley. Some humble ledges on the lower slopes of Mount Direction became a sheer cliff face where we clambered in search of the cave. Closest to home of all yet mentally furthest away, the cave itself hid across two lanes of highway and through the showground fence inside a shed now jointly occupied by Cadbury's and Schweppes. Three minutes after leaving the house I was in it, having prised open the concealed, overgrown door of a dream, which admits you to a secret recess within yourself.

It was an intoxicating time. Finding a cave meant for me, I now see, an evasion of ordinary life: getting off school and out of uniform, wearing a baggy green shirt and patched, fraying shorts — my costume, which for six months I had to battle to prevent my mother from washing — and growing your hair. Even after I returned to school, I kept the lank untidy mop, and whenever a teacher remonstrated with me about it — this was three years before the Beatles invented sexual intercourse and long hair — I'd say importantly that I couldn't have it cut because there might still be retakes to do. Back at school, there were other withdrawal symptoms. On our made-do sets, I'd always admired the habit of the camera man and the director, who screwed one hand into an eyehole-shaped aperture and squinted through it as if down the tunnel of a viewfinder, or made a rectangle with the extended thumbs and forefingers of both hands and surveyed the scene from inside that. They were framing life, composing it; I used to do the same from my desk in the back row of the class room, directing the teachers as they toiled through their explanations of algebra and French genders. None of them appreciated my placing a frame round them, and I can't imagine why I wasn't expelled for obnoxiousness.

Down Home: Revisiting Tasmania (1988)

Mortification

PETER ROSE (1955–) IS A MELBOURNE POET AND PUBLISHER.

I am walking down a classroom.
It is always the same, only longer,
the chalked message on the board
become daily more blurred.
On my right the good sit
unctuous hands crossed primly,
to my left the incorrigible
sailing their furtive orgasms
like the first kites of sex.
At the front a certain Mr Bull
instructs us in the gorier aspects
of devotion. History titillates
with Great Character Assassinations.
Follows recess: the lacteous spill.
Too blithe to matter, we are let out
to contemplate Lady Godiva *ad nauseam*
while great Samurai crazes give way
to mass flayings of the unconscionable.
We pair off beneath trees
and kill off aunts conversationally.

The House of Vitriol (1990)

The lunch test

SALLY MORGAN (1951–), WRITER AND ARTIST, WAS AT A PERTH STATE PRIMARY SCHOOL IN THE 1950S. SHE DID NOT THEN KNOW THAT HER MOTHER WAS ABORIGINAL.

It was early in Grade Three that I developed my infallible Look
at the Lunch method for telling which part of Manning my

class-mates came from. I knew I came from the rough-and-tumble part, where there were teenage gangs called Bodgies and Widgies, and where hardly anyone looked after their garden. There was another part of Manning that, before I'd started school, I had been unaware of. The residents there preferred to call it Como. The houses were similar, only in better condition. The gardens were neat and tidy, and I'd heard there was carpet on the floors.

Children from Como always had totally different lunches to children from Manning. They had pieces of salad, chopped up and sealed in plastic containers. Their cake was wrapped neatly in grease-proof paper, and they had real cordial in a proper flask. There was a kid in our class whose parents were so wealthy that they gave him bacon sandwiches for lunch.

By contrast, kids from Manning drank from the water fountain and carried sticky jam sandwiches in brown paper bags.

Nan normally made our sandwiches for school. She made them very neatly, and, sometimes, she even cut the crusts off. I was convinced that made our sandwiches special. There were occasions when Mum took over the sandwich-making. Her lunches stand out in my mind as beacons of social embarrassment. With a few deft strokes, she could carve from an unsuspecting loaf the most unusual slabs of bread. These would then be glued together with thick chunks of hardened butter and globules of jam or Vegemite. Both, if she forgot to clean the knife between sandwiches. We always felt relieved when, once again, Nan assumed the sandwich-making role.

In April that year, my youngest sister, Helen, was born. I found myself taking an interest in her because at least she had the good sense not to be born on my birthday. There were five of us now; I wondered how many more kids Mum was going to try and squeeze into the house. Someone at school had told me that babies were found under cabbage leaves. I was glad we never grew cabbages.

Each year, our house seemed to get smaller. In my room, we had two single beds lashed together with a bit of rope and a big, double kapok mattress plonked on top. Jill, Billy and I slept in there, sometimes David too, and, more often than not, Nan as well. I loved that mattress. Whenever I lay on it, I imagined I was sinking into a bed of feathers, just like a fairy princess.

The kids at school were amazed to hear that I shared a bed with my brother and sister. I never told them about the times we'd squeezed five in that bed. All my class-mates had their own beds, some of them even had their own rooms. I considered them disadvantaged. I couldn't explain the happy feeling of warm security I felt when we all snuggled in together.

Also, I found some of their attitudes to their brothers and sisters hard to understand. They didn't seem to really like one another, and you never caught them together at school. We were just the opposite. Billy, Jill and I always spoke in the playground and we often walked home together, too. We felt our family was the most important thing in the world. One of the girls in my class said, accusingly, one day, 'Aah, you lot stick like glue'. You're right, I thought, we do.

The kids at school had also begun asking us what country we came from. This puzzled me because, up until then, I'd thought we were the same as them. If we insisted that we came from Australia, they'd reply, 'Yeah, but what about ya parents, bet they didn't come from Australia'.

One day, I tackled Mum about it as she washed the dishes.

'What do you mean, "Where do we come from?"'

'I mean, what country. The kids at school want to know what country we come from. They reckon we're not Aussies. Are we Aussies, Mum?'

Mum was silent. Nan grunted in a cross sort of way, then got up from the table and walked outside.

'Come on, Mum, what are we?'

'What do the kids at school say?'

'Anything. Italian, Greek, Indian.'

'Tell them you're Indian.'

I got really excited, then. 'Are we really? Indian!' It sounded so exotic. 'When did we come here?' I added.

'A long time ago', Mum replied. 'Now, no more questions. You must tell them you're Indian.'

It was good to finally have an answer and it satisfied our playmates. They could quite believe we were Indian, they just didn't want us pretending we were Aussies when we weren't.

My Place (1987)

Big brothers

Hugh Lunn (1941–), journalist and author, went to secondary school at Gregory Terrace Christian Brothers School, Brisbane.

Mum took me across town to meet the headmaster of this boys' college locked in behind a series of rock walls. His name was Brother Adams, and he sat behind a wide desk with a statue of a boy in the school uniform behind him. I recognised the uniform because the statue was wearing the same clothes Jack had worn for the last year since he had left the convent: green-grey shirt, black and red tie, grey double-breasted suit, a broadbrimmed grey felt hat with a red and black hat band, and a red and black badge with a chalice and a star and some Latin writing which Jack said meant serving God always.

Brother Adams told Mum I would be admitted because I had a brother at the school, and he said how lucky I was, because so many boys had to be turned away each year. He didn't say anything about the low marks I got in State Scholarship but I felt that was what he was really talking about. Overall, I got 57.1 per cent, but in English I scored just 76 out of 150. Pretty good really, except that one mark less and I would have failed and my name would not have appeared in the paper, because if you didn't pass English you didn't pass State Scholarship.

I didn't think I was lucky to get into this college because I didn't like it at all. Ever since Jack had started school there he had changed. The school was right on the other side of town, where none of us had ever been before, and he was no longer interested in what happened at Annerley or the convent. He had even stopped playing marbles. Now Jack only cared what happened at this school, which he said was one of the nine Queensland 'Great Public Schools' and that was why it was a GPS school. And I said it couldn't be much of a school if it was named after the road outside — Gregory Terrace — instead of its real name, St Joseph's College [...]

But I had to admit their inter-school sports sounded much bigger than ours: even though I could see that with more than 150 boys in Jack's year in three classes they had lots of boys to choose from. They even got into the paper when I was in State Scholarship, because three GPS boys each jumped over six foot and one of them jumped 6ft 6 ins at the GPS sports at the Gabba cricket ground, which Jack claimed equalled the Commonwealth record, 'fair dinkum'.

Jack used fair dinkum so much after he went to Gregory Terrace that Mr Fogarty called him 'fair dinkum'.

And he learned a new way of talking so that he said things he didn't mean. If I agreed to help him roll the pastry he would say 'that's real curly of you' or 'that's really big of you', when clearly he didn't mean it. He even became friends with a former State School kid called Peterson who somehow got into Terrace and who showed Jack a new way home by walking with him up St Paul's Terrace and down Wharf Street to catch a tram.

Yet I had myself seen Jack fight him outside their house for the honour of us Catholics.

So I started calling him 'Big Boy' to show him what I thought of his new image. And he didn't like it. Every time I said

'Big Boy' he would get stuck into me but I would scream 'Big Boy' more and more and, short of killing me, there was no way he could stop me. I never ceased to marvel at how many different ways I could say 'Big Boy'.

Most of our fights were at night, when Mum and Dad were at the shop, but I got the better of him one day when I picked up a stone and let fly and hit him in the back of the head.

It might sound rough, but Jack didn't know how lonely it was for me having to get around Annerley without him. Not only had I been bashed up with no hope of calling on his help, but the whole class had laughed at me when Sister Vincent asked how Jack was doing at Gregory Terrace, and I said he had scored 96 per cent for bookmaking.

I didn't know then that the real name of the subject was bookkeeping. Fred was always backing horses with bookmakers, but for some reason he used a false name: Tim O'Halloran.

Even though he now went to this GPS college on the north side of Brisbane, Jack still kept his promise to take me to see my first cricket Test at the Gabba just a week before Scholarship. Pa had told us what fun it was, and he had predicted a big future for a new batsman called Neil Harvey. We sat in front of the public stand, leaning over the white picket fence that surrounded the Gabba ground, and watched the new English fast bowlers Tyson and Statham being thrashed by the might of the Australian team. Harvey scored 162 and Arthur Morris 153, and I wondered why England bothered to come and play us because we were so good. We heckled the sun-burned, tired Tyson whose white skin had gone pink under our hot Queensland sun. He was nicknamed 'Typhoon' because he was supposed to be so fast, but in the heat he trudged slowly back almost to the fence to begin his run-up, and Neil from next door, Jack and I called in unison 'get a Taxi, Tyson'.

Jack took me to my first day at Gregory Terrace: by bus from Annerley to North Quay and then a walk down Queen, George, and Adelaide Streets to the front of the City Hall — where there were a lot of tall palm trees and some statues of lions — for another bus to Terrace. It wasn't a good place to set out for school from, because it was opposite the Tivoli theatre which showed lots of good pictures and which had a big cool milk bar with rows of inviting shiny steel milkshake cans.

School started at 8.30 a.m. and so we had to leave home by 7.30 to get there in time, because it was so far away. That was why most of the boys on the southside went to the nearby Christian Brothers Catholic college of St Laurence's. Kenny Fletcher did. So did Johnny Summers. And so did my cousin, Johnny Duncan. And that's where I wanted to go too: but Mum wanted us to travel right across town just because she thought this was a better school.

Over the Top with Jim (1990; FIRST PUBLISHED 1989)

Interlude at a primary school

ROSEMARY DOBSON (1920–), POET, BORN IN SYDNEY, NOW LIVES IN CANBERRA. SHE EVOKES A MOTHER FETCHING HER CHILD FROM SCHOOL.

The sun struck noonday and the storm
Hitched shreds of cloud and rumbled off,
Birdsong and raindrops tumbled down
From laden leaves, and slips of light
Glanced from the puddles to the spire.

A stone's throw from the crowded street
I stood beneath the bell-tower porch,
The lazy dog snored on the mat,
One raindrop fell, then we were still:
A notice curled upon the wall.

I knocked, stepped in, and twenty heads
Curved round in twenty question-marks.

I might have been a swaggie come
For flour and tea and sugar, or
A boundary-rider at the door

So still it was in that church-hall
Where twenty children learnt their books,
So simple after rain the air,
So far, so far the troubled streets:
So much of country in the town.

I wished that I had ridden in
From the back paddocks to the church,
And hitched my horse, and held my hat;
Up-country drover with a grin
Like sudden sun and holiday
But as it was I made excuse
And thanked the teacher, took my child,
And hand in hand we wandered out
Beneath the porch and through the fence
And back into the unquiet world.

Collected Poems (1991)

Peeling onions always makes me cry

THIS SHORT STORY BY **JENNIFER STRAUSS** (1933–), POET AND ACAD-
EMIC, EVOKES THE EXPERIENCES OF THE 1970S WORKING MOTHER IN
MORNING SCHOOL TRAFFIC.

'Are you going straight to work?' Anxious. A heavy truck edging
out past the stop sign, a vividly yellow Honda approaching fast,
small, but aggressively in possession of its legal territory. Narrow
passage; not exhilarated by that today.

Negotiated. 'Yes, of course I am.' Sharp; resentment of
repeated failures to take her going to work as being 'of course'.

'Why?' Rising inflection, apprehensive. 'I think I've forgotten my gym bag.' Naked statement, awkward with shame. The younger would have cried first, forestalling anger. Chess-player, he knew it was largely a matter of moves.

Exaggerated calm. Signals. 'You'd better get out and look.' Slam of the bootlid tightening the morning's headache; woken too early by her husband's nightmare. Not there. Once, she thought, you were not there either; I made you. The function of mothers is to materialize; to fetch flesh from the womb; to fetch from whatever cupboards they can find food, love, clothes, discipline, toys, wisdom. How long, oh Lord, how long? He is bigger than me now, and stronger and *younger* ...

'I suppose I'll have to go back and get it for you. Friday morning, all this traffic, it's too bad of you. Do you *realize* this will take half an hour out of my day?' Image of the day and its tasks like a jigsaw scattered by heedlessness; sound-track, hateful voice, hysteria rising under reasonable accusations; visuals, his eyes reddening, tears swelling under the lids. Bang goes Rule One: No Recriminations. And coming up, the right hand turn that must be respected under all circumstances.

Negotiated. 'OK, OK.' Willed neutrality. 'I'll leave it at the School Office. Will you be able to pick it up there?' 'Yes.' Statement; nothing more; under difficulties, sorry and thanks and all the small easers of situations stuck stonelike in his adolescent maw. Sometimes, beneath irritation at ineptitude she felt panic on his behalf. What might the world do?

Silent, they clambered out of the car; sobered. She wished she had not detected a glimmer of pleasure in the face of the younger; she wished her leaden tongue had moved to say goodbye; she wished that since she was going to fetch the wretched bag anyway, she had offered it gracefully. But surely it was right to make him realize his responsibilities. 'The school aims to make your sons self-reliant.' The Headmaster, masked in academic regalia, flanked by lieutenants, fortified by loudspeakers.

'We expect parental co-operation in this.' Mean mother; weak mother. Guilt at every level.

Back to the house, fighting for 'proportion': What a production over a forgotten gym bag. Car ostentatiously controlled; doors definitively unslammed. Into the Office, light, poised, inviting to a conspiracy of amused adult indulgence. Theatrical. A crumb of comfort though in the self-disgust; converse of the princess and the pea. Theatricality was part of the discipline game; ritualized indignation, ritualized repentance. Perhaps, though refusing his part, he had perceived nothing else today. But those tears? She had thought of the ritual as protecting them all from the violence of anger; now, beneath anger she recognized a buried, more pungent violence, that of despair. Not just the familiar, half-flattering despair at the endlessness of demands upon accomplishment; something older, colder, more impersonal. Sin against the Holy Ghost. Not Recommended for Children. Post under Plain Wrapper. Had she really let him get a whiff of that? Those tears?

She *must* not … But ever since she had seen herself doubly caged, moral bars of action and consequence slotting into amoral bars of randomness and temporality, energy had drained away from her. If she could not do what she would, why should she do what she could. It was like the woodchuck rhyme: If a woodchuck *could* chuck wood, a woodchuck would chuck as much wood as a woodchuck could chuck if a woodchuck could chuck wood. Well, what the hell for? Dumb chuck …

She let the familiar road take her automatically away. Somewhere, briefly, she considered some compensatory treat — book, record, favourite food. No good; not for this one. The younger, sense of connections still imperfect, could take a day's end pleasure untainted by morning's pain; this one would take it sullenly or, worse, refuse until the offer was withdrawn and then want it. There was nothing to be done; which was another way of saying that there was everything to be done and no way to do it.

She let the familiar road take her away. Somewhere, behind her, a car pulled out carelessly from the kerb, another coming too fast to stop. Collision; traffic flowing on past a minor disaster; figures frozen in her rear-vision mirror while she waited for the green light; gestures of accusation and self-justification.

There was still something to uncover. Watch me play Peer Gynt and his metaphysical onion. He had an option, she thought: The just, impersonal displeasure of the system. He preferred my anger. But what does this mean? And why should it seem to offer comfort? Flatters my vanity? Ah, *vanitas vanitatum*. Is it all vanity? I would like to get to the end.

Tuna (1978)

The long road

GARRY DISHER (1949–), WRITER, WAS BORN IN SOUTH AUSTRALIA. HE PUBLISHED HIS FIRST NOVEL FOR CHILDREN, *The Bamboo Flute,* IN 1992.

'Good morning, Paul.'

I jump in fright. I turn to face the front. Mr Riggs then says, 'Good morning, school.'

'Good morning, Mr Riggs,' like words in a prayer.

'Be seated.'

And we sit. The same thing every day. Seven years of it.

The room never changes. It smells of chalk dust and dirty pants and kids from families who never wash. The initials *AG*, carved in my desktop, belong to Arthur Goss, Margaret's father, so badly wounded in the war that no one has ever seen him. Every desk bears years of scars and ink stains. There are wall-maps, coloured drawings marked ten out of ten, numbers nought to twelve, letters A to Z, dusty crossed flags above a varnished wall plaque naming the war-dead, seven rows of kids, and, at the front, Mr Riggs and his desk, the big blackboard behind him.

The morning drags by. The little kids practise the alphabet, the middle kids do dictation, Grade Sevens do arithmetic. Then recess.

Now we're doing adverbs and adjectives.

Another thing about Mr Riggs: he is missing the fingers of his left hand. His habit is to hook one end of his cane into the stub of flesh, the other end into his good palm, and push inwards.

Stillness settles on us when he does that. We sit, watching the cane bow and straighten, bow and straighten, then *whap!* — he slams the blackboard, and we all jump and look down at our work.

Adverbs and adjectives.

I am lost in words: walking *hurriedly*; talking *unhappily*; *stormy* sea; *crumbling* rock.

Then Mr Riggs says, 'Have you finished, Margaret Goss?'

We all look up. Behind me, Margaret says, 'Sorry, sir,' and we all return to our work.

The minutes pass. More scrapes and whispers at the back of the room. Then the crack of the cane.

'*Margaret.* If it's so interesting, perhaps you would like to share it with the whole school?'

Margaret *never* gets told off. I feel half-pleased and half-sorry.

'Please, sir,' says her friend Joy Bailey, the policeman's kid, 'it was Margaret's birthday on the weekend.'

'Was it, indeed? How old are you, Margaret?'

'Please, sir, twelve, sir.'

'Did you have a party?'

There is another stir of giggling, of feet shuffling on the floor. 'Yes, sir.'

A party. I feel hot inside. What did they do? Where did they go? Did they take their clothes off?

'Back to work,' Mr Riggs says. 'All of you.'

I look down at my workbook. I can't write anything.

I've got pictures in my head: the kids at the party, waiting for the mothers to go away, then racing down the broad, slow streets, past the dusty gum trees whose bark peels and branches crack on hot days, to places only they know about. Places where no one can see them. They dare each other: who will do it first? If Margaret is ever dared, she will do it, she's not afraid. I can see her bright eyes and her hot face and her skin.

I don't realise it, but I'm humming, and it's a jumpy, out-of-breath tune.

I wake up to all their terrible laughter. Mr Riggs's eye is glittering at me like broken glass.

But, 'It's lunchtime,' is all he says.

We march out in orderly lines. Fresh air. We scatter to the ends of the yard.

I always sit under the pepper trees with other farm kids. Lunch today is an apricot jam sandwich. Sometimes my mother packs a rock bun too, but not today. Just lately she's been trading all our eggs.

The trouble with the farm kids is that all they talk about is engines and bags-per-acre. The trouble with the town kids is that they have secrets and no place for me. I sit, with my back against a tree trunk, looking across the yard at the town beyond the school fence, and the flat empty land and the long road stretching north and south.

The Bamboo Flute (1992)

Smoke screen

TIMOTHY CONIGRAVE (1959–94), ACTOR AND PLAYWRIGHT, WROTE ABOUT HIS SCHOOLDAYS AT XAVIER COLLEGE, MELBOURNE, IN HIS AUTOBIOGRAPHY, *Holding the Man.*

Out of this landscape appeared a boy called Damien. He was from a working-class family; his father and brothers were in the army, but he was a rebel. His hair was long, his attitude defiant. He thought football was stupid. With a shock of glossy black hair tumbling into his eyes, he looked like Mowgli from *The Jungle Book*. Our point of contact was born of this rebelliousness: smoking.

I had already been experimenting. One Friday night I sat on my parents' bed watching a St Trinian's movie. Two girls were smoking in the toilets. I lit a match, blew it out and drew back the fumes. I felt sophisticated despite the sulphurous burning in my throat. Another time I filled a paper straw with lawn clippings and nearly set my lungs on fire as I drew back the burning grass.

Damien and I were going up to the park when I spied a cigarette butt on the ground and put it in my mouth. He pulled out a whole pack of Craven As and some matches.

'You smoke?'

'Der.'

'Wow. What's it like?' He offered me one.

'Not here!'

'Where?' He was testing me. I showed him a couple of hollow pine trees that were hiding places for local kids, their branches smooth from years of polishing by children's bums.

This sanctuary was to become ours. We were partners in crime, a secret society in our secret headquarters. Our ritual always started with a cigarette. The smoke provided safety as we talked about school, what a dickhead so-and-so was, or the time Gilligan built that car out of coconuts.

I liked Damien, and I was happy that he liked me. Although we weren't in the same class we always found each other at breaks and played handball in the concrete squares of the playground, practised tricks with Coca-Cola yoyos or climbed over the back of the green shed to have a cigarette.

The bench I was sitting on was slowly being torn from its place by the roots of the liquidambars that surrounded the lunch quadrangle. All around me the broken asphalt said that these trees were winning a war. I was trying to finish my lunch before English. I hadn't done my homework and had spent the break composing a poem about 'scraping away to the inner essence'.

Sitting nearby was the sunglasses boy. I was thinking about his looks. *What makes me think he's handsome? I like the way he is. Calm, and cool. Would the other guys think he was handsome?* As I lobbed the soggy remainder of my lettuce-and-Vegemite sandwich into the bin, I spied Damien walking across the playground. *He's really good-looking. Even the way he walks is really good.* He walked towards me, smiling.

He sat on the bench, opened his hand and revealed a superball. 'It's Andy's.'

'God, he'll be spewing!'

He put his arm around me. There was a kind of stirring, a buzz coursing through me. I wanted to break away from him but I also wanted to put my head on his shoulder. The electronic bell pealed.

I headed off to the toilets. Damien said he'd save me a place in the assembly hall.

Friday afternoons were a bludge. Mr Steed the science teacher would show us documentaries — about Campbell's attempt at the land-speed record in his futuristic Bluebird, or the development of the Merino by CSIRO. It was a strategy to stop us sleeping our way through the last period of the week, but it gave us a chance to play up as the excitement of the weekend loomed.

The assembly hall was a fibro hut, painted pale green like a public toilet. The carpet was a splotchy synthetic red. It resembled pizza and smelt like pizza. Black curtains were drawn across windows that were wide open. The roof was corrugated iron and even in winter the heat could be smothering. On this summer day the room was an oven filled with boys basting in their own juices.

I could make out the short figure of Mr Steed fumbling at the projector. We sat totally still until he squatted down beside the machine, and then the room became a snowstorm of paper balls and planes. Mr Steed stood up and the storm abruptly stopped.

The projector threw a white square of light onto the screen, which immediately came alive with rabbits, dogs, thumbs-up, and peace signs. Someone did the VO-5 symbol from the television ad. The rabbit became a two-finger salute.

Where is Damien? I heard a whispered call and turned to see him on his own, up the back behind the projector. He patted the seat next to him.

Mr Steed was agitated. As he lifted an arm to brush his oily fringe off his thick glasses I could see the sweat stains in the pit of his mustard-coloured shirt. The projector jumped into life and the screen read, *The Prickly Menace.*

Damien took my arm and put it around his waist, smiled and turned to the screen. The film was about a cactus getting out of hand somewhere and the moth that was helping to keep it under control. It could have been about Auschwitz. All I could think of was my arm around Damien's waist. It felt like it had found its home. It felt right. It felt safe.

We sneaked looks at each other and smiled. Then he put his lips to my cheek and let them sit there until I whispered, 'Don't!'

He smiled and whispered, 'I wish you were a girl.' I wasn't sure what he meant but said I wished he was a girl too.

We stayed entwined until the film whipped out of the gate and slapped the projector, stirring Mr Steed awake. He fumbled to turn the machine off. Damien stretched and released me. The darkness was broken by boys pouring out of the assembly hall.

'Come back here until the bell goes,' barked Mr Steed. As if to make a fool of him, the bell went.

A couple of Grade Fives stood on the footpath waiting for someone to pick them up. One grabbed the other's bag and lobbed it over the wall back into the playground. The victim kicked his friend's bag into the traffic and ran back into the grounds.

'Got any durries?' I turned to see Damien coming out of the school ground with his cap pulled to one side. He put his arm around my shoulder. I showed him the pack of Escorts inside my bag.

'Are you two boyfriends?' An older boy with carrot-red hair was leaning against a wall, hands in pockets, feet crossed at the ankles.

Damien turned to confront him. He picked Damien's cap off his head and threw it onto the road. Damien went to snatch the redhead's cap but was gripped by the wrist and shoved. 'Poofters!' jeered the redhead and sauntered across the road in triumph.

Holding the Man (1995)

Pudge

PHILIP HODGINS (1959–95), POET, WAS BORN NEAR SHEPPARTON AND EDUCATED AT GEELONG COLLEGE, VICTORIA.

I don't know what it was about the two
of us. We just didn't hit it off.
Eventually we had this vicious blue
outside the dining room and he lost.

After that I thought he'd given up.
We'd pass each other in the corridor
without a look or anything and at
the Easter break he shifted to another dorm.

One afternoon in second term I chased
a ball behind the gym when just like that
something yellow went whizzing past my face.
What could have made a whizzing noise like that?

I went to where it landed in the shade
and found an apple stuck with razor blades.

Down the Lake with Half a Chook (1988)

Early birds

SAM SEJAVKA (1960–), MUSICIAN, PLAYWRIGHT, AND ACTOR, HAS PUBLISHED A NUMBER OF SHORT STORIES IN WHICH CHILDHOOD EXPERIENCE IS CENTRAL.

His mother let go Tunny's hand and left him staring at a nest of 49 foetal personalities.

What distinguishing features there were amongst the 49 only hinted at the possibility of character. Nervous eyes betraying an eagerness to guard the perimeters of their infantile herd. Soft, anxious eyes declaring a promiscuous willingness to obey. Forty-nine unfinished units, of which Tunny was to be the fiftieth.

He recognised no one from the year before. Nor did he recognise the classroom with its one wall of windows and one wall of neatly executed projects on zirconium mining. He recognised none of the starkly coloured fingerpaintings on the pinboard. But among the happy stick-families, with their bulbous cats and sweetly smoking chimneys, were some pleasingly familiar shapes: elongated ovals, downy softnesses, roundnesses evolving from stem to mysterious duct.

When he turned, his mother was gone, and Miss Loculus stood facing him across the room.

She asked him to sit, but Tunny was transfixed by the sight of his peers. Their expressions were startlingly uniform. Each bore an identical message of empty judgement. When Loculus repeated her command, Tunny looked and saw that expression mirrored in her face. He could see nowhere to sit.

At once, it was twilight. The room was a roosting place for 49 shrilling birds with electrocuted mouths and their twittering spread quickly, like a virus. Tunny shuddered. Their laughter, pure laughter, untempered by sympathy, was frighteningly automatic.

'There's a seat at the front, Tunny.'

He did not want to sit there, wedged between his fellows and Loculus, and when he hesitated the laughter thickened. They laughed as they would at the sad threshing of Krang's robot body, the incinerated husk of Daffy Duck, the ultra-violent crimes of The Skipper. He was the Simpson child, snapped at the spine by a blustering father. Tunny had dreaded coming back to school.

Loculus took Tunny's hand. Her flesh felt nothing like his mother's. It was unpleasant and unyielding. He suffered in the corrosive scent of hair that fell in heavy red shoals to her waist, and he did not like the frame on which her rayon summer dress was slung. It hinted at softness, but on a second glance seemed harsh.

He tried to struggle from her grip. Her smile dissolved and she half dragged him to his seat. The class quietened, but Tunny could not relax. He wanted to open his desk and pour in the contents of his satchel. He wanted to eat his lunch, or at the very least assess its composition. But he did nothing and waited, stiffly.

'Each of you has a partner at your desk,' intoned Loculus. 'You have a minute now in which to introduce yourself.'

Tunny turned to confront the girl beside him.

'I'm Utri,' she giggled. Utri wore a pale-green gingham dress, and a dark-green ribbon in her hair. Her cheeks were flushed.

'I'm Tunny,' he replied, guardedly, and was rewarded with another giggle. He looked from Utri to the drawings on the pin-board. Her chin, her pronunciation of the vowels in her name, particularly the 'u', had something in common with the more agreeable of the shapes there, a capacity to fill the elongated ovals and complete the softnesses.

'I don't think I like you, Tunny.'

Utri turned away and giggled in concert with a female friend. Tunny felt ashamed, a little annoyed. Abandoning the intro-duction, he boldly transferred the contents of his satchel to the desk. Inside, there were messages scrawled in nervous haste: 'Alan was here', 'Debbie is stupid', 'Miss Loculus is a worm'.

As the class chattered, Tunny listened to the sound of Loculus's chalk grating on the blackboard. He registered her indifference without comprehension.

'Take your exercise books and pencils.'

Tunny obeyed. As he opened to the first page of his book, he heard massed breathing behind him, a wet ticking of minds.

'Now copy what you see on the board.'

With an air of relief, Loculus sat, and began to leaf through a glossy magazine. Her fifty charges studiously transferred her work into their 32-page books. The atmosphere in the room relaxed and, to some extent, so did Tunny. Yet he experienced difficulties. Though he was close to the board, he could not see it clearly. He squinted.

Some minutes later, Loculus rose and asked the class to hold up their work. She nodded, returned to the blackboard and copied out a series of sentences for duplication. It was Summer, they learnt, it was February and today was Tuesday.

Utri pinched and kicked Tunny when he tried to read her large childish script. Loculus heard her giggle.

'Tunny!'

He desisted. He recommenced his squinting.

Presently, they were visited by Miss Vesicle from 4B. Tunny found her indistinguishable from Loculus. Her hair, though a different colour, was similarly styled, and similar scents followed in her wake. Loculus closed her magazine as Vesicle perched herself lethargically on the edge of the desk. In each other's company, their listlessness was apparent, and they made no effort to disguise their shared disinterest in schoolteaching. They chattered brightly at first, but their conversation quickly dwindled and they sat for a moment in leaden silence, before Loculus shifted her gaze to Tunny and cocked a painted eyebrow. A whispered exchange took place, punctuated by giggles not dissimilar to Utri's or her friends'.

Tunny was not oblivious to this. Though his conscience was clear, Tunny was apprehensive. He was guilty of no crime he knew, but that did not absolve him. No one of his age could reasonably claim familiarity with all the myriad laws and by-laws of his world. His only response was to work harder. It was the only means he could think of to save himself from trouble and it was a mistake. Concentration distorted his face into a comic mask.

George Papaellinas (ed.), *Homeland* (1991)

Minding your language

Kim Scott (1957–), writer, bases this story on the experience of Aboriginal children taken from their families and sent to mission schools in north-western Australia.

'My name is Fatima Nangimara. I am the first one born in the mission …

'I grow up in the mission. I grow up by the Spanish monks, you know, the Fathers.

'When I was bigger they sent me to school because there's no school in here. No sisters or no anybody to teach anybody.

'Myself and Mary we went to Beagle Bay school by *Kuringa*, by big ship.

'They didn't tell us nothing, they hide the clothing. They pack it up, gave it to one of the Fathers, and tell us that we were just going to see the people on that boat, *Kiringa*.

'But it wasn't true. They play tricks on us. We might cry, or my mother might take me to the bush and hide me, see. So they didn't tell anybody.

'So. We went on the boat, we met the crew. They were unloading and Father told us to go up so we went up. We were in that ship and the lady brought us cake. That's Mrs Johnson and Mrs Thompson, they look after us.

'We thought that boat was moving, maybe. But we thought, they said, we were stopping in there, in that Pako Bay. But it wasn't Pako Mission, we were in Wyndham already, you see. Or same as.

'We were thinking of Mummy and Daddy and sad because I didn't say 'bye to Daddy because Daddy was fishing. And Mummy was at home. So.

'We were in that boat with no good air. Then, when it sun setting time, we came out of the place to see outside, you know, and they told us, "This is Wyndham". Those two British nurses, they look after us. They did not let us off the ship. We stayed inside long time. They thought we might jump out of the boat I suppose.

'We were scared of it.

'Out on the water we used to dance corroboree for them. We were happy to do that. I used to sing, Mary dance. She used to sing for me, and I used to dance. Well we were children. We didn't feel shame or anything like that you know.

'I think the lady told us. You know the nurse, from us? She told us to dance, so we dance corroboree for them.

'They used to be happy with us you know, make us not to think for our parents, you know? And they used to be with us, clapping their hands when we danced.

'There were many ladies in the ship. This was big ship. They used to come and make our beds, clean nice undywear, shower. They used to be good for us. Nice food they used to give us, nice bed. They were nice people.

'And from there we went to Darwin. We were only crying for Mummy and Daddy, still crying. We were in Darwin in the morning time. We saw one Aborigine woman, and man. They talk in pidgin you see, they told us, "Where you come from?" And we told them we come from Dresfield. "We know that place. Where are you going?" We told them we didn't know where we were going.

'See, we didn't know where we were going.

'On the ship they thought we might jump out I suppose. But they were nice people. Gave us nice food, nice bed.

'But this Darwin. That Aborigine man was talking with us. He said, "I am from that side too, from this part of the country". But we don't know, see? We were not big people to know everything.'

Again again again. Out on the blue sea, them ladies in their many dresses, their pink skins scrubbed, they clap chapped hands at the two dark girls dancing dancing dancing like shadows in the hard sun. The sun and sea hurt eyes, the sea slaps at the hull. The ropes and timbers creak.

Splinter of wood, scrap of sail, tiney zig-zags across all that blue. We can hear the singing, little bit. Just faint, you know.

'We left Darwin, we went back, and we started to go to Broome. And there we get out.

'The lady told us, "You are going out now, with this man here". We said "No!" many times. We didn't know he was

Bishop, Bishop Somebody. He told us, "I'll take you". We used to say "No!" We used to say no.

'After all he took us for a train, from the jetty you know. We went on the train, we get out, and one of the nuns was working in the garden just watering the place. Stop us. Then she take us to the girls. We take two, three days in Broome. Then after Brother took us to Beagle Bay Mission.

'There were three boys there waiting for us that was from Pako Mission. They went in front of us, before us, you know. One of the luggers took them there. They didn't know.

'Like we didn't know. We didn't think. I didn't know anything. Nothing!

'We met one boy, one Aborigine boy, in the road. Give him a letter. It was a letter to that Bishop and when the boy said, "Yes Father," we just looked at each other, Mary and me. We said, "This is Father who we say no no no?" We said to one another, you know, "This is Father?" Oh no, we made a mistake he's a Father and we just say no no no for him.

'We went to Beagle Bay. We stayed there. We used to be sorry, but too many girls there so that make us happy.'

'We came back here, we were grown-up girls, like the big girls you teach. We got out of the lugger and Mother, Father, uncles and anybody, they were waiting for us. They were waiting for us. Some people in the camp, they said, "The two girls are coming back". They just knew.

'So they were ready for us and they cried for us. We didn't know how to speak the language. We forgot about our language. We talk in English. I couldn't understand my mummy. I forgot all about our language. We forget about it.

'Back then, you would be able to talk their language in no time. They would get sugarbag, bush honey, and sing it and give it to you to eat. When you had eaten that honey you would be able to talk their language just the same as they do. But with us we did just forget, so after a time we getting it little by little so we can talk now.

'My mummy said that she cannot understand, to other people. Telling them that we cannot understand them and that they cannot talk, when they were talking to us in language. Mummy told them, "They don't talk, they forgot about their language".

'Mummy took me to the dormitory where we have to live. I was already a big girl, see, because I couldn't stay with them. In the law of the Aborigine, from the bush, you know, their fathers don't like big girls to live in their mummy's place.

'They don't like me to stay with them. Not like here now they live with their parents.'

True Country (1993)

Homelands

MANDAWUY YUNUPINGU (1956–) IS AN INTERNATIONALLY FAMOUS
ROCK MUSICIAN AND AN EDUCATIONIST.

My own education was a Yolngu education. It took place with our large family group living in the places on our land that hold special importance for us. With Mum and Dad, we went from place to place, and every place had its stories. Some of these were sacred stories that we heard sung in ceremonies. Some were family stories, like Mum's stories of when she was a little girl in this place or that. We knew that my grandad had been here, and his grandad before him did these things, and right back to the ancestors who made the land as they went about doing just the same sorts of things we did in our ordinary life and in our ceremonial life.

Mum and Dad travelled long distances with us kids. Just by going and living in the various places, we were respecting those ancestors of ours who made the world. My father followed the seasons in his lands. Sometimes Mum took us over to her places.

Like during April, when it was starting to get chilly at night, we would be inland. We were in covered places where it was sheltered; all those cosy places. We would camp there in the jungle and get honey from beehives in the rocks — rock honey. When the cold snap was coming on, after April into May/June, when it is almost going into the dry season, that's when we'd start hanging around there.

Even when we were camped inland, we would come down to the beach. There were good spots there. We would get Mum to come and help us collect oysters and get honey — rock honey — and fruit, traditional fruit in season. Just like now, when we go to places to collect fruits, say at Galaru just north of where Nhulunbuy township is, it's a form of homage and recognition for the Djankawu sisters, those ancestral women who did the same thing there in their world-making activity.

Each move was a change of context as far as my education was concerned. Each new place has new concepts associated with it. Each place is connected to other places in deep ways. And I learned about that, both from being in the place and by associating it with the songs and dances of our ceremonies. In this way, the more abstract knowledge of how places are connected was linked with the practical and emotional knowledge of actually living in a place.

My father would teach me to be a man and take me hunting, spear fishing. He taught me all the fish names. And he would tell me off for doing naughty things too. I remember the nighttimes best. We would listen to stories at night by the campfire. All the stories had a strong lesson for us kids. They would be stories to get us to stay put by the fire and not wander about. They would get us frightened and get us to sleep much faster.

This is the '50s and early '60s I'm remembering. But, as I grew, our Yolngu world was no longer ours alone. Changes in my family's lifestyle were taking place. Influences outside the family and clan were being felt. Both Yirritja and Dhuwa people were being moved around by white people. Clans were being assembled here and encouraged to leave there. The missionaries had been around all my life. Somehow they started to have more impact on us all.

About this time, my fathers and uncles and my older brother were involved with the court challenge to the government of Australia and NABALCO, the big foreign mining company that wanted our land. The struggle was to find ways of explaining our laws and beliefs to white Australia in an attempt to retain all that is important and sacred in Yolngu life — our land. That struggle to explain our laws and beliefs is what you hear in Yothu Yindi's songs today. In our songs we have found a way to help people hear us today. But back then it wasn't possible.

After my initiation, I began to go to school regularly. It was all quite funny to me at the time. But it had its exciting bits. As I see it now, I needed this different sort of energy, different learning. But a whole lot went along with it, like having to wear clothes. Sometimes when I had no shorts, I'd wear *naga*. It didn't worry me. The missionaries had their 'young ladies', the Yolngu girls' sewing class, make our uniforms for us.

Sometimes I found aspects of education really good; I learned something new. It was like every day you were looking at things, and then you were challenged. I'd try to match it. I could practically hear my brain working. But sometimes I found the classroom isolated, cut off from everything I knew and loved. I'd sit in that school for five hours or twenty minutes and then go back home and play to our own rules.

School worked for me. For my type of thinking, western education could fit in. I think my parents had it fixed in their minds, too, that I should be schooled in order to give me a good balanced education. Learning English just kept me coming back for more. I remember learning lots of bible words. Learning English was a pleasure. I already knew ten or so clan languages and English was a great new challenge. I remember coming back to the family with new English words which I'd try out on them. I distinctly remember showing off to my sisters by reciting 'The house that Jack built'.

But looking back now, I can see that the teachers probably saw things differently to me. Many of their demands were quite incomprehensible. They weren't just teaching me 'useful things'; they had a theory, an ideology. I see now that it was a curriculum driven by the ideology of assimilation. I marvel at the ways we knew how to resist it. I see now that a lot of what motivated those white teachers was the view that it was only when Yolngu stopped being Yolngu that we could become Australians.

But what about schooling now? Have schools stopped being the instrument of assimilation? My children are in school. I became the principal of the school where I once sat at a desk with the other Yolngu kids. Are my kids having a Yolngu education comparable in depth and rigour to what my parents gave me? I would answer a firm yes. But I can only answer yes because for nearly a quarter of a century people, both Yolngu and Balanda, have worked to achieve this. We have transformed the missionary, assimilation ideology into an authentic Yolngu schooling. It took a lot of imagination and struggle.

The changes which we have introduced into our schools did not just happen. Since the early 1970s, a large group of people have made them happen. They have had a different vision and have struggled with those whose imaginations are more limited. Yolngu and Balanda who are now old men and women have been involved. I'm thinking of people like our old Balanda friend, Nugget Coombs, who recently spoke at a Melbourne University graduation ceremony at Yirrkala. He recalled his involvement with our community over the past twenty-five years. I'm thinking of people like my relation, Dambalipu, who told education department officials we needed schools in the new homelands settlements we were establishing in the 1970s. They just could not understand why we wanted to leave the big mission settlements for our traditional homelands. But still we started schools in those homelands with our own people as teachers. The department officials were puzzled and amazed.

Each of our clans has its own homelands. And in the 1970s we began to establish different life-ways in our own homelands, blending old ways and new. Naturally we want our children to be reared at home. But should a child have to miss out on schooling just because the family wants him or her to grow up at home with the family? In the bureaucratic minds of education department officials, schools were associated with being away from all things Aboriginal. Schools in homeland centres upset all their categories. And I know from painful experience that when you upset white people's categories, you'd better watch out [...]

Now this is the place for me to sum things up.

Like many people of my age all over the world, I see that my children's lives are different from my life as a child. My children are in Yolngu schools taught by Yolngu teachers.

Like me, my wife, Yalmay, is a teacher. We are both trained in the Balanda sense, but we are also guided by Yolngu elders. We are gradually making our schools into Yolngu institutions.

It seems to us that the most important thing is language. Our children study their clan languages in school. They learn to understand the deep meanings and to read and write in their mother's and father's languages. We also think that the study of English language is important for our children. It holds a significant place in our curriculum. But it is placed within a curriculum of multiple balances. Balances that our children must learn if they are going to be active Aboriginal members of our contemporary Australia.

Mathematics is important, too. In fact, we have spent a lot of time and words developing a maths curriculum for our kids, a genuine Aboriginal mathematics. We have called this a Gamma Maths Curriculum and it is in the process of being officially recognised as an approved course of study in mathematics. It enables our children to work intellectually with the balances they must achieve in their lives.

Yolngu education is a balanced, active process. We have come a long way since I was a child.

'Yothu Yindi: finding balance' (1994)

Home game

David Bateson (1921–), a Sydney writer, tells the story of a Korean student arriving in an Australian school with no common language except that of the soccer ball.

In a few seconds you could pick him out from the two hundred boys in the playground. Nearly all the others wore plain grey shorts or trousers. He wore flared denims with orange trimmings down the side, a red jacket and yellow sneakers.

It was his first day at this school. His name was Yang Jim Su. The name Jim could be useful if he was willing to drop his Korean name, Yang, but Su could be a real drawback. There were three girls called Sue in the school.

It was 9.25 on a bright but windy morning. The bell had been sounded. All the pupils were moving towards the veranda to arrange themselves in straight lines. There was another Korean three lines away. He was wearing the school uniform. He called out something to Yang Jim Su. Yang started to reply but sensed that the children had stopped talking and were staring at him. He went quiet.

A tall man on the veranda started talking into a microphone. In all that he said, there was only one word that Yang could distinguish. It was *shoes*. Every time the man said *shoes* all the girls and boys started laughing. He did not understand why *shoes* was funny, but after he had heard the word six times he tried to smile with the others. It was very difficult to smile.

It so happened that the tall teacher was saying:

'Yesterday at the athletic carnival two children took off their *shoes* to run. After the races they went to collect their *shoes*. When he arrived home one boy tried to put on his *shoes*. To his astonishment he discovered that he had two left *shoes*. Well, as you all know, two left *shoes* are not much use except to some-body with two left feet. So, do we have anybody out there who went home with no left *shoes* but two right *shoes?*'

There was a long silence until a boy three places in front of Yang Jim shuffled uneasily before putting up his hand a little bit at a time until it was upright. The tall teacher looked stern at first, then started to grin. He talked for a while as the unhappy boy took his bag up to the veranda to produce the two right *shoes*.

Not long after that, Yang followed the other children into a classroom. Five minutes passed before he found himself sitting at a desk. The teacher spoke to the class for a while, smiling now and then though never saying the word *shoes*. Soon she began to chalk things up on the board. The pupils started writing in their books. A few minutes passed. Yang sat there, not knowing what to do. The teacher stroked her long hair into position, then came to his desk. She picked up a pencil and an exercise book, making signs that he should try to write.

Yang took hold of the pencil. She smiled. It was a kind smile, warm like spring sunshine, but he could not smile back. He could not think why he ought to smile, for she had not said *shoes*. He tried to copy the patterns on the board. He was only trying to be polite, for he could not understand why it was nec-essary to do the writing.

A long time afterwards he heard the sound of a bell ringing. The children stood at their desks. The teacher spoke. Everyone grabbed biscuits or apples or packets of chips, then hurried out of the door. Only Yang was left there. The teacher pointed towards the playing area. Yang went out, glad to be in the free-dom of the breeze and bright sun.

Out on the back paddock he looked for the other Korean boy. He was not in sight. Everybody seemed to be busy. Girls were throwing basketballs, boys were passing oval-shaped balls around; some children were hopping and kicking at flat stones on a cement area marked out with chalk lines, while others were thumping a tennis ball against a wall where there was a makeshift squash court.

There came a moment when Yang realized that a huge boy was shouting at him and shaking his fist. Without realizing, he had walked between two boys who were throwing the oval ball to each other. He hurried off in another direction.

Two children with fair hair pointed at him and giggled. He stared at them, bewildered. Suddenly they started swishing a skipping rope, forgetting all about him. The wind came chilling round the corner of a building. Yang felt he wasn't part of anything. He shivered.

Then a familiar-looking round leather ball came rolling along the ground towards him, almost as if by magic. A soccer ball, just like many he had played with in Seoul! Almost unthinkingly he used his foot to flip the ball up on to his knee, then bounced it up on to his head before letting it tumble back on to his instep, where he let it rest for a few moments, before passing it back to the boy who had sent it in his direction.

He became aware that about seven boys were looking at him. Yet they were not regarding him like a stranger from an alien land. Their faces expressed total admiration. His skill had impressed them. It was a sort of international language.

No sounds came from their mouths. They made signs. The signs said clearly: 'Come and join our game'.

Slowly, nervously, he moved into the zone where they were playing. It was not a familiar zone, but at that moment he felt that he was not such a frighteningly long distance from the home he knew best.

'YANG JIM', JIM KABLE (ED.), *An Arc of Australian Voices* (1990)

Behind the masks

Ted Egan (1932–) taught in the Northern Territory in the 1960s and at Groote Eylandt where the Australian Government took over a mission school.

Among most tribal Aborigines there's an avoidance pattern that says there's about ten per cent of the people that you can't talk to, look at or have any dealings with. On Groote the avoidance taboo applies to about seventy-five per cent of the people, which makes life very tough. And the Groote Eylandters are tough and surly by our standards. They're aggressive.

In the past the women had to get down and hide behind a bark blanket which they were required to carry at all times. I'm of the opinion that Groote Eylandt women still mentally carry those things. The minute you put them under pressure, they hide behind them. And the same applies to the boys, but much less so. You couldn't say, 'Abel, what is ...?' You couldn't even say, 'Six times seven? Michael, what do you think?' Because immediately he'd yell at you, 'Don't single me out!' So you didn't ever do it.

If you put a kid under any pressure as an individual that kid would invariably stand up, stalk — bang, bang, bang — out of the bloody room. The other kids would immediately put their fingers over their ears because he would predictably go outside, grab the biggest handful of rocks and just let them go — whack whack — straight at the school. We had boxes of glass louvres. We had to change the windows every bloody morning.

Then he would go home and get Mum and Dad. They would come with a handful of spears. Now I've seen one of these fellows hit a banana palm with a spear five times out of eight from nearly one hundred yards. Of course Dad wouldn't throw the spear at you. He would throw it symbolically, either over the roof or through the wall. Then he and Mum would give everybody, the teacher and every other kid, the greatest serve.

So I had to come to terms with this. How could I teach them when they wouldn't look directly at me. It was a bit of a fluke, but for oral English I hit on a device. We made papier mâché masks: crocodile heads, or pigs' or frogs' heads. They were nice masks, and the kids with these masks on would talk their heads off. So I thought, 'Well bugger it, we'll have oral English with the masks.' I could say to Michael, 'How are you, Mr Crocodile?' And he'd say, 'Oh, pretty good, Mr Egan.' 'What's six times seven?' 'Forty-two.' He'd answer because he had the mask on. He was a pig or a rabbit or a clown.

HANK NELSON, *With Its Hat About Its Ears* (1990; FIRST PUBLISHED 1989)

World within world

ROBERT DESSAIX (1944–), WRITER AND CRITIC, PUBLISHED HIS AUTOBIOGRAPHY, *A Mother's Disgrace*, IN 1994.

When I was about eleven I started reading up on artificial languages — Esperanto, of course, but also Volapük, Pirro's Universal-Sprache, Interlingua and other concoctions. I was starting to learn Latin and Russian, already spoke a little French, and for £2/1/6 I bought myself a copy of Frederick Bodmer's *Loom of Language: A Guide to Foreign Languages for the Home Student*. So while other little boys were playing cricket in the street after school or going to Scouts or torturing small animals, I was comparing Greek script with the Cypriotic syllabary, musing on sound changes in medieval French and learning quite a lot about the differences between Swedish and Danish, not to mention Dutch, from the fascinating word lists in the Language Museum at the back of the book. All this must have been having some effect on the sort of teenager I was becoming.

One effect, apart from a complete lack of interest in cricket or indeed in playing any kinds of games with little boys, even cards, was the immediate need I felt to create a Pure Language for my Pure Land. I would set up my own loom and weave my own language. Now, many children make up private languages, I know — sisters talk with brothers in secret codes, only children compile private vocabularies, prepubescent fraternities have their ritualistic gobbledygook and so on. But starting from the age of about eleven I began to do something much more ambitious and, I suppose, eccentric: I began to construct an Indo-European language of enormous grammatical and morphological complexity, with a history going back to pre-Roman times in Asia Minor, sound shifts, three scripts (one syllabic, thanks to the Cypriots), two main dialects and several regional variations on those dialects. If I'm alone and in a compulsively Pure-Landish mood, I'll chat to myself in this language (the dialect depends on the persona I'm entering) and certainly all my dogs have heard a lot of it. As far as I know, no one else has ever heard or read a word of it. (Well, you've actually read one word, *mokkd* (n., neut. sing. nom.): 'a small keep' (from the root *mok-* 'to close off'.)

A Mother's Disgrace (1995; FIRST PUBLISHED 1994)

Radio days

ROSA SAFRANSKY (1948–), DAUGHTER OF POLISH MIGRANTS, WAS AT A STATE PRIMARY SCHOOL IN MELBOURNE. THE FOLLOWING IS AN EXTRACT FROM A SHORT STORY.

'I've got eyes in the back of my head Danny A-a-rons!' Evil Eyes grabs the racing form away from Danny who wants to be a bookie, and hauls him out to the front of the room.

'Stick out your hand!' Evil Eyes raises the strap. Danny refuses.

'Don't give cheek to me. Stick out your hand!'

'You always pick on me!' Danny cries. Real tears wash down his cheeks.

'Just wait till I get my old man onto you!' Danny bursts out of the room. When? I couldn't wait.

Evil Eyes, a short ugly man with a butcher's face and an RSL badge stuck to his lapel, arrives at eight on the dot each morning. A few pieces of rotting driftwood and a dead snake in a pickle jar are carefully arranged on the nature study bench. The snake is a warning. In Evil Eyes's classroom, nature is dead.

'Now is that the way to do short division?' he smiles as he drives his fist into my exercise book. I can see the black points of stubble on his nose and smell the whiskey on his breath as he positions his ruler at an angle and smashes it into the palm of my hand. He rips the pages out of my exercise book and throws them across the room. The figures on my page blur in and out of focus but only cissies, weakies and girls cry in public. Who cares if he's got eyes in the back of his head, he looks ugly enough the way he is. I complain constantly to my mother about him but she refuses to listen and regales me with tales of her education in Poland which finished in the sixth grade.

'Mr Gallagher wouldn't be a teacher if he didn't know what he was doing. He is an educated man.'

Evil Eyes is a gorilla! And I HATE 'A Sunburnt Country' by D-O-R-O-T-H-E-A M-A-C-K-E-L-L-A-R! Why do we have to keep repeating this poem day in and day out? Melbourne is wet and bitterly cold. I shiver as an icy wind blows under the door of the toilet block where I sit, freezing to death, trying to avoid wiping myself with the government issued waxed toilet paper supplied in tiny cardboard boxes by the Education Department. I prefer my mother's cut up newspapers which she slices up neatly with a ruler, then impales on a large nail.

My mother is washing the kitchen floor.

'Now it's clean, you can get it dirty again,' she propels the mop under my feet while I try to memorise my Education Day speech. Our principal, Mr Conroy, says I sound like the Queen.

Mr Conroy shares his office with a portrait of the Queen, Albert Namatjira's 'Ayer's Rock' and a loudspeaker system. The names of ex-students killed in two world wars hang outside his office on polished wooden boards in gold lettering. Faces on faded photos of school football teams stare defiantly down the corridor. Our school boasts an enormous concrete yard with an incinerator outside the boys toilets. The yard is segregated, boys in one half, girls the other. A model garden maintained by the horticulture class and carefully fenced off from the rest of the concrete, decorates the front of the administration block.

Education Day arrives at last and my mother, the Polish immigrant, stands in the quadrangle silently watching me.

'Welcome to the school.' I enunciate each syllable distinctly and clearly as if State School 458196 were Buckingham Palace.

'Where did you learn such good English?' Mr Conroy smiles. From Kid Grayson, Superman and the Shadow and Harry Dearth, George Foster and Grandpa in 'Laugh Hoo-Hoo-Ha-Ha-Ha, Till You Cry' and 'When you're on a good thing', a fly spray commercial I love which says, 'Stick to it!' At night I took the mantel radio to bed and listened to an ancient music critic called Dr Floyd. I knew the second an 'h' was dropped. I even thought some of my teachers couldn't speak English properly themselves.

'You're a good sport!' I tell my father. At school it was a great compliment. He hit the roof.

'Is that what they teach you at school? Is this what comes from getting an EDUCATION?'

'Queen of the parasites', R.F. Holt (ed.), *Neighbours: Multicultural Writing of the 1980s* (1991)

Mr Twitch

PELHAM COBBETT (1953–) SURVIVED THREE YEARS AS A SCHOOL TEACHER IN VICTORIA, AND NOW LIVES AND WRITES IN MELBOURNE. THIS IS AN EXTRACT FROM AN UNPUBLISHED CHILDREN'S STORY SET IN THE 1970S.

'In your class,'
said Sandra,
'we never see any films.
Last year
in Mr Jock's class
we saw lots of films
and we were good.'
'Is that true?'
said Mr Twitch.
'I am sure you didn't see many films
with Mr Jock.'
'Yes, yes,'
said the other children.
'With Mr Jock
we watched films all the time.'
'And were you good?'
asked Mr Twitch.
'Yes, yes,'
cried all the children.
'With Mr Jock we were very good.
If you showed us films
we would be good all the time.'

Next day Mr Twitch took the children
into the film room.
'If any children talk
while the film is on,'
said Mr Twitch,
'they will be in trouble.'

It was not the film
that the children had asked for,
but as soon as it began
Mr Twitch knew
that it would be very interesting.
It was all about butterflies.
It showed how they began as caterpillars,
when they did nothing but eat and grow.
Then they made themselves into cocoons,
where they couldn't move
and they couldn't see,
and then they changed into butterflies
and flew away.

When the film was almost finished
there was a knock on the door.
It was Peter's mother.
She had come to take Peter
to the doctor.
'Peter has been a good boy today,'
said Mr Twitch.
He felt in the dark for the light switch
and turned it on.
But the window was open
and the children were not there.

UNPUBLISHED MANUSCRIPT (1980)

Copy cats

Simon French (1957–) published his first novel for children, *Hey Phantom Singlet*, when he was still at school in Sydney.

Math clattered down the stairs, the maroon Qantas airline bag in one hand and a pair of suede boots in the other. At the front door he dropped the bag, then sat down and put the boots on. Once he'd laced them up, he checked through the bag to make sure he'd packed the right books for school.

Mrs Roxon came down the stairs, then walked out towards the kitchen.

'See you this arvo,' Math called after her, as he picked the bag up and opened the door.

'What shoes have you got on?' she called from the kitchen.

'My desert boots.'

'Why aren't you wearing your school shoes?'

'Too small for me.'

He was about to step out the door when she called again: 'And don't forget to pick Ivan up from kindergarten this afternoon.'

'Righto.'

'You forgot to last week.'

'Yeah. See you.' He stepped outside, clicking the door shut behind him. He started off down the footpath, then stopped and waved back at Steve Kerr who was still out on his verandah, painting. Steve waved back and grinned.

Math walked down the hill, past the Cullens' house, past the two little kids who were once more playing out on the footpath.

On the street corner at the bottom of the slope, Stuart Young waited. He and Math had known each other practically since they'd first started school; and somehow, through all their fights and minor hassles, they'd stayed the best of mates. Stu had a serious, freckled face and dark brown hair that curled its way down over his head. He had a weird sense of humour which showed through all of his jokes — most of which were so sick, Math laughed anyway.

'Hi Stu.'

'Hi.'

'You do the science homework?'

'What science homework?'

'Those questions we had t'do for Mad Dog. Jeez, you've got a great memory.'

'I know. Well, can you lend us your book and I'll copy 'em all up at recess?'

'Yeah, okay.'

[…]

They came to Oxford Street. Being one of the main roads into Sydney, it was pretty crowded with traffic. Math and Stu waited a moment, then crossed over to the bus stop on the other side.

'Hope Stan's driving the bus today. Can't stand that other guy.'

'The mad pom?'

'Yeah. Boy, he's a rat.'

Since Stan was the only bus driver who called the kids by their proper names and let them smoke if they wanted to, he'd easily become the most popular driver on the school run.

[…]

The high school crouched in readiness for the eight forty-five stampede.

The buildings were old: two storey brick, with tall windows and dark classrooms. The playground was a cramped and barren stretch of asphalt; at one corner, a lone gumtree struggled for survival.

It was a pretty dismal place — a concrete nothing.

Stan brought the bus to a grinding halt, opened the doors, then watched as the kids piled out onto the footpath.

Math, Stu and Greg walked along towards the school entrance, talking about the previous night's homework. As they walked through the gate, a car came up behind them, its horn blasting. Hustler, a burly sixth former, leant out the driver's window and shouted, 'Outa the way you first form cruds!'

The three boys scattered, and the mauve Holden panel van roared past. Hustler was one of the few kids in the school who owned a car, and he was the only student who took the liberty of parking it with the teachers' cars.

'Not a bad car that,' Greg said, watching Hustler swinging the van into a parking space.

'Nuh,' Stu answered, also watching. 'Wouldn't mind it myself.'

They entered the main playground. A lot of kids were already around, either playing handball or standing in groups. Some cleaners were still there, getting the last of yesterday's dirt out of sight. One ageing cleaner, armed with mops, bucket and duster, charged across the quad in the direction of the cleaners' annexe.

Math dumped his bag on a seat. 'You handing that poetry work in, Greg?'

'Not now. I wanna check my answers and see what Stu's got.'

'Fair enough. I'm handing mine in now before I forget.'

Stu nodded. 'Tell Boony we're still working on it.'

Hey Phantom Singlet (1975)

Bits of goss

JOHN MARSDEN (1950–) WRITES NOVELS FOR CHILDREN AND ADO-LESCENTS, SET IN VICTORIAN PRIVATE SCHOOLS. THESE EXTRACTS FROM *Take My Word for It* ARE FROM THE DIARY OF A YEAR 9 BOARDER, LISA.

April 25:

Rikki and I went to the Anzac Service in town. It was OK, not as boring as I thought it would be, and it did get us out of an

Astronomy test in Science. A few weeks ago we had that film, 'For Valour', and that changed my attitudes a bit. One of the guys in the film, who was killed in the evacuation from the beach, looked so like Peter. I was looking at the old diggers at the Cenotaph and trying to imagine them as the young guys in the film, but it was hard. They seemed so serious and responsible. In the film they were casual and carefree, not giving a stuff about anything. They were different from us, I think. In those days I don't think people our age questioned anything or analysed what was happening. Seems like the government said, 'OK, there's a war, you blokes grab a uniform and get over there.' And they said, 'Oh yeah, righto, we'll have a bash at that.' Nowadays we'd say, 'Well, what's the war for? Who's fighting and why? What other ways out of it did you try before you declared war? Why don't you go yourselves if you're that keen on it?'

I admire those guys who went though, and I felt really sad for them having so many mates killed or wounded, and I know we wouldn't be living in the kind of country we're in now if they hadn't gone.

July 13:

[...]

Second bit of goss is not so good. Kate got picked up by the cops last Saturday night. It's the first time I've seen her really worried, and believe me, she is packing her daks. She wasn't going to tell anyone about it, but needless to say the whole Year 9 knew by lights out. She was caught in a stolen car with a guy who was expelled from Brentwood last year. Kate says she didn't know it was stolen but she still might be charged.

Originally she was going to the snow, but when she took that illegal before mid-term her parents cracked a bit of an aggro and cancelled the skiing. Probably would have been better if she'd gone; she wouldn't have got into so much trouble.

The other thing is, she reckons she might get expelled from here, but I can't see how she can, for something that happens during the holidays. You'd think that what she does in her spare time is her own business. Still, I suppose that's not always true. I mean if you got arrested for murder or drug-running or something the school'd have to expel you.

My mid-term wasn't as dramatic as these others. It was OK though. The Year 9 dance was a disaster for me — I spent the whole night trying to avoid these complete drop-kicks from St Patrick's, two guys called Duncan and Wayne. God, they were losers. Plus they would have registered about 0.8 on the breathalyser scale. Then, when I tried to crack onto a guy from St Luke's I crashed and burned badly. Turned out he was with Laura Johns, so that was a popular move with Laura, who would have nuked me if she'd had a button handy.

Take My Word For It (1993; FIRST PUBLISHED 1992)

Multiple choice

MELINA MARCHETTA (1965–) SET HER NOVEL FOR CHILDREN, *Looking for Alibrandi*, IN A SYDNEY CONVENT SCHOOL.

Panic was my first reaction to the multiple choice options which lay on my desk in front of me. I glanced at the students around me before turning back to question three. I hated multiple choice. Yet I didn't want to get question three wrong. I didn't want to get any of them wrong. The outcome would be too devastating for my sense of being.

So I began with elimination. 'D' was completely out of the question as was 'A', so that left 'B' and 'C'. I pondered both for quite a while and just as I was about to make my final decision I heard my name being called.

'Josephine?'

'Huh?'

'I think you mean "I beg your pardon" don't you, dear?'

'I beg your pardon, Sister.'

'What are you doing? You're reading, aren't you, young lady?'

'Um … yeah.'

'Um, yeah? Excellent, Josephine. I can see you walking away with the English prize this year. *Now stand up.*'

So my final school year began. I had promised myself that I would be a saint for this year alone. I would make the greatest impression on my teachers and become the model student. I knew it would all fail. But just not on the first day.

Sister Gregory walked towards me and when she was so close that I could see her moustache, she held out her hand.

'Show me what you're reading.'

I handed it to her and watched her mouth purse itself together and her nostrils flare in triumph because she knew she was going to get me.

She skimmed it and then handed it back to me. I could feel my heart beating fast.

'Read from where you were up to.'

I picked up the magazine and cleared my throat.

'"What kind of a friend are you?"' I read from *Hot Pants* magazine.

She looked at me pointedly.

'"You are at a party",' I began with a sigh, '"and your best friend's good-looking, wealthy and successful boyfriend tries to make a pass. Do you: A — Smile obligingly and steal away into the night via the back door; B — Throw your cocktail all over his Country Road suit; C — Quietly explain the loyalty you have towards your friend; D — Tell your friend instantly, knowing that she will make a scene".'

You can understand, now, why I found it hard to pick between 'B' and 'C'.

'May I ask what this magazine has to do with my religion class, Miss?'

'Religion?'

'Yes, dear,' she continued in her sickeningly sarcastic tone. 'The one we are in now.'

'Well…quite a lot, Sister.'

I heard snickers around me as I tried to make up as much as I could along the way.

Religion class, first period Monday morning, is the place to try to pull the wool over the eyes of Sister Gregory. (She kept her male saint's name although the custom went out years ago. She probably thinks it will get her into heaven. I don't think she realises that feminism has hit religion and that the female saints in heaven are probably also in revolt.)

'Would you like to explain yourself, Josephine?'

I looked around the classroom watching everyone shrugging almost sympathetically.

They thought I was beaten.

'We were talking about the Bible, right?'

'I personally think that you don't know what we've been talking about, Josephine. I think you're trying to fool me.'

The nostrils flared again.

Sister Gregory is famous for nostril-flaring. Once I commented to someone that she must have been a horse in another life. She overheard and scolded me, saying that, as a Catholic, I shouldn't believe in reincarnation.

'Fool you, Sister? Oh, no. It's just that while you were speaking I remembered the magazine. You were talking about today's influences that affect our Christian lives, right?'

Anna, one of my best friends, turned to face me and nodded slightly.

'And?'

'Well, Sister, this magazine is a common example,' I said, picking it up and showing everyone. 'It's full of rubbish. It's full of questionnaires that insult our intelligence. Do you think they have articles titled "Are you a good Christian?" or "Do you love your neighbour?". No. They have articles titled "Do you love your sex life?" knowing quite well that the average age of the reader is fourteen. Or "Does size count?" and let me assure you, Sister, they are not referring to his height.

'I brought this magazine in today, Sister, to speak to everyone about how insulted we are as teenagers and how important it is that we think for ourselves and not through magazines that exploit us under the guise of educating us.'

Sera, another friend of mine, poked her fingers down her mouth as if she was going to vomit.

Sister and I stared at each other for a long time before she held out her hand again. I passed the magazine to her knowing she hadn't been fooled.

'You can pick it up from Sister Louise,' she said, referring to the principal.

The bell rang and I packed my books quickly, wanting to escape her icy look.

'You're full of it,' Sera said as we walked out. 'And you owe me a magazine.'

I threw my books into my locker and ignored everyone's sarcasm.

'Well, what was it?' Lee grinned. 'A, B, C, or D?'

'I would have gone with him,' Sera said, spraying half a can of hairspray around her gelled hair.

'Sera, if they jailed people for ruining the ozone layer, you'd get life,' I told her, turning back to Lee. 'I was going to go for the cocktail on the Country Road suit.'

The second bell for our next class rang and with a sigh I made another pledge to myself that I would be a saint. On the whole I make plenty of pledges that I don't keep.

Looking for Alibrandi (1992)

Our daily bread

Sonia Mycak (1964–) describes her experiences as a Ukrainian migrant child in a Sydney convent and that of her brother, a few years earlier, in a state primary school.

It's first period, Monday morning. Religion with Sister Margaret Mary.

'Who can tell me what Father O'Malley's sermon was about?' Her eyes are scanning the room. Somehow I know they will land on me.

'I don't know, Sister,' I reply meekly.

'Didn't you go to Mass on Sunday?'

'Yes, sister. But I went to Ukrainian church, and we don't really have sermons, not until the end, and they are about Ukraine.'

Sister Margaret Mary's eyes widen with disbelief. If only I had the nerve to tell her that I had also taken first communion but that it was in our church, and that we also have nuns who are as pious as her except that they teach us in Ukrainian, and that my father had been instrumental in establishing the Ukrainian Catholic Church in Sydney and had been elected to go to Rome as a representative of our community before he died. If only all of that actually mattered, if only all of that could match that look of disbelief on her face.

It's 1954. I haven't been born yet, but my brother is five years old and standing at the gates of the local school, about to embark on his first day there. He speaks no English — at this stage my parents' use of the language is functional but not sophisticated. So, as well as facing the expected trauma of separation from his mother, he is confronting a new culture in a language he cannot speak and can only fleetingly understand. At midday the other children crowd around his lunchbox:

'Ugh…yuk. He's eating a dirty sandwich.'

The young teacher comes over to see why the new boy is crying and the others are laughing at him. She takes one look at his half-eaten sandwich, and throws it in the bin.

'Come on, we'll get you a nice vegemite sandwich from the canteen.'

She takes his hand and they walk to the next building. She's only trying to be helpful. After all, she's never seen black bread before, and as for that smelly salami — well, how is a child meant to eat such spicy food? It's a wonder the child doesn't throw it all up, she says to the ladies putting away the tubs of peanut butter. It's no wonder he's such a pale, spineless thing, she says, if he has to live on *that* kind of food.

'Well, they don't know much about nutrition in *those* countries, do they?' says one of the ladies by way of explanation.

Of course, no-one told Miss Campbell that she would have a little 'New Australian' in her class. She's not sure what to do with the wide-eyed fragile looking boy with his funny baggy shorts and unpronounceable name. His eyes plead insecurity; this type of profound fear is something she can't deal with. She's used to kids weeing on the floor, and crying for mummy — not this. And somehow he must learn English. It's embarrassing for her, and no good for him, either. So, for his own good, she instigates a system whereby she slaps his wrist good and hard every time he uses one of *those* foreign words. She even sends him out of the class when he finally starts crying in sheer confusion and utter misery. Eventually his survival instinct takes over, his skin thickens somewhat and his English improves. It improves so much that six years later he becomes dux of the school and wins a place at the selective high school. It improves so much that now, thirty-seven years later, he speaks not one word of Ukrainian.

By the time I was a teenager, a certain conflict of interests was beginning to dominate my life. Allegiance to two cultures was dividing my intellect from my emotions, my days from my nights, my weekends from my weekdays. Two languages meant two names and two signatures; two schools meant two sets of report cards and sports days; two calendars meant two Christmases and two Easters. Of course this did not always pose a problem. As a child, two sets of Christmas presents seemed a distinct advantage. And the beauty of Ukrainian cultural life was something that every child could adore. Every year I eagerly awaited the time when the women in my family would start baking the rich Easter bread known as *paska*, in anticipation of the feast which would follow on Easter Sunday. Then the vodka would flow freely and accompany the various *zakusky* of herrings and horseradish; the roasted meats, cooked to perfection, would lie on the table along with meat and sauerkraut-filled *pyrozhky*, and the dishes of potato and cheese dumplings known as *varenyky* would tempt even the youngest of the family. Easter Sunday would be a time of celebration, of merriment and gaiety, where the oldest generation would entertain the youngest, and a time of nostalgia, where those old enough to remember would think of those left behind or lost altogether. All this frivolity came after an entire night spent in church, the conclusion of which was the blessing of the Easter baskets, a ritual in which the priest, adorned in an ornate gold and silver gown, would bless the wicker baskets laden with breads and meats and cheeses which each family had brought to symbolise the prosperity of the season of the risen Lord. Nestling amongst the food and the embroidered linen lay the multifarious colours of the *pysanky* — eggs decorated with wax and dyed in bright colours, adding to the sheer brilliance of the spectacle.

But being Ukrainian was not always so easy. At school, on the television, amongst Australian friends, the assumption was that there was a definable quintessential Australian culture which was at the centre of our lives. And yet for my family, the Ukrainian community was the pivot of our existence. I longed to belong to the first but was inextricably part of the second, and the problem of dual allegiance only increased as I got older.

'A DUAL EXISTENCE IN A SEEMINGLY SINGULAR COUNTRY', KAREN HERNE, JOANNE TRAVAGLIA, ELIZABETH WEISS (EDS), *Who Do You Think You Are?: Second Generation Immigrant Women in Australia* (1992)

Santa at the Hindmarsh Hall

HELEN O'SHEA (1951–) IS A MELBOURNE WRITER. THIS EXTRACT COMES FROM HER FORTHCOMING BOOK ABOUT A VICTORIAN COUNTRY DISTRICT IN THE 1990S.

Alongside the exhilaration of harvest and the anticipation of Christmas, there was anxiety. The humid weather gave way to hot northerlies, and the district was already dry. Betty Marles was in the store on the morning of the Christmas Tree. She said it was always like that, ever since the fires. 'It's the northerlies, they really put the wind up people. No-one says anything but everyone knows, and you're just watching, keeping an eye out.'

Geraldine Helmer blew into the store, leaving the baby in the car, and bought a gift for the Tree. And why not? Bill asked. The baby's arrival might have stirred up the local gossips, but no child should be left out at the Christmas Tree, not in his opinion.

Every year the Christmas Tree and school concert were held at the district hall. The concerts had been going since the school opened over a hundred years ago, but the Tree was newer. Betty Marles thought it must have come in Depression times, when she was a child.

'As long as I can remember there was a Christmas Tree, and as long as I can remember my grandfather was Santa Claus. He was a great big bloke, a jovial sort of a fellow, and he loved kids. The presents were all put up in Grandma's house, up on the big bed in the spare bedroom. And we'd be always trying to sneak up and have a look under the blanket. But these days, every mother buys her own kiddy's present. And we always had a concert at the same time. We did a Teddy Bear's Picnic one year, and we were all dressed up in hessian bags. Another year we had satin frog suits, green with yellow hands.'

'Yairs,' Bill consulted his memory. 'One of us was a frog, it might've been Mercy. The mothers did a marvellous job with those costumes.'

'And, Bill, didn't the hall used to always be packed! You were lucky to get a seat, you know. I suppose when I went to school there would've been about thirty children, there might've been more. And now it's down to nine. But that's the way it goes. I've been really hoping when the school closes somebody'll still run a Christmas Tree.

'There's always been lollies and balloons, and always a lovely supper: cream sponges, éclairs, cream puffs and all those sorts of things. And they used to make coffee out the back in coppers, didn't they, Bill, milk coffee. One person would take the cups around, and along would come another person and they'd have a big pot of coffee, and then the next person would have one of tea, and then there'd be somebody with a bit of milk and sugar, all around the hall. Then would come the big trays of sandwiches, and the cakes. Hindmarsh was always known for good suppers, wasn't it?'

Betty and her husband Wal brought the pine tree up to the hall after lunch. The tree came each year from the plantation behind the school, the result of decades of Arbor Day plantings. The big fire ten years ago had missed it, and burnt down the store instead. Betty wondered what would happen to the trees now. To think of all those meetings where the School Council had decided not to sell the timber, to save it for an emergency, and now there was one, the trees couldn't make any difference.

'It was all bush over there behind the school, right up to the fifties. We've got a bush block on our place still, thirty acres, and we'll leave it that way while I'm alive. I love trees; I love them, yeah. I used to come down with Dad and he'd cut wood, and the kookaburras'd be there with him, and I'd help him stack it. I didn't have any brothers, so I suppose I had to help Dad. At first he used to sell to the factory and later just for firewood. There'd be a fortune in it now with all these wood heaters.'

Looking southwards to the Marles' place beyond the school, it was hard to imagine those bare flats bristling with rushes had once been bush. Hard to imagine a young girl working down there. The girls round here stayed at home generally, scarcely ever went beyond the garden or the cowyard.

At the back of the hall the men were setting up the tree, holding it in a rubbish bin filled with sand while they tried to jam it upright with a few bricks. The trunk kept falling sideways, and in the end they propped it against the wall so the women could get on with the decorating. Stuart, the schoolteacher, was up on the ladder untangling the streamers the kids had made. The rest of the men gathered down the back of the hall, giggling as they filled balloons from a helium dispenser.

That evening it seemed as if every car in the district was parked outside the hall. The men, scrubbed and brushed, had congregated by the door, stubbies already on the go. The schoolkids were giggling and whispering and eyeing the Christmas tree. Mothers sat in groups while the pre-schoolers screeched up and down, knocking over bassinets and working themselves into a lather. The schoolteacher looked once more at his watch and clapped his hands. 'All right, everyone.' The pupils of Hindmarsh School gathered on the stage for the last time ever.

The children looked a bit nervous but played to their audience, smiling at grandparents and acting coy. The little boy with Down's Syndrome boomed out of tune, but people just listened more intently. The audience roared at the 'Doctor, doctor' jokes that the kids had been rehearsing on everyone for the past six weeks; but when one of the Little Teapots tipped right over, there was hardly a titter.

Stuart turned on the electronic keyboard for the carols and soon we were back there. 'The First Noël', 'Away in a Manger', 'Silent Night', 'O Come All Ye Faithful'. The ghosts of a hundred Christmases hovered around us, the glittering tree before us. It was like church; here was the centre, or the idea of a centre. This was home, where we came from. People like us had come to this outpost of swamp and scrub, had planted pines to show that they had arrived and would prosper. And they had, or some had. The others had left.

Outside the hall Santa had arrived in his ute from a Christmas Tree a few miles up the road. Tipping a stubby carefully between layers of cotton wool, he was having trouble getting over the kids who had chased him, trying to rip off his beard.

'The little buggers. I nearly burst my boiler getting back to the old sleigh. I tell you what, the reindeer were pretty thirsty by the time I got here!' Inside the kids sang 'Jingle Bells' for all they were worth, but Santa was playing hard to get.

'Come on, school,' Stuart egged them on, 'Santa can't hear you. Let's sing the first verse again.' The kids were at such a pitch they were squealing in anticipation.

'Ho, ho, ho, little children! Ho, ho, ho!' Santa hammed it up, asking if they'd been good boys and girls as he gave out the presents, ignoring the snatches of envious siblings. He made a discreet getaway just as the bags of lollies were being handed out.

Children with overstuffed mouths rushed the tables for more sugar: fizzy drinks and fairy bread. For the adults there were cups of tea and cream puffs (the district's best). There were plates of sandwiches, party pies, scones, slices, a couple of sponges. It was the last chance to catch up on most of the neighbours before Christmas, and people stayed on for a while. The Baptist pastor's squeaky laugh rose above the chatter, and fractious children with sticky fingers clambered for attention. Only

Geraldine Helmer left early, carrying the sleeping baby with a new pink rattle beside her in the basket.

'TREEVINES', *Meanjin* (1994)

Speaking Australian

LUCIA, DAUGHTER OF ITALIAN IMMIGRANTS, WHO LEARNED AUSTRALIAN WAYS IN MELBOURNE SCHOOLS, TOLD HER STORY TO MORAG LOH DURING THE LATE 1970S.

I was born in Italy, in Abruzzo, but I haven't got much memory of it, just vague little pictures of Grandpa and a little house. I was five and a half when I came and I started school. I started in Grade One, I missed out on Preps.

Well, the first two years were very sad. I didn't make friends very easy, it wasn't until Grade Three that I really had a friend. I used to sit at lunch time under the staircase, I always remember sitting under there and waiting for the bell to go to resume class. I couldn't communicate. I didn't know the language as yet. There was a lot of Italians at the school but I can't remember any special efforts being made to teach English. I was the only one that couldn't speak Australian and I suppose all the other children were too young to realise that they had to make a special effort to fit me in.

I remember crying and Mum sending me off. Mum pushed me out of the front door every morning, saying, 'Well, you're off to school.' It wasn't until about Grade Three that I was happily going to school; until then I'd always be very upset.

Strangely enough I never had any Italian friends, never. I could never accept an Italian friend, I always wanted to have an Australian friend. Do you think it might be I wanted to be accepted by Australians? Then I didn't speak Italian, always a dialect, and the other Italian kids spoke dialect too, so we had to speak English. Even to this day I'm very quiet when there's an Italian group around, I keep well out of it, just in case … I can understand Italian OK but I'm very embarrassed to talk, I don't feel as though I could go up and have a good conversation with somebody. I speak to Mum and Dad always in dialect and I never feel comfortable in Italian. I always say to Giovanni, my husband, that I don't fit into the Italian way and I don't fit into the Australian way, I'm not one or the other. He came here at fifteen so he has got more of the Italian in him.

I became quite popular at school, believe it or not. That was later on, and it was really good. But I always felt different, oh yes. I'd try to hide the fact that I was Italian, although I could never really hide it with my dark hair. I never felt pretty, I always felt as if I was the ugly duckling. I always thought I'd have to have blonde hair for the boys to like me. I'd have given anything to have had lighter hair and lighter skin and to have been passed as an Australian. It would have been marvellous.

I never wanted Mum to come into the school because she always wore dark clothes and never wore make-up. I didn't want the other kids to say 'Ooh — there's your mother.' I think all the Italian mothers looked very much the same. They never took much part in the school and I never wanted them around, never.

In primary school I remember having these pair of very colourful socks, they were all triangles, Italian socks, very lairy looking things. And every time Mum would send me off to school in those — oh — I'd cry, because the kids would pick on me for wearing them.

The food. That was my biggest problem. We never had sliced bread. Mum and Dad wouldn't eat it, and we'd buy these big loaves and of course it was very hard to cut them thin, so I'd end up with two inch thick sandwiches. And Mum's fillings! They were nothing like ham. I'd have *mortadella* and then there was *frittata*, omelet I suppose you'd call it now, and the bread would become a bit greasy. I'd have to hide those sandwiches because everyone'd laugh at me eating them. I'd have to eat them when nobody was looking, which is very hard in primary school when you all have to sit in a big hall. I'd always try to find a little corner and eat my sandwiches in there. I don't think I ever told Mum. Perhaps I might have and she said, 'Oh well, that's all you're getting.' As soon as I was old enough to make my own lunch I'd go out and buy myself a roll and put in a slice of ham and a bit of tomato. That was much more acceptable at school.

Mucking around

Roberto, another child of Italian immigrants, told his story of Australian schooling to Morag Loh.

I'm at the high school now. I started off at the state school, then I went to St J's, that's Catholic, in Grade Three. My parents wanted a better education or something. I used to get the strap every day for no reason at all. If I didn't go to mass I'd get the strap on the Monday. I hated mass, because it was boring, just listening to the priest you'd fall asleep. Then I changed to a college and that was really hard. If I picked a ruler up and let it fall on the ground it would be, 'Come out the front,' and they'd sprinkle sand on the platform. We used to wear shorts in Form One and you'd have to kneel on the sand for about half an hour until the end of the period and you'd get the strap at the end as well. You'd get out of line when you've got line-up and you'd get the strap. Just for anything wrong, anything. If your shoes were dirty you'd have to polish them then you'd get your name marked down. If your name's written down five times you get the strap again and Saturday detention for three hours. My parents didn't mind, they were really satisfied. They go, 'If you want to punish my son, go right ahead.' I couldn't handle it. When I went there I was kicked out of the class more than I was in it. I used to go next door and talk to the teacher there between when he was telling his class what to do. In Form Two I said to Dad, 'Let me leave. I can't handle this.'

He went to the high school and straight away I got in. It was completely different. I thought classrooms were closed off, with closed doors, but there everything was opened up and you had lockers, you could swear and you didn't get told off. I was really happy and I started swearing because I was allowed to let everything out of me. I was used to being a good boy, see. As soon as I came in the school I said to the teacher, 'Where do I go?' and he just got hold of me by the head, and started laughing, and took me along and I was having fun. It was completely different. I learnt more at the Catholic school but I'm glad I came here.

The schools in the films about the '50s, the kids used to go to schools in their cars and have the girls with them. Schools should be like that. This school's like that in a way, it's open, you can do what you like. The last two periods I was over the pinball shop, but I hope nobody tells Sir. I'd rather go to school than work. We say, 'I hope I get kicked out of school,' but when you do, you want to come back in because you have more fun at school. School doesn't train you for anything much, not really, but it's social. I reckon my school should have a dance. I suppose what I'm saying shows I'm a bit Australian. I'm Italian what I think, but I'm Australian the things I do, like not listening to my father and mucking around.

Morag Loh (ED.), *With Courage in their Cases* (1984; FIRST PUB-LISHED 1980)

Soft frilly things from the sea

AIMÉE TSE (1975–) WAS BORN IN MELBOURNE TO CHINESE PAR-ENTS. SHE IS STUDYING ARTS AT UNIVERSITY.

My mum makes soup out of soft frilly things from the sea, and boils them with herbal plants. She buys packets of dried lotus roots, mung beans and white fungus from the Chinese grocery store. The man behind the counter has a mole on his chin with stiff black hairs growing out of it. He smells like musty wooden furniture.

My mum pours the soup into a thermos and I take it to school. At lunchtime, it sits on my desk with my sandwich and my apple. One day I was eating my apple when the teacher stopped me. 'No sweetie, you have to eat your sandwich first,' she instructed. The other kids started to giggle and I put my apple away.

By the time I finished my hot, clear soup everyone had gone outside to play without me. They said I ate strange soup with worms and beetles in it. They said I had a face like a frying pan and eyes like a power point. They said I was a nip and a gook. I wanted to say something back but I didn't know what words to use. It was like looking out of a face with no mouth.

As I walked home a couple of girls, Jessica and Pauline, followed me and stepped on the heels of my shoes. I could see my mum in the distance. She was standing outside our front gate waiting for me. I focused on her through my tears and walked as quickly as I could.

I asked my mum if there were any insects in my soup, and she said it was made from crab meat. I knew about crabs. I'd seen them crowded into tanks at restaurants, bound with string at the store, and packed into the meat compartment of my own fridge. It was traditional to keep the crabs alive until just before meal time. It amazed me that no matter how they were treated, they would not rot while there was still the tiniest droplet of life left in them. I told my mum I didn't want to eat crab. 'But it's good for you, and it gives the soup flavour,' she said gently. I told her I wouldn't eat crab meat and I wouldn't bring soup to school anymore.

That night I ate all my rice but wouldn't touch anything else. Mum told Dad about my decision and he slammed his hand on the dinner table. 'You will eat what the family eats,' he shouted. Mum gave him a cross look and turned to me. She said if I wouldn't eat meat, I'd have to eat more spinach and beans than my brothers and sisters. I thought about this and agreed.

The following night, Mum separated the soup into two pots, and made mine with mushroom stock. After dinner, she poured the leftovers into my thermos and put it in my schoolbag. She did this every night even though I never drank the soup at school. I drank it in the afternoon when I came home. The smooth white fungus was my favourite bit. I loved the way it slipped down my throat.

One day we ran out of bread, so Mum put an extra apple in my schoolbag. I finished the apples at recess and still felt hungry. I knew there were lots of good things in my soup, but I was still a little frightened. I waited until everyone had gone, then I took out my thermos and quietly crept behind the bookshelves to eat. But someone was already there.

Hidden in the corner was the new boy. There were pastry crumbs all over his face and on the floor around him. In his lap were three curry puffs on a sheet of crinkly brown paper. He stopped chewing when he saw me and tried to rewrap his lunch. I smiled at him and started drinking my soup. His name was Scott.

Shortly before the bell rang people began to wander inside. Jessica and Pauline peered around the bookshelves at us. 'Eating worms again, ching-chong?' Jessica sneered. There was silence.

'She sure is …' Scott returned finally. 'And I'm eating frog's ovaries and duck's tongues in curry sauce.' He looked at me and I started to giggle. 'Would you like some lizard's eyeballs?' I offered, holding up a spoonful of spotted pearl barley. Jessica's eyes widened in horror. She grabbed Pauline's arm and dashed outside.

Scott and I had lunch together again the next day, in the sunshine.

Canberra Times (1996)

Sources and acknowledgments

The editors and publisher wish to thank copyright holders for granting permission to reproduce textual extracts. Sources are as follows:

Joan **Airey**, 'Rural Life Between the Wars', *South Australiana*, vol. 14, no. 1, March, 1975, pp. 10–13; Thea **Astley**, *A Kindness Cup*, Penguin Books Australia, Ringwood, 1989, pp. 5–6, 110–11; A.G. **Austin**, *Select Documents in Australian Education 1788–1900*, Pitman Pacific Books, Carlton, 1972, pp. 164–8; Australian Archives and the Public Record Office of Victoria, *'My heart is breaking': A Joint Guide to Records about Aboriginal People in the Public Record Office of Victoria and the Australian Archives, Victorian Regional Office*, Australian Government Publishing Service, 1993, pp. 105, 160, 162; David **Bateson**, 'Yang Jim', *An Arc of Australian Voices* (ed. Jim Kable), Oxford University Press, Melbourne, pp. 18–20, reproduced with the author's permission; Randolph **Bedford**, *Naught to Thirty-three*, Melbourne University Press, Carlton, 1976, pp. 20–1, 26–7; Annabella **Boswell**, *Annabella Boswell's Journal* (ed. Morton Herman), Angus & Robertson, Sydney, 1965, pp. 9–10; Thomas **Bowden**, in *The Evidence to the Bigge Reports*, vol. 1, 'The Oral Evidence' (ed. John Ritchie), William Heinemann, Melbourne, 1971, pp. 159–61; Martin **Boyd**, *Day of My Delight: An Anglo-Australian Memoir*, Lansdowne Press, Melbourne, 1965, pp. 27–31; Dame Mabel **Brookes**, *Crowded Galleries*, William Heinemann, Melbourne, 1956, pp. 45–6; Mary Grant **Bruce**, *Norah of Billabong*, Angus & Robertson, Pymble, 1992, pp. 12–15; Prince **Charles**, 'Beating About the Bush', *Gordonstoun Record*, 1966 (Gordonstoun School magazine), reproduced with permission of the Prince of Wales Charities Trust; Nan **Chauncy**, *The Roaring 40*, Oxford University Press, London, 1963, pp. 9–13; Eliza à Beckett **Chomley**, *My Memoirs,* 1920, La Trobe Library, State Library of Victoria, MS 9034; Manning **Clark**, *The Puzzles of Childhood*, Penguin Books, Ringwood, 1989, pp. 192–6; Pelham **Cobbett**, 'Mr Twitch' (unpublished MS), reproduced with the author's permission; Joan **Colebrook**,

A House of Trees, Transworld Publishers, London, 1989, pp. 36–9; Timothy **Conigrave**, *Holding the Man*, McPhee Gribble, Ringwood, 1995, pp. 6–9; Peter **Conrad**, *Down Home: Revisiting Tasmania*, Chatto & Windus, London, 1988, pp. 192–4; Jill Ker **Conway**, *The Road from Coorain*, Minerva/Reed Books, London, 1992, pp. 93–5, copyright © 1989 Jill Ker Conway, reprinted by permission of Alfred A. Knopf Inc.; Evelyn **Crawford**, *Over My Tracks*, Penguin Books, Ringwood, 1993, pp. 12–14; Graeme **Davison**, *The Unforgiving Minute: How Australia Learned to Tell the Time*, Oxford University Press, South Melbourne, 1993, pp. 24–5, 27; Bruce **Dawe**, 'Public Library, Melbourne', *No Fixed Address: Poems*, F.W. Cheshire, Melbourne, 1962, p. 9; Peter **Dawson**, in *Adelaide Chronicle*, 1 June 1993, p. 66; Robert **Dessaix**, *A Mother's Disgrace*, Angus & Robertson, Pymble, 1995, pp. 30–1, reproduced with the permission of the author and Australian Literary Management; Garry **Disher**, *The Bamboo Flute*, Angus & Robertson, North Ryde, 1992, pp. 42–6; Rosemary **Dobson**, 'Interlude at a Primary School', *Collected Poems*, Angus & Robertson, North Ryde, 1991; Geoffrey **Dutton**, *Out in the Open: An Autobiography*, University of Queensland Press, St Lucia, 1994, pp. 37–8, 44–5; Chester **Eagle**, *Play Together, Dark Blue Twenty*, McPhee Gribble, Melbourne, 1986, pp. 11–12, 73; Ted **Egan**, *With Its Hat About Its Ears: Recollections of the Bush School* (ed. Hank Nelson), ABC Enterprises, Crows Nest, 1990, p. 183, reproduced with the author's permission; June **Epstein**, *Woman with Two Hats: An Autobiography*, Hyland House, Melbourne, 1988, pp. 6–10, reproduced with the author's permission; Kathleen **Fitzpatrick**, *Solid Bluestone Foundations: Memories of an Australian Girlhood*, Penguin Books, Ringwood, 1986, pp. 85–9, 91–2; Miles **Franklin**, *My Brilliant Career*, Angus & Robertson, Sydney, 1990, pp. 183–6; Simon **French**, *Hey Phantom Singlet*, Angus & Robertson, Sydney, 1975, pp. 10–12, 14–15; Gwen **Friend**, *My Brother Donald: A Memoir of Australian Artist Donald Friend*, Angus & Robertson, Pymble, 1994, pp. 19–20; Mary E. **Fullerton**, *Bark House Days*, Melbourne University Press, Carlton, 1921, pp. 8–13; John **Funder**, 'Melbourne Millefeuilles' (unpublished manuscript), 1996, reproduced with the author's permission; Helen **Garner**, *True Stories: Selected Non-fiction*, Text Publishing, Melbourne, 1996, pp. 48–9; Dorothy **Gilbert**, 'Country Life in the Later Nineteenth Century: Reminiscences', *South Australiana*, vol. 12, no. 2, September

1973, pp. 58–60; Dame Mary **Gilmore**, *Old Days: Old Ways: A Book of Recollections*, Angus & Robertson, Sydney, 1934, pp. 86–90; Germaine **Greer**, *There's Something About a Convent Girl* (eds Jackie Bennett & Rosemary Forgan), Virago Press, London, 1992, pp. 87–90, reproduced with the permission of Watson, Little Ltd; Barbara **Hanrahan**, *The Scent of Eucalyptus*, Chatto & Windus/Hogarth Press, London, 1985, pp. 38–42; Gwen **Harwood**, 'The Spelling Prize', *Bone Scan*, Angus & Robertson, North Ryde, 1988, pp. 3–4, reproduced with the permission of ETT Imprint; Paul **Hasluck**, *Mucking About: An Autobiography*, Melbourne University Press, Carlton, 1977, pp. 31–3, reproduced with permission of Nicholas Hasluck QC; James S. **Hassall**, *In Old Australia: Records and Reminiscences from 1794*, R.S. Hews & Co., Brisbane, 1902; Shirley **Hazzard**, *The Transit of Venus*, Penguin Books, Ringwood, 1981, pp. 43–5, 47–8; Dorothy **Hewett**, *Wild Card: An Autobiography 1923–1958*, McPhee Gribble/Penguin Books, South Yarra/Ringwood, 1990, pp. 59–62; Philip **Hodgins**, 'Pudge', in *Down the Lake with Half a Chook*, ABC Enterprises, Crows Nest, 1988, p. 21, reproduced with the permission of Janet Shaw; Donald **Horne**, *The Education of Young Donald*, Penguin Books, Ringwood, 1975, pp. 54–5; Janette Turner **Hospital**, 'Turning Points', the *Age: Saturday Extra*, Melbourne, 5 November, 1994, pp. 5–6, reproduced with permission of the author and Hickson Associates; Robert **Hughes**, 'Flying the Black Mamba', *London Magazine*, vol. 9, no. 8, November 1969, pp. 14–17; Barry **Humphries**, *More Please*, Viking, London, 1992, pp. 13–15; Amirah **Inglis**, *Amirah: An Un-Australian Childhood*, William Heinemann, Richmond, 1989, pp. 90–3; Clive **James**, *Unreliable Memoirs*, Jonathan Cape/Pan Books, London, 1980, pp. 114–16; John Stanley **James**, *The Vagabond Papers* (ed. Michael Cannon), Hyland House, Melbourne, 1983, pp. 178–80; Frances **Kerr**, *Glimpses of Life in Victoria by 'A Resident'*, Melbourne University Press, Carlton, 1996, pp. 274–8; John **Kickett**, 'My Children Want to Learn', in *Westralian Voices: Documents in Western Australian Social History* (ed. Marian Aveling), University of Western Australia Press, 1979, pp. 192, 194; Henry **Kingsley**, *The Recollections of Geoffry Hamlyn*, Rigby, Adelaide, 1975, pp. 178–9; C.J. **Koch**, *Crossing the Gap: A Novelist's Essays*, Hogarth Press, London, 1987, pp. 28–9, 93; Moira **Lambert**, *A Suburban Girl: Australia 1918–1948*, Macmillan, South Melbourne, 1990, pp. 30–2, © Moira Lambert 1990; Ruby **Langford**,

Don't Take Your Love to Town, Penguin Books, Ringwood, 1989, pp. 35–8; Henry **Lawson**, 'A Fragment of Autobiography', in *The Bush Undertaker and Other Stories* (ed. Colin Roderick), Angus & Robertson, Sydney, 1989, pp. 233–6; Brian **Lewis**, *Our War: Australia During World War I*, Melbourne University Press, Carlton, 1980, pp. 200–1, 203; Joan **Lindsay**, *Picnic at Hanging Rock*, Hill of Content, Melbourne, 1978, pp. 2–3, 8–11; Norman **Lindsay**, *My Mask: For What Little I Know of the Man Behind It*, Angus & Robertson, Sydney, 1970, pp. 60–3, reproduced with permission from Barbara Mobbs; Graham **Little**, 'The Happiest Days of Your Life', *Meanjin*, 1/1987, pp. 19–20, 22, 26–8, reproduced with the author's permission; Mary Rose **Liverani**, *The Winter Sparrows: Growing Up in Scotland and Australia*, Thomas Nelson, 1977, pp. 224–6; Rosaleen **Love**, 'The Hidden Curriculum' (unpublished MS), 1996, reproduced with the author's permission; Adelaide **Lubbock**, *People in Glass Houses: Growing up at Government House*, Thomas Nelson, West Melbourne, 1977, pp. 141–2; '**Lucia**: Life Shouldn't be Hard for Kids' and '**Roberto**: I'm Italian What I Think But I'm Australian the Things I Do', in *With Courage in Their Cases* (ed. Morag Loh), Italian Federation of Emigrant Workers and Their Families (FILEF), Coburg, 1984, pp. 109–10, 114–15; Hugh **Lunn**, *Over the Top with Jim*, University of Queensland Press, St Lucia, 1990, pp. 160–3; Morris **Lurie**, *Whole Life: An Autobiography*, McPhee Gribble, Melbourne, 1987, pp. 140–3; Elizabeth **Macarthur**, 'Elizabeth Macarthur to Betsy Kingdom, 1 September 1795', MS A2908, State Library of New South Wales; Louise **Mack**, *Teens*, Angus & Robertson, Sydney, 1897; Kenneth **Mackenzie**, *The Young Desire It*, Angus & Robertson, Sydney, 1963, pp. 42–3, reproduced with the permission of ETT Imprint; John **Mackrell**, in *No Privacy for Writing: Shipboard Diaries 1852–1879* (ed. Andrew Hassam), Melbourne University Press, Carlton, 1995, pp. 214–16; George Gordon **McCrae**, 'Fragment of a Diary' in *Georgiana's Journal: Melbourne 1841–1865* (ed. Hugh McCrae), Angus & Robertson, Sydney, 1992, pp. 232, 235–7; F.M. **McGuire**, *Bright Morning: The Story of an Australian Family Before 1914*, Rigby, Adelaide, 1975, pp. 150–1, reproduced with permission of the Estate of Frances Margaret McGuire; Graham **McInnes**, *The Road to Gundagai*, Hogarth Press, London, 1985, pp. 51–3; Rhyll **McMaster**, 'Kindergarten Bus' from *Flying the Coop: New and Selected Poems*

1972–1994, William Heinemann Australia, 1994, p. 207; Eugénie McNeil, *A Bunyip Close Behind Me: Recollections of the Nineties by Eugénie (Delarue) McNeil*, Penguin Books, Ringwood, 1985, pp. 37–9, 67–8, reproduced with permission of the Trust Company of Australia Ltd; David **Malouf**, *Johnno*, University of Queensland Press, 1975, 1989, pp. 56–8; Tony **Maniaty**, *All Over the Shop*, Penguin Books, Ringwood, 1993, pp. 81–4; Melina **Marchetta**, *Looking for Alibrandi*, Puffin, Ringwood, 1992, pp. 1–4; John **Marsden**, *Take My Word for It*, Pan Australia, Chippendale, 1993, pp. 45–6, 87; Louisa Anne **Meredith**, *Tasmanian Friends and Foes, Feathered, Furred and Finned: A Family Chronicle of Country Life, Natural History, and Veritable Adventure*, J. Walch, 1880; Alan **Moorehead**, *A Late Education: Episodes in a Life*, Hamish Hamilton, London, 1970, pp. 12–15; Sally **Morgan**, *My Place*, Fremantle Arts Centre Press, Fremantle, 1987, pp. 37–9; Les **Murray**, *With Its Hat About Its Ears: Recollections of the Bush School* (ed. Hank Nelson), ABC Enterprises, Crows Nest, 1990, pp. 12–13; Sonia **Mycak**, 'A Dual Existence in a Seemingly Singular Country', *Who Do You Think You Are?* (eds Karen Herne, Joanne Travaglia & Elizabeth Weiss), Women's Redress Press, Broadway, 1992, pp. 50–2; Penelope **Nelson**, *Penny Dreadful*, Random House, Milsons Point, 1995, pp. 72–5; John **O'Brien**, 'The Old Bush School', *Around the Boree Log and Other Verses*, Angus & Robertson, Sydney, 1994, pp. 16–17, 19; Barry **Oakley**, *Scribbling in the Dark*, University of Queensland Press, St Lucia, 1985, pp. 92–7; Helen **O'Shea**, 'Treevines', *Meanjin*, vol. 53, no. 1, 1994, pp. 16–18; Jan **Owen**, 'Y-Cough', *Blackberry Season*, Molonglo Press, Canberra, 1993, p. 52; Nancy **Phelan**, *A Kingdom by the Sea*, Angus & Robertson, North Ryde, 1990, pp. 46–8; Hal **Porter**, *The Watcher on the Cast-iron Balcony: An Australian Autobiography*, Oxford University Press, Melbourne, 1985, pp. 96–9; Peter **Porter**, 'Reading MND in Form 4B', *Collected Poems*, Oxford University Press, Oxford, 1984, p. 45; Katharine Susannah **Prichard**, *Child of the Hurricane: An Autobiography*, Angus & Robertson, Sydney, 1963, pp. 29–30, reproduced with the permission of Curtis Brown Australia; Henry Handel **Richardson**, *The Getting of Wisdom*, Mandarin, Port Melbourne, 1990, pp. 48–52; Faith **Richmond**, *Remembrance*, Collins, Sydney, 1989, pp. 86–90; Andrew **Riemer**, *Inside Outside: Life Between Two Worlds*, Angus & Robertson, 1992, pp. 92–6, reproduced with the permission of ETT Imprint;

Jill **Roe**, *With Its Hat About Its Ears: Recollections of the Bush School* (ed. Hank Nelson), ABC Enterprises, Crows Nest, 1990, p. 151; Peter **Rose**, 'Mortification', *The House of Vitriol*, Picador, Sydney, 1990, p. 18; Dick **Roughsey**, *Moon and Rainbow: The Autobiography of an Aboriginal*, Lansdowne Publishing, Sydney, 1995, pp. 38–9; Dorothy **Roysland**, *A Pioneer Family on the Murray River*, Rigby, Adelaide, 1977, pp. 36–7; Elizabeth **Salter**, *Helpmann: The Authorised Biography of Sir Robert Helpmann, CBE*, Angus & Robertson, Brighton, 1978, p. 28; Rosa **Safransky**, 'Queen of the Parasites', *Neighbours: Multicultural Writing of the 1980s* (ed. R.F. Holt), University of Queensland Press, St Lucia, 1991, pp. 168–70, reproduced with the author's permission; Kim **Scott**, *True Country*, Fremantle Arts Centre Press, Fremantle, 1993, pp. 30–3; Sam **Sejavka**, *Homeland* (ed. George Papaellinas), Allen & Unwin, North Sydney, 1991, pp. 48–50; Mary Turner **Shaw**, 'Education of a Squatter's Daughter', *The Half-open Door: Sixteen Modern Australian Women Look at Professional Life and Achievement* (eds Patricia Grimshaw & Lynne Strahan), Hale & Iremonger, Sydney, 1982, pp. 287–90; Ella **Simon**, *Through My Eyes*, Seal Books, Sydney, 1995, pp. 59–61; Bernard **Smith**, *The Boy Adeodatus: The Portrait of a Lucky Young Bastard*, Penguin Books, Ringwood, 1985, pp. 209–11; Gavin **Souter**, *The Idle Hill of Summer*, Collins, Melbourne, 1972, pp. 111–14; Catherine Helen **Spence**, *Clara Morison: A Tale of South Australia During the Gold Fever*, in *Catherine Helen Spence* (ed. Helen Thomson), University of Queensland Press, St Lucia, 1987, pp. 52–6; Christina **Stead**, 'The Old School', *Ocean of Story: The Uncollected Stories of Christina Stead* (ed. R.G. Geering), Penguin Books, Ringwood, 1985, pp. 23–6; Bruce **Steele**, 'Hotchin's Hothouse' (unpublished MS), 1996, reproduced with the author's permission; Mary **Steele**, 'Beside the Lake, Beneath the Trees: A Ballarat Childhood' (unpublished MS), 1996, reproduced with the author's permission; Meg **Stewart**, *Autobiography of My Mother*, Penguin Books, Ringwood, 1985, pp. 79–81, reproduced with the author's permission; Randolph **Stow**, *The Merry-Go-Round in the Sea*, Penguin Books, Ringwood, 1979, pp. 78–80; Jennifer **Strauss**, 'Peeling Onions Always Makes Me Cry', *Luna*, 1978, reproduced with the author's permission; Lady **Tennyson**, *Audrey Tennyson's Vice-Regal Days 1899–1903* (ed. Alexandra Hasluck), National Library of Australia, Canberra, 1978, p. 255; Aimée **Tse**, 'Soft Frilly Things from the Sea' (unpublished MS), reproduced with the author's permission; Margaret **Tucker**, *If Everyone Cared: Autobiography of Margaret Tucker MBE*, Ure Smith, Sydney, 1977, pp. 90–3; Ethel **Turner**, *Seven Little Australians*, Walter McVitty Books, Montville, 1994, pp. 46–51; George **Turner**, *In the Heart or in the Head: An Essay in Time Travel*, Norstrilia Press, Carlton, 1984, pp. 46–9; W.J. **Turner**, *Blow for Balloons*, J.M. Dent & Sons, London, 1935, pp. 207–13; R.E.N. **Twopeny**, *Town Life in Australia*, Penguin Books Australia, Ringwood, 1973, pp. 83–4, 87–9; Joseph **Verco**, 'A Colonial Boy-hood: Some Recollections of Sir Joseph Verco, 1858–1867' in *South Australiana*, vol. 2, 1963, pp. 64–5; Mary Howitt **Walker**, *Come Wind, Come Weather: A Biography of Alfred Howitt*, Melbourne University Press, Carlton, 1971, p. 214; Russel **Ward**, *A Radical Life: The Autobiography of Russel Ward*, Macmillan, South Melbourne, 1988, pp. 9–11, reproduced with the permission of Curtis Brown Australia; M.E. **Ware**, unpublished memoir, 1996, reproduced with the author's permission; Jack **Waterford**, 'The Best Days of My Life', *Eureka Street*, vol. 2, no. 2, March 1992, pp. 30–1, reproduced with the author's permission; Patrick **White**, *Flaws in the Glass: A Self-portrait*, Jonathan Cape, London, 1981, pp. 12–14, reproduced with the permission of Barbara Mobbs; Tim **Winton**, *Cloudstreet*, Penguin Books, Ringwood, 1996, pp. 138–40, reproduced with the permission of the author and Australian Literary Management; Virginia **Woolf**, *The Waves*, Penguin Books, Ringwood, 1931, p. 16; Mandawuy **Yunupingu**, 'Yothu Yindi: Finding Balance', *Race and Class*, vol. 35, no. 4, 1994, pp. 114–16, 119.

Every effort has been made to trace the original source of copyright material contained in this book. The publisher would be pleased to hear from copyright holders to rectify any errors or omissions.